Early Mathematics Learning

Ulrich Kortenkamp • Birgit Brandt
Christiane Benz • Götz Krummheuer
Silke Ladel • Rose Vogel
Editors

Early Mathematics Learning

Selected Papers of the POEM 2012
Conference

Editors

Ulrich Kortenkamp
Institut für Mathematik
Martin-Luther-Universität Halle-Wittenberg
Halle (Saale)
Germany

Birgit Brandt
Inst. für Schulpädaogik und
Grundschuldidaktik
Martin-Luther-Universität Halle-Wittenberg
Halle (Salle)
Germany

Christiane Benz
Institut für Mathematik und Informatik
Pädagogische Hochschule Karlsruhe
Karlsruhe
Germany

Götz Krummheuer
FB 12 Informatik und Mathematik
Goethe-Universität Frankfurt am Main
Frankfurt am Main
Germany

Silke Ladel
Fachrichtung 6.1 Mathematik
Universität des Saarlandes
Saarbrücken
Germany

Rose Vogel
FB 12 Informatik und Mathematik
Goethe-Universität Frankfurt am Main
Frankfurt am Main
Germany

ISBN 978-1-4614-4677-4   ISBN 978-1-4614-4678-1 (eBook)
DOI 10.1007/978-1-4614-4678-1
Springer New York Heidelberg Dordrecht London

Library of Congress Control Number: 2013955388

© Springer Science+Business Media New York 2014
This work is subject to copyright. All rights are reserved by the Publisher, whether the whole or part of the material is concerned, specifically the rights of translation, reprinting, reuse of illustrations, recitation, broadcasting, reproduction on microfilms or in any other physical way, and transmission or information storage and retrieval, electronic adaptation, computer software, or by similar or dissimilar methodology now known or hereafter developed. Exempted from this legal reservation are brief excerpts in connection with reviews or scholarly analysis or material supplied specifically for the purpose of being entered and executed on a computer system, for exclusive use by the purchaser of the work. Duplication of this publication or parts thereof is permitted only under the provisions of the Copyright Law of the Publisher's location, in its current version, and permission for use must always be obtained from Springer. Permissions for use may be obtained through RightsLink at the Copyright Clearance Center. Violations are liable to prosecution under the respective Copyright Law.
The use of general descriptive names, registered names, trademarks, service marks, etc. in this publication does not imply, even in the absence of a specific statement, that such names are exempt from the relevant protective laws and regulations and therefore free for general use.
While the advice and information in this book are believed to be true and accurate at the date of publication, neither the authors nor the editors nor the publisher can accept any legal responsibility for any errors or omissions that may be made. The publisher makes no warranty, express or implied, with respect to the material contained herein.

Printed on acid-free paper

Springer is part of Springer Science+Business Media (www.springer.com)

Contents

Part I   Introduction

1 Introduction 3
   Christiane Benz, Birgit Brandt, Ulrich Kortenkamp, Götz
   Krummheuer, Silke Ladel and Rose Vogel

2 A Dance of Instruction with Construction in Mathematics
   Education 9
   Norma Presmeg

Part II   Case Studies

3 It is quite confusing isn't it? 21
   Judy Sayers and Patti Barber

4 Mathematical Teaching Moments: Between Instruction and
   Construction 37
   Troels Lange, Tamsin Meaney, Eva Riesbeck and Anna Wernberg

5 "I have a little job for you" 55
   Birgit Brandt

6 The Relationship between Cultural Expectation and the
   Local Realization of a Mathematics Learning Environment 71
   Götz Krummheuer

7 The Reflection of Spatial Thinking on the Interactional
   Niche in the Family 85
   Ergi Acar Bayraktar

Part III Children's Constructions

8 **The Roots of Mathematising in Young Children's Play** 111
   Bert van Oers

9 **Non-canonical Solutions in Children-Adult Interactions—A Case Study of the Emergence of Mathematical Creativity** 125
   Melanie Münz

10 **The Interplay Between Gesture and Speech: Second Graders Solve Mathematical Problems** 147
   Melanie Huth

11 **Children's Constructions in the Domain of Geometric Competencies (in Two Different Instructional Settings)** 173
   Andrea Simone Maier and Christiane Benz

12 **Identifying quantities—Children's Constructions to Compose Collections from Parts or Decompose Collections into Parts** 189
   Christiane Benz

Part IV Tools and Interaction

13 **Children's Engagement with Mathematics in Kindergarten Mediated by the Use of Digital Tools** 207
   P.S. Hundeland, M. Carlsen and I. Erfjord

14 **Mathematical Situations of Play and Exploration as an Empirical Research Instrument** 223
   Rose Vogel

15 **Number Concepts—Processes of Internalization and Externalization by the Use of Multi-Touch Technology** 237
   Silke Ladel and Ulrich Kortenkamp

Part V Intervention

16 **Intentional Teaching: Integrating the Processes of Instruction and Construction to Promote Quality Early Mathematics Education** 257
   Jie-Qi Chen and Jennifer McCray

17 **Professionalization of Early Childhood Educators with a Focus on Natural Learning Situations and Individual Development of Mathematical Competencies: Results from an Evaluation Study** 275
Hedwig Gasteiger

18 **Employing the CAMTE Framework: Focusing on Preschool Teachers' Knowledge and Self-efficacy Related to Students' Conceptions** 291
Pessia Tsamir, Dina Tirosh, Esther Levenson, Michal Tabach and Ruthi Barkai

19 **Early Enhancement of Kindergarten Children Potentially at Risk in Learning School Mathematics—Design and Findings of an Intervention Study** 307
Andrea Peter-Koop and Meike Grüßing

Erratum E1

Index 323

Contributors

Patti Barber University of London, Institute of Education, U.K.

Ruthi Barkai Tel Aviv University, Israel

Ergi Acar Bayraktar Goethe-University Frankfurt am Main and Center for Individual Development and Adaptive Education (IDeA), Germany

Christiane Benz University of Education Karlsruhe, Germany

Birgit Brandt Martin-Luther-Universität Halle-Wittenberg and Center for Individual Development and Adaptive Education (IDeA), Germany

Martin Carlsen Department of Mathematical Sciences, University of Agder, Norway

Jie-Qi Chen Erikson Institute, Chicago, U.S.A

Ingvald Erfjord Department of Mathematical Sciences, University of Agder, Norway

Hedwig Gasteiger Ludwig-Maximilians-University Munich, Germany

Meike Grüßing Leibniz Institute for Science and Mathematics Education (IPN), Kiel, Germany

Per Sigurd Hundeland Department of Mathematical Sciences, University of Agder, Norway

Melanie Huth Goethe-University Frankfurt am Main and Center for Individual Development and Adaptive Education (IDeA), Germany

Ulrich Kortenkamp CERMAT, Martin-Luther-Universität Halle-Wittenberg, Germany

Götz Krummheuer Goethe-University Frankfurt am Main and Center for Individual Development and Adaptive Education (IDeA), Germany

Silke Ladel CERMAT, Saarland University, Germany

Troels Lange Malmö University, Sweden

Esther Levenson Tel Aviv University, Israel

Andrea Simone Maier University of Education Karlsruhe, Germany

Jennifer McCray Erikson Institute, Chicago, U.S.A

Tamsin Meaney Malmö University, Sweden

Melanie Münz Institute for Mathematics Education, Goethe-University Frankfurt am Main and Center for Individual Development and Adaptive Education of Children at Risk (IDeA), Germany

Bert van Oers Department Research and Theory in Education, VU University Amsterdam, The Netherlands

Andrea Peter-Koop IDM, University of Bielefeld, Germany

Norma Presmeg Illinois State University, U.S.A.

Eva Riesbeck Malmö University, Sweden

Judy Sayers The University of Northampton, U.K.

Michal Tabach Tel Aviv University, Israel

Dina Tirosh Tel Aviv University, Israel

Pessia Tsamir Tel Aviv University, Israel

Rose Vogel Goethe-University Frankfurt am Main and Center for Individual Development and Adaptive Education (IDeA), Germany

Anna Wernberg Malmö University, Sweden

About the Editors

Christiane Benz is professor of mathematics and mathematics education at the University of Education Karlsruhe. Her research interests lie in early mathematics education, in particular in the domain of arithmetics and in professional development.

Birgit Brandt scientific assistant for primary school education at Martin-Luther-University Halle-Wittenberg and member of the research center IDeA (Individual Development and Adaptive Education of Children at Risk). Her research interests are interaction processes and the use of language in early mathematical education and in primary school.

Götz Krummheuer is a professor in the Institute of Mathematics and Informatics Education, Department of Mathematics, at Goethe-University Frankfurt am Main, Germany. His general research interest involves the development of an interactional theory concerning mathematical learning in the early years and in primary school.

Ulrich Kortenkamp is professor of mathematics education at Martin-Luther-University Halle-Wittenberg, Germany. His research interests lie at the interface between mathematics, computer science and didactics of the sciences, resulting in a focus on ICT in mathematics education for all ages. Together with Silke Ladel he is directing CERMAT, the Centre for Educational Research in Mathematics and Technology.

Silke Ladel is professor of primary mathematics education at Saarland University in Saarbrücken, Germany, Faculty of Mathematics and Computer Science. Her main research interest is the meaningful use of ICT in primary math education.

Rose Vogel is a professor of mathematics education in the Institute of Mathematics and Informatics Education, Department of Mathematics, at Goethe-University Frankfurt am Main, Germany. Her research interests are multimodality in learning mathematics, the development of mathematical concepts for children aged 3 and older, and the significance of feedback for learning processes.

Part I
Introduction

Chapter 1
Introduction

Christiane Benz, Birgit Brandt, Ulrich Kortenkamp, Götz Krummheuer, Silke Ladel and Rose Vogel

This book is the result of a conference that took place from February 27 to 29 in Frankfurt am Main, Germany. Following up the Congress of the European Society for Research in Mathematics Education (CERME) conference 2011 in Rzészow, Poland, we, a group of German researchers from Frankfurt and Karlsruhe in early mathematics education, were faced with the question: In which way—and how much—should children be "educated" in mathematics before entering primary school. The European conference in Poland demonstrated that there are many opinions and research results, and the topic itself deserves further attention. We decided to organize an invitation-only workshop-conference to further investigate this question.

We wanted to address this question from a mathematics education perspective on early mathematics learning in the strain between instruction and construction. The topics of the conference included research on the design of learning opportunities, the development of mathematical thinking, the impact of the social setting and the professionalization of nursery teachers.

At the conference, we created a focused working atmosphere in the spirit of the CERME conferences, with only few paper presentations and allowing for more inter-

---

U. Kortenkamp (✉)
CERMAT, Martin-Luther-Universität Halle-Wittenberg, Halle, Germany
e-mail: kortenkamp@cermat.org

B. Brandt
Martin-Luther-Universität Halle-Wittenberg, Halle, Germany
e-mail: birgit.brandt@paedagogik.uni-halle.de

G. Krummheuer · R. Vogel
Goethe-University and IDeA-Center Frankfurt am Main, Frankfurt am Main, Germany
e-mail: {krummheuer|vogel}@math.uni-frankfurt.de

C. Benz
University of Education Karlsruhe, Karlsruhe, Germany
e-mail: benz@ph-karlsruhe.de

S. Ladel
CERMAT, Universität des Saarlandes, Saarbrücken, Germany
e-mail: ladel@math.uni-sb.de

action and exchange between the researchers. This book collects revised and extended versions of the conference papers, grouped in four parts that reflect major strands that emerged. These parts follow an introductory chapter by Norma Presmeg, "A dance of instruction with construction in mathematics education." Presmeg highlights in a very personal exposition the main theme of the book: The dual nature of instruction and construction, with each being necessary for the other, or as she phrases it, "Instruction and construction can mutually constitute each other in a fine-tuning awareness that I have called a dance." To us, there could not be a better description for the fundamental question of perspective on early mathematics (POEM) than this poetic one.

In the first part, the relation between instruction and construction is illuminated by case studies in different social settings. Case studies from three European countries with different curricular concepts for early (mathematics) education and with different institutional embedding of the interaction processes between children and adults are gathered in this part. Although the studies use different methodological approaches and theoretical backgrounds, they all use videotape as database and focus on situational aspects and different roles of the participants within the interactions.

Three of these contributions are concerned with interaction processes in institutional settings and particularly deal with the role of the teacher. Sayers and Barber examine one experienced teacher's practice in relation to the centrally imposed English mathematics curriculum. Within the framework of pedagogical content knowledge (Shulman 1986)[1], they focus on pedagogical issues related to the use of manipulatives and language emphasized when teaching place value to young children in a whole class interaction. Similarly, the contribution of Lange, Meaney, Riesbeck and Wernberg is concerned with one teacher's practice in relation to the national curriculum for early education. Using Anghileri's (2006) model of scaffolding, this case study focuses on how one teacher in a Swedish preschool recognizes and builds on mathematical teaching moments that arise from children's play with glass jars in a guided play set up by the kindergarten teacher. Brandt also discusses the acting of kindergarten teachers in guided play situations. Within the framework of folk pedagogy (Bruner 1996), she examines the pedagogical ideas of three kindergarten teachers arranging learning opportunities in the mathematical domain patterning and describes three basically different instruction models. The two last contributions of this part leave the institutional embedding of the interaction processes in preschool or kindergarten. Krummheuer examines the interface between cultural expectation and local realization in the social context of encounters that "serve" as mathematical learning opportunities for children. For this reason, he analyses peer interactions guided by an adult and a play situation in a family. Tracing back Super and Harkness (1986), he employs the concept of the "developmental niche in the development of mathematical thinking". This concept is adopted by Acar-Baraktar for her investigation of the interaction processes between children and adults and the reconstruction of mathematics learning in the familial context. In her contribution, she carries out the support system of a German–Turkish family in the domain of spatial thinking while playing a rule-based game.

---

[1] See the respective chapters for full references.

1 Introduction

Thus, the cultural impact of early mathematical teaching and learning and the "dance of instruction and construction" become apparent through these case studies.

In Part 2, the focus will be on children's constructions. By investigating children's constructions, the learner's perspective will be focused on. The different insights in children's constructions can help to provide a basis for instruction in terms of realizing and using learning opportunities and creating learning environments within mathematical early childhood education. So the "dance between construction and instruction" also underlies this part, although the aspect of construction will be more exposed.

In the introductory chapter, Bert van Oers highlights the aspect of construction, using the term of "productive mathematising" in contrast to mathematical activities with a re-productive aspect. Based on the cultural–historical activity theory, van Oers defends the position that "the activity of mathematising basically is a form of playful mathematics, embedded in young children's play". Regarding different aspects of play as a form of productive mathematising, both the aspect of children's construction and the aspect of instruction will be presented.

The productive and creative aspect in children's constructions is also analyzed by Melanie Münz. In her chapter, she focuses especially on the aspect of mathematical creativity. Mathematical creative ideas, which emerge in the interaction between children and the accompanying person, are illustrated. By including the analyses of the interaction of the accompanying person, the aspect of mathematical instruction is also mentioned.

A special expression of children's constructions are gestures. In the chapter by Melanie Huth, the interplay between gestures and speech used by second graders is illustrated while they are occupied with a geometrical problem in pairs. Constructions regarding the geometrical domain are also the subject of the chapter of Andrea Maier and Christiane Benz. Here, children of two educational settings, England and Germany, were interviewed. In addition to insights in children's geometrical competencies concerning shapes, hypotheses are formulated how the introduction of shapes might additionally influence the concept formation of the children. Another discernment of individual's constructions is given in the chapter of Christiane Benz. Here, different processes by recognizing or perceiving collections of objects and by identifying quantities of collections are investigated. On the basis of insights about children's constructions, different conclusions for instruction in early mathematics education will be drawn.

The third part concentrates on tools and interactions. There are three chapters in this part that all have a view on learning as a socio-cultural process. Therein, instructions are given as orders from the teachers to the students. The role of the teacher is to orchestrate mathematical learning opportunities for the children. The child has to construct the mathematical meaning. The artefacts determine this construction. They mediate between the subject, the child, and the object, the mathematical content. In the first and third chapter, the artefact is a digital tool. They focus on the use of technology to support mathematical teaching and learning. In the second chapter, mathematical conversation situations, impulses of the guiding adult, and of the materials are used as the starting point of the interaction.

Martin Carlsen, Ingvald Erfjord and Per Sigurd Hundeland analyse the children's engagement with mathematics in kindergarten mediated by the use of interactive whiteboards. In the research project, they survey in what ways digital tools may nurture children's appropriation processes relative to mathematics. In particular, they focus on the use of a digital pair of scales in kindergarten for comparison of weights. In the long-term study 'early Steps in Mathematics Learning' (erStMaL), Rose Vogel explores mathematical situations of play and exploration as an empirical research instrument. An especially developed description grid in the form of "design patterns of mathematical situations" achieves a comparability of the situations.

Silke Ladel and Ulrich Kortenkamp use information and communication technology (ICT), in particular multi-touch technology, to survey and to enhance the development of children's concepts of numbers. A special focus lies on the processes of internalization and externalization that constitute the construction of meaning. Also the instructions given by the (nursery) teacher as well as the partners have an influence on the child's internalization and externalization. As a basis for the design and analysis this research project refers to Artefact-Centric Activity Theory (ACAT).

In Part 4, "interventions" are presented that integrate both the principle of instruction and the principle of construction into processes of early mathematical education. Jie-Qi Chen and Jennifer McCray describe a yearlong training program for preschool teachers. The program "Early Mathematics Education" was launched in 2007. Starting with mathematical "Big Ideas", preschool teachers shall be enabled to understand children in their mathematical thinking and support children to build up mathematical knowledge. A variety of teaching strategies were developed in the program to encourage the preschool teachers.

Hedwig Gasteiger presents a professionalization program of early childhood educators as part of the project "TransKiGs Berlin". Early childhood educators are enabled to support the individual mathematical learning of children, here particularly in everyday learning situations. The further education program includes three modules in the domains number/counting/quantity, space and shape, and measurement and data. The fourth module is concerned with methodological components like observation, documentation and intervention measures.

Pessia Tsamir, Dina Tirosh, Esther Levenson, Michal Tabach and Ruthi Barkai examine 36 practising preschool teachers with regard to their mathematical knowledge and their self-efficacy. Based on the results of their study, they develop professional courses for preschool teachers. One important aspect of the program is to discuss with the teachers the different aims of mathematical tasks. In addition, the authors assume that the teacher's own learning experiences are important in supporting the children's learning.

All training programs presented focus on the development of mathematical and special methodological knowledge to support the learning of mathematics in early education.

Andrea Peter Koop and Meike Grüßing focus on the children themselves. Their study examines 5-year-old preschoolers. By different methods of testing, they identify 73 children out of 947 that are "potentially at risk learning school mathematics". The 73 children are split in two groups, which are promoted with different programs in prior to school entry. The results of the study are examined in detail, with a special interest in children with a migrant background.

We hope that this book will be able to carry over not only the results of the conference, but also its spirit and atmosphere to a broader audience. May we ask you for the next dance?

Chapter 2
A Dance of Instruction with Construction in Mathematics Education

Norma Presmeg

Setting the Scene

Our field, our baby field that is brand new in comparison with the millennia for which mathematics has existed as a discipline, has seen some dramatic changes in its half-century of being a field in its own right, with its own journals and conferences. We have come a long way, even since the early 1980s, when "illuminative evaluation" (McCormick 1982) was slowly replacing or, initially at least, supplementing the psychometric experiments that used "subjects" (*people*) who were being taught mathematics. Before that period, in the old paradigm, no research that did not aim for objectivity by means of carefully controlled experiments and statistical analysis was considered scientific in our field. In connection with the research methods of this period, Krutetskii (1976) gave a pungent critique:

> It is hard to understand how theory or practice can be enriched by, for instance, the research of Kennedy, who computed, for 130 mathematically gifted adolescents, their scores on different kinds of test and studied the correlations between them, finding that in some cases it was significant and in others not. The process of solution did not interest the investigator. But what rich material could be provided by the process of mathematical thinking in 130 mathematically able adolescents! (p. 14)

Krutetskii's interview methods, in Soviet Russia, were in many ways a precursor to the qualitative methodologies that followed this early period. Slowly, the qualitative research paradigm gained credence. After all, we are dealing with human beings in their teaching and learning of mathematics, with all the complexities and uncertainties that that fact implies! Even Krutetskii (1976), aware as he was of individual differences, wrote of "perfect teaching methods" (p. 6), terminology that we might use more circumspectly today. With regard to useful and believable research (rather than reliable and valid experiments), initial crude attempts at quality control became strengthened. Thus, *triangulation* of various types (Stake 1995) was needed to ensure that research results and insights reported more than merely the researcher's opinions. We learned to go back and ask the mathematics teachers and their stu-

---

N. Presmeg (✉)
Illinois State University, Illinois, USA
e-mail: npresmeg@msn.com

dents whether they agreed with the results of our observations and interviews, in "member checks" that were a means of respondent validation. By the 1990s, such qualitative research was the prominent methodology, and it was in this climate that radical constructivism became the dominant theoretical framework for research in our field. Radical constructivism was salutary in its critique of the behaviorism that had preceded it. And this theoretical precedence leads me to the topic of this talk.

Construction and Instruction

I remember, in the early 1990s sitting on a stone seat in the garden of The Florida State University with Ernst von Glasersfeld and asking him about the status of *conventional* knowledge in mathematics education according to radical constructivism. It seemed obvious that attempts by teachers to give their students space to construct their ideas of mathematics in more personal ways (e.g., by discussion in groups) would lead to a kind of knowledge that could be more *meaningful* to learners in terms of their mathematical identities and ownership. It is *not* that some kinds of instruction lead to construction and others do not. What other ways of "appropriation of knowledge" (van Oers 2002) do we have than by construction? We are constructing even in the choice of what we make of a straightforward lecture as we sit and listen. We may listen, but what do we *hear*? It was concerns such as these, in part, that caused debates on whether or not radical constructivism was epistemological, and whether or not it made claims about the ontology of mathematical knowledge. Nell Noddings, in the 1990s, called it "post-epistemological" (Janvier 1996).

But to return to my conversation with Ernst von Glasersfeld in the garden, Ernst acknowledged that there are different kinds of knowledge, and that knowledge of conventions had a different status, belonging as it does to accidents of cultural historicity rather than to the logic of rational thinking. Even the ability to use conventional knowledge would entail construction by an individual; but telling by somebody who knows the convention (aurally or in written form) is required, simply because there is no logical necessity for this kind of knowledge, except perhaps in a historical sense. Why, for instance, do we have 360° in a complete revolution? 100 degrees would be much more convenient. Reporting on some of his work with Les Steffe, in one of his many publications during this period, von Glasersfeld (1994) gave a short synopsis of the radical constructivist position concerning early mathematics concepts such as number; and early mathematical learning is of particular relevance in this conference, although it is clear that mathematics learning between the poles of instruction and construction is an important topic at all levels.

The founders of theoretical edifices, such as von Glasersfeld, are thus aware of the contingencies and intricacies inherent in building theories. But Peirce (1992) had insight into what happens to such theories over time. He cast light on what he meant by continuity in his *law of mind*:

> Logical analysis applied to mental phenomena shows that there is but one law of mind, namely, that ideas tend to spread continuously and to affect certain others which stand to them in a peculiar relation of affectability. In this spreading they lose intensity, and especially the power of affecting others, but gain generality and become welded with other ideas. (Peirce 1992, p. 313)

Some followers of radical constructivism took the theory to be a prescription for instruction. The mantra became, "Teachers mustn't tell!" (I have an anecdote about a professor and her primary school mathematics education prospective teachers, who just smiled and moved on when her students decided in groups that doubling the length of a particular similar figure must, automatically, double the area.) It is to the credit of deep scholars in our field, such as Paul Cobb and Erna Yackel (e.g., Yackel and Cobb 1996) that they recognized even in the heyday of radical constructivism, that instruction has an indispensable role, and that there is a delicate blending of instruction and construction that is a fine-tuning of the teacher's craft. It is this blending that I am calling the *dance* of instruction with construction.

In an email conversation with Götz Krummheuer, it emerged that when we considered the metaphor of the dance in this regard, we were viewing different aspects of dance that had relevance. He was interested in the swirling motion as the dancers moved—and certainly there is movement if we are considering teachers and their pupils in interaction in a dynamic way that leads to deep contemplation of mathematical ideas and changes in cognition, ideally also with a positive affective component. I had been thinking more of dance involving canonical moves by people in interaction—although both aspects are relevant to instruction and construction in mathematics education. Within the set moves of a particular dance there is freedom, creativity, and vigor. Certainly, a dancer can decide to construct a different set of movements, and they may be harmonious and beautiful, but if they are too far from the set moves, that dancer cannot be considered to be doing that particular dance. As is the case with all metaphors, there are elements in which the source domain (in this case dance) resonates with the target domain (mathematics education), and this common structure constitutes the *ground* of the metaphor. But every metaphor also involves ways in which the source and target domains are different, and these constitute the *tension* of the metaphor (Presmeg 1997). The dance metaphor does not take into account that there is a knowledge differential between teachers and their students who are learning mathematics. Teachers know the conventions of reasoning and representation that are involved in the patterns of mathematical thinking: Students initially may not have this awareness. There is also thus a power differential involved. However, effective instruction can facilitate students' making of constructions that lie within the canons of mathematically accepted knowledge, and yet there is room for creativity and enjoyment. I present two examples of such instruction in the next sections.

An Example of the Dance

As an example of an effective dance, I would like to highlight the doctoral research of Andrejs Dunkels (1996) in Luleå in the north of Sweden, in the mid-1990s. But for the untimely and tragic death of Andrejs, it is likely that he would have been the very first mathematics *education* professor in Sweden, who was appointed at the University of Luleå in 2001. After establishing his credibility as a mathematician with publications in pure mathematics (which was a necessity in that academic climate), Andrejs set out to teach his section of an engineering calculus course in a way that was very different from the traditional lecture format. Of the 5 or 6 sections of the course, with students arranged in the sections according to their previous accomplishments, Andrejs chose a section for his research that was just one up from the bottom in the hierarchy (i.e., many of these students had experienced difficulty in mathematics courses previously). He collected baseline data, so that he could compare these data with the achievements of his class at the end of the course, using exploratory data analysis (EDA) as well as observations and interviews. Thus, the research design used mixed methods (quantitative and qualitative), prefiguring a balanced swing of the pendulum to methodologies that became more common in the 2000s.

How did Andrejs teach his class? Firstly, he arranged them in groups of four for ease of communication. Secondly, he told them in advance what would be the mathematical topic of a particular class session, and he expected them to read and try to make sense of the relevant material in the textbook of the course. Thirdly, they were expected to come to the session prepared to talk about their current constructions. Finally, in the session, he circulated among the groups, listened to their conversations, and answered their questions although not always directly; he sometimes answered a question by posing another question. He sometimes pointed the group in directions they had not considered—with suggestions, not as the all-knowing teacher, and without taking away their ownership and agency. He had instinctively mastered the difficult and delicate dance of instruction with construction.

At the end of the course, the statistical EDA revealed that his students had improved their accomplishments so significantly that their section was now almost at the top of the hierarchy, second only to one other section. But even more convincingly, the analysis of data from interviews with students showed that the *quality* of the mathematical knowledge the students had constructed had improved immeasurably. There was no longer memorization of *rules without reasons*; they knew *why* the rules worked, and above all, they experienced greater enjoyment of the mathematical content, and more self-confidence than previously. This doctoral research study thus provided convincing evidence, both quantitative and qualitative, of the efficacy of balancing instruction with construction in mathematics education.

The Purported "epistemological paradox"

An issue that is relevant at this point is the oft-quoted paradox of instruction and construction (e.g., Simon 1995) that students can actively work only with what they have *already* constructed: How then is new knowledge possible? I shall argue shortly that there really is no paradox; the seeming paradox hinges on a false dichotomy. However, let me first give an example of a related phenomenon from my own research on ethnomathematics. I asked students in a masters-level course in mathematics education to take a personally meaningful cultural activity, and to construct mathematics from it. I gave examples from ethnomathematics literature and my own experiences to show them how to use several steps of semiotic chaining (Presmeg 2006a) to build connections between a cultural activity and mathematical ideas suitable for teaching at some level in a mathematics classroom. The process is akin in many ways to the horizontal mathematization, followed by vertical mathematization, used by the Freudenthal group (e.g., Treffers 1993; Gravemeijer 1994) in *Realistic Mathematics Education* (RME). The students in my course took ownership of the project, and the activities they chose were diverse and personally meaningful to them. However, it was evident that the mathematical ideas that students recognized in their chosen cultural activities depended heavily on what mathematics they already knew. For example, Vivienne, a primary school teacher, did not recognize the hyperbola that resulted when she analyzed the gear ratios and distances traveled by her mountain bicycle: Vivienne called the graph "a nice curve." In contrast, David constructed a "dihedral group of order 4" when he analyzed the symmetries of a tennis court: He was a teacher of college-level number theory. And in the data there were many more examples of this phenomenon. How then might teachers use the connections of horizontal mathematization to facilitate students' construction of *new* mathematical ideas? This question might be particularly vexing for a teacher who feels under pressure to 'cover' the topics listed in a mathematics syllabus.

I can do no more here (the topic has been addressed in several papers or book chapters, e.g., Presmeg 1998, 2007) than to report that the ethnomathematics course had the effect of broadening participants' beliefs about the *nature of mathematics*, which was no longer seen as a "bunch of rules to be memorized" (initial student characterization of what mathematics is), with or without understanding. Many students expressed in reflective journals that after the course they saw mathematics as inherent in patterns and regularities that they could identify also in their daily lives and activities. This change of beliefs prefigures what Tony Brown (2011) is accomplishing in his "weekly session centred on broadening the students' perceptions of mathematics and of how mathematics might be taught" (p. 18). Brown does not use the conceptual framework of semiotics, but the contemporary theoretical lenses of Zizek and Badiou, in his work, but the aim of his teaching resonates with a dance of instruction with construction.

To return to the so-called *learning paradox,* as I hinted, there really is no paradox at all if mathematics education is reconceptualized as a dance of construction with instruction. The crux of the matter is the relationship between the constructions made by an individual, and the broader societal context, the culture in which established mathematical ideas reside: These might be characterized as Karl Popper's (1974, 1983) worlds 2 and 3, respectively. Radford (2012) has trenchantly pointed out that the seeming dilemma results from what he calls the "antinomies" in epistemological views that we have accepted: "Unfortunately, we have become used to thinking that either students construct their own knowledge or knowledge is imposed upon them" (p. 4). As he points out, this conception is a misleading oversimplification. Radford poses the paradox in terms of *emancipation* in mathematics education rather than in terms of construction, but the ideas are relevant to both. He points out that the antinomies reside in two epistemological ideas: "First, knowledge is something that subjects *make*. Second, the making of knowledge must be carried out free from authority" (p. 102, italics in original). What is problematic is the relationship between freedom and truth. Radford points out convincingly that the paradox results from "a subjectivist view of the world espoused by modernity (a world thought of as made and known through the individual's deeds) and the cultural regimes of reason and truth that precede the individual's own activity" (p. 104). Although Radford does not cast it in these terms, it is the mistaken notion that Popper's worlds 2 and 3 are colliding. But all individual constructions (world 2) are made in the *context* of a cultural milieu (world 3). This relationship is inescapable. Seen in this light, the paradox disappears, and this relationship has its practical manifestation in a delicate blending of freedom and truth, a dance of instruction with construction. It is not necessary for the teacher's role to conform to an irreducible and contradictory dichotomy of "the sage on the stage" versus "the guide on the side," because elements of both these metaphors are evident in the dance, as the following example illustrates.

Blending Popper's Worlds in the Teaching of Trigonometry

I would like to present here an instance of teaching high school trigonometry that uses the dance of instruction and construction to the fullest, thereby—at least in some measure—resolving the apparent paradox suggested in the previous section.

Sue Brown (2005) carried out a powerful dissertation study in which she analyzed high school students' understanding of connections among trigonometric definitions (particularly of sine and cosine) that move from right triangles to the coordinate plane and unit circle, and then to definitions that establish sine and cosine as functions. Following this research (which involved quantitative as well as qualitative methods), she and I set out to examine further, pedagogy that might facilitate the students' constructions of such connections in trigonometry. In this postdoctoral phase, I served as the researcher in Sue's trigonometry class in the spring of 2006, in Chicago, USA. The research question was as follows: *How may teaching facilitate students' construction of connections among registers in learning the basic concepts of trigonometry?* The main goal in Sue's trigonometry class was to foster skill in converting among signs as students build up comprehensive knowledge of trigonometry concepts.

The methodology of this teaching experiment included cycles of joint reflection based on interviews with students, followed by further teaching. Early in our collaboration, Sue listed ways in which she tried to facilitate connected knowledge in her class—actions that were confirmed in my observations of her lessons, and in documents such as tests and quizzes. In the analysis of data, her list was compared with the connections constructed—or the lack of connections—by four students in a series of six interviews conducted with each student at intervals during the semester. The four students were purposively chosen by the teacher in collaboration with the researcher to ensure a range of learning styles and proficiency.

Some of Sue's facilitative principles that have the intent of helping students to move freely and flexibly among trigonometric registers are summarized as follows:

- Connecting old knowledge with new, starting with the "big ideas," providing contexts that demand the use of trigonometry, allowing ample time, and moving into complexity slowly
- Connecting visual and nonvisual registers, e.g., numerical, algebraic, and graphical signs, and requiring or encouraging students to make these connections in their classwork, homework, tests, and quizzes
- Supplementing problems with templates that make it easy for students to draw and use a sketch, or asking students to interpret diagrams that are given
- Providing contextual ("real world") signs that have an iconic relationship with trigonometric principles, e.g., a model of a boom crane that rotates through an angle θ, $0° < \theta < 180°$, on a half plane
- Providing memorable summaries in diagram form, which have the potential of becoming for the students prototypical images of trigonometric objects, because these inscriptions are sign vehicles for these objects
- Providing or requiring students to construct static or dynamic computer simulations of trigonometric principles and their connections, in many cases giving a sense of physical motion; and
- Using metaphors that are sometimes based on the students' contextual experiences, e.g., a bow tie and the boom crane, for trigonometric ratios in the unit circle.

An analysis of the complete corpus of data in terms of Sue's full list (abridged here) assessed the effectiveness of these principles in accomplishing their goal, at least for the four students who were interviewed (Presmeg 2006b). On the surface, Sue's list appears to relate to the *instruction* pole of the dance; however, it was her long experience of students' *constructions*—informed also by her intensive doctoral research—that formed the foundation for her principles of instruction in this list. And many instances were present of ways that Sue incorporated idiosyncratic constructions of students in her teaching. An example of this inclusion is the bow tie metaphor, which was introduced in class by Sue, but originated in interviews with students in a task in which they were finding the sine of angles in the second and third quadrants. Sue's pedagogy provides an illustration of principles that alternate flexibly and sensitively between instruction and construction in learning trigonometry.

Some Conclusions

In this introduction to the topic of *a mathematics education Perspective On Early Mathematics learning between the poles of instruction and construction (POEM)*, I have introduced a brief overview of the way our field has moved from a behaviorist emphasis on instruction, to an opposite concern with pupils' constructions, and further to the realization that instruction and construction can mutually constitute each other in a fine-tuning awareness that I have called a dance. Other writers have used different terminology, although the ideas resonate with the notions of construction and instruction: Hewitt (2012) makes the distinction between arbitrary and necessary knowledge, which he characterizes as knowledge that has the function of assisting memory and knowledge that is necessary in educating awareness of the accepted canons of a discipline, respectively. In any case, learning mathematics involves not only becoming aware of conventions and standards of the mathematics that has been accepted as such through the ages but also making sense of the logic of these canons in a personally and individually meaningful way.

I tried to initiate conversations on the topic with reference to two examples: one in a university-level calculus class and the other in a high school trigonometry class. I look forward to examples our colleagues will present in early childhood teaching and learning of mathematics. But I hope the cases presented here exemplify my belief that the topic is important at all levels of learning mathematics and that attention to this topic is required at both theoretical and empirical levels, the former, for example, with regard to the so-called paradoxes of our field and the latter in the day-to-day lives of teachers and students.

References

Brown, S. A. (2005). *The trigonometric connection: Students' understanding of sine and cosine.* Unpublished Ph.D. Dissertation, Illinois State University, USA.

Brown, T. (2011). *Mathematics education and subjectivity.* Dordrecht: Springer.

Dunkels, A. (1996). *Contributions to mathematical knowledge and its acquisition.* Doctoral dissertation, University of Luleå, Sweden.

Gravemeijer, K. (1994). *Developing realistic mathematics education.* Utrecht: CdB Press.

Hewitt, D. (2012) Young students learning formal algebraic notation and solving linear equations: Are commonly experienced difficulties avoidable? *Educational Studies in Mathematics, 81*(2), pp. 139-159. doi:10.1007/s10649-012-9394-x.

Janvier, C. (1996). Constructivism and its consequences for training teachers. In L. P. Steffe, P. Nesher, P. Cobb, G. A. Goldin, & B. Greer (Eds.), *Theories of mathematics learning* (pp. 449–463). Hillsdale: Erlbaum.

Krutetskii V. A. (1976). *The psychology of mathematical abilities in schoolchildren.* (trans: Kilpatrick, J. and Wirszup, I.) Chicago: University of Chicago Press.

McCormick, R. (Ed.). (1982). *Calling education to account.* London: Heinemann

Peirce, C. S. (1992). *The essential Peirce* (Vol. 1). In N. Houser & C. Kloesel. Bloomington: Indiana University Press.

Popper, K. (1974). *The philosophy of Karl Popper.* (trans: Schilpp, P. A.) LaSalleL: Open Court.

Popper, K. (1983). *A pocket Popper.* (trans: Miller D.) Oxford: Fontana.

Presmeg, N. C. (1997). Reasoning with metaphors and metonymies in mathematics education. In L. D. English (Ed.), *Mathematical reasoning: Analogies, metaphors, and images* (pp. 267–279). Mahwah: Lawrence Erlbaum Associates.

Presmeg, N. C. (1998). Ethnomathematics in teacher education. *Journal of Mathematics Teacher Education, 1*(3), 317–339.

Presmeg, N. C. (2006a). Semiotics and the "connections" standard: Significance of semiotics for teachers of mathematics. *Educational Studies in Mathematics, 61*(1–2), 163–182.

Presmeg, N. C. (2006b). A semiotic view of the role of imagery and inscriptions in mathematics teaching and learning. In J. Novotna, H. Moraova, M. Kratka, & N. Stehlikova (Eds.), *Procee-

dings of the 30th Annual Meeting of the International Group for the Psychology of Mathematics Education (Vol. 1, pp. 19–34). Prague, July 16–21, 2006.

Presmeg, N. C. (2007). The role of culture in teaching and learning mathematics. In F. Lester (Ed.), *Second handbook of research on mathematics teaching and learning* (pp. 435–458). Charlotte: Information Age Publishing.

Radford, L. (2012) Education and the illusions of emancipation. *Educational Studies in Mathematics, 80*(2/3), pp. 101-188.

Simon, M. (1995). Reconstructing mathematics pedagogy from a constructivist perspective. *Journal for Research in Mathematics Education, 26*, 114–145.

Stake, R. E. (1995). *The art of case study research*. Thousand Oaks: Sage.

Treffers, A. (1993). Wiscobas and Freudenthal: Realistic mathematics education. *Educational Studies in Mathematics, 25*, 89–108.

Van Oers, B. (2002). The mathematization of young children's language. In K. Gravemeijer, R. Lehrer, B. van Oers, & L. Verschaffel (Eds.), *Symbolizing, modeling and tool use in mathematics education* (pp. 29–57). Dordrecht: Kluwer.

von Glasersfeld. (1994). A radical constructivist view of basic mathematics concepts. In P. Ernest (Ed.), *Constructing mathematical knowledge: Epistemology and mathematics education* (pp. 5–7). London: The Falmer Press.

Yackel, E. & Cobb, P. (1996). Sociomathematical norms, argumentation, and autonomy in mathematics. *Journal for Research in Mathematics Education, 27*, 458–477.

Part II
Case Studies

Chapter 3
It is quite confusing isn't it?

Judy Sayers and Patti Barber

> *Implications of a national policy on mathematics teaching on the dance of instruction and construction of knowledge in the teaching of place value through manipulatives.*

Introduction

Firstly, it is important to distinguish between two different constructs of place value; namely, the 'quantity' value aspect and 'column' value aspect. Thompson (2009) informs us that using manipulatives, such as base ten apparatus, reinforces the 'column' aspect of place value, while emphases on partitioning reinforce the quantity aspect. However, there are important questions about whether we should be teaching column value to young children at all, for it is not a necessary prerequisite for early calculation, whereas an understanding of quantity value is (Thompson 2009).

In this chapter, we discuss how Jane, an experienced teacher with good mathematics subject knowledge and considered locally to be effective, presented the topic of place value to 5–6-year-old children. We wanted to examine the various resources, including manipulatives, she used and the specific language she privileged in her support of her young children's mathematical thinking. In so doing, we wished to understand how her practice was constructed by the curriculum discourse imposed centrally on teachers in England. The depth of case study colleagues' subject knowledge was an important defining characteristic, not least because it is an essential prerequisite for good mathematics teaching (Rowland and Ruthven 2011). In particular, deep pedagogical subject knowledge (Shulman 1986) is needed to understand the developmental stages of number sense (Howell and Kemp 2005) foundational to place value and its relationship to quantity. Thus, the dance between the instruction and construction of knowledge could be identified through the case.

J. Sayers (✉)
Stockholm University, Stockholm, Sweden.
e-mail: Judy.sayers@mnd.su.se

P. Barber
Institute of Education, University of London, London, UK

The Context

In England, since the introduction of a national curriculum in 1987, there has been substantial change in the teaching of mathematics, culminating in the launch of the National Numeracy Strategy and the adoption by primary schools of the 'daily mathematics lesson' in 1999. There was much debate over many years prior to its introduction about the teaching and learning of mathematics, but this was the first shift towards a public education emphasis which decreed equal treatment for all students and all teachers (Brown 2010). It was also the first time a pedagogical prescription was introduced, which emphasised whole class, or direct, teaching, and specified modes of instruction. However, the research base for the innovation was weak (Brown et al. 1998) and, in the years that have followed, further government-sponsored pedagogical intervention has been introduced to the extent that teachers no longer appear to trust their own judgement, believing themselves compelled to follow their interpretations of the national strategy.

Theoretical Background

A long, and still current, debate in education questions whether a constructivist approach is sufficient in teaching and learning, for example, Kirschner et al. (2006) question the efficacy of all constructivist approaches to learning, whether discovery, experiential, problem-based and inquiry-based teaching. Tobias and Duffy (2009) challenge this view. Drawing on the research foundations of Vygotsky (1978), Piaget (1952) and Bruner (1966), and more recent perspectives such as situated learning (Resnick 1987) and its derivative, communities of practice (Lave and Wenger 1991), they suggest that there are many, not unrelated, characteristics of constructivist approaches to learning.

Recent research into early years practice in England, for example, the Effective Practice of Preschool Education (EPPE) project (Siraj-Baltchford 2002), refers to the continued work of Weikart's (2000) model, as a typology of commonly applied 'early childhood education curriculum models' where high teacher initiative is described in terms of the highly structured pedagogy and high child initiative in terms of the learner's control of the curriculum. The model is based on two continua reflecting the interactions of both teacher and child perspectives in the ownership of the learning trajectory, implying there should be a balance between the two, where an instructional orientation can interplay, or dance, with a constructivist approach (Siraj-Baltchford 2002).

What the early years literature appears to suggest is that effective early childhood pedagogy must still be 'instructive', but should be interpreted as incorporating all of those processes that occur within the classroom that aim to initiate or maintain learning processes, and to be effective means to achieve educational goals (Creemers 1994). This does not mean the rejection of a constructivist approach, on the contrary. According to the English system education guidance for teachers

(DfES, 1999), effective teaching encompasses direct teaching that makes effective use of unexpected and unforeseen opportunities for children's learning. This will include both instructive and constructive approaches to learning. When considering the guidance, the message to teachers in England is clear, there are structured opportunities to be identified and planned which should provide a balance of approach between instruction and construction in order to be an effective practitioner.

In general, primary teachers in England do not study early years educational philosophy in their training; they receive a general training delivered through the curriculum subjects and a national strategy. However, recent independent reviews of primary practice in England have shown how the national strategy has failed to provide an appropriately meaningful pedagogy for early years teaching (Williams 2008), in its offering just a series of notes that implicitly adopt a broadly constructivist approach to teaching mathematics. The Cambridge Primary Review (2009) also reported on the need for a proper debate about primary education, in particular research-based approaches to how mathematics should be presented to children for deep learning experiences.

A significant issue of the national strategy model of planning is that 'teaching starts to be assumed to be the reality of learning. Children are not assessed on what they have learned, but on whether they have learned very specific objectives. Rather than the attained curriculum—in the sense of what children actually learn—being a guide to help shape further teaching it has become a tick list' (Askew 2011, p. 23). Furthermore, Aubrey et al. (2006) reported how the national strategy advantages some pupils more than others, with low attainers in particular, being least advantaged. Although primary mathematics teaching was presented as informed by constructivist, in reality it appeared to have become an impoverished list of things for the teacher to do.

Importantly, Askew et al. (2002) also found that if the emphasised mental mathematical images suggested in the guidance did not fit with those predetermined for the lesson then these were, at best, judged by teachers as not so relevant, rather than being a resource for the class to discuss and build upon, and were often ignored. Askew and Brown (2004) later confirmed that informed interpretation of the given objectives, and a move to more strategic ways of working, were challenging for teachers to understand and implement. Although professional development training was offered by the national strategy department, different interpretations were conceived by those training and by those being trained.

Knowledge for Teaching

The understanding of subject knowledge necessary for teaching mathematics is not disputed; effectiveness of mathematics teaching is not only due to the depth of a teacher's knowledge but also to how explicit connections are made within the subject (Askew et al. 1997). Importantly, teachers should have a deep knowledge of mathematics at the level they were teaching rather than having knowledge of advanced mathematics' (Ma 1999, p. 120).

Furthermore, Ball et al.'s (2001) view is that not only should mathematical conceptual knowledge be revisited but also pre-service teachers may need to unlearn what they know about teaching and learning of mathematics. Indeed, case studies, such as Goulding et al. (2002), report that an early years specialist with good subject knowledge does not guarantee successful teaching of mathematics. Their case of Frances revealed that a lack in confidence was also an issue, for although she knew the theory behind the teaching of subtraction, due to problems with her management, she resorted to time-filling activities.

In 1986, Lee Shulman et al. introduced different kinds of knowledge, in particular 'pedagogical content knowledge'. This term called attention to a special kind of teacher knowledge that links content and pedagogy. Ball and Bass (2000) describe how pedagogical content knowledge characterises the representations of particular topics and how children tend to interpret them. Children will often have difficulties with mathematical ideas or procedures and so teachers will need a unique subject-specific body of knowledge highlighting the need for close interweaving of subject matter and pedagogy in teaching (Ball and Bass 2000).

Teaching Place Value

Place value is taken to mean the value assigned to a digit according to its position in a number, e.g. 2 represents 2 units in the number 42, 2 tens in the number 125 and 2 hundreds in the number 274. Teaching place value has been a part of the mathematics curriculum since the introduction of a numeracy strategy (Department for Education and Employment (DfEE) 1999). With respect to early mathematics, it has been emphasised through extensive work on partitioning and recombining two or more digit numbers. Young children, who are only just developing an early understanding of quantity value while working with two-digit numbers, are expected to recognise a more formal perspective on these numbers, in order to prepare them for the formal written method.

English teachers are encouraged to support young children's mathematical thinking by taking a constructivist approach and provide a range of manipulatives that will model the concepts under scrutiny and support mathematical thinking, but little guidance on why this might be done. Documentation available encourages teachers to use a range of models and images to support the teaching of mathematics to young children. What they appear not to have achieved is the provision of appropriate pedagogical content knowledge and guidance as to how best to teach the contradictory elements of place value. In England, young children are expected to develop and refine counting skills, which are then abandoned in favour of a completely different approach based on place value through partitioning the tens from the units. Research contradicts this perspective (Sugarman 2007; Thompson 2000; Beishuizen 2004), in that young children need to bridge this understanding of quantity value and column value, but much later in their development, when they are fluent in their understanding of quantities (Beishuizen 2004).

Manipulatives have the propensity to provide representations of mathematical concepts and structures, and are used widely to support children's thinking, but they are not sufficient to guarantee meaningful learning (Clements and Samara 2009). Askew (2011) discusses how learners cannot go directly from not knowing about place value to knowing about it. Teachers provide tools and artefacts that mediate this, through which the learning is assumed to be enabled. Thus, part of that mediation has to come through appropriate use of language and specific vocabulary which will enculturate children in learning to think and speak mathematically (Lerman 2001). Teachers' guidance has promoted the use of some manipulatives, such as, base ten apparatus, to reinforce the 'column' aspect and to an extent the partitioning of quantity aspect. Consequently, teachers will draw on what they have used in the past, what they have seen others use or what their institutional scheme of work or textbook (if they have one) suggests. It is assumed that teachers will know what manipulatives are best to use for place value, drawing on their subject or pedagogical content knowledge. However, Rowland et al. (2009) show that whichever manipulatives are used, the examples provided by a teacher ought, ideally, to be the outcome of a careful process of choice because some examples work better than others.

As stated above, this approach has been called into question. Thompson (2009) argues that teachers need to distinguish between the two different interpretations of place value the 'quantity' value aspect and 'column' value aspect. Furthermore, research indicates that place value understanding needs to develop over time, possibly years (Thompson and Bramald 2002; Liebeck 1984; Anghileri 1995). They question why we (the English) teach column value as soon as children begin to recognise and calculate with two-digit numbers. Beishuizen (2004), summarising Freudenthal's earlier work, wrote 'instead of introducing formal structures like place value with concrete materials to children, Freudenthal (1973) advocated the more radical view of linking-up early maths activities to children's own informal (counting) strategies, and postponing the more formal aspects till later' (2004, p. 19).

Bruner's (1966) work on enactive, iconic and symbolic learning provides us with a warranted framework from which to analyse how place value could be introduced and developed with young children. More recent work (Thompson 2009, Thompson and Bramald 2002; Sugarman 2007; Tall and Vinner 1991) reinforces how imagery and representation (Bruner's iconic stage) can explicitly, and implicitly, develop deep understanding of partitioning. Examples of effective imagery can be seen in Clements and Samara's (2009) work, and in particular in the Australian Maths Recovery work by Wright et al. (2006).

Here are some examples of the type of imagery that might be used to support children's understanding if used consistently through instruction (Sugarman 2007) (Fig. 3.1).

A fives dot rack, where ten discs are placed in a line can provide an intermediate grouping for ten. This can reinforce the partitioning of numbers such as six, which is five and one more, seven is five and two more, etc. developing a consistent structure for the children to follow that they can build upon.

The bead string shown in Fig. 3.2 provides a similar model, where numbers that go beyond five either form a new line or change colour.

Fig. 3.1 Fives rack.

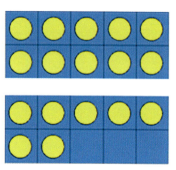

Fig. 3.2 String beads.

The images become a powerful mental picture for children to develop number structures mentally, such as the number 17 illustrated above. Children will see that 17 can be made up or broken down into parts, all of which will be familiar to them at that stage, e.g. a ten, made up of two fives, and five and two more, just as the Soroban discs for Japanese and Chinese children offer (Frank and Barner 2012). This will support children moving onto calculation, for example, when two numbers are placed together for adding, 4+3, after several physical movements of the discs, or beads, children will be able to mentally move the discs and know that 4+3 becomes (4+1)+2, thus five and two more. This becomes even more effective when they begin to bridge ten.

Essentially, it would appear that carefully selected manipulatives can be a crucial part of the process of learning. Conducted under careful instruction by the teacher, but developed through constructive models where patterns, combinations and parts of numbers can be seen and discussed explicitly with the children. However, if not selected or used appropriately, manipulatives may become simply a motivational pieces of apparatus. Indeed, Moyer's (2001) research found that some teachers' perspectives and 'behaviours indicated that using manipulatives was little more than a diversion in classrooms where teachers were not able to represent mathematics concepts themselves.' (p. 175). In such circumstances, the emphases were on fun rather than the necessary support for learning in general and mathematical thinking in particular.

The research reported here is to analyse how one experienced teacher, with good subject knowledge, orchestrates the dance between instruction and construction in teaching this challenging concept of place value through partitioning of numbers with models and images, to young children.

Methodology

A number of studies (Thompson 1984; Goldin 2002; Beswick 2007) have shown how case study can greatly enhance our knowledge and understanding of the relationship between teachers' espoused beliefs and enacted practice. In respect of this study, six primary teachers, considered locally to be effective teachers of mathematics, participated in a series of observations and post-observation video-stimulated recall interviews. It was decided to work with teachers who were essentially ambassadors of the subject in order to eliminate, as far as possible, lack of confidence or enjoyment in teaching the subject. This chapter reports on the findings of one of the six teachers (Jane), who, when involved in this research, taught children of ages five and six, to illustrate pedagogical issues related to the use of manipulatives and language emphasised when teaching fundamental number structures to such young children.

Prior to any observations, a semi-structured interview was conducted to elicit colleagues' mathematical backgrounds. The intention was to examine how their early experiences of school, university and, for example, family had influenced their perspectives on mathematics and its teaching. Following the initial interview, each teacher was observed over a period of 6–12 weeks. Each lesson was videotaped and after an initial analysis, where questions and issues were identified, followed by a stimulated recall interview (SRI) (Perkins 1982). During these interviews, colleagues were invited to discuss the whole class episodes of the lessons in relation to their professional decision-making in respect of the chosen task and the manner in which the episode played out. Foci for this elicitation included, for example, their mathematical objectives and the pedagogical approaches they used. Importantly, teachers' topic choices were assumed to have been predetermined by the statutory National Curriculum requirements and so SRIs focussed on the rationales colleagues' gave for the ways in which they engaged their children during the whole class episodes of their lessons. Thus, the data for each teacher comprised a pre-observation background interview and between three and six paired observations and SRIs. Data were analysed qualitatively drawing on, but not exclusively, the constant comparison exploited by grounded theorists (Strauss and Corbin 1998).

The Study and Discussion

What follows is a summary of what Jane presented to her class and her rationale for using the manipulatives to model the learning objectives, and the activity children were expected to do in independent work. Jane's utterances are in italics.

As presented earlier, the context in English mathematics classrooms has continued to draw from the National Strategy guidelines (DfEE 1999; DfES 2003) where the learning objectives for a lesson are displayed together with success criteria. This objective-driven approach is a procedure adopted by most teachers in England, and indeed in this case by Jane. Her lesson listed two mathematical learning objectives lifted straight from guidance papers:

Fig. 3.3 Place value cards

Fig. 3.4 Place value cards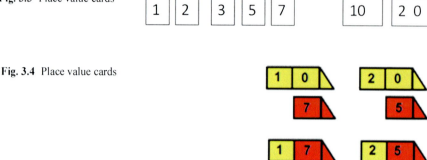

- To partition numbers into tens and units
- To begin to order two-digit numbers

Although the children had started to partition numbers earlier that week, they could not remember what the word 'partition' meant. Jane explained to the children that it meant splitting the number into tens and ones, and that would be what they do in independent work later.

Jane's success criteria were:

- We will understand how to partition two-digit numbers
- We can show a two-digit number by using cubes
- We can order two-digit numbers

The criteria emphasised the use of cubes to show understanding of a two-digit number, which Jane saw as a model for the learning of partitioning. She explained, in the SRI (interview) that followed the lesson, that the idea of partitioning was still new to the class and so the lesson '…was like one of their first steps to understanding how to partition a two-digit number'.

The first resource Jane used to illustrate partitioning was on the class interactive whiteboard (IWB) where a set of number (place value) cards, numbers 1–9 and 10–50, were displayed like the ones in Fig. 3.3.

When prompted, some of the children were able to offer examples of one-, two- and three-digit numbers which she acknowledged and praised. She then used the IWB to construct a two-digit number, and moved a ten and a seven, placing the seven on top of the zero of the ten. She asked the children what is the number. Many of the children called out the number 70. She corrected them by reiterating that it was a 17 not 70 as it was a teen number, because 'all numbers with a one in front were teen numbers'. She continued to demonstrate and explain that the number could be split apart, back to the ten and the seven again, and moved the seven card away from the ten. She repeated the process by covering the zero by the seven card, reiterating that ten and seven make 17.

Jane reflected later that her resources were not ideal but because she did not have any arrow cards, she had found the IWB card activity online so decided to use this as her model to demonstrate partitioning. The place value cards, like the ones shown in Fig. 3.4, are commonly used in primary schools.

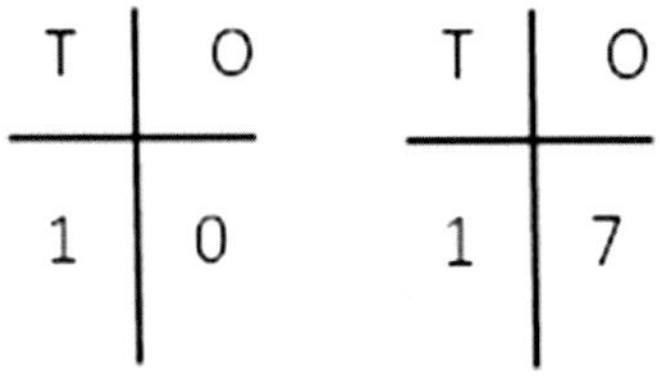

3   It is quite confusing isn't it?

Fig. 3.5 Column representation of a two-digit number

T	O		T	O
1	0		1	7

The teacher will use a large dimensioned set, and the children would have a small-sized set to use individually or in pairs. The Primary National Strategy guidance (DfES, 2003) and DfEE (NNS 1999) suggest to teachers that they 'should use place value cards to partition and combine numbers with zero as place holder' (p. 4). The resource is an abstract image rather than a more concrete one but no clear rationale is evident in the documentation for this preferred choice.

It could be argued that using the number cards on the IWB or physically by the teacher would have made little difference to the presentation of partitioning numbers; they simply appear on screen rather than in the teacher's hand. The representation of number still remains an abstract one. Therefore, the language the teacher uses here to describe the process of partitioning is crucial in the exposition. Jane did not emphasise any connection to the order of numbers, where number 17 sits within the system, this was entirely left for the children to implicitly understand, which is problematic. As Lampert (1986) and Gelman (1986) highlight, teaching implicit understanding can have the adverse effect on the development of children's mathematical thinking. Jane had found the place value cards free online and 'thought that would be good to use, but they were only small ones and only one set of them. So I would have preferred to use giant hands-on ones…so I could show them, together, take them apart, etc. I would have preferred that…but this was the best I could find at short notice'.

After repeating the splitting up and recombining of the cards to illustrate partitioning of number 17, Jane explained to the children that the numbers were in columns called ones and tens. And reiterated 'seven ones go into the ones column and one ten goes into the tens column', just as illustrated below, stating to the children that this was 'where all two-digit numbers go' (Fig. 3.5).

She repeated the process with 25, showing a 20 card and a five card and placed the five over the zero of the 20. She repeated that 'the five is in the ones column and the two is in the tens column' and partitioned them as she did before. She reinforced the idea by asking the children what this means, as she makes hand gestures of pulling something apart. She repeats, 'It means to split the number apart.' as she moves the five away again from the 20. Jane asks, 'What are we left with?' To which the children shout out 'Twenty!'

Jane's progression to draw column lines onto her board above the number 17 she believed reiterated that the one represents one ten in the tens column and the seven represents the seven in the ones column. Interestingly, she provided no explanation to what these columns meant, or why they were important. After repeating the same statement, that the seven goes in the ones column and the tens go into the tens column, she qualified this fact saying 'where all the two-digit numbers go'. Her

Fig. 3.6 Linking cubes

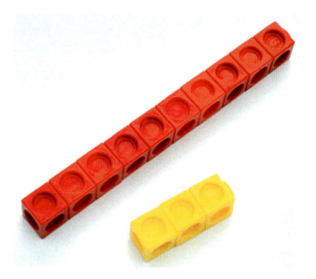

qualifying statement here is problematic; she does not expand on what she means by 'all the two-digit numbers go...' She did not explain what two-digit numbers have in common. Instead, she introduced a new number to look at, 25, and repeated the explanation. Jane believed that this is what was required of her. She believed that drawing the columns supported the children's understanding of place value, and therefore partitioning. As Askew (2011) argues 'learners cannot go from not knowing to knowing about place value', teachers need to provide tools and artefacts that will mediate this notion, through which the learning is assumed to be enabled. Jane was convinced that drawing the columns helped the children understand place value, she said 'I have used this before, it works well'.

The lesson changed to an instruction of what the children were expected to do at their tables independently. Jane introduced linking cubes, as shown in Fig. 3.6.

Jane showed the children ten cubes attached to each other in a rod, and said:

Jane: One tower of ten cubes here and this represents the tens column. This is a block of ten (as she shows a number of cubes fixed in a rod). It's just one block of ten. (She then held up seven orange cubes attached in a shorter length.)

Jane: The orange cubes, how many cubes have I got here? (showing the children the smaller length of cubes).

Class: Seven

Jane: You think seven? Yes I have, (and counts them). These cubes show us the number 17 in those columns. We have one block of ten but seven little ones. You are going to do that soon at your tables in a minute.

In the SRI, Jane was asked why she called the small rod of seven cubes the 'little ones'? She said '...for practicality really, for showing them on the carpet. It's difficult to show them seven individual ones in your hand so ideally, that's what I would have liked them to see, and on reflection I could have perhaps stuck them with blu-tack on the little white board...so they could see them better, but I think that was the main reason it was difficult to show them seven individual ones'.

3 It is quite confusing isn't it?   31

Jane repeated the procedure with the number 25, again reiterating the column she asked 'we have then number two in our tens column, how many cubes of ten will I need now?' She pointed to the 20 in 25. The class response was quite mixed, they shouted out:

Class: Nine...two...ten.

Jane: *It's quite difficult isn't it! With our 17...ok I have one in the tens column. And one block of ten, how many do I need in this one? (Pointing to the number seven. She then points back to the number two in 25.)*

Lisa: *'We need two blocks of ten,' to which Jane praises, 'We do, good girl!'*

Jane agreed and reiterated that 'in the tens column we need two blocks of ten'. One child called out 'Two more?' which she rejected and repeated that they need two blocks of ten in the tens column. She again counted the two blocks in her hand and repeated they need two blocks of tens in the tens column. She turned to her box to get some more cubes, and a child shouted out 'we need five cubes'. She turned with her cubes and said, 'That's right just five,' and announced that they need, 'five ones for the ones column', pointing to the ones column on the board 'but two blocks of ten for our tens column. It is, quite confusing isn't it!', she stated. The children appeared to be confused with this different model, having demonstrated understanding of the abstract of splitting two digits apart and then recombining, they were moved onto column value and then swiftly followed by quantity value in the cubes.

The independent work lasted for nearly 12 minutes and when children appeared to struggle with making the tens and 'little ones' to partition their numbers given to them. Jane called a halt to this section of the lesson and tried to explain the process again. She asked what they found difficult about the task, but the children did not appear to be able to articulate what they found difficult, consequently Jane re-taught the idea using the linking cubes but changing the vocabulary from blocks of ten and little ones saying, 'One group of ten or one tower of ten'. She repeated that the number one represented number ten and that it was not the number one, and explained the ones column asking another child (Tom) to select the right number of cubes to show this number (seven). She reiterated that Tom was not getting 'two big towers out of the box, but just seven on its own'. She placed the two towers (ten and the seven) together to show the cubes and asked the children to help her count on from 10 to 17. The lesson ended, the topic would not be picked up again until the following term, nearly 3 months later.

Jane had clearly believed that to reconstruct a two-digit number, she would need a model for the children to gain understanding of partitioning through 'accessible concrete materials that illustrate' the concept of 'partitioning' she had previously illustrated abstractly on the board. The linking cubes were presented as one 'block' of ten, linked together and seven 'little ones' which were also linked in a rod, but smaller. Jane's rationale for this approach was:

> '...I've used those two (place value cards and cubes) together before and it's been successful. This was good because you could see how the numbers began in their tens and units and you could put them together and partition them again and to try to relate the partitioning and like making towers of ten to relate to the numbers.'

Jane recognised that the children were struggling with the task she had set them of partitioning and recombining numbers with cubes so changed the vocabulary she had used in her previous explanation and instruction. She said:

...if children don't understand the word 'block' then they might understand the word 'tower' or they might understand 'lots of' or they might understand other vocabulary. So I tend to throw different vocabulary at them, because some children might not understand just one of those words.

Her reflection indicated her understanding of the difficulties children experience with certain vocabulary, yet she did not seem aware of the more complex difficulties the children were having with the instruction she gave them. Her focus (learning objective) was to partition numbers into tens and ones. This she did by deconstructing the digits of a two-digit number and partitioned the seven from the ten card. She immediately followed this by instructing the children to see the two-digit number by its column value, one ten and seven ones. The children did not respond to this new idea of columns. To reiterate the partitioning and recombining of two-digit numbers, the children were instructed to construct the quantity value of the numbers shown, then attempt to reconstruct new numbers at their tables independently using the cubes. The difficulties the children had were between the teacher's abstract instruction and concrete re-construction of what a two-digit number is, was confusing to the children. Jane believed the construction of a two-digit number with cubes was to scaffold the children's learning, just as the teacher guidance suggests when partitioning and recombining numbers.

Evidence in this study reveals that these 'blocks' of cubes do not easily lend themselves to becoming tools for thinking with. People's mental models of number seem to be linked to the ordinal aspects of number where numbers are placed in order and with respect to each other, as on a linear scale or number line (Dehaene 1999). Jane had not considered the implication of using an abstract form of number cards followed by the introduction to column value, then scaffold the idea with a concrete form of quantity. She believed she was supporting children's thinking by constructing the quantity value to reinforce the partitioning. However, the confusion began with mixing the abstract form alongside the column value, followed by the quantity value together with informal language to complicate the situation. The dance of instruction with construction (Presmeg 2014) was a confusing dance for these children, who were still unsure of the quantity value of numbers.

This study is not presented to criticise one teacher's exposition or lack of pedagogical content knowledge. For this case is not atypical, when analysing the national strategy documentation (DfEE 1999, 2003) the guidance to English teachers informs them that abstract representations are to be favoured over more concrete materials without any clear rationale. Jane conveyed no knowledge that there could be an issue in using concrete materials (cubes) alongside the abstract form. She followed the national strategy training and documentation and interpreted the suggested advice closely. She was successful and considered to be an effective teacher of mathematics, totally committed to doing well by the children in her care, working hard to follow the system in which she was working.

Sutherland (2007) argued that the practitioners are no longer being treated as intelligent professionals, whose teaching would be enhanced by knowing the reasons for using a particular teaching approach. She views the framework as 'dumbing down' the teachers, which is likely to lead to a 'dumbing down' of their pupils. This study would concur with this idea, the relationship between the instruction and construction appears to no longer be in the hands of the teacher, for Jane trusted the guidance materials she used, as is the expectation.

Jane assumed that if she showed her class the number cards to represent the two digits, and then cubes, it would help to illustrate the number symbols by offering a concrete sense of size and quantity of the number, thus the mathematical concept of place value. Research informs us that resources do not in themselves convey knowledge; the teacher should explicitly make the connections between the abstract and the concrete idea. Yackel (2000), Cobb et al. (1992) and Holt (1982) state, only those who already understand the mathematical concepts being modelled will perceive the mathematics in them, as the interpretation of the individual will be constrained by prior experiences. Jane appeared not to be concerned with this idea. She assumed that the children were simply not ready for partitioning, and not, the exposition itself may have been the difficulty children were having. She changed her vocabulary indicating that she was aware of some misunderstandings but little sense was made by the children of how these two ideas linked.

Conclusion

Although the exposition described here appears to imply that Jane had limited mathematical subject knowledge, the fact is she trained as a specialist of mathematics and achieved a very good grade in her degree. What she appeared not to demonstrate was a deep pedagogical knowledge (see Shulman 1986), however, we argue that she had placed her trust in the national strategy and followed the guidance carefully.

Where the lesson failed, it seems to us, was in her ambition of supporting children's mathematical thinking, particularly in respect of making explicit the connections between quantity value and column value. She understood how teaching place value through the use of digit cards links with the partitioning of two-digit numbers and introduced column value. Jane attempted to support her class' understanding by the use of informal language: 'block of, and tower of (tens) and little ones'. In this respect, Jane was confident that her chosen words were familiar to her children, and yet our observations indicated that these words meant little to the children in this context, which is a problem well rehearsed in the literature (Clements and Samara 2009; Lansdel 1999).

Significantly, Jane works in a system that expects an unquestioning adherence to centrally prepared pedagogical guidelines. These guidelines, which do not suggest postponing work on tens and units/ones with column headings T and U, expect teachers to teach this idea to young children. Jane made the decision to support children's understanding of partitioning through her cube-related representation. In so doing, she assumed that mathematical meaning was embodied in her representations but failed to make explicit her objectives in this regard.

In sum, place value is difficult to understand and to teach. Jane's teaching of mathematics is expected to comply with a national strategy that presents mathematical content as lists of learning objectives and success criteria. She attempted to provide her children with meaningful opportunities to develop conceptual understanding through her use of manipulatives and language in order. Yet the dance—to use Presmeg's (2014) metaphor—as presented here, shows that teachers need an awareness of how these opposing pedagogical approaches interplay. Until a system offers teachers, the pedagogical training and guidance necessary for the development of an awareness of the subtleties of the dance between instruction and construction, we cannot expect those who teach young children mathematics to participate in the dance. It simply becomes confusing, doesn't it?

References

Anghileri, J. (Ed.) (1995). Children 's mathematical thinking in the primary years. London: Hodder & Stoughton.

Askew, M. Brown, M. Rhodes, V. Wiliam, D. Johnson, D. (1997). Effective teachers of numeracy in primary schools: Teachers' beliefs, practices and pupils' learning. British Educational Research Association Annual Conference, University of York.

Askew, M., & Brown, M. (2004).The impact of the national numeracy strategy on mathematics attainment and learning in year 4. Paper presented at International Congress of Mathematics Education, Copenhagen, July, 2004.

Askew, M. (2011).Transforming primary mathematics. London: Routledge.

Aubrey, C., Dahl, S., & Godfrey, R. (2006). Early mathematics development and later achievement: Further evidence. Mathematics Education Research Journal, 18(1), 27–46.

Ball, D. L, Lubienski, S., & Mewborn, D. (2001). Research on teaching mathematics: The unsolved problem of teachers' mathematical knowledge. In V. Richardson (Ed.), Handbook of research on teaching (4th ed.). New York: Macmillian.

Ball, D., & Bass, H. (2000). Interweaving content and pedagogy in teaching and learning to teach: Knowing and using mathematics. In J. Boaler (Ed.), Multiple perspectives on mathematics teaching and learning. Westport: Ablex.

Beishuizen, M. (2004). Two Types of Mental Arithmetic and the Empty Numberline. British Society for Research into Learning Mathematics. Conference Proceedings. 17. 1&2. Oxford.

Beswick, K. (2007). Teachers' beliefs that matter in secondary mathematics classrooms. Educational Studies in Mathematics, 65, 95–120.

Brown G. (2010). Equality Act 2010. London: HM Stationery Office.

Brown, M., Askew, M., Baker, D., Denvir, H., Millett, A. (1998) Is the National Numeracy Strategy Research-Based? British Journal of Educational Studies, Vol. 46 (4) pp. 362–385

Bruner, J. S. (1966). Towards a theory of instruction. New York: Norton.

Cambridge Primary Review. (2009). Towards a new primary curriculum part 2 summary of main points. http://www.primaryreview.org.uk. Accessed: 050612.

Clements, D. H., & Samara, J. (2009). Learning and teaching early math: The trajectories approach. Abington: Routledge.

Cobb, P., Yackel, E., & Wood, T. (1992). A constructivist alternative to the representational view of mind in mathematics education. Journal for Research in Mathematics Education, 23(1), 2–33.

Creemers, B. P. M. (1994) The Effective Classroom. London, Cassell.

Dehaene, S. (1999). The number sense: How the mind creates mathematics. Oxford: Oxford University Press.

DfEE (Department for Education and Employment). (1999). *The national numeracy strategy: Framework for the teaching of Mathematics.* QCA.

DfES (Department for Education and Skills). (2003). *Excellence and enjoyment: A strategy for primary schools.* London: DfES.

Frank, M., & Barner, D. (2012). Representing exact number visually using mental abacus. *Journal of Experimental Psychology: General, 141*(1), 134–149.

Gelman, R. (1986). Toward an understanding-based theory of mathematics learning and instruction, or, in praise of lampert on teaching multiplication. *Cognition and Instruction, 3*(4), 349–355.

Goldin, G. A. (2002). Affect, meta-affect and mathematical belief structures. In G. Leder, E. Pehkonen, & G. Törner (Eds.), *Beliefs: A hidden variable in mathematics education*? (pp. 59–72). Dordrecht: Kluwer.

Goulding, M., Rowland, T., & Barber, P. (2002). Does it matter? Primary teacher trainees' subject knowledge in mathematics. *British Educational Research Journal, 28*(5), 689-704.

Holt, J. (1982). *How children fail.* New York: Dell.

Howell, S., & Kemp, C. (2005). Defining early number sense: A participatory Australian study. *Educational Psychology, 25*(5), 170–218.

Kirschner, P. A., Sweller, J., & Clark, R. E. (2006). Why minimal guidance during instruction does not work: An analysis of the failure of constructivist, discovery, problem-based, experiential, and inquiry-based teaching. *Educational Psychologist, 46*(2), 75–86.

Lampert, M. (1986). Knowing, doing and teaching multiplication. *Cognition and Instruction, 3*, 305–342.

Lansdell J. M. (1999): Introducing Young Children to Mathematical Concepts: Problems with 'new' terminology, Educational Studies, 25:3, 327–333

Lave, J., & Wenger, E. (1991). *Situated learning: Legitimate peripheral participation.* Cambridge: Cambridge University Press.

Lerman, S. (2001). Getting used to mathematics: Alternative ways of speaking about becoming mathematical. *Ways of Knowing, 1*(1), 47–52.

Liebeck, P. (1984). *How children learn mathematics.* Harmondsworth: Penguin Books.

Ma, L. (1999). *Knowing and teaching elementary mathematics.* New Jersey: Lawrence Erlbaum.

Moyer, P. S. (2001). Are we having fun yet? How Teachers use Manipulatives to teach mathemaitcs. *Educational Studies in Mathematics, 47*, 175–197.

Perkins, D. C. (1982). *The Mind's Best Work.* Cambridge Ma.: Harvard University.

Piaget, J., (1952). *The Origins of Intelligence in Children* (M. Cook, Trans.). New York: International University Press.

Presmeg, N. (2014). A Dance of Instruction with Construction in Mathematics Education. In: U. Kortenkamp et al. (eds.), *Early Mathematics Learning,* (pp. 9 –17). New York: Springer.

Resnick, L. (1987). Learning in school and out. *Educational Researcher, 16*(9), 13–20.

Rowland, T. & Ruthven, K. (2011). *Mathematical Knowledge in Teaching.* London: Springer.

Rowland, T., Turner, F., Thwaites, A., & Huckstep, P. (2009). *Developing primary mathematics teaching. Reflecting on practice with the knowledge quartet.* London: Sage Publications Ltd.

Shulman, L. S. (1986). Those who understand: Knowledge growth in teaching. *Educational Researcher, 15*(2), 4–14.

Siraj-Baltchford, I., Sylva, K., Muttock, S., Gilden, R., & Bell, D. (2002). Researching effective pedagogy in the early years. The EPPE Research Report no: 356. London: DfES.

Strauss, A. L., & Corbin, J. (1998). Basics of qualitative research: Techniques and Procedures for developing Grounded Theory (2nd ed). Thousand Oaks Calif.: Sage Publications Ltd.

Sugarman, I. (2007). The Same Difference. *Mathematics Teaching.* Association of Teachers of Mathematics. 202. pp16–18.

Sutherland R (2007) *Teaching for learning mathematics.* Maidenhead: Open University Press.

Tall, D., & Vinner, S. (1981). Concept image and concept definition in mathematics, with special reference to limits and continuity. *Educational Studies in Mathematics, 12*, 151–169.

Thompson, A. G. (1984). The relationship of teachers' conceptions of mathematics and mathematics teaching to instructional practice. *Educational Studies in Mathematics, 5*, 105–127.

Thompson, I. (2009). What do young children's graphics tell us about the teaching of written calculation Ch 11. In Thompson (Ed.), *Teaching and learning early number*. Open University press.

Thompson, I., & Bramald, R. (2002). *An investigation of the relationship between young children's understanding of the concept of place value and their competence at mental addition* (Report for the Nuffield Foundation). Newcastle upon Tyne: University of Newcastle upon Tyne.

Tobias, S. & Duffy, T. M., Eds. (2009). *Constructivist instruction. Success of failure?* Oxford, UK: Routledge.

Vygotsky, L. (1978). *Mind in Society: development of Higher pyschological processes.* Cambridge Mass: Harvard University Press.

Williams, P. (2008). *Independent Review of Mathematics Teaching in Early Years*. London: DCSF.

Wright, R., Martland, J., Stafford, A. K., & Strange, G. (2006). *Teaching number in the classroom with 4–8 year olds*. London: Paul Chapman Educational Publishing.

Yackel, E. (2000). Creating a mathematics classroom environment that fosters the development of mathematical argumentation. International Congress of Mathematical Education. Paper prepared for Working Group for Action 1. July 31–August 6, 2000, Tokyo.

Chapter 4
Mathematical Teaching Moments: Between Instruction and Construction

Troels Lange, Tamsin Meaney, Eva Riesbeck and Anna Wernberg

Mathematics Through Play in Swedish Preschools

Sweden, like other countries such as New Zealand (Haynes 2000), is faced with a tension of wanting to ensure that children begin school with stronger mathematical understandings, while also wanting to adhere to the philosophy that preschool children should learn through play. This is a tension that some see as irreconcilable (Lee and Ginsburg 2009; Carr and May 1996), often because it is reduced to an either–or scenario—either children's own interests are followed or they are directly instructed by an adult (Dijk et al. 2004). In this chapter, we explore how one teacher developed children's mathematical curiosity from their play. Through respectful listening, including watching carefully what children do, the teacher was able to ask questions that simultaneously engaged the children's mathematical curiosity and supported their play.

As is the case in many countries around the world, in Swedish preschools play is considered the foundation for children's learning experiences (Skolverket 2011). This is reflected in the curriculum:

> Play is important for the child's development and learning. Conscious use of play to promote the development and learning of each individual child should always be present in preschool activities. Play and enjoyment in learning in all its various forms stimulate the imagination, insight, communication and the ability to think symbolically, as well as the ability to co-operate and solve problems. (Skolverket 2011, p. 6)

Connecting play with enjoyment assumes that learning will produce more easily "imagination, insight, communication and the ability to think symbolically, as well as the ability to co-operate and solve problems". However, in a study of Swedish teachers and parents' perceptions of the relationship between play and learning in very young children, learning was taken for granted and considered as something that always occurs in play (Sheridan et al. 2009). It was not something that had to be planned for. At the same

---

T. Lange (✉) · T. Meaney · E. Riesbeck · A. Wernberg
Malmö University,
205 06, Malmö, Sweden
e-mail: troels.lange@mah.se

time, play was assessed as being of low quality, although exactly how this quality was judged was unclear. Still, it would seem that the assumption of the connection between play, enjoyment and learning needs more investigation.

One reason for the difficulty in assessing the quality of play may be because it is difficult to define (Samuelsson and Carlsson 2008). Alan Bishop (1988), in discussing the addition of play to his list of universal mathematical activities, used Norbeck's (1977) reflections on the work of Huizinga to suggest the following list of characteristics:

- Voluntary, free
- Not a task, not ordinary, not real
- Essentially unserious in its goals although often seriously executed
- Outside the immediate satisfactions itself, but an integral part of life and a necessity
- Repetitive
- Closely linked with beauty in many ways but not identical with it
- Creates order and is order; has rules, rhythms and harmony
- Often related to wit and humour but is not synonymous with them
- Has elements of tension, uncertainty, chanciness
- Outside the antitheses of wisdom and folly, truth and falsehood, good and evil, vice and virtue, has no more moral function (p. 42)

More succinctly and combining many of the features also identified by Samuelsson and Carlsson (2008), Dockett and Perry's (2010) stated:

> The process of play is characterised by a non-literal "what if" approach to thinking, where multiple end points or outcomes are possible. In other words, play generates situations where there is no one "right" answer.... Essential characteristics of play then, include the exercise of choice, non-literal approaches, multiple possible outcomes and acknowledgement of the competence of players. These characteristics apply to the processes of play, regardless of the content. (Dockett and Perry 2010, p. 175)

These definitions share several ideas. They include a sense of play being voluntary so that children have a choice of whether to engage or not as well as having choices about how to participate. It could also be said that the uncertainty that is integral to play provides the opportunities for multiple possible outcomes. The "what-if" and "non-literalness" nature of play resonates with play being outside the "antitheses" mentioned by Bishop. While the Dockett and Perry (2010) definition includes the "acknowledgement of the competence of players", the characteristics discussed by Bishop (1988) do not include any which are related to characteristics of the participants. Play can be considered as an essential component of children's experiences as they explore, try out and interact with aspects of the world around them.

The Swedish curriculum for preschools (Skolverket 2010) does not define play as such, except by choosing to use the word *lek,* meaning play without predetermined rules. (Playing of rule-based games, such as football, bridge and Monopoly, is denoted by the word *spel.*) The choice of the word *lek* indicates an alignment with Dockett and Perry's (2010) idea that the characteristics of play are about the process, rather than outcomes. In the characteristics discussed by Bishop (1988), rules are mentioned but in the sense that they arise out of the play—"creates order and is order; has rules, rhythms and harmony"—rather than being imposed on the play.

We consider that there are predominantly two kinds of situations which can be described as play in preschools: free play, in which children use the resources around them without adult intervention, and guided play where a teacher sets up a situation but allows children's own interests to form the play. Both of these kinds of play are in alignment with the use of *lek* in the preschool curriculum. Although researchers used these terms, for example, Coltman et al. (2002), Edo et al. (2009), Lamberty (2007), the differences between the terms generally remain undefined.

Although it has been documented that mathematical learning has arisen from free play (Coltman et al. 2002), Lee and Ginsberg (2009) suggested that children are likely to gain only limited mathematical understandings from it. For them, the role of the teacher is of paramount importance. Björklund (2008) showed that adults set the parameters for children's opportunities to engage with mathematical ideas. An adult watching or participating in a child-initiated play can develop children's mathematical ideas by stimulating their curiosity and language use (Doverborg 2006). Anderson (1997) in investigating parent interactions with preschool children wrote:

> Adherence to social constructivist principles implies that parents be encouraged to share in determining and carrying out activities with their children rather than to expect children to work alone with the materials. Likewise, it suggests that young children are capable explorers who actively seek meaning from and aptly structure their own engagement with the materials and significant others. (p. 485)

As an alternative to the two types of play, direct instruction also can occur in preschools. In this case, the teacher prescribes what actions the children should engage in. Children may still enjoy this learning but they can make limited, if any, choices about what they do (see Emilson and Folkesson 2006). In recent years, particularly in English-speaking countries, several intervention studies have involved teachers presenting preschool children with set activities. For example, Papic, Mulligan and Mitchelmore (2011) implemented an intervention program on repeating and spatial patterning in one preschool over a 6-month period. Children were grouped according to how they performed on an initial diagnostic interview and then provided with tasks for their level. A combination of individual and group time was provided. Children progressed to the next level if they showed competency in their current level.

Although learning through play can be juxtaposed with learning from direct instruction, such a juxtaposition limits the types of discussions that can result. Consequently, we see it as being more valuable to focus on the teaching process and the features most likely to lead to learning. To us, teachers, or other adults, who engage with children around mathematical concepts are teaching. Therefore, teaching can occur both in guided play as well as in direct instruction. The relationship between teaching and learning is complex, making it difficult to determine causality (Krummheuer 2012). However, by understanding how a teacher interacts with children within a guided play situation, we will be more able to understand which features in the interaction contribute to children's learning mathematics.

In this chapter, we first present two models for the organisation of learning before describing how the Swedish preschool teacher engaged with a small group of children around the mathematical ideas in a set of glass jars. We then use the models to analyse the teacher's role in developing children's mathematical curiosity through building on mathematical teaching moments.

The Teacher's Role in Preschool Children's Learning

The importance of scaffolding, where adults gradually reduce their level of support so children become competent, is often raised in discussions about young children learning mathematics. Frequently, this discussion is framed in relation to children solving problems (Wood et al. 1976). Using her own and others' work on scaffolding, Anghileri (2006) distinguished between different teacher strategies for scaffolding mathematics learning. These strategies can be seen in the three-level model represented in Fig. 4.1. Each level is in a hierarchical relationship to the others:

> At the most basic level, *environmental provisions* enable learning to take place without the direct intervention of the teacher. The subsequent two levels identify teacher interactions that are increasingly directed to developing richness in the support of mathematical learning through *explaining, reviewing and restructuring* and *developing conceptual thinking*. (Anghileri 2006, p. 38)

Examples of different strategies are provided at each level. The strategies in the centre are those that Anghileri (2006) considered were seen most frequently in classrooms, while the strategies on the sides were the ones that were more likely to be connected to effective mathematics classrooms. Although situated within the school context, much of the work that Anghileri drew on in developing this model came from research on 4–6-year-olds. Given that Swedish children are in preschools for most of this age period, Anghileri's model has the potential to be a valuable resource in analysing the teacher's role in developing children's mathematical curiosity.

Although Anghileri (2006) acknowledged the importance of the interactions between teachers and students as leading to learning, her model focuses on what the teacher does and the children's actions are less visible. As indicated by Anderson (1997), children are active investigators of their world and thus their contributions to the interactions must be considered, especially when it is from their play that the teacher identifies teaching moments. In a study of toddlers in a Swedish preschool, Emilson and Folkesson (2006) used the ideas of Bernstein to suggest that a teacher, "instead of keeping control by the selection of communication, its sequencing and its pacing, she is responsive, observant and confirming, and she develops the ideas of the children" (p. 237). In so doing, she was able to support children to make decisions about their learning and consequently be involved in genuine participation. The child's contribution to the interaction was the basis on which learning opportunities were developed. Therefore, although Anghileri (2006) provides valuable insights, there is a need for a broader model with which to analyse interactions between the teacher and the children.

In many ways, the description of Emilson and Folkesson's (2006) teacher's interactions with toddlers resembles what Rogoff et al. (2003) described as *intent participation*. Rogoff et al. (2003) acknowledge that there are many ways to organ-

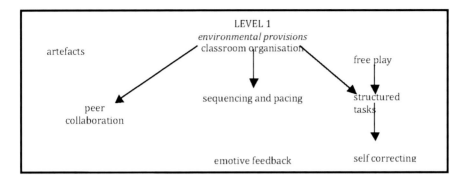
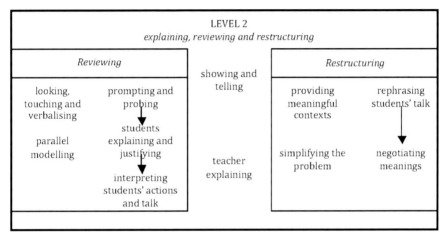
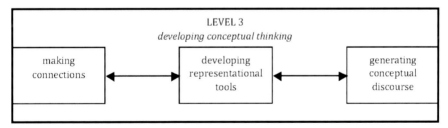

Fig. 4.1 Teacher strategies for scaffolding learning. (From Anghileri 2006, p. 39)

ise learning, but in their article they distinguished between *intent participation* and *assembly-line instruction*. Table 4.1 shows the main differences between these two types of learning. *Intent participation* often occurs when "people engage together in a common endeavour" (p. 183) and *assembly-line instruction* is used when there is a "transmission of information from experts outside the context of purposeful, productive activity" (p. 183), something which they perceived as being common in schools.

Table 4.1 Multifaceted traditions for organising learning. (From Rogoff et al. 2003, p. 185)

	Assembly-line instruction	Intent participation
Participation structure	Hierarchical participation structure with fixed roles	Collaborative, horizontal participation structure with fluid responsibilities
Motivation	Motivation in extrinsic rewards, threats. Relation of steps to purpose often unknown	Motivation in importance of activity. Relation of steps to purpose understood
Assessment	Assessment separate from learning, to test receipt	Assessment during shared endeavours to aid learning
Communication	Communication mainly in words; questions to quiz learners	Communication through joint action, and words and gestures about needed information
Learning	Learning through lessons, exercises, out of purposeful endeavours	Learning through observation during participation in shared endeavours
Roles	Experts manage, dividing task, not participating. Learners receive information	Experienced people guide while participating. Learners take initiative

Although not specifically on preschool teaching, Rogoff et al.'s (2003) model, like that of Anghileri (2006), drew on extracts from interactions between adults and preschool-aged children to exemplify the different components. Rogoff et al. (2003) considered that it is the integration of the components which contributes to the different traditions for organising learning. Certainly, the components of *intent participation* recognise the role of the child or learner in the interaction. There is an overlap in some aspects of both models; for example, Anghileri's model highlighted the need for a teacher to identify meaningful contexts whilst Rogoff et al. suggested that in *intent participation,* "motivation is generally inherent in the obvious importance and interest of the activity". However, there are also differences. Anghileri concentrated on the teacher, whereas Rogoff et al. viewed the roles of the participants as being fluid. We have primarily drawn on Rogoff et al.'s model and used the teacher scaffolding strategies of Anghileri's model to unpack the teacher's role in the interactions with the children.

The Data

The research was undertaken in a private preschool in a large city in southern Sweden. Filming was undertaken with different classes/groups over several days. In this chapter, we report on one episode of guided play. Although initially the teacher had not nominated it as being a mathematical activity, this focus became evident as the children engaged with the jars. Therefore, it was chosen because it exemplified how the activity was developed from the children's own interests. The whole episode lasted about 11 min. Extracts of the transcript are provided in the original Swedish with an English translation.

After first describing the episode, we then analyse how the teacher identified and then elaborated on children's interests by discussing each of the components in Rogoff et al.'s (2003) multifaceted models and connecting them to Anghileri's (2006) teacher strategies for scaffolding for learning.

Playing with Glass Jars

In this episode, three children, Marie, Mia and Lena, all pseudonyms, played with some glass jars. The teacher (L in the transcripts) provided the opportunity for this exploration, although the main purpose of the activity was for the children to put coloured paper on the jars and make them into candleholders.

The teacher placed herself on the side of the group and so was at a similar height to the children. This seemed to contribute to them focusing on the jars in the centre of the space. The children continually touched the jars, putting their hands and feet inside and exchanging the jars between themselves.

Most of the time, the teacher sat away from the jars, allowing the children to take the lead. However, when she wanted to ask specific questions or highlight particular aspects of the jars, she would touch or point to them. Although the teacher asked questions, she did not model answers, nor force the children to answer her questions when they showed reluctance.

The teacher began by asking the children if they thought that the jars looked the same. The children explained how they perceived the jars as rectangular, thick or thin. The teacher then asked one of the children, Lena, why she thought her jar was thick.

| L: Och din är lite tjock. På vad sätt är den tjock Lena, hur är den tjock? | And yours is a bit thick. In what way is it thick Lena, how is it thick? |
| Lena: Den är tjock på denna bredden. [barnet har en burk som blir tjockare nertill som hon visar på] | It is thick at this width. [the child has a jar that gets thicker at the bottom which she demonstrates] |

The teacher then continued by asking if the children had noticed other shapes

| L: Har den någon annan form någon annanstans? | Does it have any other shape elsewhere? |

This helped the children to focus on different shapes both between the jars as well as within the jar. After a while, the teacher asked if the children could put the jars in some sort of order. Lena placed all but one together in a group and explained how the odd jar was rectangular and therefore did not fit with the others.

After a short while, Mia tried to put her foot in one of the jars and Lena and Marie copied her immediately.

4 Mathematical Teaching Moments: Between Instruction and Construction

This went on until the teacher again asked the children if they could put the jars in order but this time she specified that the order was to be according to size. The children started to arrange the jars, with the teacher asking questions as they were doing it.

L: Vilken kan komma efter den här om den är högst och sen kommer den vilken kan komma efter den här? [Marie flyttar dit en högre burk] Om man tänker att man hitta nått som är lägre än den?	What can come after if this is the tallest and then what could come after this? [Marie moves a taller jar into the line] Do you think that you could find one that is lower [smaller] than that?
Marie: Större	Bigger
L: Den är högre	It is taller
[Mia ändrar på burkarna så att de går från högre till lägre.]	[Mia changes the jars so they go from tallest to shortest.]

On the initiative of Marie, they divided the jars between them. Marie said that everyone could have two each. The teacher then asked if they could have three each.

L: Om vi gör så att vi ställer tillbaka dom också ser vi om vi alla kan få, ställ tillbaka dom Marie allihopa, om alla kan få tre var?	If we put those back too, we will see if everyone can get, put them back Marie all of them, if everyone can get three each
Marie: En, två, tre [Marie räknar när hon tar sina, de andra bara tar]	One, two, three [Marie counts as she takes hers, the others just take theirs]
…	…
L: Det gick inte att få tre var	Could not get three each.

Then they counted the jars. Marie counts seven whilst Lena counts eight.

L: Åtta. Hur många fick du det till, kommer du ihåg det? [till Marie] när du räknade alla tillsammans? [Marie skakar på huvudet]	Eight. How many did you get it, do you remember that? [Marie] when you counted all together? [Marie shakes her head]
Marie: Sju	Seven
L: Marie fick det till sju	Marie got it [the answer] to be seven
Marie: Nej, jag fick det till åtta	No, I got it to be eight
L: Aha, du fick det till åtta sen, mm. Det är åtta tillsammans och vi har två var nu. Om vi gör så här att vi försöker ställa alla små burkar i en hög och alla stora burkar i en hög	Aha, you got it to be eight, then, mmm. There are eight together and we have two each n. If we do like this that we try to put all the small jars in a pile and all the big jars in a pile

By contrasting the answers, the teacher made the girls aware that there were two different answers. However, Marie did not want to take this any further and then said that she got eight as well.

Then the teacher asked the girls to sort the jars with the small jars in one group and the tall ones in another group. Although it began as a discussion about size, all of a sudden Marie says *fyrhörning* (meaning a figure with four corners, i.e. a quadrilateral). This comment occurred when she was touching a jar with a square cross section. The teacher focused on this and they started to talk about the different shapes.

Throughout the episode, the teacher followed whatever the children were interested in. However, the repeated requests for the jars to be sorted according to some criteria, suggested that she did have a specific intention for the activity. Nevertheless, she followed the children's own interests and did not insist on them continuing to arrange the bottles according to different kinds of attributes. By being sensitive to the children's interest in the jars, she both caught and missed opportunities to challenge the children's understanding. For example, she was able to suggest seeing if it was possible for each person to have three jars each after Marie's suggestion of having two each had been investigated.

Analysis

In the analysis, we look at each of Rogoff et al.'s (2003) components to see how representative the various incidents are of *intent participation* or *assembly-line instruction*. In making this analysis, we use Anghileri's (2006) strategies—*environmental provisions; explaining, reviewing and restructuring; developing conceptual thinking*—to identify how the teacher developed the learning opportunities for the children.

Participation Structures

The teacher set out the jars so that the children could make candleholders. Possibly, because the children began to handle the jars immediately, she invited them to play before the main task of making the candleholders. At different times, she requested the children to talk about the jars and to order them in different ways. However, in responding to the teacher's suggestions the children took control of how the activity developed through their actions or comments. Although the participation structures did not have the fluidity described by Rogoff et al. (2003) for *intent participation;* neither did they have the fixed roles of the *assembly-line instruction*.

This fluidity of control was supported by "provision of artefacts", a scaffolding strategy, from the *environmental provision* level, which was the lowest level of Anghileri's (2006) hierarchy. The provision of artefacts, the glass jars, scaffolded the children into playing which then lead to learning opportunities. The jars attracted and retained the children's interest and consequently they explored them in a variety of different ways, sometimes with teacher guidance but also by themselves. Providing the jars resulted in the children immediately touching and playing with them, which exemplifies level 2 of Anghileri's (2006) teacher strategies identified as "looking, touching and verbalising". The teacher could build on these tactile sensations by asking different children to verbalise what they noticed, thus bringing mathematical ideas such as shape and number into focus.

At times the children engaged with the jars individually, or in parallel, but at other times they worked together as was the case when they ordered the jars from shortest to tallest. According to Anghileri (2006), grouping as a way of working together is a form of scaffolding at the environmental provision level. Children's working together in this way, with the teacher sitting on the side, was a result of collaborative, horizontal participation structures. However, it may be that the value that the participants gave to this way of working then supported the use of those structures at other times. The control of the activity flowed between the different participants during these group work sessions.

Roles

In *intent participation*, "experienced people play a guiding role, facilitating learners' involvement and often participating alongside learners—indeed often learning themselves. New learners in turn take initiative in learning and contributing to shared endeavours, sometimes offering leadership in the process" (Rogoff et al. 2003, p. 187). In the activity, the teacher did not participate in the same way as the children and so her role was closer to that of a manager in *assembly-line instruction*. On the other hand, although she suggested activities, such as ordering the jars, she did not force the children to carry them out. Several times, the children took the initiative in suggesting activities and so their role could be considered to be closer to that of *intent participation*. To structure their interactions, they used the ideas of each other, such as placing their feet in the jars, as much as they did the ideas of the teacher. Although they did not verbally interact with each other like they did with the teacher, they constantly watched and copied each other's actions.

Many of the teacher's questions focused the children on mathematical aspects of their jars. As part of her level 2 strategies, Anghileri (2006) identified the need for teachers "to interject questions that focus on the most critical points in an explanation and take the understanding forward. Here the purpose is to gain insight into students' thinking, promoting their autonomy and underpinning the mathematical understanding that is generated" (p. 42–43). Without the questions, these aspects may have been missed by the children. Therefore, the teacher's role as the one with expert knowledge was important. However, as noted earlier, the play situation meant that it was not always possible to push children's thinking because they were not required to answer the teacher's questions, as occurred when Mia was counting the jars.

Although the teacher may have known the answers to some of her questions, her way of listening to the children suggested that she was opening a learning space which accommodated their reflections. Thus, not only did the teacher ask prompting and probing questions but she also left the children to interpret and answer the questions, which meant that children's autonomy was supported. Thus, her "listening style" was as important as her questioning style.

Motivation and Purpose

After the children had begun to handle the jars, the teacher suggested that the beginning activities were play—"Men innan vi börjar med att göra de här ljusen tänkte jag att vi kunde leka lite med de här burkarna. Tycker ni att alla burkar ser likadana ut?" ("But before we start making these candles, I thought we could play around with these jars. Do you think that all the jars look alike?"). The video of the episode showed that the children continued to play with the jars, even though the teacher asked a school-like question. The characteristics of play identified by Dockett and Perry (2010), "the exercise of choice, non-literal approaches, multiple possible outcomes and acknowledgement of the competence of players" (p. 175) can be seen in how the children explored the jars. Consequently, the purpose of the activity was clear to all. By agreeing on the activity being one of play, the children were free to make choices about what they would do. It would not have been appropriate for the teacher to expect responses to her questions as in a school-like initiation–reply–evaluation format (Rogoff et al. 2003) as this would have clearly changed the activity. The confining of participants' actions to those consistent with play can be seen as a significant contributor to the children engaging eagerly in the activities.

However, with the activity being labelled as play, many of the teacher scaffolding strategies identified by Anghileri (2006) were inappropriate unless they were adapted, such as was the case with teacher listening. One of Anghileri's level 2 strategies is "identifying meaningful contexts", which constitutes finding a shared context which makes the mathematical problem more accessible to students. This episode with preschool children suggests that working in a context that is meaningful for the children, that of play, and conforming to its characteristics, contributes to children engaging actively. When children have control over deciding if and how they want to engage then there is no need for a teacher to search for a meaningful context. Rather it is the level 1 strategies, connected to environmental provisions, which are more important, as the teacher needs to provide materials with which the children will want to engage.

Sources of Learning

Rogoff et al. (2003) stated that "in intent participation, learning is based on participation in ongoing or anticipated activities, with keen observation and listening" (p. 22). The glass jar activity was not an adult activity where the children learnt from watching experts. Simply reading the transcript could suggest that the children merely responded to the teacher's questions as would be the case in *assembly-line instruction*. However, the video shows that in addition to listening to the teacher, the children at the same time manipulated the glass jars and watched each other. Simultaneously noticing different behaviours is common in play, as the focus shifts frequently. Therefore, as in *intent participation,* the children paid attention to multiple ongoing events. In *assembly-line instruction,* the focus is supposed to be concentrated on only one action. Children, who focus widely, are labelled as distracted and are likely to have problems learning (Rogoff et al. 2003). Thus, because the activity was acknowledged as play, focusing widely provided a variety of sources for learning opportunities.

With the children focusing widely, there were opportunities for them to make connections between visual imagery and spoken words, a scaffolding strategy, developing representational tools, that Anghileri (2006) saw as being part of level 3.

Mia used the discussion between Marie and the teacher about "bigger" and "taller" as well as looking at and touching the jars to rearrange them from shortest to tallest.

Forms of Communication

In the episode, the children's actions were often connected to language as a result of the teacher's questions. As discussed previously, the teacher's questions were sometimes about information that she already knew. As such, Rogoff et al. (2003) would consider that they were test questions and a form of communication linked to *assembly-line instruction*. Yet, the children responded to them as though they required genuine investigation. For example, the first request was about whether the children thought the jars were alike. Although the children and the teacher could see that there were differences, the children picked up the jars, felt them and then made comments about them. The teacher was not judgemental about the comments, but instead asked for clarification. The children made choices about whether to respond or not. This format for interaction would not be considered typical of *intent participation* where the expert provides explanations only within the context of the process being learnt. Nevertheless, the format for interaction made the mathematics visible in the exchange but kept the conversation within the children's control. For example, in suggesting that the children order the jars according to size, the children's actions in placing the jars in a row, provide the teacher with an opportunity to bring in comparison terms, an important component of measurement.

Most of Anghileri's (2006) scaffolding strategies can be considered forms of communication, as they are concerned with how a teacher interacts with students. As already noted, many of the strategies were seen in this episode. At the highest level of scaffolding, Anghileri included "generating conceptual discourse" in which the teacher identifies for the students valuable ways of thinking mathematically, "thus enabling students to become aware of more sophisticated forms of mathematical reasoning" (p. 49). In the jar episode, the teacher's requests for clarifications rather than providing judgements about the children's answers may have supported them to see that their explanations were what the teacher valued, rather than a specific, correct answer. This is likely to contribute to them gaining "intellectual autonomy" (p. 49). However, there were opportunities for the teacher to request more information from the children about their mathematical thinking, and similar was the case with the sharing of the jars so that each child had two each. It is interesting to note that she did not recognise or chose not to take up the possibility to have children think more about why sharing in twos was possible while sharing by threes was not and so missed an opportunity to push them into thinking more about the numbers and how they were related.

Assessment

In *intent participation,* assessment occurs continually during the performance of the activity with the intention of ensuring that children gain "the important skills and ways of their community" (Rogoff et al. 2003, p. 196). By being in a play situation, assessment requirements are not connected to the performance of a particular practice and do not determine the children's retention of set information, as is the case in *assembly-line instruction*. Yet, the preschool teacher was involved in continual assessment both of the children's willingness to engage, important in *intent participation,* and of the mathematical information that they showed. Having children show the mathematics that they knew was not an end in itself but rather contributed to the play being continued and the mathematics becoming visible.

Anghileri (2006) suggested that negotiating meaning is one strategy that involves the teacher having to listen carefully:

> It is time consuming and demanding on a teacher's skills to elicit the true meaning of their students' responses, respecting the more outlandish contributions as their students work at developing their personal understandings, and not simply opting for responses that are "in tune" with their requirement. (Anghileri 2006, p. 46)

Anghileri queries the need for teachers to insist that children always provide the "correct" meaning. Similarly, Krummheuer (2012) suggests that negotiating meaning occurs in every interaction:

> From an interactionist's stance, all interaction situations principally entail the potential of developing in a *non-canonical* way so that the participants cannot easily refer to routinized and/or standardized knowledge applications. In such cases, the participants have to interactively negotiate a novel "shared meaning". (p. 321)

When two children arrived at different total numbers of the jars, the teacher highlighted that there were differences but when Marie did not want to discuss the difference, but changed her answer to that of Lena, the teacher did not insist on Marie recounting. The teacher could assess the children's knowledge and note for future reference that it might be useful to provide activities where it was likely that Marie would need to count to eight again. Requiring Marie to count immediately after she had rejected an offer to discuss her answer may have decreased her willingness to participate in further activities and changed the activity from one of play to one of direct instruction which would be more closely aligned with *assembly-line instruction*.

Using Play for Teaching Mathematics

Too often, discussions about learning of mathematics in preschools are positioned as being a choice between direct instruction and free play. Although the importance of the teacher interactions in preschools have been noted in many studies, a clear description of what the teacher does to facilitate learning often remains unclear, especially within guided play situations. Our study indicates how conforming to the context of play affected both the children and the teacher's ways of interacting. Our analysis of each of Rogoff et al.'s (2003) components shows how the effect of the particular kinds of interactions which occurred then affected the possibilities for learning.

The play context supported the children's engagement, but also restricted how the teacher could interact with the children and the scaffolding that she provided. Level 1 scaffolding strategies were more important for setting up learning opportunities than Anghileri (2006) suggested, because the organisation of the environment is what supported the children to play. The play undertaken with the jars also resulted at level 2 in reviewing, rather than restructuring, strategies being used frequently by the teacher because they conformed more easily to the need for the children to have control of the activity. As the children controlled the activity, level 3 strategies had to build on what was offered by the children through their actions or words and so could not be easily initiated by the teacher independently.

At first glance, play and teaching mathematics do not seem to be compatible. Mathematics is often considered to be something that can only be learnt from direct instruction (Lange and Meaney 2011). Yet, this example of a preschool interaction shows that guided play can provide rich opportunities for learning mathematics. It could be said that the teacher guided the children's actions, but was respectful of the children's control over the direction of the activity. The teacher was able to stimulate children's mathematical curiosity about shapes, their attributes and about number, including division. This curiosity, as well as the children's enjoyment, could be seen in the way that the children played with the jars and the mathematical ideas that they discussed. This episode does seem to illustrate the Swedish preschool curriculum's suggestion that play and enjoyment produces learning that would lead to "imagination, insight, communication and the ability to think symbolically, as well as the ability to co-operate and solve problems" (Skolverket 2011, p. 6).

Nevertheless, by placing the teaching in a play situation the teacher's actions are constrained. Direct instruction also constrains the teacher's possibilities for interacting with the children, but in different ways. As was illustrated in this episode, play means that children have as much opportunity as the teacher, if not more, to control what happens. The focus of the activity can switch frequently supporting children to take note of a wide range of stimuli simultaneously. The teacher can offer suggestions for activities and ask questions about what the children are engaged in but the children can ignore the invitation or decline to participate. The teacher cannot insist that her suggestions are accepted, as this would move the activity from one of being play into something more closely resembling Rogoff et al.'s (2003) *assembly-line instruction*. Consequently, the teacher must watch and listen very carefully to the children so that her suggestions build on the children's interests and also what they have previously shown about mathematical ideas. The questions and suggestions should raise the children's curiosity, if children are to engage with them willingly. If the teacher is successful in doing this, then the mathematical aspects of children's actions are made visible.

Thus, it is clear that the context has a substantial influence on children's possibilities for learning. This is not to suggest that play is a negative influence. Rather, like direct instruction, the possibilities for learning are constrained as well as enabled by the contexts in which these possibilities arise. In Sweden, the role of play as the context for learning is a long-standing belief, heavily supported within the curriculum (Skolverket 2010, 2011).

However, this small study of one teacher's interactions suggests that for learning to develop over time, the teacher's understanding about mathematics and how to develop children's mathematical curiosity within a play context is very important. Teachers need to both recognise mathematical learning opportunities and formulate challenging questions, matching both children's interest and their current knowledge of mathematical ideas, if the joint aims of using play as the context for learning and to develop children's mathematical understanding are to be achieved. When the teacher is able to do this as happened in this episode, the children will make use of the control that they have from the activity being one of play and this is likely to contribute to learning being connected to enjoyment.

References

Anderson, A. (1997). Families and mathematics: A study of parent-child interactions. *Journal for Research in Mathematics Education, 28*(4), 484–511. http://www.jstor.org/stable/749684.

Anghileri, J. (2006). Scaffolding practices that enhance mathematics learning. *Journal of Mathematics Teacher Education, 9*, 33–52. doi:10.1007/s10857-006-9005-9.

Bishop, A. J. (1988). *Mathematical enculturation: A cultural perspective on mathematics education*. Dordrecht: Kluwer.

Björklund, C. (2008). Toddlers' opportunities to learn mathematics. *International Journal of Early Childhood, 40*(1), 81–95. doi:10.1007/BF03168365.

Carr, M., & May, H. (1996). The politics and processes of the implementation of Te Whaariki, the New Zealand national early childhood curriculum 1993-6. In M. Carr & H. May (Eds.), *Implementing Te Whaariki* (pp. 1–13). Wellington: Institute for Early Childhood Studies.

Coltman, P., Petyaeva, D., & Anghileri, J. (2002). Scaffolding learning through meaningful tasks and adult interaction. *Early Years: An International Journal of Research and Development, 22*(1), 39–49. doi:10.1080/09575140120111508.

Dijk, E. F., van Oers, B., & Terwel, J. (2004). Schematising in early childhood mathematics education: Why, when and how? *European Early Childhood Education Research Journal, 12*(1), 71–83. doi:10.1080/13502930485209321.

Dockett, S., & Perry, B. (2010). Playing with mathematics: Play in early childhood as a context for mathematicsl learning. In L. Sparrow, B. Kissane, & C. Hurst (Eds.), *Shaping the future of mathematics education: Proceedings of the 33th annual conference of the Mathematics Education Research Group of Australia* (pp. 715–718). Freemantle: MERGA Inc.

Doverborg, E. (2006). Svensk förskola (Swedish pre-school). In E. Doverborg & G. Emanuelsson (Eds.), *Små barns matematik (Small children's mathematics)* (pp. 1–10). Göteborg: NCM Göteborgs Universitet.

Edo, M., Planas, N., & Badillo, E. (2009). Mathematical learning in a context of play. *European Early Childhood Education Research Journal, 17*(3), 325–341. doi:10.1080/13502930903101537.

Emilson, A., & Folkesson, A.-M. (2006). Children's participation and teacher control. *Early Child Development and Care, 176*(3–4), 219–238. doi:10.1080/03004430500039846.

Haynes, M. (2000). Mathematics education for early childhood: A partnership of two curriculums. *Mathematics Teacher Education & Development, 2*, 93–104. http://www.merga.net.au/node/43?volume=2.

Krummheuer, G. (2012). The "non-canonical" solution and the "improvisation" as conditions for early years mathematics learning processes: The concept of the "interactional nichein the development of mathematical thinking" (NMT). *Journal für Mathematik-Didaktik, 33*(2), 317–338.

Lamberty, K. K. (2007). *Getting and keeping children engaged with a constructionist design tool for craft and math*. Unpublished PhD thesis. Atlanta: Georgia Institute of Technology. http://smartech.gatech.edu/jspui/bitstream/1853/14589/1/lamberty_kristin_k_200705_phd.pdf.

Lange, T., & Meaney, T. (2011). Preservice teachers learning mathematics from the internet. In J. Clark, B. Kissane, J. Mousley, T. Spencer, & S. Thornton (Eds.), *Mathematics: Traditions and (new) practices: Proceedings of the 34th annual conference of the Mathematics Education Research Group of Australia and the Association of Mathematics Teachers*, (pp. 438–445). Adelaide: AAMT and MERGA. http://www.merga.net.au/node/38?year=2011.

Lee, J. S., & Ginsburg, H. P. (2009). Early childhood teachers' misconceptions about mathematics education for young children in the United States. *Australasian Journal of Early Childhood, 34*(4), 37–45. http://www.earlychildhoodaustralia.org.au/australian_journal_of_early_childhood/ajec_index_abstracts/ajec_vol_34_no_4_december_2009.html.

Papic, M. M., Mulligan, J. T., & Mitchelmore, M. C. (2011). Assessing the development of preschoolers' mathematical patterning. *Journal for Research in Mathematics Education, 42*(3), 237–268.

Rogoff, B., Paradise, R., Arauz, R. M., Correa-Chávez, M., & Angelillo, C. (2003). Firsthand learning through intent participation. *Annual Review of Psychology, 54*, 175–203. doi:10.1146/annurev.psych.54.101601.145118.

Samuelsson, I. P., & Carlsson, M. A. (2008). The playing learning child: Towards a pedagogy of early childhood. *Scandinavian Journal of Educational Research, 52*(6), 623–641. doi:10.1080/00313830802497265.

Sheridan, S., Samuelsson, I. P., & Johansson, E. (2009). *Barns tidiga lärande: Et tvärsnitsstudie om förskolan som miljö för barns lärande (Children's early learning: A cross-sectional study of preschool as an environment for children's learning)*. Göteborg studies in educational sciences 284. Göteborg: Acta Universitatis Gothoburgensis. https://gupea.ub.gu.se/handle/2077/20404.

Skolverket. (2010). *Läroplan för förskolan Lpfö 98: Reviderad 2010*. Stockholm: Skolverket.

Skolverket. (2011). *Curriculum for the Preschool Lpfö 98: Revised 2010*. Stockholm: Skolverket.

Wood, D., Bruner, J. S., & Ross, G. (1976). The role of tutoring in problem solving. *Journal of child psychology and psychiatry, 17*(2), 89–100.

Chapter 5
"I have a little job for you"

Birgit Brandt

Instructional practices in interaction processes between kindergarten teachers and young children in Germany

Introduction

With the publication of international comparisons, early education has attracted the interest of scientists and the general public. In Germany, new plans for the education of children's daycare centres are being devised, and most of the German states include mathematics as its own educational discipline within different curriculum approaches (e.g. Niedersächsisches Kultusministerium 2000; Hessisches Sozialministerium 2007). In most German countries, mathematical education is demanded as a specific activity in kindergarten, but there are relatively few insights into the current practices and the daily routines of mathematical instruction of kindergarten teachers. Thus, one part of the research project erStMaL investigates the everyday practice of mathematical interaction processes in kindergarten settings.

The aim of this chapter is to describe different practices of mathematical instruction in the German kindergarten. As theoretical background for the descriptions serve the idea of folk pedagogical concepts (Bruner 1996; Olson and Bruner 1996) and the concept of instructional models (Rogoff 1994; Rogoff et al. 1996). In micro-sociological analyses of video data, relations between these pedagogical aspects of the interaction process and the emerging opportunities for mathematical learning are illustrated.

---

erStMaL is integrated into the Research Center IDeA (Individual Development and Adaptive Education of Children at Risk). The preparation of this chapter was funded by the state government of Hesse.

B. Brandt (✉)
Martin-Luther-Universität Halle-Wittenberg, Halle, Germany
e-mail: birgit.brandt@paedagogik.uni-halle.de

The Theoretical Framework

Following the interactionistic perspective on learning processes, as implemented by a group of German and American researchers to mathematics education (Bauersfeld 1994; Cobb and Bauersfeld 1995), the way of participation in interaction processes is a crucial aspect for learning processes. In this approach, the interaction serves as a place for joint negotiation and thus individual cognition is bound to the participation in the construction of (taken as) shared meanings (Brandt and Tatsis 2009). Theoretically, this approach is based on the symbolic interactionism and the idea of negotiation of meaning (Blumer 1954, 1969) as well as on the ethnomethodological concept of local production (Garfinkel 1967) and situational perspective (Goffman 1983) (cf. Brandt and Tatsis 2009; Krummheuer 2011, 2012). In addition, this approach is aware of the role of culture in teaching and learning mathematics, whereat culture is seen *"as webs of significance (which) may be central also in the societal, institutional, and pedagogical aspects of mathematics education considered as a social process"* (Presmeg 2007, p. 437).

As a consequence of the situational perspective, the research focus of this chapter is on the current "how" of the everyday practice and the attempt to understand its underlying rationality.

The Development Niche of Mathematical Thinking

Harkness and Super (Super and Harkness 1986; Harkness et al. 2007) elaborate a developmental theory from a cultural perspective which is in line with the ecological model of child development (Bronfenbrenner 1979). The central concept of their theory is the *"development niche"* (Super and Harkness 1986; Harkness et al. 2007), *"which provides a framework for examining the effects of cultural features on child rearing in interaction with general developmental parameters"* (Super and Harkness 1986, p. 546). The child and their *"particular set of inherited dispositions"* (Harkness et al. 2007, p. 34S) are in the centre of the development niche, encompassed by a system of cultural constructed environmental circumstances, which influence the child's development:

a. Physical and social settings
b. Customs of child care and rearing
c. Caretakers' psychology (ibid.; see Fig. 5.1)

Enclosed to aspects of the larger culture, children will be involved in different social and physical settings (1), different customs will be livened up by the participants of the social interactions (2), and the adults will have different ideas of how children in general or a specific child "is like" (3).

In adoption of this theoretical model, Krummheuer developed the *"Interactional Niche in the Development of Mathematical Thinking"* (NMT; cf. Krummheuer

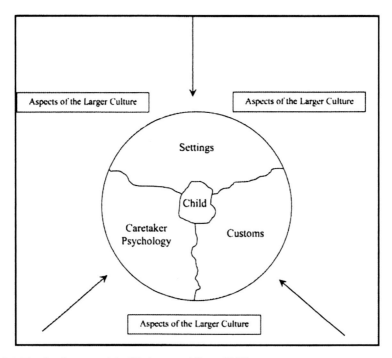

Fig. 5.1 The development niche (Harkness and Super 2007)

2012, 2014). The three components of Super and Harkness were combined to *cooperation* (personal grouping) and *pedagogy respectively education*. Due to the focus on mathematical learning, the component *content* is added.

According to the theoretical consideration of situational aspects of learning, these components are considered in two dimensions (see Table 5.1):

- The aspect of allocation, given by canonical knowledge, institutional arrangements, or theories of education
- The aspect of the situation, which refers to the emerging performance of these three components by the negotiation process of the participants (see Krummheuer 2012, 2014)

In the project erStMaL, this model of NMT serves as basis for theory-driven reconstruction of interaction processes in different contexts (cf. Acar 2014). Engaging in pedagogical aspects of concrete interaction processes between kindergarten teachers and children, this chapter will focus on the situational aspects of education and pedagogy, which is the marked cell of the NMT in Table 5.1. As van Oers (2002) outlined, the teacher's epistemology of mathematics contributes to the monitoring and guidance of mathematical thinking of pupils. In a certain manner, the perspective of this chapter is the inverted one: The pedagogical beliefs of the kindergarten teacher will contribute to the mathematics which emerges in the interaction processes.

Table 5.1 Components and dimension of NMT (cf. Krummheuer 2012)

NMT	Content	Cooperation	Education/Pedagogy
Allocation	Mathematical domains, tasks	(Institutional) settings of cooperation	Theories of (mathematics) education, pedagogical concepts
Situation	Interactive negotiating of the theme	Emerging structure of participation	Folk theories of education, every-day routines in mathematical instruction

For the empirical reconstructions of the interaction processes I refer to the concept of folk pedagogy (Bruner and Olson 1996; Bruner 1996) and to the instruction models described by Rogoff (1994) and Rogoff et al. (1996) (cf. Brandt and Tiedemann 2011). These concepts will be linked to the developmental niche. Folk pedagogy can be located in the caretakers' psychology and in the pedagogical aspects of general customs of care (see Fig. 5.1), which are combined in the component *education/pedagogy* in the NMT. Based on observations of caretakers' activities, the concept of folk pedagogy pertains to the situational dimension.

Folk Pedagogy

With his concept of folk pedagogy, Bruner (1996) deals with the ancient problem of applying theoretical knowledge to practical problems, especially *"applying psychological theories to educational practice"* (ibid., p. 44).

> There is one 'presenting problem' that is always with us in dealing teaching and learning.... It is the issue of how human beings achieve a meeting of minds, expressed by teachers usually as 'how do I reach the children?' or by children 'what's she trying to get at?'. (ibid., p. 45)

He argues, that we use *"everyday intuitive theories about how others minds work"* (ibid.) in the interaction with others. He calls these theories "folk psychology", which are affected by culture. Employing the intuitive theories of everyday acting to the question of helping children growing up and learning, he introduces the notion of "folk pedagogy" (Bruner 1996, p. 45 f.; cf. Olson and Bruner 1996):

> ...we are steered in the activity of helping children learn about the world by a body of assumptions that make up what we may call 'folk pedagogy'. ...Watch any mother, any teacher, even any baby-sitter with a child and you will be struck at how much of what they do is guided by notions of what children's minds are like and how one may help them learn, even though they may not be able to verbalize their pedagogical principles. (Olson and Bruner 1996, p. 10)

Bruner (1996; cf. Olson and Bruner 1996) describes four everyday educational concepts that are distinguished by the convictions about how teaching and learning work and the manner in which the knowledge should be taught and learnt. The point of reference for the designation of the concept is the child as the subject of learning, towards whom the activity of the adult model has been oriented:

- *"Children as imitative learners"* (Bruner 1996, p. 53) and *"children as doers"* (Olson and Bruner 1996), including learning as *"the acquisition of 'know-how'"* (ibid. p. 16)
- *"Children as learning from didactic exposure"* (Bruner 1996, p. 55) and *"children as knowers: the acquisition of propositional knowledge"* (Olson and Bruner 1996, p. 17)
- *"Children as thinkers: the development of intersubjective interchange"* (ibid. p. 18)
- *"Children as knowledgeable: the management of 'objective' knowledge"* (ibid. p. 21)

The first concept is more oriented towards the apprenticeship and a craftsman-like learning process. We can observe situations of writing numbers and letters in the kindergarten, which can be assigned to this concept. However, in general, this simple *"theory of imitative learning suits a 'traditional' society"* (Bruner 1996, p. 54) is not suitable for teaching and learning advanced ideas and concepts like mathematics. The other three concepts are more oriented to advanced mental abilities. Thus, these concepts will be described in more detail in their situational realisation in mathematical interaction processes by empirical data.

Instruction Models and their Relation to Folk Pedagogy

The three concepts for advanced mental abilities of folk pedagogy can be compared with the instruction models, which were described by Rogoff (1994) and Rogoff et al. (1996), observing parents in school settings. They describe three different instruction models:

- Transmission
- Acquisition
- Community-of-lerners

The interrelations between the different concepts of folk pedagogy and the instruction models are summarised in the following overview (see Brandt and Tiedemann 2011 for more details) (Table 5.2):

For the instruction model *transmission,* an adult or an expert is compulsorily necessary for learning processes, as it is in the concept *children as knowers* or learning from didactic exposure: The participation of the adult causes the learning process, whereas the child is more or less seen as passive and not responsible for its own learning. The child is seen as an empty vessel, which has to be filled by the adult. As explicitly described by Rogoff et al. (1996), this delimited the possibilities of the children in their participating in the current situations as well in the participating in prospective interactions.

> Students learn how to solve problems but not how to set them. They can produce correct answers but do not have experience examining how to determine what is correct. (Rogoff et al. 1996, p. 393)

Table 5.2 Relationship between folk pedagogical concepts (Bruner 1996) and instructional models (Rogoff 1994)

Folk pedagogy (Olson & Bruner)	Instruction model (Rogoff et al.)	Main idea of learning and teaching
Children as doers	–	Learning as acquisition of "know how"—demonstration and imitation of activities
Children as knowers	Transmission	Learning as acquisition of propositional and objective knowledge by transmission of facts and rules
Children as thinkers	Acquisition	Learning as individual construction of knowledge in exchange with others
Children as knowledgeable	Community-of-learners	Learning by participating in cultural practises with support from experts (in interaction with more knowledgeable)

The instruction model *acquisition* corresponds to the concept *children as thinkers*. Both concepts can be described as different forms of constructivism. The concept of Bruner (1996), respectively Olson and Bruner (1996), is oriented to socio-constructivism with more emphasis to the exchange with others for the construction process:

> Their understanding is fostered through discussion and collaboration, with each child encouraged to present her own way of constructing the subject at hand to achieve some meeting of minds with peers and teachers. (Olson and Bruner 1996, p. 18)

On the contrary, the dedicated instruction model *acquisition* emphasises the individual part of construction as a kind of autodidactic processes and reminds more to radical positions of constructivism (e.g. von Glasersfeld 1996).

The concept *children as knowledgeable* and the instruction model *community-of-learners* correlate in their orientation to cultural aspects of learning. The learning process is seen as a re-construction of culturally approved knowledge, which is in principal modifiable; thus, the (re-)constructions of the child are culturally delimited but not definite by objective knowledge. These concepts emphasise *"the importance of knowledge accumulated in the past"* (Bruner 1996, p. 60) and the distinction of canonical, personal, and idiosyncratical knowledge.

Data Basis: The Kindergarten Settings of erStMaL

As mentioned above, the research study erStMaL aims to the development of mathematical thinking in different social contexts. It is a video-study with a longitudinal design. Following the interactionistic perspective, we observe the children in interaction processes accompanied by different adults: research students, kindergarten teachers, and parents (for more details of the project cf. Acar Bayraktar 2011). In this chapter, I will focus on settings which were designed by the kindergarten teachers themselves.

We asked the kindergarten teacher to design settings for different mathematical domains: (1) numbers and operations, (2) geometry and sizes, (3) pattern and structures, (4) measurements, and (5) data analysis (Konferenz der Kultusminister 2004; cf. Sarama and Clements 2008). Designed by the kindergarten teacher as "settings with specific mathematical learning opportunities", these different situations will be used for working out daily kindergarten routines of planed mathematical activities. Focussing on the educational concepts and the embedded mathematical ideas, insights can be gained into the current mathematical teaching processes—omitting more open approaches of everyday routines in unplanned mathematical activities using favourable occasions.[1]

Analysis of the Empirical Data

The situational production of instructional practices by the participants will be carried out with micro-analytical methods, based on a turn-by-turn analysis of transcribed sequences (Krummheuer 2007, Brandt and Tatsis 2009). For this reason, selected episodes were transcribed verbally, completed by some screen shots of the video.

Blumer distinguished between *"sensitizing"* and *"definitive"* concepts; thereby, *"sensitizing concepts merely suggest certain directions along which to look"* (ibid. p. 7). Using *"sensitizing concepts"* for the analysis of empirical data, these concepts describe a framework for the interpretation process:

> Empirically related research questions ask less whether these concepts come to view in 'reality', but rather, how they orient one's perspective in order to interpret this 'reality'. (Krummheuer 2011, p. 82)

Looking to the local production of pedagogical aspects of observed situations, the folk pedagogical concept of Bruner and the instruction models of Rogoff serve as *"sensitizing concepts"* for the interpretation process. As argued above (Sect. 1), both concepts are similar in the main idea of teaching and learning and the role of the adult person in the interaction process. Concerning the emerging participation structure of the interaction processes (situational aspect of the component *cooperation* in the NMT, Table 5.1), I will refer to both concepts. In addition, the different concepts of folk pedagogy of Bruner (1996) are linked to different concepts or ideas of *"mind" and "knowledge"* in general (Bruner 1996, p. 50 f.), which offer the opportunity for content-related deliberations of different instruction practices (situational aspect of the component *content* in the NMT).

In the dimension of allocation of the NMT, the examined interaction processes are similar in all components:

---

[1] In German kindergarten, you can find both forms in different conceptions of 'kindergarten' (Thiel 2009). Especially, in the last year before entering school, more planned mathematical activities will be offered to the child. Looking at the videos, there is an impression of 'routine' with such more formal settings by the participants (children and kindergarten teachers) in most of the institutions of our sample.

- Component content: The selected settings are allocated to the mathematical domain pattern by the kindergarten teachers, although they choose different aspects within this domain and use different materials.
- Component cooperation: All of them are comparable due to the institutional embedment and the isolation to other activities in the kindergarten: they take place on specially prepared tables or in separate rooms and not in the area for free play activities. All children are aged 4–5. The settings differ in the number of participating children (two versus four).
- Component pedagogy: The situations are forms of planned activities within the kindergarten but not part of a special training course.

The situational dimension of the last component (pedagogy) is the focus of the following analyses. Thereby, aspects of the situational dimension of the two other components are addressed too. The situations are named by the materials, which the kindergarten teachers select for the settings.

Coloured Pins

In this situation, the kindergarten teacher selects coloured pins (red, yellow, and green), which normally were used for creating free patterns or designing pictures with concrete objects (flower, house, etc.) on a pinboard. The kindergarten teacher (TE) prepared a paper with lines of dots (red, yellow, and green) and a box with the material. After entering the room with two boys (F and N, both 4 years old), she starts to arrange the prepared material from the box at the table as shown on the first picture of this scene.

F + N: (both are grasping in the individual pin box)
TE: don't start yet . I have a little job that I prepared for you (showing the sheet of paper with the coloured dots)

Afterwards, she introduces the children to the task to copy her lines of coloured dots with the pins. Then, she guides the children line by line, covering the other lines and deciding, when the next line will occur.[2] She recognises, that N (boy on the right side) copies the fourth line from the right side, but she explicitly allows this

---

[2] This is neither the case of using the same number of pins on the pinboard as dots on the sheet of paper nor the case of building a line from the one side to the other on the pinboard as on her drawing. The decision seems situational and more or less accidental, perhaps oriented to the time.

5 "I have a little job for you"

procedure "this is the other direction, but it's all right". Thus, she sets and controls the rules for the conducting of the task.

N copies the four coloured dots of the last line with pins, again starting on the right side (red, yellow, green, and red) and leans back after the forth pin. He seems satisfied with his conduction, but the kindergarten teacher intervenes:

TE: so, here is free (showing on her drawing) but you have to fill it now, you have red yellow green and now you have to start again here (showing the red plugs one after the other) red and what is coming next (showing the yellow plug and the „gap" at the end of his line) N: well, there you need green TE: no, what is the next, what is next to red, look at your line, what did you put after red here	

Whereas the children were obliged to copy the previous lines, the idea of the last line is the continuation of a pattern. Thereby, the teacher has a definite idea how to continue the "objective given pattern": starting again at the beginning of the line, whereas her last (red) dot belongs to the first iteration of the pattern (red, green, yellow)—changing the direction (red, yellow, green) seems again not important for her. N fits in to the idea of proceeding, but taking a green pin he adduces an own idea for continuation: a possible assumption is "going backwards" (which means to produce a symmetric colour sequences).[3] Although the teacher confirms her interpretation, a few minutes later, N suggests to take a red pin at the fifth position (which could mean to iterate the whole colour sequences of the kindergarten teacher). But the teacher confirms again her idea and requests him to take a yellow pin in an interaction pattern, which reminds to the *"funnel pattern"* (Bauersfeld 1980; cf. Brandt 1997).

TE: well, (showing the yellow plug) what's the name of this colour N: yellow TE: then take it	

In this second part, again the kindergarten teacher sets and controls the rules of the procedure. Furthermore, she "transmits" her idea of continuation as a kind of objective knowledge, although from a mathematical view, this is not the fact. Thus, she rejects the divergent ideas of N. These divergent ideas will not become the topic of the interaction, but are substituted by the "objective knowledge" enforced by the adult as the knowledge agent.

---

[3] It is not sure that he has any idea of a pattern by choosing the green pin.

Generally, this situation could be assigned as a prototype of *children as knowers* and the instruction model *transmission: "Teaching is not a mutual dialogue, but telling by on to the other"* (Bruner 1996, p. 56).

Thus, learning mathematics within this concept means to cumulate facts and rules. The conception of mathematics, which is related to this instructional practice, is the traditional, formalist characterisation of mathematics as *"objective knowledge"* and *"immutable truths and unquestionable certainty"* (Nickson 1994, p. 11; cf. Presmeg 2007, p. 437).

Lot of Things

In this situation, the kindergarten teacher selects an accumulation of different things in various numbers (diverse glassy stones, dices, counter, wooden sticks, etc.) and a special kind of placemats. She prepared all of these materials in the middle of the room. Entering the room with four children (U, S, B (girls) and K (boy), all 4–5 years old), she asks the children to choose a placemat and opens up the "room" for the children's ideas: "Come have a look and see if you have an idea about what you can do with this." Then, she sits down on the floor a little bit apart. In fact, all children start to arrange different things on their own placemat. The following table gives an overview of the beginning phase (Principle, this kindergarten teacher comments only very few of the children's activities).

time: 1:35 U: (puts a big, red glassy stone in the middle of her round placemat) look TE TE: fantastic you have found a centre, like a Mandala, yes time: 2:06 B: (puts a big, green glassy stone in the centre of her round placemat) I have the big one time: 2:24 B: (singing) and I make a centre, too (puts a big, green glassy stone in the middle of her round placemat) TE: You have a centre, too, where is your centre, B B: (showing the big green glassy stone) there TE: that is the centre of the circle time: 2:40 K: where are the big one (stands up, retrieves a big green glassy stone) S: (at the same time: puts a big red glassy stone in the centre of her squarish placemat, without any comment) K: I have a centre too. TE: and you have also a centre, a tetragon has also a centre, and Sara has found her centre too	

Within 1 min, all children implemented the idea of "centre" in their arrangement, which U inserts to the interaction by her acting. It is the teacher who makes it explicit in the discourse by her comment of this acting. This was one of the kindergarten teacher's few utterances. She reacts directly and extensively; thus, she emphasises the mathematical idea of the centre of a geometrical figure. However, she ties her comments to the activities and utterances of the children. Afterwards, the children create a very different arrangement integrating "the centre". The children named their arrangements "clown", or "like a face", but nobody grasps the idea of "Mandala", which the kindergarten teacher linked to the centre of the figure—the figures are not symmetrical at all.

A few minutes later (time: 6:20), she starts an own "mandala-like" pattern on a quadratic placemat, but without any comment (see below). K starts to rearrange his pattern to a "mandala-like" pattern (time: 6:45). A little bit later (time: 7:45), the kindergarten teacher clears up her own placemat and comments: "You will have your own ideas to continue". K was the only child in this situation, who grasps the idea of symmetry of the Mandala, starting with the centre and he worked 20 min to finish a very complex, almost symmetric pattern, whereas the three others pursue to produce figurative arrangements and finish much earlier.

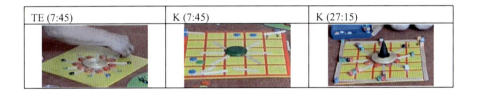

| TE (7:45) | K (7:45) | K (27:15) |

In general, this situation is formed by very free pattern creations of the children. Several times, the kindergarten teacher ties mathematically oriented comments to the utterances and activities of the children. She does not insist on following her suggestions and the children are not pushed directly to elaborate their ideas or arrangements to a "mathematical" one. In particular, she emphasises that everyone has to try out his/her own ideas—and the children did so. The individual constructions were affected by individual examination with the material, in reciprocal awareness, but not in extensive interchanges of ideas. Thus, describing this situation as a "learning opportunity", constructivist assumption of learning and mind are required, which is the basis for the concept *children as thinkers*. Regarding the concentration on the individual process and the minor emphasis on interpersonal exchange of ideas, radical constructivism as in the instruction model *acquisition* (Rogoff et al., see above) seems to be the underlying learning concept.

For this instructional practice, mathematical learning is a child-centred, active process, a kind of "learning by doing" in a very autonomous way. Children are seen as constructing their own mathematics—and it is a question of discourse to achieve a sufficient degree of intersubjectivity and to reach justified beliefs, viable theories, and conventional knowledge.

Butterfly Puzzle

In this situation, the kindergarten teacher selects a butterfly puzzle of a set of symmetric puzzles for the setting. Before entering the room with the two boys (B and N, both 4 years old), she prepared the puzzle, putting the shape of the puzzle and coloured wooden triangles (equilateral; red, blue, and yellow) in the middle of the table. She starts the situation questioning the children "Do you know what we will do today?" The children uttered some incomprehensible words, thus, the teacher goes on:

TE: let's make a butterfly together. We will colour the wing in a nice way N: I know TE: with which colour you will start	
N: with the blue one TE: we will start together with one (...) B will also participate B: with here . I make the red one TE: okay (...) You can put them together in this way (rearranging the triangles of the boys), look	

Just from the beginning, the children were encouraged to participate in the realisation of "shared endeavors" (Rogoff et al. 1996, p. 389), where it seems that the kindergarten teacher has an idea of a symmetrical puzzle ("we will start together with one"—referring to the left wing of the butterfly), but she only implicitly informs the children about the idea of colouring the butterfly symmetrically ("we will design the butterfly in a nice way"). First, the focus is on the practice of parqueting the area with equilateral triangles. Thus, the teacher regulates the first attempts ("you can put them together in this way, look"). Later on, the teacher follows her own colouring ideas, which seems to be guided by the second part of the whole project: She supplements the pattern of the two boys in a way that small plain-coloured areas occur (e.g. "lines" of yellow triangles).

After finishing the first wing, she introduces the second part of the project to the children:

TE: look, do you know how a butterfly looks like outside, when he is sitting on a flower N: yes B: (puts a triangle in the right wing) TE: B, wait a moment, this side (showing the coloured left side) looks the same as the other one (showing the empty right side) B + N: (nodding)	
TE: oh, look, it starts again, what did you need now a lot N + B: yellow (both grasp a yellow triangle) N: but I will start at the bottom TE: but then you must look there, we did not need yellow what will we need then N: ah, (a lot) red (both boys take red triangles and start the third line at the bottom)	

In the second part of the joint problem solving, she refers several times to the plain-coloured areas as orientation for copying the whole pattern. Thereby, the children are free in a certain degree. Instead of starting the third line with the lot of yellow at the top, as suggested by the kindergarten teacher, the boys decided to start at the bottom with red triangles.

The kindergarten teacher covers parts of the finished wing and points on triangles in the finished wing, as other forms of managing the realisation of a symmetrical pattern. Both forms structure the process of problem solving. At the end, the children reflect the finished puzzle with two "equally coloured wings".

Thus, this situation can be seen as a type of *children as knowledgeable,* whereas the children were encouraged and enabled to participate in the "practice of producing a symmetrical pattern"—and the kindergarten teacher participates as an expert, organising the problem-solving process in a *community-of-learners:* Within the joint process of fulfilling this specific problem which was set up by the kindergarten teacher, she established several forms of ordering and organising the puzzle. She adjusted these forms to the activities of the children and the children adopted their own ideas to her management process. Thus, on the one hand, the children are not as free in their ideas and constructions as in the situation *"A lot of things"* but on the other hand, they are not so strictly bounded to the ideas of the kindergarten teacher as in the situation *"Coloured pins"*. Thus, the conception of mathematics in this instructional practice is mathematics as a (symbolic) tool for setting and solving problems in a specific way. The way to learn mathematics as a tool for problem solving is to participate in problem-solving processes with more experienced human beings.

Final Remarks

The goal of the comparison of the three different everyday practices is to highlight differences in mathematical instructions and the emerging opportunities for mathematical learning processes.

The everyday educational concept of *children as knowers* leads to very strict methods of processing the tasks determined by the teacher in small steps. Along with that, folk pedagogical idea mathematics emerges as composed of prepositional knowledge from guidelines—and this practice fails in the examination of different ideas to a given task. Of course, skilfulness in the organisation of the learning settings and the motivation of the children for the pre-determined tasks is often demonstrated in these situations. Especially in the episode *"Coloured pins"*, the children are very proud in the end to finish such a "difficult task".

Even if the adult sets up the environment, the concept of *children as thinkers* is building up on the ideas of the participating children; the kindergarten teacher provides the objects and tasks and the children have time to explore themselves—and to discover mathematical concepts on their own. However, an outward proclivity for further discovery is often missing from the creations of the children. The teacher hopes for the situational evolvement of specific mathematical ideas from the provided materials. In the examined episode, only one child works discernible on the complex mathematical idea of symmetry. The other children were limited to the already known "fact" of identifying the centre of a simple geometric figure—and lose the interest in the material after some figural arrangements (which indeed do not reach the attention of the kindergarten teacher).

In situations that can be classified under the concept of *children as knowledgeable*, potential mathematical learning momentum can only arise if the teacher focuses on the mathematical content of the cultural practice as part of the mutual mastery. The adult as an expert has to guide the common attraction to mathematical aspects of the problem solving practice, which can be observed in the examined situation by providing strategies for copying the wing symmetrically. But we also observed several settings with missing attention to the mathematical aspect of the cultural practice.

From the examined episodes, it seems clear that it is neither the specific mathematical domain nor the kind of materials which causes the pedagogical orientation of the interaction, but the embedding of the material into a content-related task. It is an open question if the different emerging instruction models can be seen as a characteristic of the teacher, since we did not observe all kindergarten teachers repeatedly. But we have more settings with the kindergarten teachers of the episodes *"Coloured pins"* and *"A lot of things"*—and we reconstructed similar pedagogical orientations in their other interaction processes independent from the mathematical domain of the settings. Thus, for vocational training it could be a fruitful approach to analyse videotaped episodes due to the underlying folk pedagogical ideas and contrast them with other episodes. This approach for enhancements of the mathematics education in kindergarten would build on the current practices and their different strengths and weaknesses.

References

Acar Bayraktar, E. (2014). The Reflection of Spatial Thinking on the Interactional Niche in the Family. In: U. Kortenkamp et al. (eds.), *Early Mathematics Learning*, (pp. 85–107). New York: Springer.

Acar, Bayraktar E., Hümmer, A. Huth, M. Münz, M., & Reimann, M. (2011). Forschungsmethodischer Rahmen der Projekte erStMaL und MaKreKi. In B. Brandt, R. Vogel, & G. Krummheuer (Eds.), *Die Projekte erStMaL und MaKreKi. Mathematikdidaktische Forschung am "Center for Individual Development and Adaptive Education" (IDeA)* (pp. 11–24). Münster: Waxmann.

Bauersfeld, H. (1980). Hidden dimensions in the so-called reality of mathematics classroom. *Educational Studies in Mathematics*, *11*(1), 23–29.

Bauersfeld, H. (1994). Theoretical perspective on interaction in the mathematics classroom. In Biehler et al. (Eds.), *Didactics of mathematics as a scientific discipline* (pp. 133–146). Dodrecht: Kluwer Academic Publishers.

Blumer, H. (1954). What is wrong with social theory? *American Sociological Review*, *19*(1), 3–10.

Blumer, H. (1969). *Symbolic interactionism: Perspective and method*. Englewood Cliffs: Prentice-Hall.

Brandt, B. (1997). Reconstructions of "Possibilities" for learning with respect to the participation in classroom interaction. In H. Weigand et al. (Eds.), Selected papers from annual conference on didactics of mathematics, Leipzig. http://www.fmd.uni-osnabrueck.de/ebooks/gdm/annual1997.html. Accessed 28 Nov 2012.

Brandt, B., & Tatsis, K. (2009). Using Goffman's concepts to explore collaborative interaction processes in elementary school mathematics. *Research in Mathematics Education*, *11*(1), 39–56.

Brandt, B., Vogel, R., & Krummheuer G. (Eds.). (2011). *Die Projekte erStMaL und MaKreKi. Mathematikdidaktische Forschung am "Center for Individual Development and Adaptive Education" (IDeA)*. Münster: Waxmann.

Brandt, B., & Tiedemann, K. (2011). Alltagspädagogik in mathematischen Spielsituationen mit Vorschulkindern. In B. Brandt, R. Vogel, & G. Krummheuer (Eds.), *Die Projekte erStMaL und MaKreKi. Mathematikdidaktische Forschung am "Center for Individual Development and Adaptive Education"* (pp. 91–134). Münster: Waxmann.

Bronfenbrenner, U. (1979). *The ecology of human development*. Cambridge: Harvard University Press.

Bruner, J. (1996). *The culture of education*. Cambridge: Harvard University Press.

Bruner, J. (1986). *Actual minds, possible worlds*. Cambridge: Harvard University Press.

Cobb, P., & Bauersfeld, H. (Eds.). (1995). *The emergence of mathematical meaning: Interaction in classroom cultures*. Hillsdale: Erlbaum.

Garfinkel, H. (1967). *Studies in ethnomethodology*. Englewood Cliffs: Prentice-Hall.

von Glasersfeld, E. (1996). *Radical constructivism: A way of knowing and learning*. London: Falmer Press.

Goffman, E. (1983). The interaction order. *American Sociological Review*, *48*, 1–17.

Harkness, S., & Super, C. M. et al. (2007). Culture and the construction of habits in daily life: Implications for the successful development of children with disabilites. *OTJR: Occupation, Participation and Health*, *27*(4, Supplement), 33S–30S.

Hessisches Sozialministerium und Hessisches Kultusministerium. (Eds.). (2007). Bildung von Anfang an. http://www.bep.hessen.de/irj/BEP_Internet. Accessed 28 Nov 2012.

Krummheuer, G. (2007). Argumentation and participation in the primary mathematics classroom. Two episodes and related theoretical abductions. *Journal of Mathematical Behavior*, *26*, 60–82.

Krummheuer, G. (2011). Representation of the notion "learning-as-participation" in everyday situations of mathematics classes. *ZDM Mathematics Education*, *43*, 81–90.

Krummheuer, G. (2012). The "Non-canonical" solution and "improvisation" as conditions for early years mathematics learning processes: The concept of the "interactional niche in the development of mathematical thinking" (NMT). In *Journal für Mathematikdidaktik*, *33*(2), 317–338, doi:10.1007/s13138-012-0040-z.

Krummheuer, G. (2014). The Relationship between Cultural Expectation and the Local Realization of a Mathematics Learning Environment In: U. Kortenkamp et al. (eds.), *Early Mathematics Learning*, (pp. 71–83). New York: Springe

Krummheuer, G., & Brandt, B. (2001). *Paraphrase und Traduktion. Partizipationstheoretische Elemente einer Interaktionstheorie des Mathematiklernens in der Grundschule*. Beltz: Weinheim.

Konferenz der Kultusminister. (2004). Bildungsstandards im Fach Mathematik für den Primarbereich (Jahrgangsstufe 4). München: Luchthand. http://www.kmk.org/fileadmin/veroeffentlichungen_beschluesse/2004/2004_10_15-Bildungsstandards-Mathe-Primar.pdf. Accessed 28 Nov 2012.

Nickson, M. (1994). The culture of mathematics classroom: An unknown quantity? In S. Lerman (Ed.), Culturale perspective on the mathematics classroom (pp. 7–35). Dodrecht: Kluwer.

Niedersächsisches Kultusministerium. (2000). Bildung und Erziehung im Elementarbereich niedersächsischer Tageseinrichtungen für Kinder. http://www.mk.niedersachsen.de/portal/live.php?navigation_id=25428&article_id=86998&_psmand=8. Accessed 28 Nov 2012.

van Oers, B. (2002). Teachers' epistemology and the monitoring of mathematical thinking in early years classrooms. *European Early Childhood Education Research Journal, 10*(2), 19–30.

Olson, D., & Bruner, J. (1996). Folk psychology and folk pedagogy. In D. Olson & N. Torrance (Eds.), *The handbook of education and human development* (pp. 9–27). Cambridge: Blackwell.

Presmeg, E. (2007). The role of culture in teaching and learning mathematics. In F. K. Lester (Ed.), *Second handbook of research on mathematics teaching and learning* (pp. 435–458). Charlotte: Information Age Publishing.

Rogoff, B. (1994). Developing understanding of the idea of community of learners. *Mind, Culture, and Activity, 1*(4), 209–229.

Rogoff, B., Matusov, E., & White, C. (1996). Models of teaching and learning—participation in a community of learners. In D. Olson & N. Torrance (Eds.), *The handbook of education and human development* (pp. 388–414). Cambridge: Blackwell.

Sarama, J., & Clements, D. H. (2008). Mathematics in early childhood. In O. N. Saracho & D. Spodek (Eds.), *Contemporary perspectives on mathematics in early childhood education* (pp. 67–94). Charlotte: Information Age Publishing.

Super, C. M., & Harkness, S. (1986). The developmental niche: A conceptualization at the interface of child and culture. *International Journal of Behavioral Development, 9*, 545–569.

Thiel, O. (2009). Prozessqualität mathematischer Bildung im Kindergarten. In M. Neubrand (Ed.), *Beiträge zum Mathematikunterricht 2009* (pp. 395–398). Münster: WTM.

Chapter 6
The Relationship between Cultural Expectation and the Local Realization of a Mathematics Learning Environment

Götz Krummheuer

> *Momma used to say that life is like a box of chocolates: you never know what you're gonna get*
> —Forrest Gump

Introduction

I would like to talk about the interface between *cultural expectation* and *local realization* in the social context of encounters that "serve" as mathematical learning opportunities for children. In the analyses of several episodes from a German kindergarten or from family observations dealing with different mathematical domains, we were confronted with an interpretation of certain scenes, in which somehow something "went wrong." Obviously, local productions of a solution can take another path than anticipated by "normal" expectations about how the given problem is supposed to be coped with. It was a remark of Newcombe and Huttenlocher (2003) about the child's development of spatial representation and reasoning, stressing the factor or necessity of "mishaps resulting from ambiguous communication" for this development that gave me food for thought:

> Presumably, in the course of normal development, feedback from confused listeners and/or from mishaps resulting from ambiguous communication drive the development of organized description strategies and explicit marking of frames of reference. (Newcombe and Huttenlocher 2003, p. 205)

My first thought was: is this appropriate wording, when obviously crucial conditions of the child's development connote a negative outcome, like the word "mishap." I do not mean to idealize the conditions of learning mathematics in everyday situations—the kinds of normal interaction with parents, adults, nursery teachers, siblings, and peers. I would rather support a position, which might be similar to what Garfinkel calls the "ethonomethdological indifference":

G. Krummheuer (✉)
Goethe-Univesity Frankfurt a.M. and IDeA-Center Frankfurt a. M., Germany
e-mail: krummheuer@math.uni-frankfurt.de

> Administering Ethnomethodological indifference is an instructable way ... to pay no ontical [sic!] judgemental attention to the established corpus of social science. (Garfinkel 2002, p. 171)

From a socio-constructivist perspective I am interested in reconstructing the ways and modalities, in which the situationally emerging form of participation of a child in a social encounter can be conceptualized as a moment in the child's development in mathematical thinking.

This way of looking at the process of interaction is based on a long discussion in the science of mathematics education that resulted in "my" conceptualization of learning as a dual process, as the individual's cognitive construction of knowledge, and as his increasingly autonomous participation in social situations. Tomasello (2003) speaks of the "dual inheritance" (p. 283; see also Krummheuer 2011a, b; Voigt 1995).

Referring to my initial remarks, the following issues might be helpful in finding an appropriate wording for the theoretical concepts:

1. If one looks into mathematics learning processes of young children of preschool and kindergarten age, one cannot assume that the attending adults have a sufficient mathematical background to serve as experts who can help avoid the occurrence of such mishaps. Neither the nursery teacher nor the parents or elder siblings of a child necessarily possess the desirable mathematical competence. Referring to the epigram, one could say: Forrest Gump cannot be sure, what kind of chocolates are in the box.
2. From an interactionist's stance, all interaction situations principally entail the potential of developing in an *unexpected* way where the participants cannot easily refer to routinized and/or standardized applications of knowledge—they have to interactively negotiate a novel "shared meaning." Forrest Gump, who is going to get a box of chocolates, might have another understanding of what such a box is going to be.

In order to deepen this issue theoretically, I will introduce the concept of the "interactional niche in the development of mathematical thinking" and thereafter apply this concept to several episodes that were analyzed in our projects early Steps in Mathematics Learning (erStMaL) and Mathematische Kreativität bei Kindern mit schwieriger Kindheit (MaKreKi, Mathematical Creativity of Children at Risk). Finally, I will draw some conclusions about the question how much one could or should instruct small children in the development of their mathematical thinking.

The Concept of the "Interactional Niche in the Development of Mathematical Thinking"

The theoretical perspective of the generation of mathematical thinking taken here is one of socio-constructivism. This perspective encompasses two research traditions: one strand is based on the phenomenological sociology of Alfred Schütz (Schütz and Luckmann (1979) and its expansion into ethnomethodology (Garfinkel (1972) and symbolic interactionism (Blumer (1969)[1]—usually subsumed under the name "micro-sociology"; the other tradition refers to the cultural historic approach of Vygotsky and Leont'ev, etc. (see Wertsch and Tulviste 1992 and Ernest 2010).

Generally speaking, one can characterize the cultural historic approach as one which takes culture as a given that the child adapts to by its development; an important issue hereby is the notion of language that stores and transmits the cultural accomplishments in a symbolic form allowing the child to enter into this culture, step by step, finally becoming a full participant. One can characterize this approach as structuralistic (see Gellert (2008)). In contrast, the micro-sociological approach views culture as a continuously and locally emerging course of action that is accomplished by the mutual exchange of meanings in the steady interaction among the members of a group or society. Goffman (1983) calls this a "situational perspective" (p. 8; see also Krummheuer (2007)). Hereby the child co-constructs the culture in each social event in which it is participating.

From the stance of the cultural historic approach, one can consider the child's development as a general individual progression starting with statuses of participation that are dominated by observing and imitating actions of other participants and aiming toward statuses that are rather characterized by taking active influence on the course of interaction. Respectively, the interactionistic approach implies the idea of a "leeway of participation,"[2] within which a child explores its cultural environment while co-constructing it. With respect to the child's development of mathematical thinking, I will amalgamate the two approaches in a "socio-constructivist paradigm," thus allowing the introduction of the notion of the "evolutionary spiral":

- The child individually utilizes the leeway of participation that is interactively accomplished and to be understood as a result of the culture the participants share.[3] The development of thinking is then comprehensible as an individual process of cognitively active adaptation to those aspects of the process of negotiation of meaning that are conceivable to the child.
- By these processes of adaptation, the procedure of interaction develops over time allowing the child incrementally to take over activities and responsibility for the outcome of the interaction. This might lead to modifications of the structure of interaction that eventually can become stabilized in this new mode over a longer period of time. Thus, the framing conditions of the culture for such social occasions change, in that in subsequent encounters the participants are likely to accomplish (slightly) differently structured processes of negotiation of meaning.[4]

---

[1] Surprisingly, Ernest (2010) does not mention this research tradition. For its reception in mathematics education, see Bauersfeld (1995); Krummheuer (1995); Voigt (1995).
[2] See the notion of "Partizipationsspielraum" in Brandt (2004) that is translated into English as "leeway of participation"; see also Krummheuer (2011a).
[3] Culture is taken here either as a macro-sociological global precondition or as a micro-sociological phenomenon of locally stabilized and routinized procedures of meaning negotiation.
[4] One might call this a "conceptual change" on the individual level Vogel and Huth (2010).

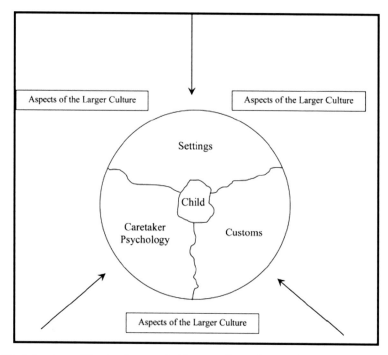

Fig. 6.1 Subsystems of the developmental niche according to Super and Harkness

For the purpose of further developing this notion of the evolutionary spiral, I refer to the concept of "developmental niche" (Fig. 6.1) from Super and Harkness (1986):

> The developmental niche...is a theoretical framework of studying cultural regulation of the micro-environment of the child, and it attempts to describe the environment from the point of view of the child in order to understand processes of development and acquisition of culture. (p. 552)

The authors introduce three subsystems for such a developmental niche:

- The physical and social settings in which the child lives
- Culturally regulated customs of child care and rearing
- The psychology of the caretakers (Super and Harkness 1986, p. 552; the diagram is published in Harkness et al. 2007, p. 34)

Super and Harkness conducted anthropological studies without focusing on the situational aspects of social interaction processes. I stress the component of the interactively local production of such processes and speak of an "interactional niche in the development of mathematical thinking" (NMT). It consists of the provided "learning offerings" of a group or society, which are specific to their culture and will be categorized as aspects of "allocation," and of situationally emerging performance

Table 6.1 Components and aspects of the interactional niche in the development of mathematical thinking (NMT)

NMT	Component: content	Component: cooperation	Component: pedagogy and education
Aspect of allocation	Mathematical domains; body of mathematics tasks	Institutions of education; settings of cooperation	Scientific theories of mathematics education
Aspect of situation	Interactive negotiation of the theme	Leeway of participation	Folk theories of mathematics education

occurring in the process of meaning negotiation, which will be subsumed under the aspect of the "situation."[5]

I modify Super and Harkness's three components of the developmental niche in that, first, I merge the categories "customs" and "caretaker psychology" to the component "pedagogy and education," second, redefine the category "settings" to the component "cooperation" and third, add the new component of the content. These modifications allow a combination of each of these novel components with either of the mentioned aspects.

In the following I would like to further explicate the details of Table 6.1:

1. *Content:* Children are confronted with topics from different domains of mathematics as they appear in their everyday life. The following data were gathered in the research project erStMaL and in everyday mathematic classroom situations. These mathematical topics are usually presented in the form of a sequence or body of tasks, which are adapted with respect to their content and difficulty to the assumed mathematical competencies of these children. On the situational level the presentation of such tasks elicits processes of negotiation, which necessarily do not proceed in concordance to the ascribed mathematical domain or to the activities that are expected in the tasks.

2. *Cooperation:* Besides this content-related component, the children participate in culturally specific social settings which are variously structured as in peer interaction or small group interaction guided by a nursery teacher or primary mathematics teacher etc. These social settings do not function automatically; in fact they need to be accomplished in the joint interaction. Depending on each event, a different leeway of participation will come forward.

3. *Pedagogy and education:* The science of mathematics education develops theories and delineates—more or less stringently—learning paths and milestones for the children's mathematical growth. In the concrete situation, however, it rather is the folk pedagogy of the participating adults and children that becomes operant. It cannot be assumed that these different theories coincide.

---

[5] For more details see Krummheuer (2011a).

Fig. 6.2 Different types of June bugs

Some Insights From our Recent Analyses in the Projects erStMaL and MaKreKi

First, some information about two projects on which my empirical analyses are based. They are a part of the Center for Individual Differences and Adaptive Education in Frankfurt am Main, Germany: early Steps in Mathematics Learning (erStMaL) and "Mathematische Kreativität bei Kindern mit schwieriger Kindheit" (MaKreKi, Mathematical Creativity of Children at Risk).[6] Both projects are longitudinal studies that range over a period of 5–6 years. Within this time frame we are in contact with the children from age 3 to 10. In erStMaL, we initiate learning opportunities for children in small groups in preschool and kindergarten and later in primary mathematics classes. Additionally, with a few children we also observe their families at home as they play with mathematically challenging material that we provide. In MaKreKi, we selected children with a seemingly extraordinary degree of mathematical creativity. In this project we integrate our analyses with psychoanalytical insights about the development of the attachment behavior of the child to his/her mother.

I will present the results of our analyses of three episodes in these two projects.

First Episode: the June Bug Problem

In a preschool, the German Kindergarten, the two children Marie (aged 4 years and 8 months) and René (4 years and 9 months) and an adult person are sitting together around a table. They have cards on the table that show June bugs, which differ in size (small and large), in color (red, green, and yellow), and in the types of spots (circle, triangle, and square and also by the sizes small and large; Fig. 6.2).

The two children invent two systems of descriptions for the size of the bodies: the size (small and large) and the family position (mom, dad, parents, and kids); for example as in Fig. 6.3.

I will refer to the end phase of a collective processing of the task. As mentioned, also a familial system of description has been invented: The small June bugs represent child-bugs and the big one mom-bugs, dad-bugs, or parents-bugs. During

---

[6] For more details of both projects see Acar Bayraktar et al. (2011).

6 The Relationship Between Cultural Expectation and the Local Realization…   77

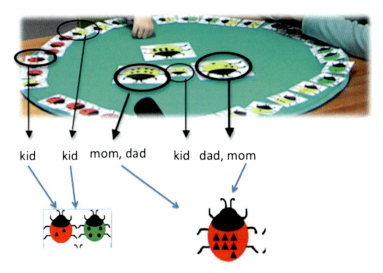

Fig. 6.3 Familial categorization of June bugs

Fig. 6.4 The three different large June bugs in the discussion

the period before this episode, they also compared the number of cards according to their size and color and found out that all these subgroups are of equal number.

After this comparison, the children realigned the cards around the round carpet, which is a kind of defined space for playing and exploring the material.

Finally, there were three cards in the center of the table as shown in Fig. 6.4.

Routinely, the adult opens this kind of constellation with the question "which one doesn't belong" (Wheatley 2008). Furthermore, routinely we expect as an answer: the June bug with the few and big triangles does not belong. But René comes up with the solution that both June bugs with the many, small triangles do not belong. His justification has two aspects:

- Comparing the figures of the small and the big cards, he concludes, that the June bugs of the small cards should also only possess small figures on their tops.
- The two cards with the many and small triangles cannot exist in the system of the cards at all.

If one interprets his explanation in terms of the invented familial system of description, one could rephrase it in this way:

- Big June bugs have big figures because they are parents,
- small June bugs have small figures because they are children, and
- so, big June bugs with small figures do not exist.

If one understands the figures on the June bugs to be, for example, people's hands, René's argument is: parents do not have hands the size of kids, this is impossible. They cannot be parents and children "at the same time," as he says.

René creates a non-canonical solution. The observing adult seems to have difficulty comprehending his approach. Possibly she assumes that he wants to say that the two June bugs with the many and small triangles are the ones that remain and therefore the third one with the few and big triangles does not belong. This constellation of misinterpretation evokes the short dialog in which Renè rephrases his solution. With respect to the interactional setting, it is René who takes over the adult's perspective of being puzzled and explains his position to her. Obviously, the adult person did not anticipate René's solution. It was beyond the canonical expectations of what a child might answer.

From the viewpoint of the design of the problem, one could argue, if the different patterns of triangles would not have been printed on the backs of June bugs but just in an "inexpressive" circle, the children would not have had the "chance" to be "confused" and to thus develop an anthropomorphic view of the problem. This might be correct, and Wheatley (2008), who developed the problem, does it with circles. But discussing the results of this scene in this inexpressive way means that a kind of deterioration occurred in the process, namely that a mishap occurred. From an interactionistic stance, however, one would rather argue: this is what happened and it was rather René who "saved" the situation by taking over the adult's perspective. (Forrest Gump got a box of something that he did not take to be a box of chocolates. So what!)

The Second Episode: The Birthday-Party Problem

In a preschool the four children and a student research assistant "B" are seated at a table.[7] The children are Karoline (4 years 11 months), Fanny (4 years), Otto (5 years 4 months), and Klara (5 years 10 months). B opens the conversation:

---

[7] This scene is first mentioned in Krummheuer (2011a).

6 The Relationship Between Cultural Expectation and the Local Realization… 79

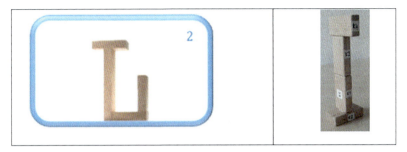

Fig. 6.5 The chosen play card and the accomplished solution

"Do you remember the chipmunk[8] that we brought with us the last time? It has its birthday today and wants to have a birthday party." B then takes off a cover from a set of dishes and eating utensils that were put on the table. It contains four cups (pink, blue, green, and yellow), four mugs, four plates all in the same four colors, four forks and knives, four teaspoons, and four tablespoons. The children take some of the items and move them around the table. Each child has a placemat in front of him/her and they group their items on it.

After 8 min of sorting out the utensils and the dishes, Otto takes his turn and says: "One thing we forgot, where is the chipmunk supposed to sit?" The group declares a part of the table to be the place where the chipmunk as a toy is supposed to sit (as a toy, it is physically not really present). The peers discover that there are no more dishes available and that only a few teaspoons remain. B comments on this situation: "We haven't got enough. But perhaps you guys can hand over some of yours."

In the following the children make several attempts to distribute their eating and drinking utensils among five participants of the party. They develop some ideas that can be seen as the very initial steps to the concept of the division in the set of rational numbers. It, however, did not merge into more tangible results.

Here again one could argue from the stance of design science, that one could have anticipated the remark that the chipmunk should sit with them at the table and one could have been appropriately prepared for this. But again: "You never know what you're gonna get."

Third Episode: The Game: "Building Bricks" in the Family Ak

In a family setting, the mother and the daughter Aleyna (aged 4 years and 8 months) play a game in which they have to rebuild a construction of bricks according to a given picture on a playing card.

At the end of a relatively intense discussion they came up with the solution shown in the right cell of Fig. 6.5. Our analysis of the interaction between mother

---

[8] The chipmunk is the mascot of the project erStMaL. It is a stuffed animal.

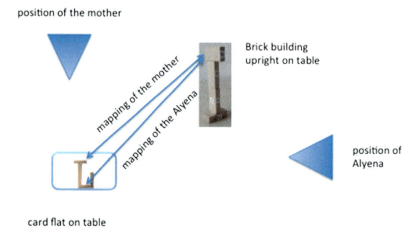

Fig. 6.6 The final joint construction of mother and daughter and their sitting positions

and daughter reveals that the two partners, sitting at different sides of the table, interpret the bricks in their final joint construction as different parts of the picture (Fig. 6.6).

Here again, we are facing a situation that developed in a surprising and unexpected way. At least Aleyna does not feel satisfied with the result, though the mother decided that their construction coincides with the picture on the card. It can be assumed that the designer of this game had not envisioned such a solution.

Conclusion: the Application of the Notion of NMT

For a deeper analysis, one can reconstruct these three examples with the help of the concept NMT. In all of these episodes a specific niche emerged, which conjointly can be characterized by the tension between the expected production of the solution and the actually realized outcome.

- With respect to the *component of content* we have to consider that the intended mathematical activities, like pattern identification, partitive division, and spatial reconstruction of two dimensional diagrams, were accomplished in the first two cases in a more elaborated way than assumedly intended by the designers of the task. René's application of two different systems of categorization combined with certain restrictions that were based on a common sense understanding of human growth is a somehow unique and not expectable solution, which from a mathematical point of view, might entail a more sophisticated mathematical potential than the expected "canonical" solution. Also the birthday-party problem advanced in a direction that, from a mathematical point of view, promises a deeper mathematical understanding of division than the expected partitive division of dishes and eating utensils. It encompasses the options of dealing with the division with a remainder, the overcoming of the positive integers, etc.

The third example appears to be different from the first two. Here the analysis leads to the insight that the negotiations between mother and daughter reach a dead end. We assume that it is not the different geometrical perspectives of mother and Aleyna that produce this calamity but the effect of interactively wiping away their differences. Finally, this leads to unclarified and unspoken discrepancies that are most unlikely to stimulate any process of cognitive (re)-construction.

- With regard to the component of cooperation we have to take into account that initially designed asymmetrical situations of interaction in which an adult is supposed to order, structure, and/or correct, emerge in a rather symmetrical discourse of co-construction. In the case of René we can even assume that he conducts himself in a more adult-like manner with the capacity of taking over the perspective of the adult.
- Referring to the component of education and pedagogy, we recognize that theories of design science overestimate the immediate and direct impact of the cognitive constructions on the learner. It is as if the wedge of the social affair of negotiating meaning in the interaction among the participants is driven between the provided problem and the mind of the child. With reference to Goffman (1983), we can speak of the "interaction order" that is somehow more or less like a thick wedge that is driven between the allocated learning material and the cognizing child. What the child is processing in his mind is not the "inherent" meaning of this material but the interactively negotiated working consensus of the definition of the situation in which this material was implemented. This interaction order is to be taken as a social institution that for the most part independently functions with its own regularities and dynamics.

Taking all this into regard, we can reconstruct NMTs in the first two episodes that do not fail but rather proceed in an evolutionary spiral. Mathematically, more sophisticated definitions of the situation and rather symmetrical forms of discourse are emerging as well. New mathematical concepts are in the incubator of these processes: the making of meaning and the potential of symmetrical co-construction can be exploited. The longitudinal design of our projects will give us the opportunity to analyze the actions of these children in later phases of their development. We also can gain insights into accomplished niches that go awry. This happens in the interaction when the emerging differences in the individual definitions of the situations are not distinguishable. It is neither the persistence of differences nor the situational impossibility of dissolving them; it is instead the act of sweeping these discrepancies under the carpet that extinguishes the NMT. Bauersfeld (1980) called it once the "hidden dimension(s)" (see also Krummheuer 2009, 2012).

The results of these first studies about the functioning of NMT allow a relatively differentiated standpoint on the question how much one should instruct children of kindergarten age in mathematics and how much one should let them have their own experience in constructing personally new insights that in the long term can be incorporated in the buildup of their mathematical knowledge (see the discussion in Tobias and Duffy (2009)). It is not so much a matter if something goes right or wrong, which from an instructional point of view would be an indicator whether the instruction needs to be improved. There is always the possibility of unexpected ways in which the actual situations emerge. The allocative components will always be mediated in the concrete encounter by the interactive process of negotiation of meaning. Both aspects together define the interactional niche, by which the child might perceive the appropriate *stimulus* and the appropriate *guidance* as well for his/her cognitive development. Stimulus and guidance are on the one hand distinguishable as allocative and situational and on the other hand they are two sides of the same coin: they are concepts that in terms of NMT appear as a whole and not as one of its aspects. Empirically, there seem to be various constellations of NMT, which "operate" differently with respect to stimulus and guidance. Depending on these realizations of NMT, the evolutionary spiral then advances along different loops and opens different options to the process of children's mathematical thinking—you never know what your're gonna get.

Further research is necessary in order to reconstruct these options and describe their effects.

The projects erStMaL and MaKreKi are funded by the Hessian initiative for the development of scientific and economic excellence (LOEWE) and are conducted in the Center of "Individual Development and Adaptive Education" (IDeA) at Frankfurt am Main, Germany

References

Acar Bayraktar, E., & Hümmer, A.-M., et. al. (2011). Forschungsmethodischer Rahmen der Projekte erStMaL und MaKreKi. In B. Brandt, R. Vogel & G. Krummheuer (Eds.), *Die Projekte erStMaL und MaKreKi. Mathematikdidaktische Forschung am "Center for Individual Development and Adaptive Education" (IDeA) (Vol. 1, pp. 11–24)*. Münster: Waxmann.
Bauersfeld, H. (1980). Hidden dimensions in the so-called reality of mathematics classroom. *Educational Studies in Mathematics, 11*, 23–29.
Bauersfeld, H. (1995). "Language games" in the mathematics classroom: Their function and their effects. In P. Cobb & H. Bauersfeld (Eds.), *The emergence of mathematical meaning. Interaction in classroom cultures* (pp. 271–291). Hillsdale: Lawrence Erlbaum.
Blumer, H. (1969). *Symbolic interactionism*. Prentice-Hall: Englewood Cliffs.
Brandt, B. (2004). *Kinder als Lernende. Partizipationsspielräume und -profile im Klassenzimmer*. Frankfurt a. M: usw.: Peter Lang.
Ernest, P. (2010). Reflections on theories of learning. In B. Sriraman & L. English (Eds.), *Theories of mathematics education: Seeking new frontiers* (pp. 39–46). Berlin: Springer.
Garfinkel, H. (1972). Remarks on ethnomethodology. In J. J. Gumperz & D. Hymes (Eds.), *Directions in sociolinguistics: The ethnography of communication* (pp. 35–71). New York: Holt.
Garfinkel, H. (2002). *Ethnomethodology's program. Working out Durkheim's aphorism*. Lanham: Rowman & Littlefield Publishers.
Gellert, U. (2008). Validity and relevance: Comparing and combining two sociological perspectives on mathematics classroom practice. *Zentralblatt für Didaktik der Mathematik (ZDM), 40*(2), 215–224.
Goffman, E. (1983). The interaction order. *American Sociological Review, 48*, 1–17.

Harkness, S., & Super, C. M., et al. (2007). Culture and the construction of habits in daily life: Implications for the successful development of children with disabiliites. OTJR: Occupation. *Participation and Health, 27*(4 (Fall Supplement)), 33S–30S.

Krummheuer, G. (1995). The ethnography of argumentation. In P. Cobb & H. Bauersfeld (Eds.), *The emergence of mathematical meaning: Interaction in classroom cultures* (pp. 229–269). Hillsdale: Lawrence Erlbaum.

Krummheuer, G. (2007). Argumentation and participation in the primary mathematics classroom. Two episodes and related theoretical abductions. *Journal of Mathematical Behavior, 26*(1), 60–82.

Krummheuer, G. (2009). Inscription, narration and diagrammatically based argumentation. The narrative accounting practices in the primary school mathematics lesson. In W.-M. Roth & N. C. Charlotte (Eds.), *Mathematical representation at the interface of the body and culture* (pp. 219–243). Charlotte: Information Age Publishing.

Krummheuer, G. (2011a). Die empirisch begründete Herleitung des Begriffs der "Interaktionalen Nische mathematischer Denkentwicklung" (NMD). In B. Brandt, R. Vogel, & G. Krummheuer (Eds.), *Die Projekte erStMaL und MaKreKi. Mathematikdidaktische Forschung am "Center for Individual Development and Adaptive Education" (IDeA) (Vol. 1 pp. 25–90)*. Münster: Waxmann.

Krummheuer, G. (2011b). Representation of the notion "learning-as-participation" in everyday situations of mathematics classes. *Zentralblatt für Didaktik der Mathematik (ZDM), 43*(1/2), 81–90.

Krummheuer, G. (2012). The "non-canonical" Solution and the "Improvisation" as conditions for early years mathematics learning processes: The concept of the "interactional Niche in the Development of mathematical Thinking" (NMT). *Journal für Mathematik-Didaktik, 33*(2), 317–338.

Newcombe, N. S., & Huttenlocher, J. (2003). *Making space. The development of spatial representation and reasoning.* Cambridge, London: Bradord, MIT Press.

Schütz, A., & Luckmann, T. (1979). *Strukturen der Lebenswelt* (Vol. 1). Frankfurt a. M.: Suhrkamp.

Super, C. M., & Harkness, S. (1986). The developmental niche: A conceptualization at the interface of child and culture. *International Journal of Behavioral Development, 9*, 545–569.

Tobias, S., & Duffy, T. M. (Eds.). (2009). *Constructivist instruction. Success of failure?* New York, Oxford: Routledge.

Tomasello, M. (2003). *Constructing a language. A usage-based theory of language acquistion.* Cambridge: Harvard University Press.

Vogel, R., & Huth, M. (2010). "…und der Elephant in die Mitte" – Rekonstruktion mathematischer Konzepte von Kindern in Gesprächssituationen. In B. Brandt, M. Fetzer, & M. Schütte (Eds.), *Auf den Spuren Interpretativer Unterrichtsforschung in der Mathematikdidaktik. Götz Krummheuer zum 60. Geburtstag* (pp. 177–208). Münster: Waxmann.

Voigt, J. (1995). Thematic patterns of interaction and sociomathematical norms. In P. Cobb & H. Bauersfeld (Eds.), *The emergemce of mathematical meaning: Interaction in classroom cultures* (pp. 163–201). Hillsdale: Lawrence Erlbaum.

Wertsch, J. V., & Tulviste, P. (1992). L. S. Vygotsky and contemporary developmental psychologiy. *Journal of Developmental Psychology, 28*(4), 548–557.

Wheatley, G. (2008). *Which one doesn't belong.* Bethany Beach: Mathematics Learning

Chapter 7
The Reflection of Spatial Thinking on the Interactional Niche in the Family

Ergi Acar Bayraktar

Interactional Niche in the Development of Mathematical Thinking (NMT) in Familial Situations

IDeA Center and Project erStMaL

One of the research projects of the Center for Research on Individual Development and Adaptive Education of Children at Risk (IDeA) is the project Early Steps in Mathematics Learning (erStMaL), which investigates the mathematical development of children in this age group. It is planned as a longitudinal study to follow children from the age of three, until the third year of primary school from a socioconstructivist perspective. While the first survey period covers kindergarten children, the second survey period covers the same children in primary school ages (see also Acar Bayraktar et al. 2011). Currently, the fifth observation phase continues in the project erStMaL. In the study erStMaL, a family study is also performed, which is designed as a longitudinal study and named erStMaL-FaSt (Early Steps in Mathematics Learning-Family Study). It deals with the impact of the familial socialization on the mathematics learning. The chapter deals with first insights of this family study.

The IDeA is conducted by the German Institute for International Educational Research (DIPF), Goethe Universität Frankfurt, and the Sigmund Freud Institute Frankfurt. The center explores the development of children at risk and the processes of individual learning in the preschool, kindergarten, and primary school age.

A Familial Study in the erStMaL Project: erStMaL-FaSt

For the family study, we choose children from our main study erStMaL according to the following three criteria: the ethnic background (German or Turkish), the duration of the formal education of the parents (more or less than 10 years), and the sibling situation within the families. From different kindergartens, 120 erStMaL

E. Acar Bayraktar (✉)
Goethe-Univesity Frankfurt a.M. and IDeA-Center Frankfurt a. M., Germany
e-mail: acar@math.uni-frankfurt.de

Table 7.1 Research design of the family study

Eight families		With sibling	Without sibling
Higher educational level	Turkish/German	1	2
	German	2	1
Lower educational level	Turkish/German	1	–
	German	1	–

Table 7.2 Observation design

Observation design	I	erStMaL child as a single child	II	erStMaL child as a sibling
erStMaL child is playing with	Ia	Mother or one member of family (e.g., father)	IIa	Mother or one member of family (e.g., father) and sibling
	Ib	Mother and one member of family (e.g., father)	IIb	Mother, sibling, and one member of family (e.g., father)

children who were about the age of 4 considering the year 2009 were selected, from among whom 49, whose families matched all three criteria, were chosen for the family study. These families were contacted and asked if they would like to participate in erStMaL-FaSt. At the beginning of the family study, eight families had agreed to participate in it.

Currently, there are eight ongoing participant families in the erStMaL-FaSt, whose children are aged seven considering the year 2012. The detailed research design is shown in Table 7.1.

Data collection comprises of recorded videos and their transcripts. Once a year, an appointment is arranged with each family. This leads step by step to a collection of data from each child.

In these appointments, the erStMaL child is video recorded together with members of the family while they are playing. By setting up a design for the observation of each child, it is also enabled to see game partners of the erStMaL child (Table 7.2).

For erStMaL-FaSt, four play situations are conceived, which refers to two mathematical domains: geometry and measurement (Acar Bayraktar and Krummheuer 2011, p. 143; see also Acar Bayraktar et al. 2011). Each play situation is constructed according to specific design patterns for erStMaL-FaSt (see also Vogel 2012; Vogel and Wippermann 2005).

In each brief description, as a specific design pattern (1) definition of play situation, (2) application field, (3) intended mathematical domain, (4) mathematical context, (5) materials and playroom, and (6) instruction manual are introduced. As an example, one specific design pattern and its translation are shown in Figs. 7.1 and 7.2.

In FaSt, there are four different play situations, which are expanded and upgraded in each year before the observations.

For data collection, an appointment must be arranged with the family by giving them the flexibility to choose place and time.

7 The Reflection of Spatial Thinking on the Interactional Niche in the Family

Spiel- und Erkundungssituation

FaSt – Bauen 01 (B01)

erStMaL-Familienstudie
(Stand: 04.03.2010)

Kurzbeschreibung der Spiel- und Erkundungssituation (1)	Wie kann die Spiel- und Erkundungssituation beschrieben werden?	
	In der Spiel- und Erkundungssituation können die Kinder und ihre Familien Quadergebäude von zweidimensionalen Abbildungen mit entsprechenden Quadern nachbauen.	
Einsatzbereich (2)	Welcher Einsatzbereich ist für die Spiel- und Erkundungssituation vorgesehen? (Familienstudie, Erstbesuch/Zweitbesuch, Altersbereich)	
	• Familienstudie • Erstbesuch • 4+ Jahre	
Mathematischer Bereich (3)	Welchem mathematischen Bereich kann die Spiel- und Erkundungssituation zugeordnet werden?	
	Geometry and Spatial Thinking	
Mathematischer Gehalt (4)	Wie kann der mathematische Gehalt der Spiel- und Erkundungssituation beschrieben werden?	
	Objektdarstellung durch einfache Mittel, Vereinfachung, Abstraktion; Zusammenhang zwischen zwei- und dreidimensionalen Darstellungen: Kavallierperspektive in ein dreidimensionales Modell übertragen	
Material und Raum (5)	Welches Material wird für die Durchführung der Spiel- und Erkundungssituation benötigt? Wie muss der Raum für die Spiel- und Erkundungssituation vorbereitet sein?	
	• Holzquader in ausreichender Anzahl • Verschieden komplexe Abbildungen von Quadergebäuden auf Spielkarten (Komplexität wird durch Punktzahlen kenntlich gemacht) • Spielanleitung „Bauen 01"	
Impulse und Hinweise für die Familien (6)	Welche Impulse und Hinweise benötigen die teilnehmenden Familien, um an der Spiel- und Erkundungssituation teilzunehmen?	
	Spielregeln: • Die Spielkarten werden gemischt und verdeckt auf einem Stapel in der Mitte des Tisches platziert. • Die Teilnehmenden ziehen nacheinander eine Karte und versuchen jeweils die darauf abgebildeten Gebäude nachzubauen. • Es werden fünf Runden gespielt. Danach vergleichen die Teilnehmenden ihre jeweils erspielte Anzahl an Punkten auf ihren Karten.	

Fig. 7.1 The specific design pattern of play Building 01

Mathematical situation of play and exploration
FaSt – Building 01 (B01)

erStMaL - Familystudy
(Date: 04.03.2010)

Definition of play situation (1)	How can the play situation be described?
	In the play, families are supposed to build three-dimensional version of the picture with wooden bricks.
Application field (2)	Which fields are scheduled at the application of the play situation?
	• Family study • First Meeting • Age 4+
Intended mathematical domain (3)	Which mathematical domain is chosen for the play situation?
	Geometry and Spatial Thinking
Mathematical context (4)	How can the chosen mathematical content de described?
	Exploration of the two-dimensional illustrations from the three-dimensional buildings and performing the relations between two- and three-dimensional representations.
Materials and play room (5)	Which materials and structures are needed?
	• Wooden bricks with the sufficient count in the same size and weight • The game cards in different levels • The given introduction manuals
Instruction manual (6)	Which impulses and information are needed for the participation of the play situation?
	Rules of the play situation on the given introduction manuals (see chapter 4)

Fig. 7.2 English translation of the specific design pattern of play Building 01

Before family members begin to play in the meeting, all plays are explained in the language family members want: either German or Turkish. At the same time, all play materials are shown to family members. In addition, it is told that they are also free to play in any language they want. Instruction manuals of each play are composed in both languages as well. These introduction manuals and game materials are provided by the author and put at the disposal of the family in the recording room. Afterwards, the family is left by themselves to make all play members feel comfortable while the video recorders are turned on. The members of the family are supposed to choose at least two games out of four and to perform them.

Theoretical Framework of erStMaL-FaSt

Parents are their children's first and continuing "educators" (Mills 2002, p. 1). Thus, the family functions as an ongoing "support system," parallel to kindergarten, preschool, and (primary) school for the learning of mathematics. By the term "support system," it is referred to the idea of socioconstructivist theory, which means that the cognitive development of an individual is constitutively bound to the participation of this individual in a variety of social interactions. Support is a type of feedback or correction, which helps the child to participate more during the play situation. With respect to Bruner's concept of a Language Acquisition Support System (LASS), we propose a similar concept for the learning of mathematics, which is analogically called the "Mathematics Learning Support System" (MLSS) (Bruner 1986, p. 77; see also Acar Bayraktar and Krummheuer 2011, Krummheuer 2011b, c, Tiedemann 2010).

> Mathematical support exists of patterns and routines of interaction, which are realized by adult and child, and also, in which the child is supported to participate in a mathematical discourse. (Tiedemann 2010, p. 154; translation by Ergi Acar Bayraktar)

Considering play situations of erStMaL-FaSt, while children experience the mathematical situations in their families, learning mathematics in early years emerges in different forms of participation (Acar 2011a, p. 1861). The research interest is to identify in which way these forms of participation is shaped by MLSS.

This support occurs not only through "correct instructions" but also through "incorrect instructions." Through the negotiation during the play situation, children and parents construct new definitions of the situation, which reflect the mode of functioning of MLSS (see Acar Bayraktar and Krummheuer 2011). Thus, MLSS is seen as part of a familial "micro cosmos" that emerges during such play situations. It is referred to here as the theoretical framework "developmental niche," which has been introduced by Super and Harkness.

Super and Harkness developed this theoretical framework as a reflection on cultural anthropology and developmental psychology:

> The developmental niche…is a theoretical framework of studying cultural regulation of the micro-environment of the child, and it attempts to describe the environment from the point of view of the child in order to understand processes of development and acquisition of culture. (Super and Harkness 1986, p. 552)

This theoretical framework is generated as a juncture of cultural anthropology and developmental psychology. The authors introduce three major subsystems of a developmental niche, which operate together and share the common function of mediating the individual's developmental experience within a larger culture: (1) the physical and social settings in which the child lives, (2) culturally regulated customs of child care and rearing, and (3) the psychology of the caretakers (Super and Harkness 1986; see also Harkness and Super 1994; Harkness et. al. 2007, p. 552).

Nevertheless, these three components of the developmental niche are deprived of focusing on the situational aspects of social interaction processes. Although they form the cultural context of child development (Super and Harkness 1986; see also Wombles 2010, p. 552), local productions of social interaction processes of mathematics education in children's development are not taken into account. Krummheuer (2011a, b, 2012) worked on this theoretical concept, modified it to the mathematical development, and named it the "interactional niche in the development of mathematical thinking" (NMT).

For the comparison among the various family situations and for the longitudinal analyses as well, the concept of the "interactional niche in the development of mathematical thinking" (NMT) can be used (Krummheuer 2011a, b, 2012). This new theoretical framework includes the advantage of a closer analysis of the relationship between mathematical learning occasions with those, which take place in preschool, kindergarten, and/or primary math classes.

Krummheuer explains NMT as follows:

> It consists of the provided "learning offerings" of a group or society, which are specific to their culture and will be categorized as aspects of "allocation," and of situationally emerging performance occurring in the process of meaning negotiation, which will be subsumed under the aspect of the "situation." (Krummheuer 2012, p. 323; see also Krummheuer 2011a, b)

While analyzing the mathematical situations according to emerging performances of participants, NMT makes it possible to analyze their learning offerings at the same time. Through the allocational aspect, the activeness and the emergence of interaction during the play can be examined in a chosen mathematical domain. Through the situational aspect, it can also be examined how players participate and what they perform during interactive negotiations in the play situation. Thus, this framework enables one to observe and examine the child development clearly through social interaction processes in mathematical situations.

With regard to the design of the family study, the general structure of the interactional niche in the development of mathematical thinking is adapted to the familial context and named NMT-Family (Table 7.3).

Due to allocation and situation aspects, the structure of three components is detailed and explained below[1]:

- **Content:** In the practice of erStMaL-FaSt, children and their families are confronted with mathematical play situations, which are in mathematical domain either "geometry" or "measurement."
  The play situations in erStMaL-FaSt are designed according to a specific design pattern, which supposedly gives the families open areas and opportunities for interactive negotiations. From the situational perspective, during play situations

---

[1] This part is translated into English from the German article (Acar Bayraktar and Krummheuer 2011).

7 The Reflection of Spatial Thinking on the Interactional Niche in the Family 91

Table 7.3 Components and aspects of the interactional niche in the development of mathematical thinking in familial context. (Acar Bayraktar and Krummheuer 2011, p. 140)

NMT-Family	Component: content	Component: cooperation	Component: pedagogy and education
Aspect of allocation	Mathematical domains: geometry and measurement	Play as a familial arrangement for cooperation	Developmental theories in mathematics education and proposals of activeness for parents on this theoretical basis
Aspect of situation	Interactive negotiation of the rules of play and the content	Leeway of participation	Folk theories of mathematics education, everyday routines in mathematics education; MLSS

interactive negotiations emerge, in which the rules of play and/or mathematical topics might be chosen as themes.

- **Cooperation:** The process of cooperation between the adult and child provides the opportunity to refine their thinking and to make their performance more effective. Depending on this cooperation, a different leeway of participation comes forward.

 "Leeway of participation" is one of the interactionistic approaches, by which a child explores his/her cultural environment while co-constructing it (Krummheuer 2012, p. 322; see also "Partizipationsspielraum," Brandt 2004). So, this is a concept belonging to the situational aspect. Brandt (2004) explains that the participants interactively accomplish different margins of leeways of participation that are conducive or restrictive to the mathematical development of a child (see also Krummheuer 2011c; 2012). Alongside contents, the children are involved in the social settings in the play situations, which are variously structured as in child–parents interaction and/or child–sibling interaction. These social settings need to be accomplished in the process of interaction.

- **Pedagogy and Education:** Developmental theories and theories of mathematics education describe and delineate learning paths for the children's mathematical growth from different points of view. With respect to folk pedagogy, the participating adults and children become situationally active and operant in the concrete interaction. During each interaction, there emerge new interpretations, which support the development of the child either in a positive or in a negative way. Thus, in this system, MLSS occurs in different ways.

With respect to all these three components, one chosen scene will be introduced as an example to show how the concept of "interactional niche in the familial context" can be clearly used to examine the social interaction processes in the play situations with respect to the functioning of MLSS.

Fig. 7.3 The game cards on different levels

Spatial Thinking and a Play: Building 01

> The play, for the child and for the adult alike, is a way of using mind, or better yet, an attitude toward the use of mind. (Bruner 1983, p. 69)

The exemplarily chosen mathematical play from the family study refers to spatial thinking and is based upon the play "Make 'N' Break" (Lawson and Lawson 2008). In the play, families are supposed to build three-dimensional version of the picture with wooden bricks, which are of the same size and weight. The play situation offers families different opportunities to perform the relations between two- and three-dimensional representations.

In each round, one player chooses one card from the deck and builds the figure, which is seen on the card as an image. The aim of play is to build a figure properly with the provided wooden bricks as seen on the chosen card, and thereby to get the most points to be a winner. To check the compatibility between the built figure and the seen figure on the card, other players should examine if the built figure is correctly built or not and give a feedback. If it is correct, then the player gets as many points as seen on the card.

In the play, cards are placed on the table face down. Each card has a difficulty level ranging from one to three, which also shows how many points each player can get after they build the card right. The cards with the number 1 are the easiest and the cards with the number 3 are the hardest (Fig. 7.3). In total, they play five rounds by turns of each player.

In the intellectual growth and everyday existence, spatial ability plays a major role (Wachs 2003, p. 534). Clements and Sarama point out that mathematics achievement is related to spatial abilities and therefore, spatial ability is an important factor for the acquisition of many topics in mathematics (2007, p. 489). By many researchers, this "complex" and "elusive" (Clements and Sarama 2007, p. 489) role of spatial ability is investigated in two parts: spatial orientation and spatial visualization (Bishop 1980, p. 259; see also Harris 1981; McGee 1979; Clements and Sarama 2007; National Research Council Committee on Early Childhood 2009). Spatial visualization means that the subject must be imagined as the rotations of objects in space and spatial orientation means that the subject must be recognized and the relationships between the various parts of a configuration and his own position are comprehended (Bishop 1980, p. 259). In their work, Clements and Sarama draw on spatial thought under the part "spatial orientation" (2007). Spatial thought is a thought that finds meaning in the shape, size, orientation, location, direction or trajectory of objects, processes or phenomena, or the relative positions in space of multiple objects, processes, or phenomena (Science Education Resource Centre 2008). The term spatial structuring is defined as the process of organizing two- and three-dimensional concepts. Furthermore, it is declared that it is related with selecting, coordinating, unifying, and registering in memory a set of mental objects and actions (Nes 2009, p. 21).

In the chosen example, it will be focused on both spatial abilities and their subparts as explained above.

For the developmental steps in spatial abilities, it will be benefited from the work of National Research Council Committee on Early Childhood (2009): Step 1 for age 2 and 3, step 2 for age 4, and step 3 for age 5. This chapter focuses on step 3, i.e., age 5. In respect of National Research Council (2009), children who are aged five can take measures of sides (simple units) and compare areas by using superimposition. Furthermore, they can identify and create symmetric figures by using motions (e.g., paper folding; also mirrors as reflections). By using a variety of shape sets (e.g., pattern blocks; rectangular grids with squares, right triangles, and rectangles, tangrams), they can also construct compositions on grids and in puzzles with systematicity and anticipation.

In the range of this age, they can substitute shapes and build complex structures. From pictured models, they can build structures as well.

Additionally, they can both understand and replicate the perspective of a different viewer. Describing both congruent faces and parallel faces of blocks in context (e.g., block building) is another ability of children in the range of age 5.

According to Clements and Sarama, 5-year-old children can metrically represent spatial information in a polar coordinate task, using the same two dimensions as adults, radius and angle (2007, p. 498). It is also reported by National Research Council Committee on Early Childhood that 5-year-old children can understand and can replicate the perspectives of different viewers. Morever, these competencies reflect an initial development at the third level of thinking, which is about relating parts and wholes level. (2009, p. 191).

As a comparison on spatial thinking among children and adults, Clements & Sarama emphasize qualitatively indistinguishability of spatial processing:

> Spatial processing in young children is not qualitatively different from that of older children or adults. However, with the age, children produce progressively more elaborate constructions. (2007, p. 512)

The richness of block building in free-play situations and explorations gives wide opportunities for discovering the basic structure of mathematics and establishing equivalencies in length, height, area, and volume, making tangible, and therefore real, what children have so far learned only symbolically (Hewitt 2001, p. 10). Kersh, Casey, and Young emphasize the reflection of block play on the social skills:

> Engaging in block play helps children acquire a diverse range of valuable competencies and knowledge, from social skills to the foundations for later math achievement. (2008, p. 237)

Moreover, blocks enable children to be illuminated in different varieties of growth areas: physical, social, emotional, and cognitive growth (Bullock 1992, p. 16; see also Cartwright 1988). Bullock draws up each benefit in each growth area, through the block play, as follows (ibid):

> **Physical Growth:** (1) Small and large-muscle development and coordination of muscles by lifting, carrying, bending, reaching, pushing, and pulling. (2) Learning hand-eye coordination by reaching, grasping, and moving blocks. (3) Learning a sense of balance and symmetry through building, stacking, and balancing blocks. (4) Developing motor coordination by moving blocks. (5) Understanding object-space relationships through placement of blocks.
> **Social Growth:** (1) Promotion of social growth through experience in interpersonal relationships. (2) Experience in taking turns, sharing, and respecting the rights of others. (3) Learning to cooperate and play together. (4) Opportunities to engage in several levels of play, from solitary and parallel to group. (5) Increased confidence and self-esteem.
> **Emotional Growth:** (1) Learning patience. (2) Increasing independence. (3) Contributing to a sense of accomplishment, which improves the child's self-image. (4) Stimulation of imagination, creativity, and joy. (5) Experimenting with a variety of roles and skills and feeling a sense of success.
> **Cognitive Growth:** (1) Exploration of sizes, shapes, distances, proportions, and weight. (2) Mathematical concepts such as "bigger than," "smaller than," or "need more or need less." (3) Counting, one-to-one correspondence, classification, sorting, and matching. (4) Experimentation, manipulation, and problem solving. (5) Communicating with others (listening, speaking, and sharing).

Correspondingly, Johnson lays an emphasis on block building and suggests that children go through different phases in each growth area (Johnson 1966). In addition to this, Bullock points out that younger or less experienced children may need more encouragement during the block-building activities (Bullock 1992, p. 18).

The Kil Family

The Kil family is a German-Turkish family who lives in a major German city. The parents, having been brought up in Germany, speak with their daughter Ayse mostly German. Ayse is a single child, aged 5 years and seven months; she speaks German and rudimentary Turkish. Her mother studied for 10 years and has a higher education qualification. Her father studied for 13 years and has a higher education qualification, too. Similar to Ayse, her parents speak both German and rudimentary Turkish.

In the chosen game, Ayse and her father play together. Although they have been informed through the instruction manual that they should play only a total of 5 rounds, they play in total 14 rounds by taking turns, in which they build up all given cards.

Up to the chosen and transcribed scene, they have played just two rounds. Mr. Kil started to play. Until the third round, they built each chosen card correctly. In the third round, Mr. Kil chooses another card and starts to build it (Fig. 7.4).

After a while, he completes the assignment as it is seen in Fig. 7.5.

7 The Reflection of Spatial Thinking on the Interactional Niche in the Family   95

Fig. 7.4 A card chosen by Mr. Kil in the third round

Fig. 7.5 A structure built by Mr. Kil

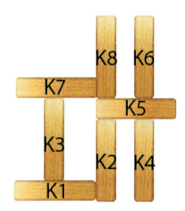

In the chosen scene, he asks his daughter if the built structure is identical with the figure on the card (Table 7.4).

By posing the question "right?" <01>, Mr. Kil probably tries to get to know, if Ayse finds his built figure proper as it is seen on the chosen card. This question also enables to spark off her spatial visualization and spatial orientation. As a reply, Ayse gives him a positive feedback, which shows a temporary agreement that her father built the picture correctly as it is seen on the card. Further, this action indicates that he can gain 3 points given on the card <01–02>.

But after she checks the card again, she realizes a discrepancy between the constructed building and the picture. She says, "But one long and one short" <04>. Actually, she does not exactly depict which wooden bricks she meant are long and short. When the card is compared with the structure of the building, it could be interpreted that she could mean what is shown in Fig. 7.6.

As can be seen in Fig. 7.6, there is a difference between the figure on the chosen card and the built structure. According to the visual discrimination, it can be said that Ayse can represent wooden bricks at the detailed level of shapes (Clements and Sarama 2007, p. 511). Topologically, she can also coordinate both structures and realize that the wooden bricks, K8 and K6, are not horizontally of the same height.

Table 7.4 The transcript of the chosen scene with Ayse and Mr. Kil

01			Father	right?
02			Ayse	Yes
03			Father	Cool
04			Ayse	But one long and one short. *looks at the card*
05			Father	Yes I think the picture is false. *bends to front*
06				And shows the card with his index finger
07			Ayse	Mmh
08			Father	Just look. this is a short block or a short
09				Piece of wood
10			Ayse	Looks at the residuary pile of wooden blocks
11	4.30		Father	Building block
12			Ayse	Leans back, looks still at the pile of blocks
13			Father	Shows the pile of wooden blocks. but there
14				Are no short blocks. I think the picture is
15				False. I would say; it is all right. O.K.?? *puts*
16				The card in his left hand and piles it on his
17				Other cards. you too?
18			Ayse	Pushes her father's building with her right
19				Hand. mhhm
20		>	Father	Good. bowls over the his building and
21				Pushes the blocks to the other pile
22		>	Ayse	Picks a new card with her right hand
23				Turns the card face, looks at it, then looks
24				At her father and laughs
25			Father	Yes
26			Ayse	Mh
27			Father	Not so difficult. scratches his face with his
28				Left hand
29			Ayse	She picks up the card and puts it on the
30				Table so that she looks on it like in line 22
31				She separates the cards from the other
32				Cards which are used in exercises they have
33				*Before*.but…one more…a long one. heh?
34				Looks at the pile of blocks on the table
35			Father	No, no it looks like that. *takes cards away*

As a reply, her father approves her critique and shows the reason of his "discrepancy" as "the chosen card" <05–09>. He says first, "Yes, I think the picture is false." Then he claims, "Just look. This is a short block or a short piece of wood…" <05–09>. These claims could be interpreted in three different ways:

- He might think that the figure on the card is less stable and would easily collapse, whereas the construction they build seems to be quite firm; especially the cross consisting of K4, K5, and K6 is statically better integrated into the entire building.

7 The Reflection of Spatial Thinking on the Interactional Niche in the Family 97

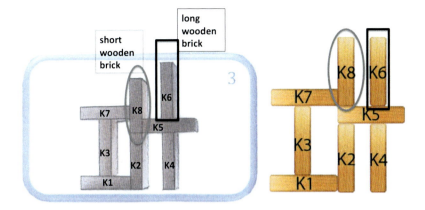

Fig. 7.6 Comparison between the figure on the chosen card and the built structure

- He sees the difference between the card and the built figure. But he does not care about the difference and jut between blocks (Ya–Yb) (see Fig. 7.7). Maybe, this difference is less important to him as compared with his daughter's opinion.
- He perceives two different blocks (K8, K6) on the card and probably comments as if he needs longer or shorter blocks, with which the figure can be properly built up as seen on the card. He just says that the card is false in spite of interpreting the fact that all the given blocks are of the same height.

He goes on explaining the mistake on the card, that one building block, most probably K8, is scratched shorter than others on the card. It could be that he does not see the "discrepancy" in his construction.

With regard to his argument, Ayse looks up to the pile of wooden bricks, probably checking whether the all-wooden bricks are of the same length and size < 10–12 >. Her father, meanwhile, repeats his statement as follows: Although there are no short wooden bricks, there is a short wooden brick on the chosen card. Hence, the card is false < 13–14 >. Then, he insists that he built the figure correctly and asks for Ayse's approval < 14–17 >. She does not argue any further and does not make any other comment. So, her father behaves as she has not rejected his argument < 18–21 >. This interaction process can be interpreted in the following way:

- Without remarking the effect of K5 (Ya–Yb), the discussion is automatically terminated that there is a need for a short wooden brick to build the figure properly as seen on the card. Because there is no short wooden brick, the card is falsely scratched and the built figure is correct. Thus, the discussion leads to unambiguous consensus (see Fig. 7.7).

There is a working consensus between the father and his daughter about this first solution. The given information by the father is not clear enough that their argument is held in suspense and therefore, comes up with an unambiguous consensus.

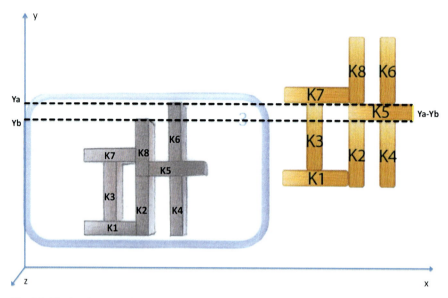

Fig. 7.7 The jut due to K5 in coordinate axis: Ya–Yb

Then, Ayse selects a new card from the deck. Hereby, Mr. Kil's turn in third round ends up and Ayse's turn begins (see Fig. 7.8).

She laughs at her father, after she looks at the card <22–24>.

Her reaction could be interpreted as that she asks her father's help to "construct" the figure, because it is difficult to build it by herself. But despite her appeal for help, the father tells her that he thinks that the figure on the card is not difficult <25–28>. With this reaction, he might encourage her to build the figure by herself.

She takes an upright position to build the card. After she checks the card, she says, "one more...a long one" <29–34>. Most probably, she mentions two blocks by using the adjectives "one more" and "a long one" in the following way:

- In her father's turn, which was just before her turn, she saw "one long" wooden brick (see Fig. 7.9) and then, on her card she sees two long wooden bricks (see Fig. 7.10). This evokes the idea that she needs one more wooden brick, because according to her father's card there was already "a long one."

Here it is seen as high attentiveness of Ayse, that she can realize the jut of Kx (X2–X1) and the jut of Ky (Y1–Y2) (see Fig. 7.11).

Actually, she repeats her arguments, what she already mentions during her father's turn and might defend it by the way. Obviously, her father cannot give a persuasive explanation why the lengths of wooden bricks are seen different in the image on his card. This might have the impact that Ayse cannot release her argument that she needs two long wooden bricks to build the figure on her card.

7 The Reflection of Spatial Thinking on the Interactional Niche in the Family

Fig. 7.8 A card chosen by Ayse in third round

Fig. 7.9 The long wooden brick on Mr. Kil's card (K6)

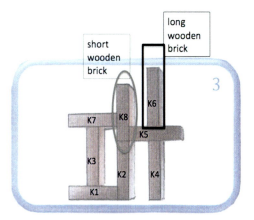

Fig. 7.10 Long wooden bricks on Ayse's card (Kx and Ky)

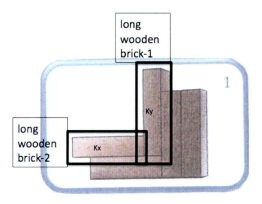

Despite all her claims, her father answers that the figure on the card looks as if two different lengths of blocks are needed to build the figure correctly, but in fact, they are not needed <35>. Furthermore, he gives her no further explanations. Hereby, two similar problems are exactly expressed as two different contrary positions. In his turn, he rationalizes that the card is false, while in Ayse's turn, he rationalizes

Fig. 7.11 Juts of Kx and Ky in coordinate axes: X2–X1 and Y1–Y2

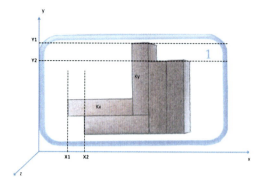

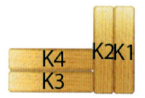

Fig. 7.12 Ayse builds the figure

that the card gives an impression as if two different lengths of blocks are needed, but actually, they are not needed. In both of his and Ayse's turn, he ascribes his "incorrectness" to the chosen cards and thereby begets a "discrepancy" between his arguments. In his turn, the difficulty level of the chosen card was three and now in Ayse's turn, a card with the lowest level of difficulty is chosen. After a while, Mr. Kil tells her that the card is easy to build and she should just get started. Through this encouragement, Ayse starts to build the figure slowly by checking with her father after each action. So far, she builds the figure as seen in Fig. 7.12.

During Ayse's check by looking at her father, he gives a clue and tells that one long wooden brick is missing. Then she takes one wooden brick (K5) from the pile and puts it vertically in between K2 and K4 on K3 as seen in Fig. 7.13.

Her father approves her action and says that she has built the figure right. Hereby, Ayse conducts her turn and gains one point as given on the card (see Fig. 7.14).

Although Ayse abstains from building this card, Mr. Kil encourages her to build it and at the end of the third round, she properly builds the figure as seen on the card (see Fig. 7.14) and conducts her turn.

As a summary, in this scene, although there is a discrepancy between Mr. Kil's arguments, there emerges a developmental niche for Ayse in the following way.

In her father's turn, she realizes the missing jut (Ya–Yb) in the built figure and the discrepancy between building and picture. Her father establishes this fact that the chosen card is falsely constructed. Furthermore, he means that different lengths of blocks are needed to build the figure on card properly. But the assigned blocks are all of the same length. Thus, he means the card is falsely constructed.

In Ayse's turn, she realizes juts ((X2–X1) and (Y1–Y2)) on the chosen card again. Through the negotiation with her father, she understands that the card is

7 The Reflection of Spatial Thinking on the Interactional Niche in the Family 101

Fig. 7.13 The built figure in Ayse's turn

Fig. 7.14 The chosen card and the built figure in Ayse's turn

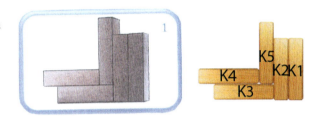

constructed correctly. According to the father, two different lengths of blocks are needed to build the figure correctly but in fact, they are not needed. The card can be built up without any long blocks.

While in her father's turn, she sees that the figure can be built up properly only with the different lengths of blocks, in her turn, she experiences that the figure can be built up properly without any blocks of different lengths. In both cases, she explores sizes, shapes, and proportion of blocks, which reinforces her cognitive growth (Bullock 1992, p. 16). Additionally, she represents the relationship between picture and built objects. Moreover, despite her argument, she builds the structure from pictured model correctly (National Research Council, Committee on Early Childhood 2009, p. 187), by the emotional agency of the father. Thus, both the turns together provide the opportunity to reinforce Ayse's spatial abilities. Furthermore, they construct new definitions in the situation, which reflect the mode of functioning of MLSS.

According to Clements and Sarama, 5-year-old children can metrically represent spatial information in a polar coordinate task, using the same two dimensions as adults, radius and angle (2007, p. 498). If this argument would be disregarded, it could be assumed that Ayse's spatial thinking is not developed enough to realize two- and three-dimensional coordinate axes. In any case, a developmental niche for Ayse due to the awareness of the relationship between the building and the picture occurs there. In her father's turn, she sees the discrepancy between the building and the picture. Thus, in her turn, she acts already on the base of a sensitization for jutted blocks (K_x and K_y). Although she tries to abstain from building the card, her father encourages her to carry on building. This encouragement is also another sensitization for Ayse that she can do something despite her assumed difficulties. She focuses on the problem and solves it. Although there is no long wooden brick, she builds the figure with juts ((X_2–X_1) and (Y_1–Y_2)) correctly. By the agency of her father, both her emotional and cognitive growth is fortified (Bullock 1992, p. 16).

This whole analysis can be structured according to the three components of an interactional developmental niche in familial context.

- **Component "Content"**

Block building provides a view of children's initial abilities to compose three-dimensional objects. Theoretically, by building blocks, five goals are pursued:

- Spatial structuring
- Operating shapes and figures
- Exploring sizes, shapes, and proportions
- Static balance between wooden bricks
- Coping with the different difficulty levels on the cards

As Clements and Sarama (2007, p. 494) point out spatial relations require attention, Ayse sensitizes and realizes the spatial relations between two- and three-dimensional objects.

According to National Research Council Committee on Early Childhood, children at the age of five can understand and replicate the perspectives of different viewers. These competencies reflect an initial development at the third level of thinking, which is about relating parts and wholes level. (2009, p. 191). Concerning this report, it can be said that Ayse can relate parts and the whole with two- and three-dimensional structures. So, the spatial structuring and operating with shapes occur during the play as an allocational aspect.

During the negotiations of the play between Ayse and her father, a "discrepancy" emerges between the father's arguments. However, they are not rejected and held in suspense (ambiguity). Thereby, an *unambiguous consensus* comes out of the interaction, in which concurrences are actually not explicit and clear enough. For father and daughter, it seems to be an unambiguous consensus, although from the perspective of the observer, it would seem to be rather an *ambiguous consensus.*

- **Component "cooperation"**

Parental scaffolding of spatial communication develops children's physical, social, emotional, and cognitive growths (Bullock 1992, p. 16; see also Clements and Sarama 2007). The chosen play situation is constant and directed by the father. By his reaction for type, a leeway of participation emerges, that limits her space of activities.

But, in her turn, he assigns an opened up leeway of participation for Ayse, that she should believe in herself and overcome the difficulties. Thus, in this play situation, different leeways of participation have been realized.

- **Component "pedagogy and education"**

The chosen play situation is constructed along a uniform didactical design pattern and refers to the spatial structuring in geometry. From pictured models, each player has to build up three-dimensional structures. Clements and Sarama call spatial structuring as a mental operation of constructing an organization or form for an object or

7   The Reflection of Spatial Thinking on the Interactional Niche in the Family   103

Table 7.5 NMT-Family Kil

NMT-Family	Component: content	Component: cooperation	Component: pedagogy and education
Aspect of allocation	Geometry, operating with shapes and figures, spatial structuring, exploring sizes, shapes and proportions, static balance between wooden bricks	Familial situation (father plays with daughter)	Development of spatial skills and transformational abilities in spatial thinking
Aspect of situation	Discrepancy between the solutions, unambiguous consensus	Different leeways of participation	The father's "discrepancy" and arguments assist Ayse to recognize feasibility of the building juts without long wooden bricks. His encouragement provides Ayse the success of spatial abilities, social and emotional growth

set of objects in space (2007, p. 498). In the chosen scene, the opportunity to sensitize two- and three-dimensional bodies (objects) has been embraced.

Her father's "discrepancy" and arguments help Ayse to recognize the feasibility of the building juts without long wooden bricks. With respect to folk theory, his encouragement provides Ayse the success of enhancing her spatial abilities. She abstains from building this card but her father encourages her to build it. Therefore, she overcomes the difficulty and builds the figure properly as seen on the chosen card. Thereby, Ayse experiments her skills, because her success can help build her confidence and self-esteem. Thus, it can be said that Mr. Kil's encouragement provides not only Ayse's cognitive and physical growth but also emotional and social growth.

These insights can be assembled in the NMT-Family table (Table 7.5).

Afterword/Conclusion

> The play under the control of the player gives to the child his first and most crucial opportunity to have the courage to think, to talk, and perhaps even to be himself. (Bruner 1983, p. 69)

The play situation "Building 01" gives an opportunity to negotiate interactively about two- and three-dimensional spaces, which enables one to reinforce the children's spatial abilities (see Miller 1986, p. 176; Acar Bayraktar and Krummheuer 2011, p. 168).

For the learning opportunities, it is not obviously commendable that the interactions lead to a consensus among the participants. In the chosen scene, there are "antagonisms" among the father's explanations. Although the structure that he builds in his turn is not proper as it is seen on the chosen card, he says that short blocks are needed to build the figure properly; according to him, the card is falsely scratched and he built the structure correctly. In Ayse's turn, he rationalizes his argument by telling that the card gives an impression as if two different lengths of blocks are needed to build correctly, but actually they are not needed. In both of his and Ayse's turn, he ascribes the "discrepancy" of his arguments to the "incorrectness" of the chosen cards. Consequently, there are "antagonisms" among the father's explanations. In this sense, despite Mr. Kil's oversights or his insufficient information, a developmental niche for Ayse on her spatial skills emerges there. Her spatial thinking is contrasted with her and her father's discrepant reasoning, which might enable her to see the potential of the building up with the blocks of the same length.

Contrary to Ayse's arguments, her father always offers another reasoning. Herewith, she experiences different kinds of building possibilities and learns to associate two- and three-dimensional coordinate axes. On the other hand, the language-based encouragement of her father provides the development of her spatial thinking as well as her personal/social skills as mentioned before. In the chosen example, eventually with the emotional motivation given by her father, Ayse builds the figure correctly. Although "antagonisms" occur toward the inputs given by her father, Ayse interprets distinctively the given instructions through his encouragement. This is an over-careful learning progress, in which the interactional developmental niche emerges for Ayse.

Five-year-old children can normally understand the substitution of shapes, replicate the perspective of a different viewer, and build complex structures (National Research Council, Committee on Early Childhood 2009, p. 187). Hereby, it could be explicated that, children in the age range of 7 are able to build two- and three-dimensional structures according to coordinates, or build up the figure by substituting different wooden bricks.

My first insight to reveal this tendency is the parent's assignment, regardless of whether they have good spatial skills or enough geometrical knowledge. In this sense, it is really important if parents give an emotional motivation to their children, although they do or do not have enough spatial knowledge. As it seen in the example, sometimes instead of spatial abilities of parents, emotional motivation of parents suffices to reinforce the spatial development of children.

On the other hand, in a long-term analysis of the development of spatial skills in familial context, based on the notion of NMT-Family, it could be declared that this development occurs slightly independent from parent's geometrical knowledge (Acar Bayraktar and Krummheuer 2011, p. 169; see also Acar 2011b). In some analysis of FaSt, it is seen that during play situations, children can potentially explore something through the negotiations, although parents do not have enough spatial abilities (Acar Bayraktar and Krummheuer 2011; Acar 2011a, b). "Mishaps" and "Aporias" reinforce the emergence of children's developmental niche during interactions in the play situations (Acar Bayraktar and Krummheuer 2011, p. 170). In another long-term analysis of FaSt, it is also seen that the construction of parents during the negotiation is independent of the educational level of parents. Not only they demonstrate and dissolve the differences of interpretations, but also they interpret the different solutions (see also Acar Bayraktar and Krummheuer 2011). During the interaction processes, participants create a communicative atmosphere and in there they can explicitly manifest their agreement and disagreement about the construction of the built figures. Hence, it seems to be that the interactional phenomenon has an essential impact by supporting the children's developmental niche in the spatial abilities (Krummheuer 2012, p. 332).

Proximately, long-term analyses of FaSt are close to introduce that the spatial development of children can be supported by either spatial abilities or non-abilities of parents, and by either negative or positive emotional motivations given by parents. It is really rare in play situations that parents serve both spatial non-abilities and emotional motivations to their children during interactions.

In this sense, it will be augmented with examples in the next 2 years. It will be exciting to find out how NMT-Family functions work on children's spatial development in the familial context.

Rules of Transcription

Column 1	Serially numbered lines
Column 2	Speech timing
Column 3	Abbreviations of the names of the interacting people
Column 4	Verbal (regular font) and nonverbal (italic font) actions
underlined	Speech is in Turkish
bold	Accentuated word
<	Indicates where people are talking at the same time
>	The next block of simultaneous speech is indicated by a change in arrow direction
#	There is no break, the second speaker follows immediately after the first
	The sides of the blocks are defined as X-side, Y-side, Z-side in the transcript

References

Acar, E. (2011a). ERSTMAL-FAST (Early steps in mathematics learning—Family study), Proceedings of CERME 7, WG13, 1861–1872. ISBN 978-83-7338-683-9, Rzeszów, Poland.

Acar, E. (2011b). Mathematiklernen in einer familialen Spielsituation, Proceedings of 45. Conference GDM (45. Tagung für Didaktik der Mathematik), Vol. 1, pp. 43–46, Freiburg, Germany.

Acar Bayraktar, E., & Krummheuer, G. (2011). Die Thematisierung von Lagebeziehungen und Perspektiven in zwei familialen Spielsituationen. Erste Einsichten in die Struktur "interaktionaler Nischen mathematischer Denkentwicklung" im familialen Kontext. In B. Brandt, R. Vogel, & G. Krummheuer (Eds.), *Die Projekte erStMaL und MaKreKi. Mathematikdidaktische Forschung am "Center for Individual Development and Adaptive Education" (IDeA)* (Vol. 1 pp. 11–24). Münster: Waxmann.

Acar Bayraktar, E., & Hümmer, A.-M., et al. (2011). Forschungsmethodischer Rahmen der Projekte erStMaL und MaKreKi. In B. Brandt, R. Vogel, & G. Krummheuer (Eds.), *Die Projekte erStMaL und MaKreKi. Mathematikdidaktische Forschung am "Center for Individual Development and Adaptive Education" (IDeA)* (Vol. 1 pp. 11–24). Münster: Waxmann.

Bishop, A. J. (1980). Spatial abilities and mathematics education—A review. *Educational Studies in Mathematics, 11*(3), 257–269. Netherlands: Springer. http://dx.doi.org/10.1007/BF00697739 doi:10.1007/BF00697739.

Brandt, B. (2004). *Kinder als Lernende. Partizipationsspielräume und -profile im Klassenzimmer.* Frankfurt a. M. usw.: Peter Lang.

Bruner, J. (1983). Play, thought, and language. *Peabody Journal of Education, 60*(3), 60–69, The Legacy of Nicholas Hobbs: Research on Education and Human Development in the Public Interest: Part 1.

Bruner, J. (1986). *Actual minds, possible worlds.* Cambridge: Harvard University Press.

Bullock, J. R. (1992). Learning through block play. *Early Childhood Education Journal, 19*(3), 16–18. Netherlands: Springer. doi:10.1007/BF01617077.

Cartwright, S. (1988). Play can be the building blocks of learning. *Young Children, 43,* 44–47.

Clements, D. H., & Sarama, J. (2007). Early childhood mathematics learning. In F. K. Lester, Jr. (Ed.), *Second handbook of research on mathemtics teaching and learning* (pp. 461–555). New York: Information Age Publishing.

Cross, C. T., Woods T. A., & Schweingruber H. (Eds.). Committee on early childhood mathematics; National research council. (2009). *Mathematics learning in early childhood: Paths toward excellence and equity.* Washington, DC: National Academies Press. http://www.nap.edu/catalog.php?record_id=12519.

Harkness, S., & Super, C. M. (1994). The developmental niche: A theoretical framework for analyzing the household production of health. *Social Science and Medicine, 38*(2), 217–226.

Harkness, S., Super, C. M., Moscardino, U., Rha, J.-H., Blom, M. J. M., Huitrón, B., Johnston, C., Sutherland, M., Hyun, O.-K., Axia, G., & Palacios, J. (2007). Cultural models and developmental agendas: Implications for arousal and self-regulation in early infancy. *Journal of Developmental Processes, 1*(2), 5–39.

Harris, L. J. (1981). Sex-related variations in spatial skill. In L S. Uben, A. H. Patterson, & N. Newcombe (Eds.), *Special representation and behavior across the life span* (pp. 83–125). New York: Academic Press.

Hewitt, K. (2001). Blocks as a tool for learning: Historical and contemporary perspectives. *The Journal of the National Association of Young Children, 56,* 6–13.

Johnson, H. M. (1966). *The art of block building.* New York: Bank Street College of Education Publications.

Kersh, J. E., Casey, B., & Young, J. M. (2008). Research on spatial skills and block building in girls and boys. In Saracho, O. N. & Spodek, B. (Eds.). *Contemporary perspectives on mathematics in early chilhood education* (pp. 233–251). Information Age Publishing, Inc.

Krummheuer, G. (2011a). *Die "Interaktionale Nische mathematischer Denkentwicklung" (NMD). Beiträge zum Mathematikunterricht 2011* (pp. 495–498). Münster: WTM.

Krummheuer, G. (2011b). Die empirisch begründete Herleitung des Begriffs der "Interaktionalen Nische mathematischer Denkentwicklung" (NMD). In B. Brandt, R. Vogel, & G. Krummheuer (Eds.), *Die Projekte erStMaL und MaKreKi. Mathematikdidaktische Forschung am "Center for Individual Development and Adaptive Education"* (IDeA) (Vol. 1 pp. 25–90). Münster: Waxmann.

Krummheuer, G. (2011c). Representation of the notion "learning-as-participation" in everyday situations of mathematics classes. *ZDM Mathematics Education, 43,* 81–90. doi:10.1007/s11858-010-0294-1.

Krummheuer, G. (2012). The "non-canonical" solution and the "Improvisation" as conditions for early years mathematics learning processes: The concept of the "interactional Niche in the Development of mathematical Thinking" (NMT). *Journal für Mathematik-Didaktik, 33*(2), 317–338.

Lawson, A., & Lawson, J. (2008). Make 'N' Break. Ravensburg: Ravensburger Spielverlag. http://www.ravensburger.de/shop/grosse-marken/make-n-break/make-n-break-23263/index.html. Accessed 5 Oct 2012.

McGee, M. G. (1979). Human spatial abilities: Psychometric studies and environmental, genetic, hormonal, and neurological influences. *Psychological Bulletin, 86,* 889–918.

Miller, M. (1986). *Kollektive Lernprozesse*. Frankfurt a. M.: Suhrkamp.
Mills, J. (2002). Early numeracy. children's self-initiated recordings (3–5 years),unpublished PG Diploma Assignment, Swift Masters Programme, College of St Mark and St John. Plymouth.
Nes, F. T. van. (2009). Young children's spatial structuring ability and emerging number sense. Dissertation, Freudenthal Institute for Science and Mathematics Education, Utrecht University, Utrecht.
Science Education Resource Center. (2008). Carlton College, Northfield, MN http://serc.carleton.edu/research_on_learning/synthesis/spatial.html. Accessed 22 Oct 2012.
Super, C. M., & Harkness S. (1986). The developmental niche: a conceptualization at the interface of child and culture. *International Journal of Behavioral Development, 9*, 545–570.
Super, C. M., & Harkness, S. (1994). Temperament and the developmental niche. In W. B. Carey & S. C. McDevitt (Eds.), *Prevention and early intervention: Individual differences as risk factors for the mental health of children: A festschrift for Stella Chess and Alexander Thomas* (pp. 115–125). Philadelphia, US: Brunner/Mazel.
Super, C. M., & Harkness, S. (2002). Culture Structures the Environment for Development. *Human Development, 45*, 270–274.
Tiedemann, K. (2010). Support in mathematischen Eltern-Kind-Diskursen: funktionale Betrachtung einer Interaktionsroutine. In B. Brandt, M. Fetzer, & M. Schütte (Eds.), *Auf den Spuren Interpretativer Unterrichtsforschung in der Mathematikdidaktik. Götz Krummheuer zum 60. Geburtstag* (pp. 149–175). Münster: Waxmann.
Vogel, R. (2012). Mathematical situations of play and explorations as an empirical research instrument. Proceedings of POEM, 27.–29. Feb. 2012, Frankfurt. http://cermat.org/poem2012/main/proceedings.html. Accessed 5 Oct 2012.
Vogel, R., & Wippermann, S. (2005). Transferstrategien im Projekt VIB – Didaktische Design Patterns zur Dokumentation der Projektergebnisse. In Ch. Bescherer (Ed.), *Einfluss der neuen Medien auf die Fachdidaktiken. Erfahrungen aus dem Projekt VIB* (pp. 39–60). Baltmannsweiler: Schneider.
Wachs, H. (2003). Visual-spatial thinking. In ICDL (Ed.), Clinical practice guidelines. Part 6: Innovative models that work with especially challenging functional developmental capacities. Chap. 20. pp. 517–536. http://www.icdl.com/dirFloortime/overview/FAQs/ClinicalPractice-Guidelines.shtml.Accessed 29 Mar 2012.
Wombles, K. (2010). Developmental Theories: Bronfenbrenner and Super & Harkness. http://www.science20.com/science_autism_spectrum_disorders/blog/developmental_theories_bronfenbrenner_and_super_harkness. Accessed 5 Oct 2012.

Part III
Children's Constructions

Chapter 8
The Roots of Mathematising in Young Children's Play

Bert van Oers

> It has not yet been sufficiently realized that present mathematical and scientific education is a hotbed of authoritarianism and is the worst enemy of independent and critical thought.
> I. Lakatos, **Proofs and refutations. The logic of mathematical discovery** (1976).

Introduction

The quality of mathematical thinking of coming generations has been a serious concern of many educators for a number of years. Since the middle of the twentieth century, mathematicians have emphasised (as in the rest of this chapter) the essential meaning of problem solving, reasoning, and the construction of communicative tools for the understanding of the nature of mathematical thought (see, for example Polya 1945; Freudenthal 1973; Lakatos 1976; Sfard 2008, to name just a few). In mathematics education in schools all over the world, however, there is nevertheless a strong emphasis on the mastery of number operations and on the formation of skills in faultless arithmetic.

Indeed, important changes have taken place in mathematics classrooms in the past few decades. Context-based problem solving has become a part of regular classroom practice for developing mathematical proficiency in pupils, but still the dominant focus is set on instruction for skill acquisition, avoiding serious efforts in promoting pupils' problem solving (Kolovou 2011) and deep conceptual understanding (Bruin-Muurling 2010). Considering the worldwide interest in accountability of schools, effective education, and skill mastery, there is no reason as yet to stop being concerned. Skill acquisition is still the main criterion in the testing of children's mathematical development, while deep conceptual understanding, argumentation, and creative problem solving more and more seem to be reserved for the gifted pupils.

B. van Oers (✉)
Department of Research and Theory in Education,
VU University Amsterdam, Amsterdam, The Netherlands
bert.van.oers@vu.nl

Many studies, however, show that the concepts and approaches for promoting children's abilities of dealing in mathematically consistent ways with reality are not exhausted (see, for example Sfard 2008). Particularly, studies on young children's thinking and learning give reasons to assume that *"mathematising"* (organising experience for mathematical purposes) may be rooted in early childhood education (see, for example Pound 1999). Picking up on young children's abilities and assisting them in their ways of dealing with number (Munn 1998), emergent notions of quantity (Carruthers and Worthington 2006), drawing (van Oers 1994, 2004), and collective reasoning (Krummheuer 2011) may provide good starting points for gradual improvements of children's mathematising abilities, beyond mere technically operating with numbers and number symbols.

In the present chapter, I will unfold an approach to early mathematics education based on a theory of playful activities, drawing from the perspective of cultural-historical activity theory (CHAT/Vygotskij). From this perspective, I will demonstrate how direct instruction of mathematical operations can be reconciled with productive mathematical problem solving. Starting out from the CHAT, I will argue that *productive mathematising* is to be conceived as an essentially playful activity that has its roots in young children's playful participation in cultural practices. Within this context, instruction of useful mathematical operations can be taught and practised, as long as it can be meaningfully embedded in children's activity. The approach that will be presented here is becoming increasingly popular in Dutch primary schools that have adopted the Vygotskian concept of *Developmental Education* (see van Oers 2012a).

What is Productive Mathematising?

The notion of "mathematising" has been introduced by Freudenthal (1973) for referring to mathematics as a human activity of organising a field (be it conceptual or material) into a structure that is accessible for mathematical refinement (Freudenthal 1973, p. 133). Organising a field of mathematical objects like circles, ellipses, parabola, etc. into the category of conic sections or quadratic functions is an example of mathematising, as well as the recognition of the growth of a plant in early childhood classrooms as a measurement problem. Mathematising is the activity of producing structured objects that allow further elaborations in mathematical terms through problem solving and (collective) reasoning/argumentation. It is the type of dialogic, inquisitive, and productive thinking that was once described as mathematical discovery by Lakatos (1976). Hence, as an expression, "productive mathematising" is basically pleonastic, but it is a useful way to contrast this mathematical activity with the *re*-productive activity of applying mathematical rules or operations for the solution of instructional tasks. By itself, there is nothing wrong, though, with reproduction in the context of mathematising (as, for example, anyone proficient in mathematics does, when immediately applying specific knowledge, e.g. the square root of, say, 81, in solving a specific problem or doing a specific task). However, reducing mathematics education to the mastery of these types of reproductions is like cutting the heart out of mathematics as mathematising.

In terms of the CHAT, mathematising can be further specified as a complex of specific human tool-mediated actions driven by a motive to know the world and organised by a series of (emergent) goals. Developing mathematical thinking from this perspective can be conceived of as a process of producing new or improved tools for the understanding and analysis of quantitative or spatial dimensions of reality that are acceptable for the mathematical community (van Oers 2001). It would not make much sense here to further characterise mathematising as an ongoing activity by specifying its goals and tools, as these latter elements always depend on the specific type of problem a person tries to solve. Rather, on a more general level, it is possible to characterise *the format* of the activity of mathematising. A format of activity refers to the general characteristics of the way an activity is carried out (see van Oers 2012b)[1]. First of all a cultural activity can be more or less strictly *rule-driven*, by object-bound rules, technical rules, and/or social rules. The number and nature of the rules determine the nature of the activity to a great extent. As a matter of fact, the rules featuring in mathematising strongly depend on the type of problem a person tries to solve, and on the mathematical rules and socio-mathematical norms available in the person. However, what basically makes an activity a form of mathematising are at least the rules of intersubjectivity and consistency, and the rules that a newly constructed object should be acceptable for the mathematical community and be accessible for further mathematical elaboration. A mathematical activity that requires strict obedience to rules has a format which is different from a mathematical activity that is based on ill-defined rules that have to be interpreted and specified by the pupils. Both are basically different mathematical activities.

A second characteristic of the format of cultural activities is the *level of involvement* of the agent. Activity settings differ as to the conditions they provide to get actors involved. At one extreme pole, an agent can be forced to carry out a procedure of specific actions (without personal involvement, as often happens in the reproduction or recitation script of schooling); at the other extreme, the activity is carried out from an intrinsic motivation and the authentic will to achieve a specific goal. Low levels of involvement require high levels of extrinsic motivation to make and keep the process going; high levels of involvement encourage pupils to get engaged in (collaborative) problem solving, to be creative, and to endure. Characteristically, mathematising is an activity that is driven by personal engagement with a personally acknowledged query that requires creativity and endurance.

Finally, the format of human activity can be characterised by more or less *degrees of freedom* allowed to the actor in the choice of goals, tools, or rules. Activities without any degrees of freedom are performances like in drill, strictly

---

[1] The notion of "format of an activity" is familiar with Lompscher's concept of "Verlaufsqualitäten der Tätigkeit" (Lompscher 1975) in its intention to further qualify human activity as a process that can have different modi of accomplishment. Lompscher's Verlaufsqualitäten and my parameters of the format both try to characterise human activities beyond the morphological model of actions, goals and operations. Lompscher, however, used other parameters in his explanation than the ones used here. It is beyond the scope of this chapter to compare different models here.

sanctioned practices, or training. On the other hand, activities that require creativity and imagination by definition require at least some degrees of freedom for the actor. As a problem-solving activity, mathematising can only be successful and productive if the problem solver is allowed to act tentatively, to make mistakes, try and re-try, and feels allowed to make wild guesses.

Hence, analysing productive mathematising as a human activity leads to the picture of this activity as a goal-oriented, tool-mediated human activity that is characterised by specific mathematical *rules* and socio-mathematical norms, by *high involvement* of the agent, and by at least *some degrees of freedom* in the choice of rules, tools, and goals. This characterisation of the general nature of cultural activities does not preclude or contradict a further microgenetic analysis of these activities in (Leont'evian) terms of motives, actions, objects, goals, tools, and operations. As said before, such analysis would only make sense when it refers to a specific task (e.g. using a number line for estimating the position of the value 17/23). I will not pursue this type of microgenetic analyses here (how illustrative and interesting they may be), as it is not necessary to complete the general argument concerning the roots of mathematising in young children's play.

Mathematics Learning and Play

On the basis of my previous research in early years' classrooms, I will argue that the activity format of mathematising as described above, can be interpreted as a specimen of a more general kind of human activity called "play". In my studies of play as a kind of human behaviour and as a context for learning, I have argued that play is basically an activity that is carried out in a specific format, i.e. as an activity that implies obeying *self-acknowledged rules*, requires *high engagement*, and allows at least *some degrees of freedom* (see for van Oers 2010a, 2012b). As a result, I defend the proposition that mathematising is basically a form of playful mathematics, embedded in young children's play. In playful activities, children can encounter situations that require special attention for the quantitative of spatial dimensions of their activity (e.g. when trading money in a supermarket play); in order to deal effectively with these aspects, children need to learn new actions that can be considered mathematical from a cultural point of view. Hence, mathematics arises in the context of play through the mathematisation of children's actions and utterances by more knowledgeable others (adults or peers). Mathematics emerges in children's development, not as an elaboration of implicit mathematics in play, but as an attribution from outside of mathematical meanings to children's actions or utterances (see van Oers 2012c).

The format of the traditional mathematics classroom activity is typically characterised by strict rules, little or no involvement of the pupils, and no degrees of freedom in the choice of tasks, objects, and rules or operations. Traditionally, the mathematical task prescribes which operations have to be carried out. This classroom gives little or no room for playing and mathematising as a productive activity.

8 The Roots of Mathematising in Young Children's Play

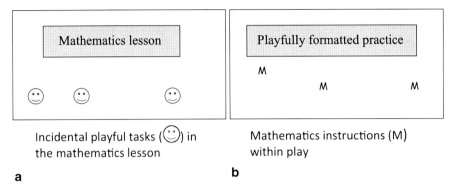

Fig. 8.1 Different relationships between mathematics and play. **a** Mathematics classrooms that follow the direct-instruction script. **b** Mathematics classrooms that follow a problem-solving script

Socioconstructivist and activity theory approaches to human learning emphasise the importance of the active involvement of pupils in their (mathematical) learning activities (see, for example Darling-Hammond 2008; Schoenfeld 2008; Leontev 1978). In the wake of the socioconstructivist approach to mathematics, several attempts have been made to make mathematics classrooms more engaging for children, particularly by introducing moments of play in the classroom. Popular versions of such attempts can be seen in the introduction of realistic contexts (like supermarkets) into the classroom, which require pupils to deal with trading money (addition, subtraction) But many other examples can be found: children sharing a pizza at parties (to evoke thinking about division), or all kinds of board games (to engage young children in counting), etc. No doubt, this has made the mathematics classes in primary schools more playful, but play in these cases was still just *embedded* in task-based classroom work within an otherwise strict classroom script that focused mainly on the mastery of operations; play functioned here merely as a stepping stone for further practising the mathematical operations outside the play contexts that initiated them.

Starting out from a cultural-historical activity point of view, a new approach is developed towards a play-based curriculum that does not just allow children to play sometimes, in addition to their task-related work, but which fundamentally implements the play format in all pupils' activities. This is essentially different from the previously described approach of integrating play and mathematics (see Fig. 8.1). In a genuine play-based curriculum, mathematising is provoked and encouraged in children as a way of dealing (collaboratively) with the quantitative and spatial dimensions of reality which surface during their participation in engaging and meaningful cultural practices. Looking for solutions to emerging problems regarding quantitative or spatial dimensions in such practices may lead to the enhancement of a child's possibilities of participating in this practice. Guided problem solving through mathematising as well as improving (mathematical) skills through practising are functional and meaningful for children's participation in this practice. In a play-based curriculum problem, solving and practising are not taken out of a playful activity, but remain functional parts of the playfully formatted practice, improving the participants' abilities to take part in this practice.

Figure 8.1 summarises the major difference between (a) mathematics classrooms that follow the direct-instruction script (with incidentally embedded games), evoking at best reproductive mathematising, and (b) mathematics classrooms that follow a problem-solving script, requiring productive mathematising, interrupted by dispersed moments of meaningful, and functional instructions.

Mathematics Learning Within Play?

When participating playfully in an engaging practice (like a restaurant, a construction site, gardener's practice, a post office, etc.), young children encounter numerous problems that demand a mathematical approach (e.g. paying three stamps in the post office, finding and comparing the dimensions of a building, figuring out the number of chocolates needed for a party, etc). In the play-based curriculum, children work out solutions to these problems collaboratively under the guidance of the teacher or a more knowledgeable peer. There are probably different dimensions of activity involved in the emergence of mathematising from playful activities. In this chapter, I will elaborate on two dimensions that we have found in our research in the past decade.

Learning to Communicate on Mathematical Aspects of Reality

An obvious feature of children's behaviour when facing a (mathematical) problem in their play is their wish to suggest solutions, to try out different solutions, to discuss different solutions, in short: to *communicate* about possible solutions. The first thing that children need in cases, where they face a problem regarding quantitative or spatial aspects of their play, is a proper language to communicate about number and spatial positions or relations. Learning to communicate mathematically is an important process to stimulate in children's play, as it is the main prerequisite for the development of mathematising in play and as play. Many researchers have already discussed the importance of language for the development of mathematical thinking (e.g. Pimm 1987, 1995), and have been able to demonstrate empirically that relationships do exist between mathematical thinking and narrative competence (see Burton 2003; Krummheuer 2011; van Houten 2011). With regard to mathematical reasoning and the construction of a mathematical space for focused communication, a number of researchers have pointed at the relevance of gestures (gesticulations) as means for communication in a mathematical discourse or teaching process (see among others Bjuland et al. 2008; Yoon et al. 2011). Similar suggestions have recently been forwarded with regard to picture books as a communicative medium

Fig. 8.2 Construction plan of a castle

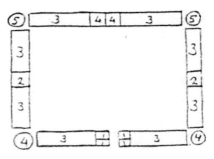

for the stimulation of young children's mathematical thinking (see, for example Elia et al. 2010). Inventing or looking for symbolic means to support communication about number, number operations, or space is common practice in many play activities of young children.

In one of my classroom visits, I witnessed two 5-year-old boys' cooperative activity of building a castle on the basis of a schematic construction plan provided by the teacher. The plan showed the floor plan of the castle and depicted the direction of the blocks and the numbers of blocks on top of each other for the reconstruction of the towers and walls of the castle (see Fig. 8.2). The teacher helped the two boys with interpreting the construction plan correctly. After that, the boys started building the castle.

However, during the re-construction of the castle the boys ran out of blocks and had to change the teacher's design for building a castle that looked similar to the teacher's design. After finalising their castle, the teacher discussed it with the boys and showed her approval. She suggested that the boys should make a drawing of their castle that could help other children build such a nice castle too. The boys liked the idea. Actually, the teacher's request put them in the position to communicate the relevant information about their castle to other children they did not even know by then.

The boys adopted the basic idea from the teacher's construction plan, but they also had to invent new communicative tools, for their castle was not exactly like the teacher's. From the perspective of learning to communicate about number, this was an interesting process to observe. One of the boys started of with drawing the blocks in the walls and towers in the way the teacher had done. However, he had trouble writing the number symbols. Immediately, he changed to an analogical representation indicating the number of blocks by corresponding quantities of small circles. So 4 was represented by four small circles. In this process, the boy was using a one-to-one correspondence rule, and he used it consistently. At a certain moment, he drew five circles in a wall with four blocks, but immediately crossed out one. These phenomena demonstrate that the boy was tentatively finding out appropriate ways to communicate about the numbers in the castle to inform future constructors.

This example of mathematical communication grew meaningfully out of the children's play. Many similar examples of children's efforts to create proper means of communication about number can be found in the work of Carruthers and Worthington (2006).

In our research programme for the study of children's symbolisations and construction of schematic representations, we have studied processes like the one described above in many early years' classrooms. We have evidence to conclude that children can produce much more sophisticated schematic representations of quantities and their relationships as long as it is meaningful for the children (and functional in the context of their play). The evolution of these representations with communicative purposes is a demonstration of how mathematising emerges in play on the basis of learning how to communicate about number (relationships). Mathematising in play develops as a playful activity, and may flourish with appropriate help towards playful mathematics. In an experimental study of Poland (see Poland et al. 2009), the researcher could demonstrate that engaging young (6-year-olds) children in this type of playful mathematising (particularly focusing on schematising) facilitates their transition into more formal mathematics in the early grades of primary school (ages 6 and 7).

Embedded Mathematics Teaching in the Context of Play

Involving children in mathematical communications in the context of their play activities is a powerful way of getting them involved in meaningful productive mathematising. Not every child, however, will immediately pick up the structure of mathematical operations through schematising alone, as some of them will not always immediately understand the action-regulating function of schematic representations or algorithms. In those cases, more stepwise instruction, explanation, and practice will be needed. Moreover, developing proficiency in mathematical communication also requires the development of automatised operations that can be used in problem solving regarding the mathematical objects or relations. Both for the support of slow learning pupils and for the development of automatised operations in all children, instruction may be unavoidable. The mastery of mathematical operations (i.e. reproductive mathematising) most of the time contributes to young children's ability to participate in role play with other children (e.g. when tending the counter of a shop).

From one of our classroom observation studies, we can report examples of both cases. In an early years' classroom (populated with pupils aged 5–7 years) a shoe shop was set up in which children were playing all kinds of shoe-shop related roles. One 6-year-old girl (who was known by the teacher to be a slow learner in maths) was highly involved in the play, and as a customer in the shop, she has bought two pairs of boots which cost € 60 each. The girl was insecure if she had enough money and said to the boy at the counter: "Wait a moment; I have to figure out, if I can pay it." She withdrew from the scene and set herself on a small bench at some distance from the counter, but next to the teacher. The teacher, however, decided to leave her alone for a moment to give her a chance to sort it out for herself. The girl opened

8 The Roots of Mathematising in Young Children's Play 119

her purse, put all her money next to her on the bank, and started counting, but she mostly had notes (notes of 50 and 10), so there was little to count: she had to calculate by adding and subtracting how much she had to pay, and find out if she had enough money. It took her a while of fiddling around with the money, but apparently she could not solve the problem on her own. The teacher had observed her from a distance and finally decided to offer help. The teacher sat next to the girl and started a conversation about her money, but she did not immediately ask what the precise problem was. The teacher started with *structuring* the girl's money in batches of 100, and showing that two times 50 is 100. With the girl, she explored different amounts of money, structured with the help of her notes of 50 and 10. Only after some examples of how to structure amounts of money with notes of 50 and 10, she addressed the girl's real problem. With some help and instruction, the girl figures out that 60 can be composed as 50 + 10, and two times 60 can be structured as two times 50 (the girl knew this was hundred) and two notes of ten. The teacher's instruction was useful for the girl, as it strengthened her ability to participate in the play.

In the same classroom, there was a small group of children interested in the shop's stock of shoes. The teacher translated this interest in a role of a book-keeper who must keep an eye on the stock of shoes available in the shop. The teacher suggests that a book-keeper must be good at calculation and should keep on practising calculations. She said: "If you want to be the book-keepers, we can play the book-keeper game. It will help you to play shop play activities in a more easy way." The children agreed and sat at the table to play the game. The teacher explained the game: there were two decks of cards (reds and greens, each with a number on it; numbers were faced down): reds are for buying shoes, greens are for selling shoes. The children understood that when you sell shoes you will earn money, but also may run out of shoes at some moment. All children are allowed 10 turns, and at each turn a child must take one card from the deck (a red or a green one). The game starts with each child drawing a red card from the deck. One child after the other may draw a card of his/her choice. They had to calculate his/her stock with the information on this card and write it down on a piece of paper as a + or a − sum. For example, one paper looked like this

5 (start quantity) − 3 − 1 + 1 + 2 + 4 − 3 etc.

The teacher was sitting at the table too, checked if it went well, that no mistakes were made; she offered help where needed for each child's successful participation in this game. For an outsider, the game may look like a traditional instruction lesson for automatisation of the elementary operations of addition and subtraction. Actually, the children performed their actions as part of their role of a book-keeper of the shoe shop. They experienced their actions as meaningful, but basically were practising addition and abstraction as well. Although from the outside the scene may look like a playful moment in an otherwise traditional mathematics classroom, it was actually experienced by the children as an instruction and practice moment in a play activity (see again Fig. 8.1).

The bottom line of the two examples above is that a playful activity including mathematical actions does not prohibit embedded instructions as long as these contribute to the child's interest in participating in the play as good as possible. Mathematising requires productive construction, but also instruction and practice. Each dimension can be made a meaningful part of coherent children's play.

Fostering a Mathematising Culture in the Classroom

Is this enough for an optimal stimulation of pupils' proficiency in mathematics? Pupils cannot keep on playing in shoe shops, restaurants, hospitals, racetracks, etc. forever. Embedding mathematising as a playful part of children's role play turns out to be a rich context for meaningful learning. However, appropriate conditions must be created for play to evolve into new activities that can be playfully formatted. By the same token, conditions must also be created to give children the chance to learn to play the role of mathematical expert who can do mathematics as an independent practice, just for the sake of mathematics, just for his/her interest in mathematics! Finally, we want pupils to master mathematical operations and understandings as meaningful "stand alone operations", originally rooted in everyday practices but finally winded up as independent accomplishments in the context of an emancipated mathematical discipline.

We are still in the middle of reflecting this issue and consider that it is even unsure that all pupils can or need to reach that high a level of disciplinary expertise for proficient participation in society and for their future jobs. Theorising on this topic from CHAT, we may conceive of this process of "emancipation" of mathematics from everyday practice as another specimen of the division of labour, an intrinsic potential of all cultural practices. In fact, the history of mathematics exemplifies this process, if we think about the origins of mathematics in practical geometry and music.

At this moment, we hypothesise that the formation of a new and autonomous positive mathematical attitude in pupils is an important condition for fostering the transition of functional mathematics in play into a playfully functioning mathematical discipline. Much is still to be found out on this issue, and elaborating deeply on this issue would go way beyond the scope of this chapter. In our approach to primary schools ("Developmental Education"), we contribute to this development by creating from the youngest grades (4-year-olds) a mathematical culture in classrooms, i.e. a culture in which communicating about number, spatial relations, mathematical games, and mathematical objects is accepted and positively valued (see for example van Oers, 2010b). Teachers try to contribute to such a culture by frequently asking questions like, "Are you sure?" (see van Oers 1996, 2001).

In Conclusion

Our argument winds up in claiming that mathematical thinking should start out as *mathematics in play* (rather than direct instruction on elementary mathematical operations), and be fostered into *mathematics as play*. Inventing and improving ways to communicate about number and spatial aspects of reality turns out to be a core issue in this process.

However, from our observations in classrooms involved in play, it is also clear that both creative construction and sensitive instruction are necessary elements for a developmentally productive organisation of play and the development of mathematical thinking. From an activity theory point of view, the differences between the two can be explained on the basis of varying degrees of freedom that are allowed to the actors ("players"). Both construction and instruction can be seen as attempts by an actor to execute his or her actions on the basis of personally and socially acceptable rules. In the instruction case, an actor receives the rules from teacher, textbook, or memory and carries out the actions strictly according to the prescriptions that follow from this rule. The girl from the example above re-constructs the conventional rule (with the help of the teacher) of how to sum 50 and 50 etc. She had no choice as to how to define the rules, but—importantly—she acknowledged the relevance of the rules for her ability to participate in the shoe shop play. The example of the book-keepers was similar: the players applied the rules as given, with minimal degrees of freedom (note that the degrees of freedom in this activity were at an another level of activity: which colour to choose?). In the construction case, the actor is more free to make decisions about how to regulate his or her actions, and to invent appropriate symbolic equipment for communication. But, here too, there is no absolute freedom due to the communicative function of the constructed symbols, or how to use the rules (see the example of the analogically represented one-to-one correspondence between quantity of blocks and the number of circles). The freedom here regards the choice of the rules or symbols to use for communication. It is important to emphasise at this point that in both cases, the actions were based on personally acknowledged (and meaningful) rules.

In the context of play and the embedded processes of creative construction and rule-driven instruction, it is important to take care that any embedded action (be it instruction or construction) is meaningful for the children and related to the psychological functions they are supposed to fulfil within the play activity (communication or mastery). The nature of the actions embedded in play can vary with respect to their degrees of freedom allowed, as long as the activity as a whole remains a playful activity, i.e. is based on personally acknowledged rules, is engaging, and preserves some degrees of freedom for the player.

Only to the extent that we succeed in doing this in our schools and families, and only to the extent that teachers and parents can receptively and purposefully participate in children's play without impairing this activity as play, we may hope that we really have harvested the best from the richness of play, and have made a start with fostering autonomous critical mathematical thinking in our children.

References

Bjuland, R., Cestari, M. L., & Borgersen. H. E. (2008). The interplay between gesture and discourse as mediating devices in collaborative mathematical reasoning: A multimodal approach. *Mathematical thinking and learning, 10,* 271–292.

Bruin-Muurling, G. (2010). *The development of proficiency in the fraction domain. Affordances and constraints in the curriculum* (dissertation). Utrecht: Freudenthal Institute for science and mathematics education

Burton, L. (2003). Children's mathematical narratives as learning stories. In B. van Oers (Ed.), *Narratives of childhood. Theoretical and practical explorations for the innovation of early childhood education* (pp. 51–67). Amsterdam: VU press.

Carruthers, E., & Worthington, M. (2006). *Children's mathematics: Making marks, making meaning.* (2nd ed) London: Paul Chapman Publishing

Darling- Hammond, L. (2008). *Powerful learning.* San Francisco: Jossey-Bass.

Elia, E., van den Heuvel-Panhuizen, M., & Georgiou, A. (2010). The role of pictures in picture books on children's cognitive engagement with mathematics. *European Early Childhood Education Research Journal, 18*(3), 275–297.

Freudenthal, H. (1973). *Mathematics as an educational task.* Dordrecht: Reidel.

van Houten, W. (2011). *Narratieve competentie en rekenvaardigheid in groep 3 en 4 van de basisschool [Narrative competence and arithmetical ability]. Masterthese Onderwijspedagogiek, Faculteit Psychologie en Pedagogiek.* Amsterdam: Vrije Universiteit.

Kolovou, A. (2011). *Mathematical problem solving in primary school* (dissertation). Utrecht: Freudenthal Institute for Science and Mathematics Education

Krummheuer, G. (1997). *Narrativität und Lernen. Mikrosoziologische Studien zur sozialen Konstitution schulischen Lernens.* Weinheim: Beltz.

Krummheuer, G. (2011). Die empirisch begründete Herleitung des Begriffs der "Interaktionalen Nische mathematischer Denkentwicklung" (NMD). In B. Brandt, R. Vogel, & G. Krummheuer (Eds.), *Die Projekte erStMaL und MaKreKi. Mathematikdidaktische Forschung am "Center for Individual Development and Adaptive Education" (IDeA).* Empirische Studien zur Didaktik der Mathematik, Band 10. (pp. 25–90). Münster: Waxman Verlag

Lakatos, I. (1976). *Proofs and refutations. The logic of mathematical discovery.* Cambridge: Cambridge University Press.

Leontev, A. N. 1978). *Activity, consciousness, personality.* Englewood Cliffs: Prentice Hall

Lompscher, J. (1975). Wesen und Stuktur allgemeiner geistiger Fähigkeiten [Essence and structure of general cognitive abilities]. In J. Lompscher (Ed.), *Theoretische und experimentelle Untersuchungen zur Entwicklung geistiger Fähigkeiten* (pp. 17–73). Berlin: Volk und Wissen.

Munn, P. (1998). Symbolic function in pre-schoolers. In C. Donlan (Ed.), *The development of mathematical skills* (pp. 47–71). Hove: Psychology Press.

van Oers, B. (1994). Semiotic activity of young children in play: The construction and use of schematic representations. *European Early Childhood Education Research Journal, 2*(1), 19–34.

van Oers, B. (1996). Are you sure? The promotion of mathematical thinking in the play activities of young children. *European Early Childhood Education Research Journal, 4*(1), 71–89.

van Oers, B. (2001). Educational forms of initiation in mathematical culture. *Educational Studies in Mathematics, 46,* 59–85.

van Oers, B. (2004). Mathematisches Denken bei Vorschulkindern. In W. E. Fthenakis & P. Oberhuemer (Hrsg.), *Frühpädagogik international. Bildungsqualität im Blickpunkt* (pp. 313–330). Wiesbaden: VS Verlag für Sozialwissenschaften.

van Oers, B. (2010a). Children's enculturation through play. In L. Brooker & S. Edwards (Eds.), *Engaging play* (pp. 195–209). Maidenhead: McGraw Hill.

van Oers, B. (2010b). The emergence of mathematical thinking in the context of play. *Educational Studies in Mathematics,* 74(1), 23–37. doi:10.1007/s10649-009-9225-x.

van Oers, B. (2012a). *Developmental education for young children: Concept, practice, and implementation.* Dordrecht: Springer.

van Oers, B. (2012b). Culture in play. In J. Valsiner (ed.), *The Oxford handbook of culture and psychology* (pp. 936–956). New York: Oxford University Press.

van Oers, B. (2012c). How to promote young children's mathematical thinking? *Mediterranean Journal for Research in Mathematics Education, 11*(1–2), 1–15.

Pimm, D. (1987). *Speaking mathematically. Communication in mathematics classrooms.* London: Routledge.

Pimm, D. (1995). *Symbols and meanings in school mathematics*. London: Routledge.
Polya, G. (1945/1973). *How to solve it. A new aspect of mathematical method*. Princeton: Princeton University Press.
Pound, L. (1999). *Supporting mathematical development in the early years*. Buckingham: Open University Press.
Poland, M., van Oers, B., & Terwel, J. (2009). Schematising activities in early childhood education. *Educational Research and Evaluation, 15*(3), 305–321.
Schoenfeld, A. (2008). Mathematics for understanding. In L. Darling-Hammond (Ed.), *Powerful learning* (pp. 113–150). San Francisco: Jossey-Bass.
Sfard, A. (2008). *Thinking as communicating. Human development, the growth of discourse, and mathematizing*. Cambridge: Cambridge University Press.
Yoon, C., Thomas, M. O. J., & Dreyfus, T. (2011). Grounded blends and mathematical gesture spaces: developing mathematical understandings via gestures. *Educational Studies in mathematics, 78*, 371–393

Chapter 9
Non-canonical Solutions in Children–Adult Interactions—A Case Study of the Emergence of Mathematical Creativity

Melanie Münz

Introduction

Attempts to define mathematical creativity seem to lead to more than 100 contemporary definitions of creativity (Mann 2006). Present empiric works measure mathematical creativity rather in the mathematical product and neglect the creative process. Especially mathematical creativity in early years is rarely examined. Thus, the first central research question is, how does mathematical creativity express itself at the age of preschool and how is it observable?

Following Urban (2003) a theory of creativity has to consider the "4P-E Structure" (Urban 2003, p. 85) of creative thinking and acting, which embodies the interactive structure of the factors: problem, person, process, product, and environment. The existence, the range, and recognizability of possible problems to be solved creatively are determined by meta-environmental factors like evolutionary and social–historical developments; macro-environment like economic, material, cultural, and political conditions; and micro-environmental factors such as socioeconomic conditions of the family (Urban 2003, p. 85–86).

From a socio-constructivist point of view, which, theoretically, this chapter is based on, the research focus is rather on the cultural and micro-environmental aspects of Urban's global approach. The main assumption of socio-constructivism states, also with respect to mathematical creativity, that the individual ability of mathematical creativity develops in the course of the various interactions with other members of the culture. Sriraman (2004) emphasizes:

> the types of questions asked are determined to a large extent by the culture in which the mathematician lives and works. Simply put, it is impossible for an individual to acquire knowledge of the external world without social interaction. (p. 21)

This chapter focuses on the mathematically creative solving process while children are working on mathematical tasks in situations of play and exploration. The

---

M. Münz (✉)
Goethe-Univesity Frankfurt a.M. and IDeA-Center Frankfurt a. M., Germany
e-mail: muenz@math.uni-frankfurt.de

situations analyzed in this chapter are designed in a way that besides the children, an adult person is also present. So the analysis highlights the processes of negotiation of meaning between the children and between the children and the accompanying person during the interactive process while coping with mathematical tasks (Bauersfeld 1995; Brandt and Krummheuer 2001; Cobb and Bauersfeld 1995; Jungwirth and Krummheuer 2006; Krummheuer 2007).

With respect to the research interest on children with social/emotional difficulties, the MaKreKi (mathematical creativity of children) project refers the psychoanalytically based attachment theory, in which these difficulties are interpreted in the light of the emerging relationship between mother and child. This theory of attachment suggests that children come into world biologically preprogrammed to form attachments with others (Bowlby 1969). The neonate develops special relationships with his/her parents. In the first years of life, the child develops an "inner working model" through child–parents interactions (Bowlby 1969). This "inner working model" contains the early individual bonding experiences as well as the expectations, which a child has toward human relationships, derived from these experiences. They conduce to interpret the behavior of the caregiver and to predict his or her behavior in certain situations. Therefore, the attachment between mother and child has a great impact on the social–emotional and cognitive development of the child. After the first year of life, this "inner working model" becomes more and more stable and turns into a so-called "attachment pattern" (Bowlby 1969, p. 364).

For the investigation of mathematically creative processes, it is relevant that children are confronted with mathematical tasks and contents from different domains of mathematics as they appear in their everyday life. In the MaKreKi project these contents are presented in the form of mathematical situations of play and exploration, which are conformly designed along a "didactical design pattern" (see Sect. "Short Description of the Sample and Empirical Approach"), which were developed for this study (Vogel 2013). Among others, this design pattern contains information for an accompanying adult person. It provides him/her with some knowledge about the mathematical content and a minimal set of instructions like questions or allegations. The competent adult also gets some hints of possible reactions and expressions of the children by these design patterns so that he/she is somehow prepared for possible solutions emerging in the context of the mathematical situation of play and exploration.

In the concrete situation, on the situational level, the initiation of these mathematical situations of play and exploration provokes processes of negotiation of meaning, which necessarily have not to be in accord with the described mathematical domain or the activities that are described in the design pattern. This principal discrepancy might be especially relevant in the context with mathematically creative children.

Summarizing, following Urban's general approach of the "4P-E structure," this chapter examines macro-environmental factors like cultural conditions, e.g., the intended mathematical domains/contents and the expected mathematical tasks and solutions presented in the mathematical situations of play and exploration as well as the interactive negotiations of these themes (micro-social factors). Besides this, the chapter also involves psychodynamic aspects of early childhood development (micro-environmental factors), like the attachment patterns of the children (see Sect. "Attachment Theory"). The attachment system is now widely studied in the life cycle, but little is said about creativity as a concomitant of this system (Brink 2000). Therefore, the second research question is which correlation exists between the attachment pattern of children and their mathematical creativity?

Theoretical Perspectives

The following section introduces theoretical perspectives of mathematical creativity in early childhood (Sect. "Mathematical Creativity") and offers psychoanalytical considerations about attachment theory and the connection to creativity (Sect. "Attachment Theory").

Mathematical Creativity

Mathematicians and researchers in mathematics education as well as psychologists have examined mathematical creativity under their various scientific viewpoints (Hadarmard 1954; Sriraman 2004). A clarification of concepts of creativity is difficult and additionally complicated by its relationship to the concepts of intelligence, giftedness, and problem solving.

With respect to the relative lack of current research, the following analyses deal with the following four aspects of mathematical creativity (Sriraman 2004):

1. Choice: Poincaré (1948) described as a fundamental aspect of mathematical creativity the ability to choose from the huge number of possible combinations of mathematical propositions a minimal collection that leads to the proof. Ervynck (1991) understands by mathematical creativity the ability to generate mathematical objects or the generation of a base idea for coping with a mathematical problem within a mathematical context. From this definition, he derives the following characteristic features of mathematical creativity:

    a. Relational: With the production of mathematical objects the individual has to discover conceptual links between two or several mathematical concepts, so that an interaction of ideas enters. The different mathematical ideas can be understood as single "blocks" (Ervynck 1991, p. 49), which can be combined differently.
    b. Selective: With competition of different mathematical blocks, the individual has to make a choice on one (at best for the most useful idea). This character is similar to Poincare's metaphor of choice.

c. Compressed/briefly presentably: The individual has to find the suitable words and symbols for the presentation of the mathematical ideas (Ervynck 1991, p. 50).

   With regard to the age group of interest under this *choice* aspect of mathematical creativity, the production of (unusual) relations between mathematical examination and experiences and the playful contact with mathematical methods is understood.

2. Non-algorithmic decision making: According to Ervynck (1991), mathematical creativity articulates itself not when routine and/or standard procedures are applied but when a unique and new way of solving a problem emerges. Ervynck refers to the creative achievement of mathematicians, who created something new for mathematics. With regard to the age group of 3–6-year-old children, there is still to clarify, what could be meant by a "unique and new" way of solving a problem? At first, one is able to shift therefore the accentuation and speak of the "divergence from the canonical" (Bruner 1990, p. 19).
3. Adaptiveness: Sternberg and Lubart (2000) characterize creativity as the ability to present an unexpected and original result that is also adaptive. Adaptiveness describes children's ability to accomplish unusual descriptions of a happening and to adapt the original core of the meaning of this description to a new situation.
4. De-emphasizing details: Liljedahl (2008) describes in his study, in which he investigates the ideas and thoughts to mathematical creativity from famous mathematicians, that the details of the problem do not play any role during the incubation[1] phase of creativity. They rather work with strategies, which allows coping with the basics of the mathematical problem. Many of the interviewed mathematicians mention how difficult it seems to them to learn mathematics by attending to the details, and how much easier it is if the details are de-emphasized.

This section has elucidated how children can express their mathematically creative ideas while coping with mathematical tasks. Regarding Urban's "4P-E Structure," it focuses mainly on the components problem, product, and process. The following section highlights the other components such as person and environment, which are also relevant for the examination of mathematical creativity in early childhood.

Attachment Theory

Attachment theory originates from Bowlby (1951) and postulates the central role of attachment behavior for individual development. Bowlby perceives the attachment system as the central source of motivation. In his approach, the antagonism between attachment and exploration has a highly relevant explanatory power. Both systems

---

[1] Hadamard has used introspection to describe mathematical thought processes. He developed the four-stage model of mathematical creative thinking: Preparation, incubation, illumination and verification (see Hadamard 1954).

cannot be simultaneously activated. If a child feels secure, he/she can activate their exploration system and explore their surroundings. If he/she perceives danger, the attachment system is activated. The child interrupts his/her exploratory behavior and seeks safety from their parent according to the developed attachment pattern between them.

Bowlby's model has subsequently been further developed. Ainsworth has created a test for the study of attachment behavior. In the so-called strange situation (Ainsworth et al. 1978), a standardized observation situation, the quality of the attachment of the child to its mother (or to their father) can be measured. Four of such attachment patterns can be described (Ainsworth et al. 1978):

a. Insecure-avoidant: The "insecure-avoidant" child (A) experiences that his/her mother feels best when he/she shows no intense reactions and behaves toward her in a controlled, distanced manner with a minimum of affect.
b. Secure: The securely attached child (B) has, thanks to his/her sensitive mother, a chance to build up a secure relationship with her in which the whole spectrum of human feelings in the sense of communication with another can be perceived, experienced, and expressed.
c. Insecure-ambivalent: The ambivalently attached child (C) has spent his/her first year with a mother, who sometimes reacts appropriately, and is at other times rejecting and overprotective, i.e., on the whole, inconsistent and for this reason she reacts in a way that is unpredictable for the child.
d. Insecure-disorganized attachment: The disorganized/disoriented attached child (D) could not build up a stable inner working model, as his/her mother (or father) suffered under the consequences of an acute trauma (for example, the dramatic loss of an important person). They were psychically so absorbed by this loss that they could hardly take up a coherent relationship with their infant.

Relating this approach to the topic of mathematical creativity of young children, the results of empirical attachment research point to the fact that the shaping of domain-specific (mathematical) creativity can be localized not only in the potentially stimulating mathematical contents in the child's milieu but also in the type of attachment of the child to his/her parents.

Grossmann describes the link between the attachment pattern of the child and the "successful cooperation" (in German: "gelingende Gemeinsamkeit") in a child–parent play situation in more detail (Grossmann 1984). The "successful cooperation" of this play situation correlates with the delicacy feeling of the mother, and a more delicacy feeling leads very often to a secure attachment pattern of the child (Grossmann 1984). Mothers of securely attached children seem to be more reserved and gentle and they show more efforts in handing over the lead to their children in play situations. In contrast, mothers of insecurely attached children are often strict and controlling and they have more instructional ratio in play situations than mothers of securely attached children (Grossmann 1984). Significant differences between children with a secure attachment pattern and children with an insecure attachment pattern in play situations are also described in the study of Grossmann. Thus, securely attached children are more often initiators of the common play and they seem to be rather more extroverted than insecurely attached children, who wait for instructions and seem to be rather introverted (Grossmann 1984).

Due to the above-mentioned antagonism between attachment and exploration behavior, it is plausible to assume that, above all, securely attached children will develop great joy in (mathematical) exploration and creativity. Nevertheless, the MaKreKi project investigates if some children, who have other attachment patterns, are also able to develop mathematical creativity. It might be possible to assume that especially children with an insecure-avoidant attachment pattern or with an insecure-disorganized attachment pattern evolve great interests in mathematics, because of the regularities and structures in the mathematical field. In this case, these children might be able to compensate their adverse attachment pattern by developing interests in mathematics and mathematical creativity.

In the research design of the MaKreKi project, children deal with mathematical problems and tasks guided by a competent adult. This adult can be seen as a representative of the parents, because it might be reasonable to assume that children show similar behavior in this situation like they would with their parents, because of their stability on the "inner working model" of their attachment pattern.

Methodology

Short Description of the Sample and Empirical Approach

The sample of MaKreKi is based on the original samples of two projects that are in the larger study IDeA (Center for Individual Development and Adaptive Education of Children at Risk[2]). One project is a study of the evaluation of two prevention programs with high-risk children regarding their attachment pattern in day-care centers (EVA[3]). It examines approximately 290 children. The second project is a study of early steps in mathematics learning (erStMaL[4]). This project includes approximately 150 children. Thus, the original sample contains 440 children.

Due to the lack of tests for identifying mathematical creativity in preschool children, the MaKreKi team developed a questionnaire in which the nursery teachers of these two original samples were asked whether they knew children in their groups who showed divergent and unusually sophisticated strategies while coping with mathematical tasks. These questions concern the interest of the children in mathematical domains as well as the children's supposed unusual dealing with mathematical situations. In the combined sample of 440 children, 40 children were identified who seemed to creatively cope with mathematical problems.

---

[2] http://www.idea-frankfurt.eu/. Accessed 6 Aug 2013.

[3] http://www.idea-frankfurt.eu/en/research/research-domains/diagnostics-and-prevention/eva. Accessed 6 Aug 2013.

[4] http://www.idea-frankfurt.eu/en/research/research-domains/resources-and-limitations-of-successful-learning/erstmal. Accessed 6 Aug 2013.

In order to analyze the children's forms of mathematical creativity, open mathematical situations of play and exploration (Vogel 2013), which were designed for the erStMaL (early Steps in Mathematical Learning) project, were applied in semi-annual surveys in pair and group settings. These situations refer to the mathematical domains of number and operation, geometry, measurement, pattern and structures, and data analysis (Sarama and Clements 2008). To ensure that the implementation is independent from specific individuals and proceeded comparably, the mathematical situations of play and exploration are described in "design patterns of mathematical situations," which follows the type of documentation of didactical design pattern (Vogel and Wippermann 2004, p. 35). The mathematical situations of play and exploration as research instruments design opportunities, in which children can demonstrate their mathematical potentials in the interaction. The composition, sparingly given verbal and gestural impulses as well as actions with the material by a guiding adult, introduce the children to the situation and the mathematical context in which they can pose or solve a first mathematical problem or work on a first mathematical assignment (Vogel 2013).

Every child participates in two different situations of play and exploration per survey date and all mathematical situations of play and exploring are videotaped. These recordings are the basis for the intended interactional analyses.

Process of Reconstructive Analysis

Regarding the theoretical considerations and the attempt to identify mathematically creative moments in mathematical interactions of preschool children, in the following an analysis of interaction is conducted, which is based on an interactional theory of learning (Cobb and Bauersfeld 1995; Brandt and Krummheuer 2001). Therefore, a method was developed, which focuses on the reconstruction of meaning and the structure of interactions (Krummheuer 2012a). The negotiation of meaning takes place in interactions between the involved individuals. These processes will be analyzed by an ethnomethodologically based analysis, in which is stated that the partners co-constitute the rationality of their action in the interaction in an everyday situation, while the partners try constantly to indicate the rationality of their actions and to produce a relevant consensus together. This is necessary for the origin of the own conviction as well as for the production of conviction with the other participating persons. This aspect of interaction is described with the term "accounting practice" (see Garfinkel 1967, p. 1). From an ethnomethodological point of view, these accounting practices are an integral component of the action itself. The interactive devices, which are necessary for securing and creating a common basis of rationality, are laid out in the actions of the participants. This claimed coincidence of the *procedures* of the realization of the action with those of the rationalization of the action is commonly referred to as the *ethnomethodological theorem of reflexivity* (Mehan and Wood 1975; Krummheuer 1995; Lehmann 1988).

To analyze these *accounting practices* of children in mathematical situations, Toulmin's analysis of argumentation (1969) has proved to be successful

Fig. 9.1 Toulmin scheme

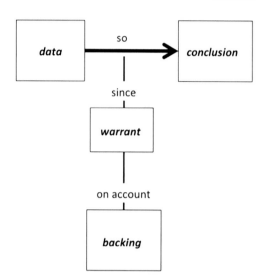

(Krummheuer 2007). Four central categories of an argumentation are "data," "conclusion," "warrant," and "backing." Toulmin (1969) returns these functional argumentation categories graphically in a layout (see Fig. 9.1).

The general idea of an argumentation consists of tracing the conclusion to be proven back to undoubted statements (data). This relationship is expressed in the first line of the layout. Therefore, this line can altogether be referred to as the inference of the argument. Sometimes, such an inference requires a legitimation. Statements, which contribute to this, represent the "warrant." Of another quality are those statements, which refer to the permissibility of the warrant. Toulmin (1969, p. 97) calls them "backings." They represent undoubtable basic convictions (e.g., the axioms in "mathematical" argumentations). Warrants and backings represent the depth of the argumentation. Arguments can be chained together in the way that an accepted conclusion can serve as data for a subsequent new argument.

Diagnosis of Attachment Style

For the diagnosis of the attachment pattern, the MaKreKi project applies the Manchester Child Attachment Story Task, the so-called MCAST (Green et al. 2000). This is a storytelling test that has good reliability and validity. A standardized dollhouse is used. The play of the child with the test coordinator is videotaped and later evaluated according to the test manual. In order to rule out the possibility that the behavior during the storytelling, for example, is not determined by an exceptionally weak, cognitive ability, the MCAST is used in combination with an intelligence test. The Hannover Wechsler Intelligence Test in preschool age (HAWIWA-III), the German adaptation of the Wechsler Preschool and Primary Scale of Intelligence (WPPSI, 2002) is implemented in the project. The international test has been shown to be reliable and valid (Petermann 2009). The test with its comparable subtests allows observing specific intellectual abilities over a longer time, for example, during phases of therapeutic or pedagogic support.

To get a deeper knowledge about the relationship between the child and his/her parents, the parents are interviewed. In the half standardized interviews conducted by experienced psychoanalysts and therapists, questions concerning the family constellation, the early development in kindergarten and school, and the mathematical creativity are focused.

First Insights

Investigating the assumption mentioned above, that not only children with a secure attachment pattern could cope creatively with mathematical tasks, the following section presents two children of the MaKreKi project with different attachment pattern while they are participating in the mathematical situation of play and exploration called "Ladybug": René (type A) and Nina (type B). Both children are examined and paired with one of their close friends and one adult person who acts as a nursery teacher.

The "Ladybug Situation"

In this situation, the children can differentiate between similar objects, which differ according to their size and color. The objects are pictures of ladybugs, which differ in size (small and large), in color (red, green, and yellow), and in spots in two ways (circle, triangle, and square and also by the amount of spots as well). The big ladybug-cards have additionally two different sizes of spots (large and small) (Fig. 9.2).

The design pattern suggests, for this situation of play and exploration, the following mathematical activities to the children through material, designated instructions, and impulses:

- Counting and determination of quantity.
- Arrangement and comparing of sets, e.g., in respect of the number of elements on the back of the ladybugs.
- Mathematical structures, i.e., the elements of sets, are associated with each other relationally and they form structures through which they differ from the other objects. The bugs are linked by social relations like in family or in kindergarten group in the eyes of the children.

The "Ladybug situation" consists of two parts. In the first part, the children are dealing with little ladybug-cards. Typical instructions of the accompanying person are: "Look what I have brought here." "Put together all ladybugs which belong to each other." "Can you find further groups or families of ladybugs?" "Why do these ladybugs belong together?"

Fig. 9.2 Little ladybug-cards

In the second part, the children are dealing with big ladybug-cards which have small and large spots on their backs. Usually the accompanying person offers a triplet of big ladybug-cards and asks: "Which one does not belong?" (Wheatley 2008).

Case Study One: René's Solution Process in the "Ladybug Situation"[5]

René is a boy aged 4 years and 9 months, who lives with his parents and his older sister in a small city. His father works full time in a computer firm and his mother remains at home.

Because of René's very sophisticated language ability, the research assistant, who contacted René first, assumed that he was older than four. In the MCAST René was very curious and highly motivated to cooperate; at the same time, however, he demonstrated in his facial mimic and body language a certain tension and restlessness. According to the nine scales of the MCAST, René shows insecure-avoidant attachment behavior (A). In the HAWIWA, René demonstrates average intellectual ability with a value of 95 points. Only in one performance subtest, "symbolic-figure", his capabilities are above average (they correspond to the abilities of a 6-and-a-half-year-old child).

Besides René, two other persons are involved in the "Ladybug situation": Lisa, a girl aged 4 years and 8 months from René's preschool and a member of our research team, who conducted the conversation with the two children as the accompanying adult person (abbreviated with B).

The presented episode refers to the end phase of a collective processing of the task. René, Lisa, and the member of the research team invented a familial system of description: The small ladybugs represent kid-bugs and the big one mom-bugs, dad-bugs, or parents-bugs. During the period before this episode, they also compared the number of cards according to their size and color and found out that all these subgroups are of equal number.

---

[5] The following extract of René's solution process refers to an analysis, which has already been published in German. For more details see Hümmer et al. (2011) and Krummheuer (2011).

9 Non-canonical Solutions in Children–Adult Interactions…

Fig. 9.3 Triplet of big ladybug-cards

After this comparison, the children realigned the cards around the round carpet, which is a kind of defined space for playing and exploring the cards.

In the center of this carpet, the adult person puts a triplet of the cards of the same size several times, but alternately of different size and number of figures on top of the ladybugs and/or of different colors of the ladybugs. Routinely, the adult always opens a new problem with the question, "Which one doesn't belong?"

In the following analysis, the guiding adult has put a triplet of three red ladybug-cards. One has 7 big triangles, one has 19 little triangles, and the last one has 23 little triangles on his back. René has mentioned that the ladybug with 19 little triangles does not belong to the group, while Marie has mentioned that the bug with seven big triangles does not belong to the group (Fig. 9.3).

The conversation continues as follows:

01			
02		B	*looks at René* why do you think that this is
03			the one *pointing to the red bug with 19 little*
04			*triangles* and why does Marie think that this is
05			the one\ *pointing to the large bug with*
06			*7 Big triangles*
07		Marie	this is the one because he has so big peaks\
08			*points to the bug with the big 7 triangles*
09		B	aha\ and you/ *looks towards René*
10		René	mhm\ *shakes his head and points to the bug with*
11			*19 Small triangles*
12	>	B	why do you think this is the one/
13	>	Marie	*puts a little yellow ladybug on the circle*
14		René	because he has too small ones\ *points to the*
15			*little triangles on the bug with 19 little*
16			*triangles*
17		B	because he has too small ones\ too small as what
18		René	too small four *looks at the little ladybugs*
19			here dots like this *points to the little*
20			*triangles of the big bug with 19 small*
21			*triangles, takes a little red ladybug with 2*

22			*small circles* like these\ like the little ones\
23		Marie	ehm René\ *looks at René's card and takes it*
24			*in her hands, together they put it back in the*
25			*circle*
26		B	but we have to come to an agreement\ well\ one
27	<		does not fit
28	<	René	hey these are, *points alternately*
29			*to one of the big red ladybugs with small*
30			*triangles* two do not belong because
31			they are coincident
32		Marie	*has 2 big yellow bugs and 1 little yellow*
33			*bug, which she arranges on the table*
34		B	these are coincident\
35		René	yes
36		B	what do you mean when you say that\
37		René	mhm this has a little bit smaller ones *points*
38			*to the bug with 19 little triangles* than this
39			*points to the bug with 23 triangles* cause
40			these are growing and these are already big
41			*points to the big bug with 7 large triangles*
42		B	aha also however they are bigger\ *points to*
43			*the big bug with 7 large triangles*
44		René	*nods slowly*
45		B	well can you warm to that we are taking Marie's
46			suggestion so we put this one away\ *puts the*
47			*bug with the 7 big triangles away*
48		Marie	*nods*
49		René	*looks at B looks at the ladybugs*
50			mhm (yes)
51		B	yes/ okay\

The interpretation presented here is based on the following constellation:

René comes up with the solution that *both* bugs with many and small triangles do not belong. His justification has two aspects:

- Comparing the figures of the small and the big ladybug-cards, he concludes, that the bugs of the small cards should also only possess small figures on their tops.
- The two cards with the many and small triangles cannot exist in the system of the cards at all.

If one interprets these two warrants of his argumentation in his familial system of description, one could rephrase it in this way:

- Big ladybugs have big figures because they are parents.
- Small ladybugs have small figures because they are children.
- So, big ladybugs with small figures do not exist.

9   Non-canonical Solutions in Children–Adult Interactions...   137

Fig. 9.4 Rene's solution

	big triangles	small triangles
parents	ok	rejected
children	rejected	ok

If one understands the figures of the ladybugs to be people's hands, René's argument is that parents do not have hands the size of kids, this is impossible. They cannot be parents and children "at the same time," as he says.

With respect to the three aspects of mathematical creativity mentioned, one can conclude: René's solution is based on a surprising *choice* of a familial system of description for the comparison of the ladybugs. Hereby, he does create a somehow *non-canonical* combination of size and family members. He restricts this 2 × 2 table as shown in Fig. 9.4.

René creates a *non-canonical* solution in which he combines the mathematical quantity "size" and the social and emotional quantity "family."

Furthermore, on the level of speech, he expresses this unusual *choice* by a linguistic adaption of the size of ladybugs by using a familial metaphor. He says that the big ladybugs would be "already big." The wording of "big" can appear in the size system of description and in a familial system of description. By combining "big" with "already," a process of change comes up: A ladybug can grow to a certain size and reach some features which ladybug kids did not possess. This switch in his formulation is seen here linguistically as an *adaptive* achievement.

The guiding adult seems to have difficulty in comprehending René's approach. Possibly she assumes that he wants to say that the two ladybugs with the many and small triangles are the ones that remain and therefore the third one with the few and big triangles does not belong. Moreover, Marie has chosen this solution. This constellation of misinterpretation evokes the short dialog in which the guiding adult asks René for explanations three times (see lines 2–3, 12, and 36). In this phase she behaves similar to the type of mother of securely attached children, she is more reserved with her own interpretation of the mathematical situation and shows efforts in handing over the lead to René. René accomplishes the warrant and backing of his argumentation mentioned above. With respect to the interactional setting, it is René who takes the part as the competent partner and explains his position to his counterpart. Being able to take this role, René shows a great autonomy in dealing with mathematical problems in social situations. Because of his great autonomy in explaining his perspective on the problem of the three big ladybugs, René can be seen as the initiator (Grossmann 1984) of his *non-canonical* solution, which he expresses and explains to the guiding adult. In this situation, he presents a very deep argumentation as the Toulmin scheme shows in Fig. 9.5 (Krummheuer 2011).

In René's argumentation, one can see that he connects the first part (finding family members, making groups of little ladybugs because of their relationships regarding their spots (amount, shape) or their colors) with the second part (separate

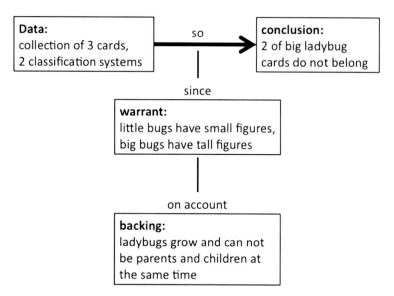

Fig. 9.5 Toulmin scheme of René's argumentation

big ladybugs, which do not belong together) of the mathematical situation. So he transforms two operations into one by disregarding the detail that only one ladybug does not belong to the triplet. He has come up with a strategy that *de-emphasizes details* (Liljedahl 2008).

In the end, the guiding adult forces an agreement and she asks if it is all right for René to take Marie's solution. Here she reacts in a more controlling way; nevertheless, she shows some kind of delicacy of feeling, because she asks René if it works for him to take Marie's solution.

Case Study Two: Nina

Nina is a girl aged 5 years and 5 months who lives with her mother in a major city. Her parents are divorced.

In the MCAST, Nina was highly motivated to cooperate and rather extrovert than introvert in her interactions. According to the nine scales of the MCAST, Nina shows secure attachment behavior (B). In the HAWIWA, Nina demonstrates low average intellectual ability with a value of 88 points in the performance IQ[6].

Besides Nina, there are two other persons involved in the "Ladybug situation": Samira, a girl aged 5 years and 10 months from Nina's preschool, and an accompanying person from the research project. At first, the children and the adult person have dealt with the little ladybugs. They have discovered various families of lady-

---

[6] Because of the difficulties conducting IQtests in early childhood, Nina has only participated in the performance test (and not in the verbal test). So these values have to be interpreted carefully.

9 Non-canonical Solutions in Children–Adult Interactions...

Fig. 9.6 Triplet of big ladybug-cards

bugs where the color and the number of spots determine to which family a ladybug belongs. At the end of this phase, Nina mentioned that all ladybugs of the same family are grown in the same stomach. After that, the little ladybug-cards are moved to the edge of the table. The presented scene begins with the second part of the ladybug situation: The guiding adult has put a triplet of big yellow ladybug-cards on the table and asked: "Which one does not belong?" Both children discuss the number of spots on the ladybugs and discover that they do not have the same amount of spots. Samira suggests putting the ladybug with six squares and the bug with seven circles together (Fig. 9.6).

0001			
0002		B	is six and seven the same/ *looks to Samira*
0003	>	Samira	ehehe *shakes her head*
0004	>	Nina	no. but there are remaining some *reaches for the*
0005			*cards which are underhanded in B's hands*
0006		B	*retains the cards* first we have to say which one
0007			is wrong of these *moves the 3 big ladybugs*
0008	<		*closer to each other* which one does not belong
0009			to the family/
0010	<	Nina	this one is away\ *sliding*
0011			*away the bug with 7 circles and the bug with 6*
0012			*squares* they are wrong\
0013		B	they are wrong/
0014		Samira	*points to the bug with 10 circles*
0015		Nina	*takes the bug with 10 circles* and this is right
0016		B	is this a one member family/
0017		Samira	yes\
0018		B	okay then we try the next ones *reaches for the bug*
0019			*with 10 circles, which Nina holds in her hands*
0020		Nina	and then it has got a baby *takes a little*
0021			*yellow bug with one triangle on his back and puts*
0022			*it next to the big bug with 10 circles*
0023		B	oohh a little ladybug\
0024	>	Nina	mhm

0025	>	Samira	yes\
0026		B	which belongs to a big one/
0027		Nina	yes\
0028		Samira	there *points to a little yellow bug with 3*
0029	<		*triangles on its back* there are many other too
0030	<	Nina	many babies
0031			*takes some little ladybugs but not the red ones*\
0032		B	not the red ones\
0033		Samira	because afterwards the red ones *points to the*
0034			*underhanded cards in B's hands* afterwards the
0035			red ones will come
0036		Nina	no, the red bugs are firebugs *slides the little red*
0037			*bugs away and puts the little yellow bugs to the*
0038			*big bug with 10 circles* and they don't like the
0039			the red ones
0040		B	these are all babies of these ones/ *points to*
0041			*the big bug with 10 circles*
0042	>	Samira	yes
0043	>	Nina	yes and he has one two three four five six seven
0044	<		eight nine ten eleven *points to each of the*
0045			*little yellow bugs*
0046	<	Samira	seven eight…eleven
0047		Nina	eleven babies\ *looks towards B and laughs*

In this scene, Samira suggests to put the big yellow bug with seven circles and the big yellow bug with six squares on their backs together. Nina and the guiding adult do not seem to agree with this solution. Before making a choice Nina tries to reach all cards of big ladybugs, which can be interpreted as the attempt to get an overview of the whole data, what is similar to the creative process of famous mathematicians mentioned in Sect. "Mathematical Creativity". The accompanying person does not permit this attempt and so Nina and Samira have to find a solution just for one triplet of big ladybug-cards. Nina comes up with the solution that two big ladybug-cards are wrong and only one ladybug-card is right. She creates a *non-canonical* solution. Her surprising *choice* can include two aspects of relationships similar to a mathematical function:

1. A relationship between the number of spots on the back of the ladybugs and the age of the ladybugs: The two ladybug-cards, which have been stated as wrong, have only six or seven elements on their backs; the right one has ten. He has a suitable quantity of elements, so he can represent an adult ladybug.
2. A relationship between the number of elements on the back of the ladybugs and the quantity of babies which belong to the bug. Each spot on the back represented one of his babies.

Following the scene, one can see that the second interpretation of Nina's *choice* (functional relationship between spots and babies) will be realized through her activities by counting the small ladybugs and her expression that the big yellow bug with 10 circles has 11 babies. She extends the functional relationship by determining the color as a feature of the functional relationship between the ladybugs: The

9 Non-canonical Solutions in Children–Adult Interactions...

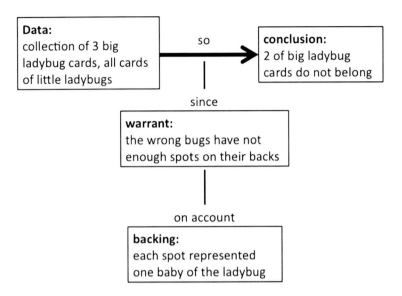

Fig. 9.7 Toulmin scheme of Nina's argumentation

big yellow bug can only have little yellow ladybug kids. Samira takes this hint and expresses an assumption that there will follow some big red ladybugs later.

By reconstructing Nina's argumentation with the Toulmin layout (see Fig. 9.7), it is obvious that she connects the first part of the mathematical situation (finding families/groups of ladybugs) with the second part (which one does not belong?).

Nina transforms two operations into one by disregarding the detail that only one ladybug does not belong to the triplet. For Samira and the guiding adult, Nina's decision of choosing one ladybug becomes clear during the scene. However, it seems that the guiding adult and Samira do not have a problem with Nina's *choice*. However, in line 16 the accompanying adult asks if the yellow bug with ten circles is a one-member family, which Nina first affirms. During this phase, the guiding person is similar to the type of mother of securely attached children (Grossmann 1984); she is more reserved with her own interpretation of the mathematical situation and shows a great interest to understand Nina's solution. She does not insist on the canonical solution to find two big ladybugs, which belong to each other. A one-member family is not possible in an ordinary context. Nina has to specify and clarify her "one-card solution" to the group, which follows in line 20. Nina lives with only a single parent and this constellation corresponds with a normal family life.[7] From a mathematical perspective, Nina's solution is now possible, too. Regarding her autonomous explanation and argumentation, Nina can be interpreted as the initiator of the *non-canonical* solution, which links the big ladybugs with the small ladybugs.

---

[7] In Germany the period of a marriage lasts 14 years on average, so many children like Nina live in a single-parentfamily.

On the level of speech, Nina is able to formulate her *non-canonical* solution with appropriate and *adaptive* expressions, so the identification of the little yellow ladybugs as babies of the big yellow ladybug can be seen as a linguistic achievement to describe the functional relationship between the little and the big ladybugs in an *adaptive* way.

Comparison of the Two Cases

The two cases show *non-canonical* solutions of children while coping with mathematical tasks. Nina as well has René offered a "one-card solution" instead of the expected "two-card solution," because of the connection they have discovered between the two parts of the ladybug situation. This endeavor is similar to the creative process of famous mathematicians (*de-emphasizing details*).

Both children show autonomy in dealing with mathematical tasks. They are initiators (Grossmann 1984) of their *non-canonical* solutions. In case of Nina as a child with a secure attachment pattern, this observation is in accord with Grossmann's results. Following Grossmann, children with an insecure-avoidant attachment pattern like René are often less autonomous in play situations. In the mathematical situations of play and exploration this is not the case for René. He often is the initiator, too. So the behavior of children in play situations may be linked to the context of the situation as well as to their attachment pattern. René is able to take the part of the competent partner because of his mathematical creativity and his great interest in mathematical situations. Another explanation for René's autonomous behavior may be his attachment type. In the MCAST, René shows a similar behavior; he reacts independently and solves the problems on his own and afterwards he returns to his mother. As an insecure-avoidant attached child, he has discovered that he emotionally gets along the best when attempting to solve his problems by himself.

In both scenes, the children provide a *non-canonical* solution by finding equivalent classes between the big and the small ladybugs. This fact leads to "improvisations" by the guiding adult (Krummheuer 2012b, p. 324). In the presented scenes, the guiding adults seem to have difficulties to understand René's and Nina's solutions so they have to claim explanations and reasons for the *non-canonical* solutions. During these phases both guiding persons behave similar to the type of mother of securely attached children; they are more reserved with their own interpretation of the mathematical situation and show efforts in handing over the lead to René and Nina. Their requests like "why" or "what do you mean by saying this" seem to support the emergence of René's and Nina's mathematically creative solutions. In case of René, there were two competing solutions by René and Marie, so the guiding adult wants to have an agreement and this leads to Marie's two-card solution. Here she reacts in a more controlling way and nevertheless shows some kind of delicacy of feeling, because she asks René if it works for him to take Marie's solution. By contrast, the guiding adult in Nina's situation is more open for Nina's idea that only one bug fits and she does not insist on the canonical solution. Thus, Nina has a good atmosphere to explore autonomously the ladybug-cards and their relationships. René has to show more effort to explain his idea because of the two competing solutions. As a child with an insecure attachment pattern, he is used to anticipate the perspective of his caregivers, because they feel better when he shows no intense affects and behaves toward them in a controlled, distanced manner. Because of his attachment pattern, he is maybe able to work autonomously and creatively although the guiding adult seems not to understand his solution. Dealing with this, René puts himself in her position and takes her perspective to elucidate his solution that can be seen in his deep argumentation. The ability of perspective taking is rather untypical for children of his age and is regarded here as a cognitive-interactional ability that he developed over time in order to compensate his insecure-avoidant behavior.

Summary

Two cases of the MaKreKi study were discussed and it has been shown that the approaches mentioned in Sect. 2 can be used to describe creative mathematical processes of young children at the kindergarten age. Regarding the first central research question, how does mathematical creativity express itself at the age of preschool and how is it observable, the two cases illustrate that children who can be seen as mathematically creative are able to change the perspective on a mathematical task, although a clear instruction from the guiding adult focuses on another perspective. Nina as well as René offered a "one-card solution" instead of the expected "two-card solution" by combining the two classification systems of big and small ladybug-cards.

Comparing René's and Nina's solution with solutions of other children in the erStMaL project, who also attended the ladybug situation, exhibits their mathematically creative potential. The other children do not discover a kind of connection between the two parts and offer accordingly the expected one-card solution. Instructions may have a strong impact on children's interpretation of mathematical tasks and so only mathematically creative children are able and have the confidence to see more possibilities and perspectives than the canonical solution, which is forced by the comments of the guiding adult.

From the guiding adult's perspectives, which are in line with the didactical design pattern of the ladybug situation, there were canonical solutions by comparing the colors of the ladybugs, the shapes on their backs, or their number of spots on their backs. In this perspective, it is easy to determine two ladybugs which belong together because of their equal features, which the third ladybug does not possess. From the situational perspective, the final definition of the problem situation is a matter of negotiation of the meaning in the concrete situation of interaction (Krummheuer 2012b).

Concerning the two poles, construction and instruction, the two cases show that some kind of instructions, especially instructions which expected arguments and reasons, support mathematically creative potential of young children. Regarding the construction of children's mathematical thinking, it is important to understand and also honor their *non-canonical* solutions, which might be the first step in the development of mathematical creativity in early childhood. As the two cases illustrated, it is not always easy for the guiding adults to see the mathematically creative potential in the *non-canonical* solutions of the children. Therefore, additional analysis of young children's *non-canonical* solutions can help to describe, understand, and identify the mathematical potential of young children. Thus, further research is necessary.

Till now the connection between mathematical creativity and the attachment pattern in early childhood is not satisfactorily investigated. Therefore, a conceptual framework has to develop which examines the cultural and the situational impact as well as the influence of the attachment pattern on the development of mathematical creativity in early childhood and connects with the creative mathematical abilities of young children.

Acknowledgments

The preparation of this paper was funded by the federal state government of Hessen (LOEWE initiative).

Appendix

Rules of Transcription

Column 1	Serially numbered lines
Column 2	Shows when people are talking at the same time
Column 3	Abbreviations for the names of interacting people
Column 4	Verbal (regular font) and non-verbal (*italic font*) actions
/	Rising pitch
-	Even pitch
\	Falling pitch
… …	Breaks of 1, 2 or 3 s
(4)	Breaks of a specified time span
Bold	Accentuated word
S p a c e d	Spoken slowly
(word)	Unclear utterance
(*remark*)	Remark, offering alternatives to unclear utterances
+	The indicated way of speaking ends at this symbol
#	There is no break; the second speaker follows immediately
<	Indicates where people are talking at the same time
>	The next block of simultaneous speech is indicated by a change

References

Ainsworth, M., et al. (1978). *Patterns of attachment*. Hillsdale: Erlbaum.
Bauersfeld, H. (1995). "Language games" in the mathematics classroom: Their function and their effects. In P. Cobb & H. Bauersfeld (Eds.), *The emergence of mathematical meaning: Interaction in classroom cultures* (pp. 271–289). Hillsdale: Lawrence Erlbaum Associates
Becker-Textor, I. (1998). *Kreativität im Kindergarten. Anleitung zur kindgemäßen Intelligenzförderung im Kindergarten* (8th ed.). Freiburg im Breisgau: Herder.
Bolwby, J. (1951). *Maternal care and mental health. A report prepared on behalf of the World Health Organization as a contribution to the United Nations programme for the welfare of homeless children*. World Health Organization Monograph Series. Geneva: World Health Organization.
Bowlby J. (1969). *Attachment. Attachment and loss* (Vol. 1). New York: Basic Books.
Brandt, B., & Krummheuer, G. (2001). *Paraphrase und Traduktion. Partizipationstheoretische Elemente einer Interaktionstheorie des Mathematiklernens in der Grundschule*. Weinheim und Basel: Beltz.
Brink, A. (2000). *The creative matrix. Anxiety and the origin of creativity*. New York: Peter Lang.
Bruner, J. (1990). *Acts of meaning*. Cambridge: Harvard University Press.
Cobb, P., & Bauersfeld, H. (1995). Introduction: The coordination of psychological and sociological perspectives in mathematics education. In P. Cobb & H. Bauersfeld (Eds.), *The emergence of mathematical meaning: Interaction in classroom cultures* (pp. 1–16). Hillsdale: Lawrence Erlbaum Associates.
Ervynck, G. (1991). Mathematical creativity. Advanced mathematical thinking. In D. Tall (Ed.), *Advanced mathematical thinking* (pp. 42–53). Dordrecht: Kluwer.
Garfinkel, H. (1967). *Studies in ethnomethodology*. Englewood Cliffs: Prentice-Hall.
Green, J., et al. (2000). A new method of evaluating attachment representations in the young school age children: The Manchester Child Attachment Story Task (MCAST), attachment and human development (Vol. 2, pp. 48–70).
Grossmann, K. (1984). *Zweijährige Kinder im Zusammenspiel mit ihren Müttern, Vätern, einer fremden Erwachsenen und in einer Überaschungssituation. Beobachtungen aus bindungs- und kompetenztheoretischer Sicht*. Regensburg: Universität Regensburg.
Hadamard, J. (1954). *Essay on the psychology of invention in the mathematical field*. Princeton: Princeton University Press.
Hümmer, A., et al. (2011). Erste Analysen zum Zusammenhang von mathematischer Kreativität und kindlicher Bindung. Ein interdisziplinärer Ansatz zur Untersuchung der Entwicklung mathematischer Kreativität bei sogenannten Risikokindern. In B. Brandt, R. Vogel, & G. Krummheuer (Eds.), *Empirische Studien zur Didaktik der Mathematik. Die Projekte erStMaL und MaKreKi. Mathematikdidaktische Forschung am 'Center of Individual Development and Adaptive Education' (IDeA)* (pp. 175–196). Münster: Waxmann.
Jungwirth, H., & Krummheuer, G. (2006). Banal sozial? Zur Soziologisierung des mathematischen Lehrens und Lernens durch die interpretative Unterrichtsforschung. In H. Jungwirth & G. Krummheuer (Eds.), *Der Blick nach innen: Aspekte der alltäglichen Lebenswelt Mathematikunterricht* (Vol. 1, pp. 7–18). Münster: Waxmann.
Krenz, A. & Rönnau, H. (1997). *Entwicklung und Lernen im Kindergarten. Psychologische Aspekte und pädagogische Hinweise für die Praxis* (7th ed.). Freiburg im Breisgau: Herder.
Krummheuer, G. (1995): The ethnography of argumentation. In: P. Cobb & H. Bauersfeld (Eds.), *The emergence of mathematical meaning: interaction in classroom cultures* (pp. 229–270). Hillsdale: Lawrence Erlbaum.
Krummheuer, G. (2007). Argumentation and participation in the primary mathematics classroom. Two episodes and related theoretical abductions. *Journal of Mathematical Behavior, 26*(1), (pp. 60–82).
Krummheuer, G. (2011). Die empirisch begründete Herleitung des Begriffs der „Interaktionalen Nische mathematischer Denkentwicklung" (NMD). In B. Brandt, R. Vogel, & G. Krummheuer

(Eds.), *Empirische Studien zur Didaktik der Mathematik. Die Projekte erStMaL und MaKreKi. Mathematikdidaktische Forschung am 'Center of Individual Development and Adaptive Education' (IDeA)* (pp. 25–89). Münster: Waxmann.

Krummheuer, G. (2012a). Die Interaktionsanalyse. In: F. Heinzel (Ed.), *Methoden der Kindheitsforschung* (pp. 234–247). Weinheim: Juventa.

Krummheuer, G. (2012b). The "Non-canonical" solution and the "Improvisation" as conditions for early years mathematics learning processes: The Concept of the "Interactional Niche in the Development of Mathematical Thinking" (NMT). *Journal für Mathematikdidaktik, 33*(2), 317–338.

Lehmann, B. E. (1988). *Rationalität im Alltag? Zur Konstitution sinnhaften Handelns in der Perspektiver interpretativer Soziologie.* Münster: Waxmann.

Liljedahl, P. (2008). Mathematical creativity: In the words of the creators. Proceedings of the 5th International Conference Creativity in Mathematics and the Education of Gifted Students (pp. 153–160). Haifa, Israel.

Mann, E. L. (2006). Creativity: The essence of mathematics. *Journal for the Education of the Gifted, 30*(2), 236–262.

Mehan, H., & Wood, H. (1975). The reality of ethnomethodology. New York: Wiley.

Petermann, F. (2009). Wechsler Preschool and Primary Scale of Intelligence-III (WPPSI-III, deutsche Version). Frankfurt am Main: Pearson Assessment & Information GmbH.

Poincaré, H. (1948). *Science and method.* New York: Dover.

Sarama, J., & Clements, D. H. (2008). Mathematics in the early childhood. In: O. N. Saracho & B. Spodek (Eds.), *Contemporary perspectives on mathematics in early childhood education* (pp. 67–94). Charlotte: Information Age Publishing.

Sriraman, B. (2004). The characteristics of mathematical creativity. *The Mathematics Educator, 14*(1), 19–34.

Sternberg, R. J., & Lubart, T. I. (2000). *The concept of creativity: Prospects and paradigms. Handbook of creativity. R. J. Sternberg.* Cambridge: Cambridge University Press.

Toulmin, S. E. (1969). *The uses of argument.* Cambridge: Cambridge University Press.

Urban, K. (2003). Towards a componential model of creativity. In: D. Ambrose, et al. (Eds.), *Creative intelligence* (pp. 81–112). Cresskill: Hampton.

Vogel, R., & Wippermann, S. (2004). Dokumentation didaktischen Wissens in der Hochschule: Didaktische Design Patterns als eine Form des Best-Practice-Sharing im Bereich von IKT in der Hochschule. In K. Fuchs-Kittowski, W. Umstätter, & R. Wagner-Döbler (Eds.), *Jahrbuch Wissenschaftsforschung* (pp. 27–42). Berlin: Gesellschaft für Wissenschaftsforschung.

Vogel, R. (2014). Mathematical Situations of Play and Exploration as an Empirical Research Instrument. In: U. Kortenkamp et al. (eds.), *Early Mathematics Learning,* (pp. 223–236). New York: Springer.

Wheatley, G. (2008). *Which doesn't belong.* Bethany Beach: Mathematics Learning.

Chapter 10
The Interplay Between Gesture and Speech: Second Graders Solve Mathematical Problems

Melanie Huth

In mathematical interactions, young learners express their ideas in multiple ways to interact with each other and to come in contact with the provided culture-based mathematical environment—to construct in common mathematical meaning, so to say. To deal with the complex multimodality seen in these interactions, this chapter investigates the interplay between gestures and speech used by second graders while they are occupied with a geometrical problem in pairs. In the chapter, gesture and speech are analyzed with an interaction analysis, and a detailed reconstruction of the semiotic process on a microscopic level. The main research question is: How and in what kind of modality—in gesture and/or speech—will mathematical ideas[1] be introduced, adopted, developed and/or refused by the children during their occupation with the given mathematical problem?

Introduction

During the occupation with mathematical problems in pairs, elementary school pupils gesticulate, discuss their mathematical ideas and methods, use the provided material, and possibly even write something down. In a complex kind of interplay, these diverse modes of expression do not appear sequentially, but rather simultaneously and they overlap with each other. Actions can be described in speech or

---

[1] The term *mathematical ideas* can be understood as any kind of expressed contribution of the second graders, which contain any suggestion to solve the given mathematical problem. What can be described as a *mathematical idea* emerges and is constructed in the interaction by negotiations of the participants. By dint of a detailed analysis, these *mathematical ideas* can be reconstructed.

M. Huth (✉)
Goethe-Univesity Frankfurt a.M. and IDeA-Center Frankfurt a. M., Germany
e-mail: huth@math.uni-frankfurt.de

imitated by gestures. The pupils talk about things they have written down, refer with gestures to things which were discussed before, etc. In the general view, the expressions—and also the interpretations of such expressions—are generated in a *multimodal* way. These multiple ways of expression will be analyzed in the present chapter by focusing on the special relation of gesture and speech used by the learners in mathematical interactions. Looking at gestures in mathematical situations, however, is a fairly new field of research in Germany, though it is increasingly gaining international significance (cf., e.g., Arzarello and Paola 2007; Radford 2009; Sabena 2008). Gesture and speech are seen as a single integrated language system and display a special relationship with each other (cf., e.g., McNeill 1992; Goldin-Meadow 2003). The present chapter offers a descriptive approach to the use and functionality of gesture and speech in their interplay in mathematical interactions of second graders. The theoretical frame makes use of previous approaches to multimodality as described, e.g., by Radford (2009) and Sabena (2008). These approaches emphasize the significance of bodily expression in the sense of "Embodied Cognition" (Anderson 2003), and describe the body and its interaction with signs and artifacts as central "sources of mathematics knowledge" (Sabena 2008, p. 19). A crucial role is ascribed to the body, its integration in the mathematical learning environment, and its constitution of mathematical thinking and learning.

> […] thinking does not occur solely *in* the head but also *in* and *through* a sophisticated semiotic coordination of speech, body, gestures, symbols and tools. (Radford 2009, p. 111)

A semiotic approach to the data in this chapter allows a micro-analytical examination of the relationship between gesture and speech used by second graders in mathematical interactions. A sequence out of the domain geometry will be analyzed by dint of an interactional and a semiotic perspective, and will concretize the theoretical remarks.

An interactional Approach to the Learning of Mathematics

In the present chapter, an interactional approach of mathematics education is used to understand the learning of mathematics as highly socially constituted in interaction.[2] In mathematics education this interactional view emerged out of the orientation on the radical constructivism, research traditions of the interpretative social research, and the symbolic interactionism (cf. Bauersfeld 2000, p. 117). According to Voigt (1984, p. 7), Krummheuer (1992), and Krummheuer and Brandt (2001, p. 13), the learning of mathematics is incomprehensively seen, if learning is exclusively

---

[2] Please note that the interaction theory is the leading approach according to the learning of mathematics in the present chapter. In some sections in the chapter, other approaches will be described to clarify the current state of research according to the theme of the chapter. In some of these other approaches, the conception of the learning of mathematics is quite different from the interactional point of view. For example, the mismatch theory according to Goldin-Meadow (2003) in the section about gestures in the learning of mathematics is ascribed to the psychological view and brings into focus the individual rather than the social constitution of learning.

viewed as an individual process. With this in mind, research in mathematics education is highly interested in the conditions of mathematics learning in interaction, as well as in the structure and organization of these social processes. In interactions, humans create—commonly by dint of processes of negotiation and subject to mutually coordinated behavior—"taken-as-shared meaning[s]" (Krummheuer 1992, p. 18). Thus, argumentations which are created rather of *the social "we"* than of *the individual "me"* can emerge. Through the participation in these argumentations, the individual has the possibility to achieve more and more autonomy and get the chance to assume responsibility for mathematical activities. With regard to mathematics learning, this process is described by Krummheuer and Brandt (2001) as the "social phenomenon of the collective genesis of meaning" (ibid. p. 15, translated by M. Huth).

The perspective of the emergence of meaning in interaction does not examine or focus the individual mental schemes of the interlocutors, which are difficult to access. As Sfard (2003) states:

> we should be less interested in explanations based on such unobservables as mental schemes, than in descriptions of the processes of learning, their patterns and mechanisms. (ibid. p. 24)

Furthermore, it rarely contains the idea of any fixed and objective given meaning of, e.g., mathematical terms, which can be taught to learners. An interactional perspective rather asks about the processes of interpretation and negotiation of the interlocutors which are created in and simultaneously constitute the interaction. Through the mutually interrelated behavior of the interlocutors, mathematical meaning emerges in interactionally generated negotiation processes. Brandt and Höck (2011a) describe these mathematical negotiation processes in peer interactions or in interactions between an expert and learners (e.g., teacher and pupils) as *co-constructions* (ibid. 245 f.). These co-constructions have mainly an impact on the individual constructions of meaning and facilitate the learning of mathematics. A precondition for individual learning in the frame of co-construction processes is the participation in the technical constitution of these interactions (cf. ibid. p. 246).

> [...] the result of a joint constructed process can become more than an addition of different ideas or propositions. (Brandt and Höck 2011b, p. 1)

Successful mathematical learning and the creation of mathematical meaning are thus more than the discussion or exchange of information about word-meaning-pairs, e.g., between teacher and learners, but rather collectively constructed *mathematical argumentations* (cf. Krummheuer and Brandt 2001, p. 18). They are described as specific processes of interaction that facilitate the learning of mathematics. It is important for learners *to be a part of* and *to take part* in[3] these interaction processes

---

[3] *To be a part of* means that learners orient themselves on the behavior of others. *To take part* means that the own behavior is used as orientation for others. Whereas the former can be described as a receptive behavior, the latter is rather an active participation (cf. Krummheuer and Brandt 2001, 17 f.).

in mathematics (cf. Krummheuer and Brandt 2001, 17 f., according to Markowitz 1986). Sfard (2003) describes from this perspective of participation

> [...] learning is first and foremost about the development of ways in which an individual participates in well-established communal activities. (ibid. p. 23)

In this way, learners can gain more and more autonomy in their participation in interactively generated interaction patterns.[4] Their responsibility for argumentations in mathematics increases with their autonomy in these interaction patterns (Krummheuer 2011, 30 ff.).

Also, Sfard (2003) describes the learning of mathematics as constituted in communication.[5] In her "communicational approach" (ibid. p. 13), she describes that

> putting communication in the heart of mathematics education is likely to change not only the way we teach but also the way we think about learning and about what is being learned. (ibid. p. 13)

Mathematics learning in Sfard's eyes is less *acquisition* but merely *participation* in mathematics interactions (ibid. p. 22). Thinking and communication is no longer differentiated:

> [...]these two "things" are to be understood as inseparable aspects of basically one and the same phenomenon, with none of them being prior to the other. (ibid. p. 27)

The goal of mathematics education is then to become a skillful participant of interactions in mathematics. This argumentation is also found in Krummheuer (2011, 30 f.), who describes the interplay of social and individual components of successful learning in mathematics in interaction like this: The participation in collective argumentations in the frame of mathematical interactions can act as an orientation of cognitive reorganization and thus leads to a convergence of individual ascription of meaning and the interactively generated negotiation of meaning.

With these theories of mathematics learning in mind, two aspects seem to be crucial for the present chapter: First, mathematics learning takes place *in the social*, and the medium of this social world is interaction. Second, in mathematics interactions different symbolic systems of expression are used to realize the processes of negotiation. To understand the roles of gestures and speech in the creation of socially constituted mathematical meaning, the present chapter would like to offer a puzzle piece to approximate this question. In the next sections of the chapter, it has

---

[4] *Interaction patterns* emerge in interactions and are a kind of routines or structures which can be reconstructed by dint of a detailed analysis of the interaction processes. These routines contain implicit and, for the interlocutors, rather unconscious rules which determine the process of interaction (cf. Voigt 1984, Krummheuer 2011). The benefit of those patterns is to stabilize the progress of the mathematical interaction and to guarantee the functionality. Mutual coordination of the interlocutors (cf. Krummheuer 1992, 40 ff.) can be realized. Interaction patterns are no (teaching) methods which are available or can be applied consciously. Both, the rules and the patterns emerge in these interactions between the interlocutors.

[5] *Communication* in Sfard's (2003) sense is understood as any instance of doing it and thus includes gestures as well: "whether diachronic or synchronic, whether with others or with oneself, whether predominantly verbal or with the help of any other symbolic system." (Sfard 2003, p. 28).

to be clarified, how the modalities gesture and speech which are used in mathematics interactions can be described in the frame of an integrated language system, and which research results are already available according to the role of gesture and speech in mathematics learning.

Gesture and Speech: Two Modes, But One System

Elements of the semiotic repertoire which is used in interactions, gestures, and speech are described as two modes of one integrated language system in the most psycholinguistic-based literature (cf. McNeill 1992 and 2005, Goldin-Meadow 2003). McNeill (1992) remarks on gestures:

> They are tightly intertwined with spoken language in time, meaning, and function; so closely linked are they that we should regard the gesture and the spoken utterance as different sides of a single underlying mental process. (McNeill 1992, p. 1)

Gestures are such stable components of the semiotic repertoire that it is probably almost impossible to suppress them for any length of time. But not only for the *producer* of gestures, but also for the *reader* or rather *interpreter* of them, they seem to be important in relation to the speech used, as indicated by Kendon (2004):

> The meanings expressed by these two components [gesture and speech] interact in the utterance and, through a reciprocal process, a more complex unit of meaning is the result. (ibid. 108 f.)

Also McNeill (2005) assumes that gestures are important for both—speaker and listener:

> I mean that an individual–social duality is inherent to gesture. A gesture is a bridge from one's social interaction to one's individual cognition – it depends on the presence (real or imagined) of a social other and yet is a dynamic element in the individual's cognition. (ibid. p. 54)[6]

Research shows that movements of the feet or head take over from hand and arm movements when the hands are artificially rested (cf. Goss 2010, p. 302). Goldin-Meadow (2003) describes this interplay between gesture and speech as having its origin in early language acquisition, where gestures acts as a facilitator and pathfinder (cf. Goldin-Meadow 2003, 17 f.).[7]

---

[6] This argumentation, although rather from a perspective of psychology, is in line with the above-mentioned aspects of the relation of individual and social learning in interaction as described by Krummheuer (2011) and Sfard (2003). Maybe the examination of gestures can thus provide a bridge between approaches of psychology and psycholinguistics and the theory of interaction in the learning of mathematics.

[7] The specific interplay of gesture and speech leads to the here described research focus. This does not mean that other expression modes as well as the influence of the given material on mathematical interactions are ignored or disregarded. Those aspects are considered analytically by dint of the interaction analysis and are integrated in the interpretation of gesture, speech, and their relation to each other.

For the research described in the present chapter, one can apply the definition of gesture used by Goldin-Meadow (2003). She describes gestures as movements of hands and arms during speaking:

> The criteria for a gesture thus stipulate that the hand motion (1) be produced during the communicative act of speaking [...] and (2) not be a functional act on an object or person. (ibid. p. 8)

Thus in the present chapter, those gestures are focused which are produced intuitively and spontaneously during speech.[8] Previous analysis in the frame of the research project described here revealed that an "act on object" (ibid. p. 8) and gestures cannot necessarily always be clearly distinguished from each other at first sight. According to the multimodal paradigm, objects can be integrated into gestural argumentations without any functional act being performed upon them. For example in a situation out of the domain *combinatorics,* all sequences of three elements had to be found by two second graders. The three elements were represented by animal figures: an elephant and two tigers, which were nearly identical but only differently colored. To explain why one cannot use two identical orders out of the anima, one of the boys integrated the tiger figures in his gestural argumentation: The boy placed the two figures exactly next to each other to figure out their specific attribute of being nearly identical but only differently colored. Metaphorically, he included the two tiger figures in his explanation of sameness. At this moment, the tigers were not used as figures of animals or as elements in rows which were interpreted in a combinatorial sense. The tigers were used as an example of sameness. In such cases, these movements of hands and arms are examined in the present chapter as gestures in the analyses. The distinction between act and gesture only emerges after a detailed analysis has been carried out (cf. Huth 2011a).

In the present chapter, the gesture dimensions according to McNeill (2005) are used for descriptions in the analyses. McNeill (2005, 38 ff.) pictures four dimensions[9] of gestures: *iconic gestures* (are used to describe, e.g., form and size of objects); *deictic gestures* (are used to point at something or refer to relations); *metaphoric gestures* (are used to refer to a more abstract thought or idea); and *beat gestures* (are used to beat the rhythm of speech or to underline prominent aspects in speech). These dimensions offer a first systematic sight on the originally less or not conventionalized system of spontaneously produced gestures during speaking.

In their interplay, both modes—gesture and speech—display unique characteristics in terms of their means of expression. Neither is simply a support or accessory for the other, and neither can fully replace the other. Speech can be described as a linear, hierarchically organized grammatical system that follows conventionalized

---

[8] Spontaneously produced gestures are differentiated from those gestures which have any kind of standardized well formedness and/or can be understood, e.g., within a language community without accompanying speech, e.g., like it is described for emblems (cf. McNeill 1992, 36 ff.).

[9] These gesture dimensions are often described as "categories" (McNeill 2005, p. 41). The different features of these categories are often mixed in the same gesture. The word *categories* seems to imply a hierarchy, which is why McNeill (2005, p. 41) recommends to use *dimensions* instead of *categories*.

rules, which are fixed within a language community. Spoken words are fleeting, but once spoken cannot be changed or taken back, but they can be further specialized. They leave a kind of phonetic track in our minds which is shortly available. Speech can create a narrative context and can establish concepts that can outlast the present situation and be used in the future, e.g., as technical terminology. On the other hand, gesture, expressed spontaneously and intuitively during speech, does not follow any conventionalized parameters in the sense of a grammatically fixed system of rules within a community of language. However, it too displays a certain fleetingness, but leaves a kind of imagistic track of movements. Deictically, it can be very precise. Furthermore, it can refer to objects that are not currently present, or even thoughts. In these cases, gestures create quasi-real objects in the gesture space, which can be referred to in the further interaction. Gestures are described as complex formations of space and time (Sager 2005, p. 22), which are a kind of images created by hands and arms, and they often express space and time aspects simultaneously. Gestures which accompany speech can experience a certain degree of conventionalization if a gesture is repeatedly used by two speakers at the moment of interaction and commonly established as the representation of an object to be used over a specific period (cf. Fricke 2007, p. 196).

Thinking of interactions, interlocutors, on the one hand, cope with these particular possibilities of expression in a sophisticated way, and, on the other hand, also handle nearly perfectly the task of the interaction itself with its various requirements of coordination and monitoring, turn-taking, and fulfilling of social norms and expectations, etc.

> [...] conversations are a testimony to the remarkable skill by which people are able to coordinate their actions with one another. (Clark 1996, p. 325)

If gestures, in this sense, are a part of language, and language is used mainly to interact, and interaction is the place in which learning of mathematics emerges, the question for the next chapter is, which role gestures play in the learning of mathematics during interactions.

Gestures in the Mathematical Learning Process: "Stepping Stones" of Learning

With relation to the significance of gestures in mathematics learning as an overarching research interest, mathematics education can use results of psychological and psycholinguistic studies (cf., e.g., McNeill 1992, Goldin-Meadow 2003). This chapter will introduce some studies which are relevant to the described research[10]

---

[10] Please keep in mind that those studies are not necessarily compatible with the introduced interaction theory, especially with regard to the conception of mathematics learning. First, regardless of these differences, the approaches will be described. At the end of this section, these approaches will be discussed with regard to the interactional approach used in the present chapter.

and interpret them using perspectives of mathematics education. The chosen scene for the following analysis is taken out of the domain *geometry,* which underlines the significance of bodily expressions, and the interplay of gesture and speech in particular. Different studies in gestures and mathematics showed that gestures particularly are suitable to describe spatial relations. Furthermore, gestures are more frequently used during tasks to define spatial words than non-spatial words and have an impact on spatial reasoning of young learners (cf. Ehrlich et al. 2006, p. 1260; Elia et al. 2011; Krauss 1998, p. 7).

In relation to the learning of mathematics from a psychological point of view, Goldin-Meadow (2003) describes the theory of "matches" and "mismatches" (ibid. 25 ff.). Where gesture and speech express the same information, this is described as a *match*. With *mismatches,* gesture and speech convey different pieces of information that do not overlap. These pieces of information are not necessarily in contrast or even in conflict to each other, but rather often mutually compensatory (ibid. p. 26). Goldin-Meadow (2003, p. 51) was able to show that children who produced *mismatches* during the occupation with mathematical problems (e.g., while solving equation problems) were in a transition phase of learning.[11] At first they showed *matches* with correct or incorrect strategies in speech and gesture. Then they produced *mismatches* with various correct and incorrect strategies in gesture and speech. A short time later, they showed *matches* with correct mathematical strategies. Furthermore, they often used gestures to express mathematical ideas *before* they were able to explain these strategies within their speech repertoire. Thus, gestures also can act as facilitators, e.g., in the development of a technical language in mathematics (cf. Givry and Roth 2006). Goldin-Meadow (2003) noted from her observations that *mismatches* are an important step in the mathematical learning process (cf. ibid. p. 54) and facilitate insights into the benefit of instructions[12] (cf. ibid. 124 ff.). Children who produced *mismatches* were "ready to learn" (ibid. p. 47) and especially open for instructions, which they were able to use for increasing their constructions in mathematics. It needs to be noted that these results were generated by investigations with individuals in relatively clearly structured mathematical situations. According to Goldin-Meadow (2003), *mismatches* are evidently relevant for the speaker's mental system, which means for the *producer* of *mismatches*. Following Goldin-Meadows description (2003) obviously utterances can be recognized as a *mismatch* if semantically different meanings can be reconstructed in the respective movements and spoken words. In my research work, I was able to reconstruct a *mismatch* according to Goldin-Meadows (2003) definition: In a measurement situation, two second graders were occupied with the volume of cubes (cf. Huth 2011a).

---

[11] The children had to solve equation problems of the following kind: $3+7+4=\_\_+4$. A match was observed, when a child said: "I add 3, 7 and 4" accompanied with a pointing gesture from the left to the right on the 3, the 4 and the 7 on the left side of the equation sign. A mismatch was observed when a child uttered the same words in speech but simultaneously showed a pointing gesture to 3 and 7 with an extended index and ring finger. In this case, the 4 on the left side of the equation sign was gesturally excluded (Goldin-Meadow 2003, p. 44).

[12] Please note that the concept of *instruction* in the here-described approach is understood rather in a narrow sense and as a kind of very clearly defined teaching sessions.

They had to answer the question, how many wooden cubes with a side length of 3 cm will fit in an edge model of a cube (side length of 9 cm). The children first filled the edge model. Then one girl suggested to count three *layers,* as she said. What she then did was rather a counting of *columns* of wooden cubes than a counting of *layers.* Her interaction partner's reaction was a kind of confusion. In the analysis it could be reconstructed that for the girl *layer* and *column* were not different ideas of counting the wooden cubes: She presumably counted *layers* of wooden cubes in each *column* of those. For her interlocutor these two concepts of volume seemed to be highly incompatible at the beginning of the sequence. In the progress of the situation, she was also able to integrate the *column* idea in her strategy of counting *layers* (she counted each side of the cube). At the end of the situation, both girls used both strategies but in quite different ways. With this in mind, the question is, when is a *mismatch* a *mismatch* and for whom, and which effect can a *mismatch* have on the level of interaction and the progress of negotiation of meaning. In the study of Goldin-Meadow (2003), the reconstruction of the *mismatches* produced by the children was made by the research team. Although they used a detailed system to carry out, what can count as a *mismatch,* the question is, which impact do *mismatches* have on the level of interaction: In the perspective of the interaction theory, like it is used in the here described research, the interactional effects of *mismatches* are of special interest, e.g., how they are perceived and handled by the interlocutors. It will also be necessary to seek to describe the specific nature of *mismatches,* and to illustrate in more detail what Goldin-Meadow (2003, p. 26) has already indicated with her description of a *continuum of matches and mismatches.*[13] McNeill (1992) investigated the effects of *mismatches* on the listener, offering various artificially generated *mismatches* as input for test persons (cf. ibid. 134 ff.). The *mismatches* were subdivided, e.g., in categories of space and form.[14] McNeill (1992) was able to show that, when the *mismatch* input they had experienced was reproduced, the test persons always tried to correct the *mismatch* in some way. The study allows one to conclude that it is evidently possible to distinguish *mismatches* according to their manner (space, form), and possibly further aspects (e.g., level of organization of the discourse, level of content, etc.). Furthermore, one can assume that *mismatches* have effects on the listener and the process of interpretation of utterances. The question with regard to these research results is, whether these can be transferred to and confirmed in relatively natural mathematical interactions of second graders, which are examined in the present chapter.

---

[13] Goldin-Meadow (2003) describes a continuum of *matches* and *mismatches* based on the degree of overlap of information in gesture and speech (cf. ibid. p. 26).

[14] *Mismatch* of space (with relation to the gesture space): In an ongoing narration, an actor is sited in a certain area of the gesture space, e.g., on the left side of the gesture space. Then the narrator uses another area as the space of reference for the same actor, which was already established for another actor. The gesture shows a shift of space, whereas the speech implies continuity of reference, e.g., by using the same pronoun "he." *Mismatch* of form: A narrator uses verbs that refer to a motion but do not convey any information about the manner of this motion, e.g., *come*. In gesture then the form of motion is shown, e.g., by bouncing up and down with the hands (cf. McNeill 1992, p. 135).

Cook and Goldin-Meadow (2006) investigated the influence of gestures in mathematical instructions[15] which were especially enriched with gestures. They noticed that learners benefited from instructions in the learning of mathematics, at first through imitation but above all through making these gestures to their own ones. Cook and Goldin-Meadow (2006) tried to find a reason for these results and latched onto some results from the field of behavioral research, describing, e.g., the imitation of actions as learning opportunities (cf. Carpenter et al. 2005). But with gestures, it was not merely a question of imitating arm and hand movements. In gestures a goal is not inherent in the movement, as it is, e.g., in imitating pressing on the light switch. Especially in mathematical situations of instructions, learners had to understand what the showed gestures represent. Cook and Goldin-Meadow (2006) were also able to show that instructions that included gestures could have long-term effects on learning, because learners were able to transfer the gestures they learned to their own repertoire and they used them to solve further mathematical tasks (cf. ibid. 226 f.).

McNeill (2005) also describes the imitation of gestures between speakers in interaction. According to McNeill (2005), an imitation of gestures between interlocutors can take place in different ways: *Mimicry* is ascribed to gestures which are imitated by the interlocutor while he or she reacts on something the speaker said. *Appropriation* is observable when, e.g., the interlocutor copies a gesture during the speaker's speech and even coordinate his own hand movement with the speech rhythm of the speaker. McNeill (2005) signifies these imitations not only as an imitation itself but above all as an insight into mental processes of the interlocutor (cf. ibid. 159 ff.).

In mathematics education, Arzarello and Paola (2007) described the imitation of gestures in mathematical interactions between teachers and pupils. They found that in a so-called "semiotic game" (Arzarello and Paola 2007, p. 18) the teacher integrates gestural "personal signs" of the pupils that show less technical terminology elements, into an adequate mathematical reasoning, called the "institutional signs" (ibid. p. 23). According to this theory, the integration of gestures showed by learners in the explanations of the teacher will foster learning, especially with regard to the development of an appropriate mathematical language. In this approach, the teacher is always seen as a role model for an adequate use of a technical language in mathematics. With relation to symmetrical mathematical interactions of learners, the question emerges whether the imitation and adaption of gestures can also be reconstructed between pupils, and what effects these assumptions of gestures have in the ongoing mathematical interaction. Can they be seen as *instructions* (in a very broad sense of a kind of *stimulus* for the development of signs) for *constructions*? In my previous research work, I was able to show that the former question may very much be answered in the positive, and that gestures then experienced a further development within the mathematical interaction. Gestural signs were taken over between the learners, they were adapted and used by the

---

[15] *Instruction* in the here-described study of Cook and Goldin-Meadow (2006) is understood as clearly structured teaching sessions with planned gesture and speech instructions.

pupils for their own strategies and emerged to more developed signs as *constructions*. In a so-called "semiotic game among equals"[16] (Huth 2011b, according to Arzarello and Paola 2007), an exchange of signs between gesture and speech could be observed: speech signs were transformed into gestural signs, and in this way they were a part of the ongoing mathematical process of negotiation and thus earn further development.

With regard to the impact of *mismatches* in mathematical interactions of learners, I was able to show that they were used as a kind of source of mathematical strategies. In the above-described example out of a measurement situation (counting *layers* and/or *columns* of wooden cubes), the *mismatch* fulfilled this role: The two strategies (*layers* and *columns*) were adopted by the two interlocutors in different ways to solve the problem. While the one girl combined them from the beginning and developed an adequate solution by dint of these strategies, the other girl first took the *layers* into focus. At the end and with a further hint of her interlocutor, she was able to add also the *column* idea in her counting process. The two strategies, which were introduced at the beginning of the situation in speech and in gesture, were adopted, further developed as well as integrated in their own strategies by the interlocutors, which displays the importance of *mismatches* in these interactions with regard to mathematical *constructions*. In this example, the relation of imitation of signs and *mismatches* is also becoming apparent. In the view of an interactional theory, *mismatches* are indeed a part of the negotiation processes of learners during their effort to generate "taken-as-shared meanings" (Krummheuer 1992, p. 18). The described studies characterize imitated gestures as important events in interaction, especially in mathematical learning environments with regard to *instruction* and *construction*.

Gesture and Speech as Signs

In order to investigate gestures and speech in mathematical utterances of learners and interpret them as signs, a theory is required that enables the description of conventionalized as well as non-conventionalized signs. Peirce's concept of signs is especially appropriate (cf. Fricke 2007, 182 f.). Peirce places the focus squarely on the sign itself and emphasizes the significance of the interpretation process, which is initiated when a sign is perceived as such. This aspect links in particular to an interactional theoretical perspective. Schreiber (2010) was able to show that Peirce's theory of signs may indeed be used to appropriately analyze mathematical

---

[16] *Among equals* means that both interlocutors were equal concerning their role in the mathematical interaction: No explicitly and previously defined role model or more advanced interlocutor of adequate mathematical reasoning participates. Both pupils take part in the interaction with their mathematical way to interpret the given problem. There is no knowing professional, and no inexperienced and unknowing novice. It is a more symmetrical interaction between peers in which, of course, these asymmetrical roles can possibly emerge and can be negotiated between the interlocutors.

Fig. 10.1 The sign triad after Peirce

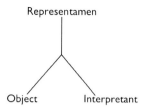

interactions of learners (cf. Schreiber 2010, 56 ff.). Peirce describes three relata as a sign: representamen, interpretant, and object (in the following often abbreviated as R, I, and O). The portrayal of this concept of signs therefore involves a triad, with the help of which all three aspects of the sign can be related to each other (cf. Fig. 10.1). Peirce describes a sign as follows:

> A sign, or *representamen,* is something which stands to somebody for something in some respect or capacity. It addresses somebody, that is, creates in the mind of that person an equivalent sign, or perhaps a more developed sign. That sign which it creates I call the *interpretant* of the first sign. The sign stands for something, its *object.* It stands for that object, not in all respects, but in reference to a sort of idea, which I have sometimes called the *ground* of the representamen. (Peirce 1931-1935, CP 2.228)

First, the representamen can be seen as an external and perceivable sign and can be a word, a gesture, etc. This representamen creates in the mind of the sign reader an interpretant, which at first can be understood as the meaning of the sign for the sign reader (inner sign). The object which the sign relates to is also related to both the representamen and the interpretant. According to Peirce a sign only becomes a sign when it is perceived as a sign and interpreted by a subject. The process of signs is never ending, since an interpretant produced in the mind of the sign reader can be expressed as a new representamen by the interpreting subject, which is obligatory for the sign process (Dörfler 2005, p. 171). In relation to the occupation of learners with mathematical problems, Schreiber (2010) was able to show that the sign process is not linear but displays a complexity. Sign processes may run parallel to each other, e.g., if one representamen leads to the creation of several interpretants (cf. ibid. 148 ff.). Schreiber (2010) developed the semiotic process cards to analyze these sign processes. In the here-described research project, these semiotic process cards were adopted on a multimodal level. In this way, the complexity can be confirmed with regard to different modes of expression (cf. Huth 2011a). In the quote above, Peirce refers to a kind of *background idea* which shows a stability over a short time: the *ground* of the representamen. This idea is used to interpret the sign and in this sense it determines the creation of an interpretant of the sign. The interpretation of Schreiber (2010, p. 37) of the *ground* concept as *frame* is affected by the frame theory of Goffman (1977) and is mainly based on the interactional approach of Krummheuer (1992). According to Schreiber (2010, 36 f.), a *frame* is activated if a sign is perceived as a sign. The *frame* offers an *interpretation background* which is determined by the number of experiences. In Schreiber's (2010) description of *frames,* the centrality of the social in line with the interaction theory becomes apparent. Schreiber (2010) describes his further developed concept out of Peirce's *ground* of the representamen, hence, in a social context as

> socially taken-as-shared and available knowledge in the sense of frames (of interpretation). (ibid. p. 59, translated by M. Huth)

In the present chapter I will not describe these frames in the later-discussed example in detail in view of an adequate number of pages and refer to Huth (2011a) concerning further remarks.

Method of Analysis and Research Focus

The data collection was based on the so-called *Didactic Design Patterns* (cf. Vogel 2014, Wippermann and Vogel 2004). These patterns of description facilitate the dispersion and communication of didactic knowledge, and enable it to be written up clearly in comparable categories and to be further developed. By dint of the *didactic design patterns,* the *instruction part* of the mathematical situation can be planned adequately according to the assumed and possible *constructions* of the learners (cf. Vogel 2014), which naturally emerges concretely when the situation takes place. Thus, the *didactic design patterns* are descriptions of didactically planned mathematical situations on a continuum between openness and closeness in the sense of didactical arrangements. Learners can bring in their ideas to mathematize the given learning environment, but there is a central theme or idea defined and described in the patterns. The mathematical situations[17] that were developed for the study can be assigned to three mathematical domains: geometry, combinatorics, and measurement. In the chapter, a sequence out of a geometrical situation will be analyzed. For the qualitative data analysis, a combined method is used:[18] In a first step, transcripts[19] of the video-recorded situations are analyzed with the interaction analysis[20] according to the interpretative research in mathematics education (cf. Krummheuer

---

[17] Each situation is accompanied by an adult who presents it to the children and gives spare impulses if needed. The concept of *instruction* in the didactic design patterns is understood in a broader sense and allocates a set of those impulses. In the planning of this set of impulses thought has been given to describe possible ideas of the children in the situation. The accompanying person can use this set of impulses to choose them adequately according to the mathematical ideas of the children.

[18] In the present paper the analyses will not be described in detail, but portrayed as summarized interpretations.

[19] With regard to an adequate number of pages, the transcript of the chosen and described sequence is not portrayed in the given paper. The produced utterances in speech and gesture, the actions of the interlocutors, as well as the whole process of interaction can be seen in the semiotic process card (cf. Fig. 10.5).

[20] The interaction analysis is based on a sequential proceeding to reconstruct the development of the theme in the progress of the interaction. In this proceeding from turn to turn, the interaction analysis leans among others on the conversation theory (cf. e.g. Eberle 1997). Aspects of the conversation analysis are adopted to focus not only the organizational aspects but mainly the development of the theme of the interaction (Krummheuer and Brandt 2001, p. 90).

and Naujok 1999, Krummheuer 2012). In order to avoid a dominance of speech in the interpretation, the two modalities—gesture and speech—are separated with each utterance, and at first only the arm and hand movements are analyzed. In the consequent procedure, the alternatives for interpreting the gestures are narrowed down through the inclusion of the interpretations of the speech used. In this process, a most probable interpretation emerges for the whole interaction. In the second step, a micro-analysis of the relationship of gesture and speech is conducted with the aid of the semiotic triad of signs after Peirce. Here the semiotic process cards from Schreiber (2010, 60 ff.) are adopted and extended on a multimodal level. Following Peirce's theory of signs, two triads are used—one for gesture and one for speech (cf. Fig. 10.5 in the present chapter)—which are linked by a common interpretant. The theoretical assumptions displayed above lead to the following overarching research focus: How and in what kind of modality—in gesture and/or speech—will mathematical ideas be introduced, adopted, developed, and/or refused by the children during their occupation with the given mathematical problem? It is particularly interesting what happens on the level of interaction if a *mismatch* appears. Previous results to these events in mathematical interactions of learners and to the above-described "semiotic game among equals" (Huth 2011b) can be used, empirically tested and possibly further developed.

The Relation of Gesture and Speech in the Empiricism

In the following chapter, an example will be described which will concretize the theoretical assumptions. With regard to the research focus, an interaction analysis as well as a semiotic analysis will be conducted to deepen previous findings and facilitate a theoretical development according to the research focus.

Introduction of the Chosen Sequence

The herein-described sequence is from a video-recorded mathematical situation which can be assigned to the mathematical domain *geometry*. The situation is called *building*. Out of a given repertoire of different LEGO® DUPLO® bricks in three sizes, each of the participating pupils Jana and Ayse should at first construct a building without any demands, except to use all of the given bricks. In the following situation, each of them should emulate the building of the partner, only regarding the speech description of the interlocutor and without seeing the original building of the partner. A dividing wall is used. In a mathematical sense, a three-dimensional object has to be built and described in speech. Then the design description of the interlocutor has to be used to construct a three-dimensional object which is congruent with the original building. Both pupils had the following LEGO DUPLO bricks

10 The Interplay Between Gesture and Speech ...   161

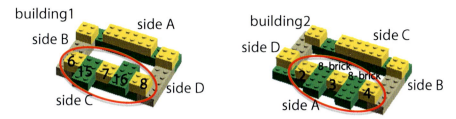

Fig. 10.2 Building 1 and building 2 at the beginning of the analyzed scene (The bricks are differently colored to illustrate the transitions between them. The girls had single-colored bricks. (figure created with LEGO Digital Designer, http://ldd.lego.com/ [27.01.2012]))

at their disposal: eight 2×2 bricks[21], eight 4×2 bricks, and two 6×2 bricks. Jana worked with a green-colored set of these LEGO DUPLO bricks; Ayse's bricks were blue. The sets were identical concerning to the numbers of different LEGO DUPLO bricks. Ayse constructed a building (building 1), which should later be emulated by Jana (building 2). A dividing wall between the two girls prevented Jana from seeing building 1. Jana had to reconstruct the original building 1 only by listening to Ayse's description in speech. After a while of trying, the dividing wall was removed as desired by the children. Jointly, Jana, and Ayse now attempted to bring building 2 more in line with building 1. In the chosen sequence, both of them can see both buildings and also gestures can be used to explain mathematical ideas.

Jana and Ayse are in the second grade of an elementary school with urban catchment in Frankfurt on the Main. About 70 % of the pupils have a migration background. Many families of the pupils have a low socioeconomic status. Jana's mother tongue is German. At the time of the video recording, Jana is 8 years old. Ayse has a Turkish background and is 7 years old. Her German proficiency is nearly on the mother tongue level. The girl's teacher describes their mathematical knowledge as being average. Both pupils were chosen as participants of the study because of their willingness to join in the offered mathematical situations in common, and according to prior consulting with their class teacher. Furthermore, 1 week before the mathematical situations were conducted, the researcher visited the class of the children to join in their daily routine in school. No math tests were conducted to choose the participants or to check their math level.

Building 1 (cf. Fig. 10.2, on the left) is the original building and building 2 (cf. Fig. 10.2, on the right) the replica at the beginning of the chosen sequence. The bricks are numbered, except the two 8-bricks at building 2. Side C at building 1 and side A at building 2 are the subject matter of negotiation in the following interaction. Obviously, the two girls do not pick out as a central theme here that already the first floors of the buildings were constructed in different ways. The girls rather try

---

[21] In the following analyses, the LEGO DUPLO bricks will be signified after the numbers of knobs they have on their upper side, e.g., the 4×2 brick is called 8-brick. Furthermore, in the buildings most of them are numbered, e.g., brick 2, brick 15, etc. (cf. Fig. 10.2).

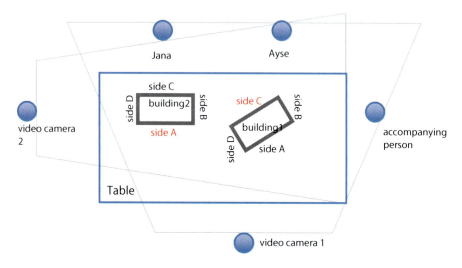

Fig. 10.3 Sketch of the setting at the beginning of the sequence

to bring the side A at building 2 more in line with the comparable part at building 1 (side C).

At the beginning of the interaction, both buildings are in front of the girls, like it is shown in the sketch below (cf. Fig. 10.3). Jana has just placed the 8-brick between brick 3 and brick 4 at building 2 (cf. Fig. 10.2).

Summarization of Interpretation—Interaction Analysis

The attempt to bring side A of building 2 more in line with side C of building 1 can be described as the main and jointly generated topic of both interlocutors in the following analyzed scene after a long period of single-working before. Especially the positions of the 8-bricks at side A of building 2 are the subject matter of negotiation in the following interaction. At the beginning of the sequence, the grasp of Ayse at the 8-brick between the bricks 3 and 4 at building 2 leads to a protest of Jana which she utters in speech. "**Ey** (inaudibly spoken) that's **right**\ I have **looked**/" is accompanied by a gesture with both flat hands. Jana's hands cover symmetrically and nearly completely side A at building 2. The hands are used as something like a flat thing to cover the building, which can be described as an iconic gesture according to McNeill (2005, 38 ff.). Further manipulations on this side of the building would not be possible any more. No one can even take a glance at this side of the building. Nevertheless, *looking* seems to be the preferred strategy of the two girls: It is observable that the utterance of *looking* at both buildings in speech often leads to changing of some bricks or marking them as set correctly or incorrectly. Obviously Jana is sure of the correct position of the grasped brick, or the whole construction of this side of her building. Jana's wording and accentuation ("**right**") underlines her wish to make this clear. Furthermore, the accentuation refers to her opinion that there are in general "right" and "wrong" positions of bricks at the building, which seems to be discovered by *looking* at both buildings (cf. "I have **looked**/"). On the first sight, the following fixed deictic gesture of Ayse on brick 15 at building 1 marks this brick as comparable to the afore-grasped 8-brick at building 2. Ayse maintains the fixation by gesture of brick 15 at building 1, even through the subsequent rotation of building 1. The index finger marks at first the point of origin of the rotation. In speech Ayse seems to agree with Jana ("yes\ (here) and now-") and refers to "here," with which obviously brick 15 is meant. It is a kind of answer to Jana's plea before. Then Ayse unfixes her index finger from brick 15 and rotates building 1 several times with both hands left and right at the building. She stops the rotation when building 1 is in the same adjustment like building 2. This action presumably leads to a better possibility of comparison. In speech Ayse states as opposed to her above-mentioned agreement: "no but not right\ **look**\." Obviously, she discovered through the rotation anything which is "not right" in her eyes, e.g., a position of a brick on side A of building 2 or the whole building. Afterwards Ayse points eight times in an energetic way on brick 16 at building 1 and obviously marks it with these gestures as "not right." Only the gesture displays the changed referent from brick 15 to brick 16. Here, a deictic or pointing gesture is mixed with the beat dimension of gesture (cf. McNeill 2005, p. 41) to underline the importance of this brick or/and the accompanying speech utterance. Only with regard to the given environment and the given mathematical problem does it become apparent that the comparable 8-brick at building 2 is meant with "not right," and not brick 16 at building 1 itself. Furthermore, her energetic pointing seems to signalize for her interlocutors that soon thereafter a crucial mathematical idea will be introduced. *Looking* is again the strategy to decide whether a brick is set correctly or not. Here it is directed through the accompanying pointing gesture. The comparison between both buildings becomes apparent through gestures and the strategy of looking, while gestures mark exactly which brick is meant. Furthermore, the herein uttered gestures seem to mark not only single bricks at one building, but refer to the relation between one brick in the original building and its comparable brick in the copying building. This seems to be implicitly clear between the two pupils, because they never discuss this aspect explicitly. In speech, Ayse obviously describes how the position has to be modified to make it "right": "(a little) in the middle" she says. This utterance can be signified as a central mathematical idea in the following scene. While Ayse is speaking, Jana brings the 8-brick at side A of building 2 between bricks 2 and 3 in a new position. Thus Jana obviously understands Ayse's utterances with regard to one brick but not with regard to the whole building, which has to be set "in the middle." Jana sets the 8-brick "in the middle," so that inside and outside at side A one row of the knobs is overlapping. The position of this 8-brick, which was denoted as "right" by Jana before, is obviously no longer correct. The rotation and Ayse's utterances of the mathematical idea to set bricks "(a little) in the middle" seem to convince Jana to change the position of this brick. How to place something/a brick "in the middle," is not necessary to be discussed between the two girls. One can interpret that Jana mainly considers the speech utterance of Ayse and disregards the changed reference object in Ayse's gesture. Ayse's previous utterances are perhaps interpreted by Jana in the following: First, brick 15 at building 1 seems to be compared to the 8-brick on building 2 between bricks 2 and 3. Ayse says that this brick was set correctly. After a few moments, Ayse obviously changes her opinion and now says that the position has to be corrected "(a little) in the middle." This is what Jana is doing now. She does not recognize that Ayse changed the reference object in her gesture to brick 16. In speech Ayse did not reveal that another brick was meant, namely the pendant of brick 16, which is set between bricks 3 and 4 at building 2. Again the gesture not only marks brick 16 at building 1 but brick 16 in relation to the comparable brick at building 2. According to McNeill (1992, 134 ff.) and with regard to the level of interaction, a *mismatch* can be assumed here which is comparable to what McNeill (1992) described as a mismatch of (gesture-)space. The interpretation of Jana is based on the disregarded change of the reference object, which is not explicitly perceivable in Ayse's speech. Only in her gesture, Ayse changed the referent to brick 16. This is the reason why Jana changed the position of the 8-brick which was set between bricks 2 and 3 "in the middle" at side A of building 2. The mathematical idea "(a little) in the middle" was introduced in speech and was set in relation to the meant bricks by gesture. But only the speech utterance was adopted by the interlocutor Jana, so that a *mismatch* on the level of interaction becomes apparent.

With regard to the question what is meant by "(a little) in the middle," and Jana's interpretation of this utterance, Ayse does not raise a plea. Thus, this interpretation can be described as a "taken-as-shared meaning" (cf. Krummheuer 1992, p. 18) of the two girls: A brick is placed so that inside and outside one row of knobs overlaps. This position is called "in the middle" by both girls.

With the action of Jana, the encircled part of building 2 gets a mirror image of the comparable part of building 1 with no preserving of orientation. The imagined plane of reflection would stand between both buildings (cf. Fig. 10.4, first layer of the buildings has to be ignored). It is still not clear whether Jana recognizes that building 2 is laterally reversed in comparison to building 1, or whether she attaches importance to this at all with regard to the given mathematical problem. For Ayse, the fact that building 2 is a mirror image of building 1 obviously leads to a correction of the position of the 8-brick at building 2, which was set between bricks 3 and 4. There emerges presumably a difference in the individual definition of what is meant by *copying a building*. Ayse obviously puts her previous remark in action: She puts the 8-brick between bricks 3 and 4 at building 2 "in the middle," like it is negotiated before. In speech Ayse explains her action and points out, which brick was meant: "This is what I've done to the middle\(inaudibly spoken) (.) like this\." This is the first time that Ayse explicitly makes clear by her act on the object *brick,* what she means by "in the middle." With regard to her action, it becomes apparent which brick was meant, namely the 8-brick between the bricks 3 and 4. Jana does not cover building 2 again, so that Ayse is able to manipulate the 8-brick without any difficulty. The reticence of Jana here emerges possibly from Ayse's grasping of Jana's hand. In the next utterance Jana first points at the 8-brick between bricks 2 and 3 at building 2 with her right forefinger. Jana lays some fingertips of her left hand down on the 8-brick between bricks 3 and 4. In gesture, she obviously marks the bricks which are important

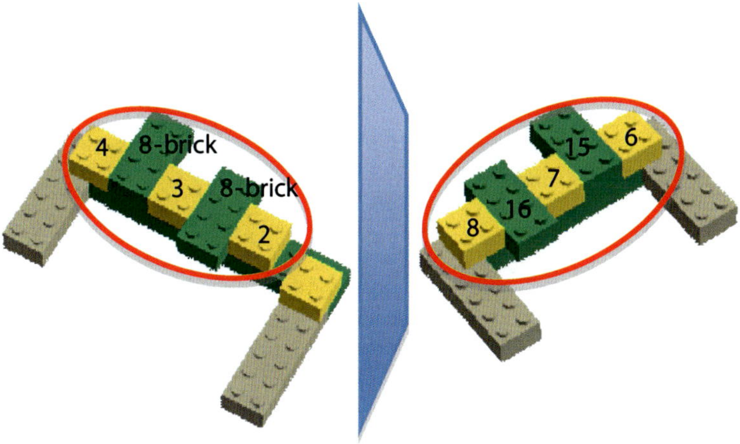

Fig. 10.4 Side A of building 2 (on the *left*) as a mirror image of side C of building 1 (on the *right*)

for her in this moment. Maybe this is an imitation and adaption of Ayse's previous behavior: Ayse also marked the important bricks by pointing several times on them. Probably Jana's fingertips at the 8-brick between bricks 3 and 4 sustain this brick for the following manipulation: Jana changes the position of the 8-brick between bricks 2 and 3 at building 2, so that outside two rows of knobs overlap. One can assume that Jana recognizes Ayse's intention to create a congruent copy of building 1 which has the same orientation, and that Jana now tries to support this plan. Also the interpretation persists that for Jana the fact that building 2 is right–left reversed to building 1 is not relevant. Jana utters in speech: "No but this-(.) this was already in the middle\," what is rather contrarily to her action. The 8-brick between bricks 2 and 3 was in the middle, but nevertheless Jana changes its position now. Maybe Jana does not want to concede this point to Ayse. It can also be more and more assumed that for Jana it is not relevant whether the copy of building 1 is preserving orientation or not. At the end of the chosen sequence and from an outside perspective with regard to the task of copying a building, the adjustment of the upper row of side A at building 2 to the upper row of side C at building 1 can be described as completed.

Summarization of the Semiotic Process: Semiotic Analysis

The semiotic process card, as is portrayed below, is used as an instrument for analysis (cf. Fig. 10.5). Furthermore, it shows the semiotic process in the described mathematical interaction of Jana and Ayse. Generally, one can see two triads[22], which are

---

[22] There is a triad for gesture (on the right) and a triad for speech (on the left). When there is no speech utterance at all, there is only one triad for gesture. The triads are numbered. Parallel utterances are portrayed by parallel triads which are marked with indices a, b,….

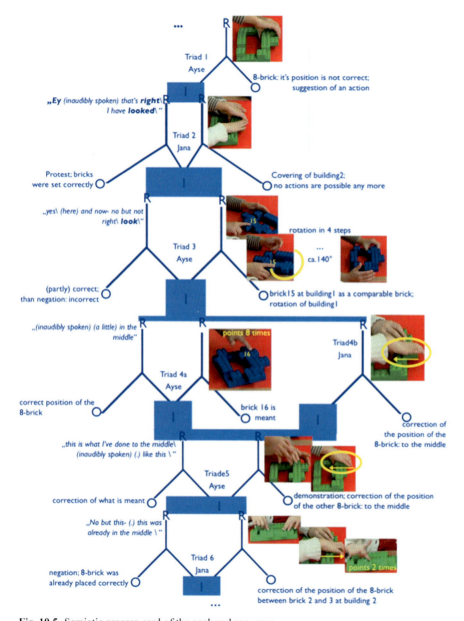

Fig. 10.5 Semiotic process-card of the analyzed sequence

linked to each other by dint of a jointly generated interpretant. The complexity of the semiotic process (cf. Schreiber 2010) is confirmed on the multimodal level, and at points in interaction where one representamen leads to more than one interpretant (cf. triads 4a and 4b in Fig. 10.5).

In the chosen sequence it is negotiated, how and which of the 8-bricks at side A of building 2 has to be changed according to their positions, to create a replica of building 1. The interaction analysis showed that an important position of these 8-bricks is called "(a little) in the middle," and means for the girls that inside and outside one row of knobs overlaps. With regard to the overarching research question, the semiotic analysis allows one to observe in detail, in what kind of modality mathematical ideas will be introduced, adopted, developed, and/or refused by the interlocutors.

In triad 1, Ayse utters as her representamen in gesture a grasping on the 8-brick at side A of building 2, which was set between bricks 3 and 4. It seems to be a suggestion of an action which is shown in gesture. Instead of repositioning the brick in fact, Ayse fixes the grasping. As an object one can assume the required correction of the position, shown as the suggested action. This representamen creates in the mind of Jana an interpretant that is expressed in the following triad 2: In speech Jana produces "**Ey** (inaudibly spoken) that's **right**\ I have **looked**\." In gesture, she fully covers side A of building 2 by dint of a nearly symmetrical gesture with both flat hands.

With this representamen Jana obviously tries to avoid any further actions at side A of building 2 which can be seen as the object of the triad. With her gesture, Jana also avoids any glance on side A. Especially with her formulation in speech in which she again refers to *looking* as an adequate strategy, this seems to be conspicuous. In the semiotic analysis, it becomes apparent that the speech representamen mainly includes the protest of Jana in relation to Ayse's suggested action. The gesture of Jana displays a short-term but effective solution by way of covering side A completely. It is evidently observable that gesture and speech are used effectively in relation to their above described special possibilities of expression. Here, the gesture seems to be a little bit faster than speech because it shows an effective solution by covering the building. In the further sign process, Ayse utters her created interpretant as a new representamen in triad 3, which seems to be contradictory at first sight: "Yes\(here) and now- no but not right\ **look**\." At first she obviously agrees to Jana, but only a few moments later, she says "no but not right\.". This discrepancy is also getting obvious in the speech object and can only be resolved with regard to the gesture used. In the gesture object, brick 15 at building 1 can be assumed as a comparable brick to a brick at building 2. Brick 15 or/and its comparable brick at building 2 are denoted as rightly placed bricks. Ayse fixes her pointing gesture at brick 15 and uses this pointing as the origin in the following rotation. Finally and through the use of further rotations, building 1 is in the same adjustment as building 2. In triads 4a and 4b, two interpretants are created out of the representamen of triad 3 which shows the complexity of the semiotic process which is already described by Schreiber (2010). Ayse obviously carries on her reasoning in triad 4a. She introduces in speech a description of what she assumes to be the correct position of the 8-brick at side A of building 2: "(a little) in the middle." This can also be assumed as the speech object. In gesture the referent is changed from brick 15 at building 1 to brick 16 at building 1, but this changing is not explicitly expressed in speech. Both objects—in speech and in gesture—seem to refer to different meant bricks. With regard to her speech only, one can assume that again brick 15 is meant. With regard to her gesture, it is clear that brick 16 is meant. Out of the interaction analysis, it is known that this is a crucial point in the interaction of the girls, where a *mismatch* becomes apparent. By dint of the semiotic analysis, it is obviously possible to document this *mismatch* in the form of different objects and interpretants in the triads in relation to one representamen.

At the same time, in triad 4b Jana creates a new representamen, which includes an action: Jana changes the position of the 8-brick at building 2 which was sited between bricks 2 and 3. The brick now is "in the middle." Jana disregards the change of the referent, which is only shown in Ayse's gesture. Jana seems to attach importance to Ayse's speech only. Thus, Jana does not integrate the change of referent in her interpretation and dislocates the 8-brick "in the middle," which presumably was not intended by Ayse. The *mismatch,* which emerges here on the level of interaction, and which is also seen in Jana's interpretation, leads to the following situation: The upper layer of side A of building 2 is a mirror image of the upper layer of side C of building 1. Obviously, Ayse recognizes the different interpretations of both girls with regard to the 8-bricks, and the question which brick has to be set in the middle. She utters a kind of correction and tries to show which brick is meant in triad 5. Her representamen in gesture refers to a kind of demonstration as the object. At first Ayse grasps Jana's hand, then Ayse accomplishes the repositioning on her own. Ayse places the 8-brick between bricks 3 and 4 at building 2 in its "right" position with an overlapping of one row of knobs inside and outside of side A. An approximation of the object in speech and the object in gesture can be observed: Both representamens refer to a correction of the brick position. At the end of the sequence, it becomes apparent that for Jana this is not a discrepancy in relation to what was done before. In speech she utters: "no but this- (.) this was in the middle already." With this negation she refers to the speech object which shows her opinion that the 8-brick, on which she now shows a pointing gesture, was already set correctly before. Maybe, it is irrelevant for Jana, whether the copy of building 1 is in the same orientation or laterally reversed. At the same time, she repositions the 8-brick between bricks 2 and 3 at building 2, so that outside two rows of knobs are overlapping. She finishes her action by pointing twice at the repositioned 8-brick, which can be described as a beat gesture according to McNeill (2005, 40 f.). The pointing and marking of the bricks are a kind of adaption of Ayse's previous behavior, and frames the action of Jana. Again, the gesture seems to be a bit further than the speech used, which can be shown in the objects of both triads.

Conclusions

In the chapter, the process of semiosis as a *semiotic game among equals* (cf. Huth 2011) is described. Signs were imitated, adopted, and negotiated between the two participating pupils in the shown example. *Instruction*[23] and *construction* within the use of signs in the described interaction are observable. One can assume that in the situation the mathematical sign "in the middle" that is introduced in speech is related to the given material by gesture, and adopted or transformed in acts on the copied building. The pointing gestures seem to be the instrument to emphasize which brick is meant for both girls. And furthermore the gestures display for what brick the currently mathematical idea is significant. The gestures are adopted between the two interlocutors to underline their own mathematical opinion about what, for them, can be regarded as a *copy of building 1* according to the expected mathematical solution of the problem. By gesture, the girls refer not only to single bricks, but rather to the relevance of the bricks concerning the given mathematical idea to put them "in the middle." They refer to bricks and their comparable brick in the other building. Only by observing the gestures is it understandable which bricks are meant and how these bricks have to be placed. The girls in the shown example have different interpretations, which brick has to be placed "in the middle." This results obviously out of the difference in the interpretation of what is considered as a *copy of a building:* Is a laterally reversed building an adequate mathematical solution or not? Furthermore, the gestures which are used by the girls relate both buildings to each other and combine comparable bricks in the buildings. A pointing (a deictic gesture) emphasizes not only one single brick but rather this brick with regard to the comparable brick in the other building. They use this pointing repeatedly and it seems to be clear for both of them what is meant by this. Pointing here is more than just creating a joint focus of attention: It is a kind of taken-as-shared mathematical meaning (cf. Krummheuer 1992) which emerges between the interlocutors: One brick is marked metaphorically as to stand for itself and for the comparable brick in the other building. The interpretation of the girls in this sense is not challenged by the girls at any time in the progress of the situation. In a mathematical sense, it is describable as a bijective mapping between the sets of bricks of buildings 1 and 2. The deictic gesture is ascribed a kind of metaphorical meaning. The environment offers a frame of interpretation of signs, which also could be described as a kind of *instruction* to read signs, which then leads to *construction* to create or develop (new) signs. The analyses also show that actions and the given environment have to be considered, especially within the described theoretical framework of the multimodal paradigm (cf. Arzarello and Paola 2007). It can be evidently assumed that the given material and the environment in total have an impact on the gestures and speech which are used by the second graders in the situation. In relation to the displayed theoretical framework of both modalities as one system, it can be further confirmed that speech and gesture have their own possibilities of

---

[23] Please keep in mind that *instruction* here is understood in a very broad sense and not exclusively as a kind of teaching by a knowing expert like a teacher. Rather *instruction* here is understandable as an impulse which can be used to foster one's own insights and further development.

expression, and both analyses confirm the special relationship of gesture and speech. Second graders are obviously able to use both modes effectively during their occupation with a mathematical problem. In the described sequence, the mathematical idea of placing a brick "in the middle" is introduced in speech and marks a critical point in interaction. In what follows, a *mismatch* (cf. Goldin-Meadow 2003) on the level of interaction appears and leads to different interpretations of the gesture-speech-utterance, or new representamens, to say it in semiotic words. In previous publications, I could reveal *mismatches* that serve as a kind of *source* of mathematical strategies in the interactions of second graders (cf. the above-described example out of a measurement situation and Huth 2011a). At first sight the *mismatch* in the herein-described situation is not comparable to this in all respects. The *mismatch* does not include different mathematical strategies itself to solve the given mathematical problem, but is rather on the level of the reference object. But in what follows, the mismatch leads to mathematically relevant aspects. Obviously, the already-negotiated taken-as-shared mathematical meaning of pointing at one brick so as to say: "*think of this brick and his features of form, position, orientation,…, and use this knowledge to position the comparable brick in the other building*" has to be clarified with regard to both modalities: gesture and speech. On the one hand, in a mathematical sense, the interlocutors rethink the positions of the critical 8-bricks at building 2, and this finally leads to different solutions so that both can be described as adequately in a mathematical sense. For Jana it is obviously irrelevant, whether building 2 is laterally reversed in comparison with the original building 1. The fact of congruency satisfies the expectation of a solution of the problem for Jana. The preserving of orientation in the congruent image of the three-dimensional object is not relevant for her. In contrast, Ayse obviously attaches great importance to the preserving of orientation to create a replica of building 1. On the other hand, the *mismatch* on the level of reference is not resolved for Jana somehow: At the end of the situation, she is still of the opinion that the bricks were already set correctly. In Jana's opinion this indeed happened before Ayse pushed for the preserving of orientation and set the proper 8-brick "in the middle." The congruent copy in the same orientation of the discussed bricks at side C of building 1 at the end of the situation seems to be more or less a result of an agreement to handle the further interaction. The girls do not look into their different interpretations of building a copy explicitly but manage the situation to go on in the interaction.

In the future research work, these results have to be confirmed in further examples and by dint of the displayed analytic instruments. Theoretically, the *semiotic game among equals* has to be described in detail, and especially in relation to the roles of *mismatches* in mathematical interactions of learners. These theoretical descriptions can be used in the future to differentiate the *mismatch* theory on the level of (mathematical) interaction, as well as concerning the question of different *mismatches,* e.g., on the level of reference with determination of the negotiated mathematical theme in the interactions. Possibly, further levels can be found with regard to the question how *mathematical* a mismatch can be or which impact it has on the negotiated mathematical theme(s) between the interlocutors.

Acknowledgments The preparation of this chapter was funded by the federal state government of Hesse (LOEWE initiative).

References

Anderson, M. L. (2003). Embodied cognition: A field guide. *Artificial Intelligence, 149,* 91–130.

Arzarello, F., & Paola, D. (2007). Semiotic games: The role of the teacher. In J. H. Woo, H. C. Lew, K. S. Park, & D. Y. Soe (Eds.), *Proceedings of the 31st Conference of the International Group for the Psychology of Mathematics Education, 2*(17–24), Seoul: PME.

Bauersfeld, H. (2000). Radikaler Konstruktivismus, Interaktionismus und Mathematikunterricht. In E. Begemann (Ed.), *Lernen verstehen – Verstehen lernen. Zeitgemäße Einsichten für Lehrer und Eltern. Mit Beiträgen von Heinrich Bauersfeld (pp. 117–145). Reihe: Erziehungskonzeptionen und Praxis* (Vol. 44). Frankfurt a.M.: Peter Lang.

Brandt, B., & Höck, G. (2011a). Ko-Konstruktion in mathematischen Problemlöseprozessen—partizipationstheoretische Überlegungen. In B. Brandt, G. Krummheuer & R. Vogel (Eds.), *Die Projekte erStMaL und MaKreKi, Mathematikdidaktische Forschung am "Centre for Individual Development and Adaptive Education" (IDeA)* (pp. 245–284). Münster: Waxmann.

Brandt, B., & Höck, G. (2011b). Mathematical joint construction at elementary grade—A reconstruction of collaborative problem solving in dyads. Proceedings of the CERME 7 Conference, Rzeszów, Poland. http://www.cerme7.univ.rzeszow.pl/WG/9/CERME7_WG9_Brandt.pdf. Accessed 28 June 2012.

Carpenter, M., Call, J., & Tomasello, M. (2005). Twelve- and 18-month-olds copy actions in terms of goals. *Developmental Science, 8*(1), 13–20.

Clark, H. H. (1996). *Using language.* Cambridge: University Press.

Cook, S., & Goldin-Meadow, S. (2006). The role of gesture in learning: Do children use their hands to change their minds? *Journal of Cognition and Development, 7*(2), 211–232.

Dörfler, W. (2005). Inskriptionen und mathematische Objekte. Beiträge zum Mathematikunterricht. http://www.mathematik.tu-dortmund.de/ieem/cms/media/BzMU/BzMU2005/Beitraege/doerfler-gdm05.pdf. Accessed 20 Nov 2012.

Eberle, T. S. (1997). Ethnomethodologische Konversationsanalyse. In R. Hitzler & A. Honer (Eds.), *Sozialwissenschaftliche Hermeneutik* (pp. 245–279). Opladen: Leske+Budrich.

Ehrlich, S. B., Levine, C., & Goldin-Meadow, S. (2006). The importance of gesture in children's spatial reasoning. *Developmental Psychology, 42*(6), 1259–1268.

Elia, I., Gagatsis, A., Michael, P., Georgiou, A., & Van den Heuvel-Panhuizen, M. (2011). Kindergartners' use of gestures in the generation and communication of spatial thinking. Proceedings of the CERME 7 Conference, Rzeszów, Poland. http://www.cerme7.univ.rzeszow.pl/WG/13/CERME7_WG13_Elia.pdf. Accessed 20 Nov 2012.

Fricke, E. (2007). *Origo, Geste und Raum. Lokaldeixis im Deutschen.* Berlin: de Gruyter.

Givry, D., & Roth, W.-M. (2006). Toward a new conception of conceptions. Interplay of talk, gestures, and structures in the setting. *Journal of Research in Science Teaching, 43*(10), 1086–1109.

Goffman, E. (1977). *Rahmen-Analyse. Ein Versuch über die Organisation von Alltagserfahrungen.* Frankfurt a. M.: Suhrkamp.

Goldin-Meadow, S. (2003). *Hearing gesture. How our hands help us think.* Cambridge: Belknapp Press of Harvard University Press.

Goss, J. (2010). Free your feet—Free your mind: An analysis of spontaneous coverbal foot gestures. *Proceedings at the 4th conference of the international society of gesture studies ISGS. Gesture—Evolution, Brain and Linguistic Structures,* Frankfurt on the Oder, 302.

Huth, M. (2011a). Das Zusammenspiel von Gestik und Lautsprache in mathematischen Gesprächen von Kindern. In B. Brandt, G. Krummheuer & R. Vogel (Eds.), *Die Projekte erStMaL und MaKreKi, Mathematikdidaktische Forschung am "Centre for Individual Development and Adaptive Education" (IDeA)* (pp. 197–244). Münster: Waxmann.

Huth, M. (2011b). Gestures and speech in mathematical interactions of second graders. Proceedings of the GESPIN Conference, Bielefeld, Germany. http://coral2.spectrum.uni-bielefeld.de/gespin2011/final/Huth.pdf. Accessed 28 June 2012.

Kendon, A. (2004). *Gesture: Visible action as utterance.* Cambridge: University Press.

Krauss, R. M. (1998). Why do we gesture when we speak? *Current Directions in Psychological Science, 7*, 54–59 (pre-editing version).

Krummheuer, G. (1992). *Lernen mit "Format". Elemente einer interaktionistischen Lerntheorie. Diskutiert an Beispielen mathematischen Unterrichts.* Weinheim: Deutscher Studien.

Krummheuer, G. (2011). Die empirisch begründete Herleitung des Beriffs der "Interaktionalen Nische mathematischer Denkentwicklung" (NMD). In B. Brandt, G. Krummheuer & R. Vogel (Eds.), *Die Projekte erStMaL und MaKreKi, Mathematikdidaktische Forschung am "Centre for Individual Development and Adaptive Education" (IDeA)* (pp. 25–90). Münster: Waxmann.

Krummheuer, G. (2012). Die Interaktionsanalyse. In F. Heinzel (Ed.), *Methoden der Kindheitsforschung, 2, 234–247)*, Weinheim: Juventa.

Krummheuer, G., & Brandt, B. (2001). *Paraphrase und Traduktion. Partizipationstheoretische Elemente einer Interaktionstheorie des Mathematiklernens in der Grundschule.* Weinheim, Basel: Beltz Wissenschaft Deutscher Studien.

Krummheuer, G., & Naujok, N. (1999). *Grundlagen und Beispiele Interpretetiver Unterrichtsforschung.* Opladen: Leske+Budrich.

Markowitz, J. (1986). *Verhalten im Systemkontext. Zum Begriff des sozialen Epigramms. Diskutiert am Beispiel des Schulunterrichts.* Suhrkamp: Frankfurt a. M.

McNeill, D. (1992). *Hand and mind. What gestures reveal about thought.* Chicago: University of Chicago Press.

McNeill, D. (2005). *Gesture and thought.* Chicago: University of Chicago Press.

Peirce, C. S. (1931–1935). *Collected papers of Charles Sanders Peirce.* (Vol. I–VI), (ed. by C. Hartshorne & P. Weiss 1931–1935; quotations, as established, according to volume and paragraph). Cambridge, MA: Harvard University Press.

Radford, L. (2009). Why do gestures matter? Sensuous cognition and the palpability of mathematical meanings. *Educational Studies in Mathematics, 70*(3), 111–126.

Sabena, C. (2008). On the semiotics of gestures. In L. Radford, G. Schubring & F. Seeger (Eds.), *Semiotics in mathematics education* (pp. 19–38). Rotterdam: Sense Publishers.

Sager, S. F. (2005). Ein System zur Beschreibung von Gestik. *Nonverbale Kommunikation im Gespräch. Osnabrücker Beiträge zur Sprachtheorie, OBST 70,* 19–47.

Schreiber, C. (2010). *Semiotische Prozess-Karten—Chatbasierte Inskriptionen in mathematischen Problemlöseprozessen. Empirische Studien zur Didaktik der Mathematik.* Münster: Waxmann.

Sfard, A. (2003). There is more to discourse than meets the ears: Looking at thinking as communicating to learn more about mathematical learning. In C. Kieran, E. Forman, & A. Sfard (Eds.), *Learning discourse: Bridging the individual and the social: discursive approaches to research in mathematics education* (pp. 13–57). Dodrecht, Netherlands: Kluwer Academic Press (also published as the special issue of *Educational Studies in Mathematics, 46*(1–3)).

Vogel, R. (2014). Mathematical Situations of Play and Exploration as an Empirical Research Instrument. In: U. Kortenkamp et al. (eds.), *Early Mathematics Learning,* (pp. 223–236). New York: Springer.

Voigt, J. (1984). *Interaktionsmuster und Routinen im Mathematikunterricht. Theoretische Grundlagen und mikroethnographische Falluntersuchungen.* Weinheim und Basel: Beltz.

Wippermann, S., & Vogel, R. (2004). Communicating didactic knowledge in university education—"Didactic Design Patterns" as Best Practices. In L. Cantoni & C. McLoughlin (Eds.), *Proceedings of World Conference on Educational Multimedia, Hypermedia and Telecommunications 2004* (pp. 3231–3234). Chesapeake: AACE.

Chapter 11
Children's Constructions in the Domain of Geometric Competencies (in Two Different Instructional Settings)

Andrea Simone Maier and Christiane Benz

Introduction

In the last couple of years, the importance of early learning has been widely discussed. Research does suggest that early learning is important in order to offer a basic education to all children, but one of the remaining questions is how education for 4- to 6-year-old children should be designed. In Germany alone, there are a number of approaches and concepts as well as new emerging programmes for preschool education, which themselves differ in their promoted way of teaching and learning. Therefore, it is not institutional or rather uniformly clarified if and how the unplanned, purpose-free playing or learning through playing or constructivist learning (Schäfer 2010, 2011; Rigall and Sharpe 2008; Puhani and Weber 2005) should be replaced by systematic, curriculum-based learning or instructional learning (Duncker 2010; Preiß 2006, 2007; Krajewski et al. 2007). On the one hand, there is a demand for protection from schoolification, especially for younger children, but on the other hand it is important to support mathematical competencies before entering school, because we know that they are predictors for later success in mathematics (Schneider 2008; Dornheim 2008), and to avoid existing learning capacities in children being exhausted.

With this in mind, the study at hand investigates the geometric competencies of children from two countries with different concepts of elementary education: Germany (Baden-Württemberg), where learning through play and with this a constructivist view of learning is, at present, the main concept for kindergarten education, and England, where the elementary education is rather systematic, curriculum based and mainly instructive, and where the competencies of the children are tested via *stepping stones* which they should have acquired. There, the children enter school in the year when they have their fifth birthday, but many children go to a reception

---

A. S. Maier (✉) · C. Benz
University of Education, Bismarckstraße 10,
76133, Karlsruhe, Germany
e-mail: benz@ph-karlsruhe.de

U. Kortenkamp et al. (eds.), *Early Mathematics Learning*,
DOI 10.1007/978-1-4614-4678-1_11, © Springer Science+Business Media New York 2014

class before that. So the entering school age is about 2 years earlier than for children in Germany.

The topic of geometry was chosen because there have been fewer studies in this area than, for example, in number and counting, but it is still a very important aspect of mathematics as is illustrated in the following quote:

> No mathematical subject is more relevant than geometry. It lies at the heart of physics, chemistry, biology, geology, and geography, art and architecture. It also lies at the heart of mathematics, though through much of the 20th century the centrality of geometry was obscured by fashionable abstraction. (Sarama and Clements 2009, p. 201)

Moreover, a geometric topic is perfectly suited for the aims of instructive learning as well as for constructive learning, for the children can easily work on their own and explore things—as can be seen, for example, in the pedagogy of Froebel (Heiland 1998; Hoffmann 1982) or Montessori (Heiland 1991; Steenberg 2008)—and also, instructions can be created in a very diversified and interesting manner, for example, by using a variety of materials.

Theoretical Background

The focus of this chapter is on the development of geometric concepts. First, it will be illustrated, what constitutes a concept, before two general theoretical models concerning concept development are presented. Following this, some empirical results concerning the development of geometric concepts are shown, ending with a brief comparison of instructive and constructive teaching methods.

Constitution of a Concept

Franke (2007) defines a concept as follows:

> We speak of a concept, if it not only represents one single object—or incidence and so on—is meant, but a category or a class is associated with it, in which the concrete object can be classified. (Franke 2007, p. 72)

According to Vollrath (1984), a comprehensive conception of geometric shapes, as a concept for objects, is shown to be able to

- Name the shapes,
- Give a definition of the shapes,
- Show further examples of this category and
- Name all properties.

Furthermore, in order to select certain shapes among others, being able to distinguish between examples and non-examples is essential, as was examined in the study by Tirosh et al. (2011).

All these aspects were included in the tasks of the study at hand. Still, it cannot be expected from children in the age of 4–6 to have such a comprehensive concept knowledge as stated by Vollrath.

Conceptualization Theories

Szagun (2008) proposes two theoretical approaches that illustrate how a concept develops. In the *semantic feature hypothesis* (*semantische Merkmals-hypothese*), general features are learnt before specific features. For example, the child has learnt the word *dog,* which is connected with one semantic feature and that is *four-legged*. Accordingly, the child would first call every four-legged animal (horse, cat, mouse, etc.) a dog. With time, other semantic features, such as *barking* are added so that the word *dog* could be distinguished from *cow* for example. The features are either present or not and apply for every member of the class, e.g. *all kinds of dogs belonging to the category "dog" are four-legged and bark*. In contrast, in the *prototype theory* (*Prototypentheorie*), which is considered as a psychologically more real theory, some members of a category are categorized as more typical than the others (Szagun 2008, p. 134). For example, a sparrow is a more typical bird than a chicken, although both belong to the subordinate concept *bird*. In addition to that, not every member of the category *bird* has the same features. Members having a lot of features in common are *prototype members* of the category bird (e.g. sparrow, robin) and members having fewer features in common are periphery members of the category bird (e.g. chicken). However, in order to give a complete picture of what we know of the geometric concept formation, how a concept develops has to be complemented by research findings on geometric concepts.

Empirical Background

In the mathematical domain, research focusing on children's concepts of space and geometric shapes began with the observations of Piaget and Inhelder (1975) and Piaget et al. (1975). Their research findings revealed that children younger than 4 years of age are not able to distinguish a circle, a square and a triangle, but consider all of these shapes as *closed* figures. With the age of 4, the children start to distinguish between curved and straight shapes but not among these classes: for example, a circle is not distinguished from an oval and a square is not distinguished from a rectangle or even a triangle. At the age of 6, the children are able to name and to distinguish between geometric shapes. Since Piaget's studies, several researches have either verified (Laurendau and Pinard 1970) or contradicted (Darke 1982; Lehrer et al. 1998) some or all of the original hypotheses of Piaget (cf. Hannibal and Clements 2008). Some studies reported, for example, that even at an earlier age children were able to distinguish between curvilinear and rectilinear shapes (Lovell 1959; Page 1959). Another body of research has focused on children's reasoning about geometric concepts that they have formed (van Hiele and van Hiele 1986). The van Hieles, who also created a hierarchical developmental description, constitute that on the first level (pre-recognition) before the age of 4, children are not able to capture all features of a geometric shape, instead only parts of the shape can be comprehended and properties cannot be explicitly realized yet. At the end of this level, children can distinguish between curvilinear and rectilinear shapes but not among these groups (in concordance with Piaget). On the next level, the visual level, up to 7 years, shapes are realized as whole entities. The following level, the analytic or descriptive level, is representative for primary school children and goes up to the age of 9/10. The shapes are now distinguished by their properties. Correlations between different classes, e.g. squares and rectangles, cannot be made yet. The other levels concern secondary school and beyond (university level).

Following these developmental models, there were several studies to prove the existence of such levels or the characteristics of such levels (e.g. Burger and Shaughnessy 1986; Gutiérrez et al. 1991; Clements and Battista 1992; Lehrer et al. 1998; Battista 2007). As a common ground, most empirical research confirmed that such levels exist and that they are useful in describing children's geometric concept development but that they are not discrete or independent. Moreover, it is difficult to relate a student to one single level, for students were on different levels for different concepts and exhibited different preferred levels on different tasks (Burger and Shaughnessy 1986; Battista 2007). Thus, the assignment to levels does not seem to be strictly related to age or theme and with this, the hierarchical order of the levels is shaken. Other researches propose that the characteristics of the single levels develop at the same time but in diverse intensity (Clements and Battista 1992; Lehrer 1998).

Apart from this, there have been studies with the single focus on the development of geometric concepts in children (Clements and Battista 1989; Clements et al. 1999; Hannibal and Clements 2008), instead of investigating geometric competencies as a whole. There also have been studies on what visual prototypes and ideas preschool children form about common shapes. Focusing on a few detailed empirical results, Clements et al. (1999) found that children identified circles quite accurately but had some difficulties in selecting squares, for they were less accurate in classifying squares without horizontal sides (Clements 2004, p. 269 f.). They had most difficulties in recognizing triangles and rectangles. The study revealed that children's prototype of a triangle seems to be an isosceles triangle and their prototype of a rectangle seems to be a four-sided figure with two long and two short sides and *close-to* square corners. Square prototypes only occur concerning position and there are no circle prototypes, for they all, except from size, look the same.

Although there have been several studies on the development of geometric concepts in children, there hardly have been any studies yet on this topic regarding different educational settings. The settings in this research differ mainly in the way learning is enhanced. In England, it is clearly defined in the national curriculum what competencies children should have acquired after each key stage. Here, the focus is on the aim of learning (cf. Gasteiger 2010, p. 78). Thus, in the school curricula starting at age 4 at the earliest, there is a focus on instructive aspects of learning in order to ensure a certain learning benefit or outcome. In Germany, there are different concepts and approaches for kindergartens in order to enhance early learning with different focuses: some focus more on instructive aspects and others more on constructive aspects of learning. In the *Orientierungsplan* of Baden-Württemberg, for example, the focus is on using children's ideas and interests in everyday situations and on letting them construct their mathematical ideas, carefully supported by an educator. Still, there are also *training programmes* (cf. Gasteiger 2007, p. 78) for enhancing learning in kindergartens, which are focusing more on instructive aspects of learning, for example, *Mengen, Zählen, Zahlen* meaning, respectively, *quantity, counting, numbers* (Krajewski et al. 2007).

Although the main focus of the study was not to compare different educational settings but much rather to illustrate children's understanding of geometric shapes in the light of different educational settings and with this the learning and teaching methods, these still play a major role for the learning benefits of the children, as is obvious in the results.

The research at hand is a descriptive study to illustrate the understanding of geometric shapes that English and German children in the age of 4–6 years have and how these competencies develop in the course of 1 year. Furthermore, it was examined whether the children of this study could be grouped into a hierarchical stage model or rather into a dynamic developmental model.

Empirical Study

Research Questions

The underlying research questions are:

(1) How do children solve some tasks of geometric conceptualization of shapes and how do they explain their proceeding?
(2) What differences in the development can be described after a year?
(3) Can hypothesis be formulated whether the educational setting, the way how early learning is enhanced, does influence the competencies of the children?

Subjects

The research gathered 81 children, of which 34 are of English nationality and were attending a local primary school, near Winchester. The age of the children in this primary school ranges from 4 to 11 years. The other 47 children were from Germany and attending a kindergarten in Karlsruhe, where children from the age of 3 up to primary school can go. The children participating in this study were from 4 to 6 years old and were all attending the school or correspondingly the kindergarten the entire week.

Method

The study was conducted in the form of clinical interviews, the origins of which coincide with Piaget's early investigations into children's thinking (Ginsburg and Opper 1998). The order of the tasks as well as the material was predetermined but in accordance with the nature of clinical interviews, this order could be altered or complemented if some of the child's answers happened to be interesting or leading into another direction worth being examined. There were altogether two points of investigation, without intervention, one at the beginning of the school year in October 2008 and one at the end of the school year in July 2009.

Tasks

In order to investigate children's knowledge of shapes and to illustrate the concept formation of the children, different tasks were conducted in the interview, of which the following will be presented in this chapter:

(1) Naming, explaining and correlating shapes
(2) Drawing shapes
(3) Identifying and discerning shapes

In the following, the selected tasks presented in this chapter are described:

Naming, Explaining and Correlating Shapes

In this task, the children were shown eight different geometric shapes. In the case of circles and squares, the shapes that were shown varied in their sizes. In the case of rectangles and triangles, there was a more prototypical example (e.g. an equilateral triangle) of the respective shape and a less prototypical example (e.g. a rectangular triangle). They were at first asked to name these shapes and then correlate them to a hole in a scarf, which had the shape of one of the geometric figures. Afterwards, they were asked to explain a triangle *to somebody who has never seen a triangle before.*

11 Children's Constructions in the Domain of Geometric ...

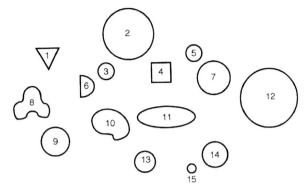

Fig. 11.1 Student marks circles. (In Sarama and Clements 2009, p. 269, from Razel and Eylon 1991)

Drawing Shapes

In order to examine the children's transfer from knowledge about a shape into a representation, they were asked to draw a triangle on a paper (cf. Burger and Shaughnessy 1986, p. 34 f.). Then they were asked to draw another triangle that would be a bit different from the first triangle. After this, again another triangle had to be drawn, differing from the first two. This was continued as long as it appeared to make sense, meaning so long until the child's way of drawing different triangles revealed something of his or her idea of a triangle and of variety. This means that, for example, if the child drew three different triangles and then again the same ones or very similar ones as fourth and fifth triangle, they were not asked to draw any more triangles. Still, all children were asked to draw at least three triangles.

Identifying and Discerning Shapes

Another task giving hints on the conceptualization of the children was a shape-selection task (cf. Burger and Shaughnessy 1989; Clements et al. 1999; Sarama and Clements 2009). The children were asked to *put a mark in each of the shapes that is a circle* on a DIN-A3 page of separate geometric figures (Fig. 11.1). After several shapes were marked, the interviewer asked questions such as the following: "Why did you choose this one?", "How did you know that one was a circle?", "Why did you not choose that one?" A similar procedure was conducted for squares, triangles and rectangles ending with circles and squares in a complex configuration of overlapping forms. The tasks for triangles, rectangles and overlapping forms are not discussed in this chapter.

Results

In the following, the generation of the categories for the evaluation of the results is presented as well as some results the children achieved at both measuring times, distinct by countries.

Table 11.1 Naming shapes

	(1) E	(1) D	(2) E	(2) D	(3) E	(3) D	(4) E	(4) D	(5) E	(5) D	(6) E	(6) D	(7) E	(7) D
2008	0%	9%	9%	5%	18%	28%	0%	37%	0%	70%	14%	0%	59%	0%
2009	0%	14%	3%	2%	9%	28%	0%	16%	0%	81%	24%	0%	68%	7%

Naming Shapes

Starting chronologically, it first will be shown what kind of categories could be generated to describe how children named the shapes. Here, six categories could be distinguished:

(1) Using terms of comparison instead of the correct name of the shape, for example, *like a ball* instead of circle or *like a cupboard* instead of rectangle.
(2) Using terms for solids (3-D shapes) for 2-D shapes, e.g. *cube* instead of square or *cone* instead of triangle.
(3) Mixing up terms, using the wrong 2-D-shape name for another 2-D shape, for example, *square* instead of triangle or *triangle* instead of rectangle.
(4) Using property names instead of the correct shape names, for example, *round* instead of square or *acute* instead of triangle.
(5) Using the generic term (quadrangle) instead of the more specific terms (square or rectangle).
(6) Using geometric terms but not for all the shapes, leaving some shapes out (often the rectangle) or using other ways (see categories before) to name the shape.
(7) Using the geometric terms for each shape. The children were only grouped in this category, if they named all the shapes with the respective geometric term.

In Table 11.1, it is illustrated how high the amount of children was for each category. For the children could be grouped to several categories at the same time, it is possible that the total percentage in each country is more than 100%. For example, if they used comparisons as well as geometric terms, they were grouped into these two categories. If the total percentage is less than 100%, this is due to the fact that some children did only use the geometric term for each shape but did not name all the shapes.

How do children name the shapes?

There were several readily discernible trends in the children's developing understanding of shape concepts. The usage of comparative terms (cat. 1) only occurred among the German children and the usage of correct geometric terms for each shape (cat. 7) occurred only (2008) or more often (2009) in England. Only German children used the generic term *Viereck* (*quadrangle*) (cat. 5), which is not frequently used in colloquial English.

As previous studies revealed (e.g. Burger and Shaughnessy 1986; Clements et al. 1999; Razel and Eylon 1991), it was more likely that the children named circles with the correct geometric term than squares, triangles and rectangles (see Table 11.2).

11 Children's Constructions in the Domain of Geometric ...

Table 11.2 Naming shapes

	circle		circle		square		square	
	D	E	D	E	D	E	D	E
2008	74%	97%	72%	100%	63%	88%	65%	88%
2009	86%	94%	81%	97%	84%	97%	70%	94%

	rectangle		rectangle		triangle		triangle	
	D	E	D	E	D	E	D	E
2008	33%	76%	30%	74%	67%	94%	53%	79%
2009	51%	91%	67%	88%	81%	94%	70%	74%

Table 11.3 Explaining shapes

	(A)		(B)		(C)		(D)		(E)	
	E	D	E	D	E	D	E	D	E	D
2008	12%	23%	6%	21%	6%	9%	9%	30%	62%	16%
2009	0%	23%	3%	7%	15%	21%	21%	49%	62%	14%

Explaining Triangles

Following the naming task, the children were asked to explain how a triangle looks like. For the explanations of the children, again several categories could be found (Table 11.3):

(A) no explanation given
(B) gestures used to explain a shape (the gestures were always applied correctly)
(C) correct comparisons used to explain the shapes
(D) correct informal ways of explaining used
(E) correct formal ways of explaining used

How do children explain the shapes?

If we summarize the research findings of this task, it becomes obvious that English children gave more often an explanation or characterization of a triangle than the German children. The latter ones used more gestures at the first point of investigation and more comparisons at the second point of investigation, like "this has the

Table 11.4 Drawing triangles

	Cat. 1		Cat. 2		Cat. 3		Cat. 4		Cat. 5		Cat. 6		Cat. 7		Cat. 8	
	E	D	E	D	E	D	E	D	E	D	E	D	E	D	E	D
2008	50%	49%	15%	9%	29%	21%	18%	7%	6%	5%	6%	7%	0%	9%	3%	3%
2009	71%	44%	24%	28%	9%	21%	12%	14%	9%	12%	6%	12%	0%	9%	3%	3%

shape of a tent or the hat of a witch". Additionally, there was a bigger tendency in Germany to explain in an informal way, meaning that they tried to explain a shape by its properties but lacked words, such as *side, corner* or *straight* or *acute*. The majority of the English children explained the shapes in a formal way, for example, *a triangle is a shape with three straight sides and three corners*. However, most English children who did not know a formal description did not try to explain the shape in another way.

Drawing Shapes

The drawings of the children were thoroughly examined and after several scans and discussions, the following seven categories for the drawings of the children were generated. Here, each child was related to at least one category, but it could also be that their drawings fit into more categories. Therefore, the overall percentages could be higher than 100% in the end (Table 11.4).

Category 1: *Area*—Child draws triangles in different sizes (but similar angles and all in an upward position).
Category 2: *Angular dimension*—Child draws triangles with different angles (from very acute ones to obtuse ones).
Category 3: *Shape*—Child draws different shapes (correct ones and "own inventions", e.g. with wavy sides).
Category 4: *Identity*—Child draws the same or similar triangle again and again.
Category 5: *Position*—Child draws triangles in different positions and directions.
Category 6: *Combination*—Child draws triangles that differ in size, area, angular size and position.
Category 7: *Objects from everyday life*—Child draws objects from everyday life having geometric shapes (for example, road signs).
Category 8: *Other examples*—Child draws a shape that is missing some critical attributes of a triangle, for example, a third side.

How do children draw different triangles?

To summarize the findings of this task, having especially in mind the concept formation of the children, it became obvious that most children connected with *different* triangles, triangles that differ in their area dimension but are all pointing upwards and are most of the time equilateral. There were more English children who drew triangles in that category; the English children drew more triangles varying in their shapes (the first triangles were usually correct ones but then other shapes, similar to triangles but, for example, with wavy sides, were drawn), but later there were more German children drawing triangles in that category. Only in England it occurred that the explanation of the triangles did not fit the actual drawing. A triangle was explained, for example, as *having three straight sides,* but in the drawings a shape with three corners and three wavy sides was described as triangle as well, just as a *different* triangle. Triangles as part of the geometric solids in the everyday life (e.g. street signs or tents instead of a simple triangle shape) were only drawn by the German children.

Identifying and Discerning Shapes

A few of the research findings at the shape-selection task are, for example, that the majority of the children in both countries could distinguish circles from non-circles correctly. Still, the children often also marked the oval shape as a circle. At the second point of investigation, there were slightly more German children (84%) than English children (76%) who marked all the correct circles and no other shapes.

According to this, in the square-selection task, there were also more German children (especially at the second point of investigation: 44%) who marked all the correct squares than English children (21%), of which most children only marked horizontal lying squares. After the children explained their selection, they often argued that "if you turn a square it becomes a diamond".

To summarize, concerning the conceptualization of the children, which were examined at the beginning and end of a school year, the following key statements can be made:

(1) In most of the tasks, German children did improve in their conceptualizations, although they were not formally instructed.
(2) The concepts of the English children were—in the majority of tasks—more prototype determined at the end of the school year than at the beginning of the school year.
(3) The competencies of the children in this research cannot be grouped into a hierarchical stage model for the children apply competencies of different stages for different tasks and children of the same age apply competencies of different stages depending on the task.

Discussion

To discuss the research findings, the differences are reflected and possible influences of the different educational settings will be hypothesized. Only the German children used terms of comparison in order to name a shape, for they were not instructed the correct concept yet and consequently had to construct their own ideas of how to name the shapes and to try to find words they connect with these shapes. Fifty-nine per cent of the English children at the first and 68 % at the second point of investigation used the correct geometric terms for each shape which is clearly due to the instruction in school. Still, using different terms could also be due to cultural differences, for example, in Germany the word "quadrangle" is colloquially often used, which is not the case in England. There, the specific terms "square" and "rectangle" are used most of the time and quadrangle is colloquially hardly ever used. When children do not know the correct concept, they try to find other logical names for the shapes, as the German children did more frequently.

The reason why English children were more eager to explain the shapes is probably because they are advanced in school to do so. They were already taught the definitions of familiar shapes and thus were able to recite them to a high degree (62 %) in the study. Most of the children there gave, for example, a formal definition of a triangle like "a triangle has three corners and three straight sides", exactly what they are taught in school, for one goal of the foundation stage curriculum is that children should be able to name and explain shapes correctly. Comprehensive definitions, like "a plane figure with three straight sides and three angles" (Oxford Dictionary) or "a flat shape with three straight sides and three angles" (Longman Dictionary), were never given, and statements like "three corners and three sides" were also counted to be correct, although the detail "straight" was missing. In the case of not knowing a definition, the English children were more likely to say nothing at all than the German children, who *made up* their own ways of explaining the shapes, through gestures, comparisons or informal explanations (using *own words* or even *made up words*) for they were not yet familiar with the correct terms because of not being instructed in the same way as the English children were.

However, as was shown before, although the children knew a correct verbal description of a concept, they sometimes had difficulty applying the verbal description correctly. This was, for example, shown in the drawing-shapes task, where the children drew all kinds of triangles, sometimes with *rocky* or *wavy* sides, although giving a perfect definition of a triangle where a triangle is described to have *three straight sides*. In the light of this finding, it should be thoroughly considered whether the construction in school could be either more extensive or completed by some constructivist activity of the children in order to explore the shapes on their own and to find out what constitutes, for example, the properties of a triangle and how the definition is linked to its representatives.

In the shape-selection task, it cannot be said whether the results here could be linked to an instructive or constructive way of teaching and learning. Still, the German children performed better in marking circles and squares as well as to some extent in marking rectangles. The English children performed better in marking triangles which clearly revealed that they are more familiar with what constitutes a triangle and what does not, presumably due to the instruction in school.

Still another influence for the concept formation that should not be left out is the material that is used in the single institutions. One reason why the English children might only describe a horizontal lying square as a square and one that stands on one of its corners as *a diamond* and not a square anymore could be the illustrations in the classroom, only showing squares in horizontal position. The reason why they preferred marking equal-sided triangles as triangles might be because the material they use for exercising only have equal-sided triangles.

Therefore, it can be concluded that the input if and how they are instructed as well as the material that is used influence the concept formation of the children.

Conclusion

Still, the question that remains is when would be the best time to actively support the children's geometric concept formation and how should this be done in order to help them to develop a comprehensive knowledge about shapes. This is not easily to be answered. Research indicates that a lot of educational materials introduce children "to triangles, rectangles and squares overwhelmingly in limited, rigid ways" (Sarama and Clements 2009, p. 216) as was assumed in the research as well, and moreover that such prototypes can rule children's thinking throughout their lives (cf. Burger and Shaughnessy 1986; Fuys et al. 1988; Vinner and Heshkowitz 1980). As the results in the study at hand also suggest, there might be a connection between the way how concepts are introduced and the perception the children acquire of each shape or correspondingly what kind of prototypes determine their perception. Consequently, teachers as well as kindergarten educators should be aware of the variety of representatives of a certain shape and let them explain what properties a shape needs to have in order to be called *a triangle* for example. An isolated memorizing of definitions is seen to be critical and more emphasis should be placed on being able to connect a concept with many representatives as examples. There are findings that one can have a correct verbal description of a concept and possess a specific visual image (or concept image) associated strongly with the concept, but still might have difficulty applying the verbal description correctly (Sarama and Clements 2009, p. 213). Altogether, the study reveals that a formal instruction might lead to a higher percentage of children acquiring geometric terms as well as formal definitions, but also to a more prototype-determined perception. So, if we think in terms of instruction of this mathematical content, it should be created in a way that children have the chance to construct a comprehensive concept of shapes and also not putting aside the constructive way of learning, for it enhances the creativity of the children. To conclude, the best way is probably to balance an instructive and a constructive teaching and learning method, as it is stated in Presmeg (2012) "a dance between construction and instruction".

References

Battista, M. T. (2007). The development of geometric and spatial thinking. In: F. K. Lester (Ed.), *Second handbook of research of mathematics teaching and learning: a project of the National Council of Teachers of Mathematics* (2nd ed.). Charlotte: Information Age.

Burger, W. F., & Shaughnessy, J. M. (1986). Characterizing the van hiele levels of development in geometry. *Journal for Research in Mathematics Education, 17*(1), 31–48 (Published by: National Council of Teachers of Mathematics).

Clements, D. H. (2004). Geometric and spatial thinking in early childhood education. In: D. H. Clements & J. Sarama (Eds.). Engaging young children in mathematics. Mahwah: Lawrence Erlbaum Associates.

Clements, D. H., & Battista, M. T. (1989). Learning of geometric concepts in a Logo environment. *Journal for Research in Mathematics Education, 20*, 450–467.

Clements, D. H., & Battista, M. T. (1992). Geometry and spatial reasoning. In: D. A. Grouws (Ed.). Handbook of research on mathematics teaching and learning. A project of the National Council of Teachers of Mathematics. New York: Macmillan.

Clements, D. H., Swaminathan, S., Zeitler Hannibal, M. A., & Sarama, J. (1999). Young children's concepts of shape. *Journal for Research on Mathematics Education, 30*(2), 192–212.

Darke, I. (1982). A review of research related to the topological primacy thesis. *Educational Studies in Mathematics, 13*, 119–142.

Dornheim, D. (2008). *Prädiktion von Rechenleistung und Rechenschwäche: Der Beitrag von Zahlen-Vorwissen und allgemein-kognitiven Fähigkeiten*. Berlin: Logos.

Duncker, L. (2010). Methodisch-systematisches Lernen im Kindergarten? Thesen zu einem schwierigen Balanceakt. In: G. E. Schäfer, R. Staege, & K. Meiners (Eds.). *Kinderwelten—Bildungswelten. Unterwegs zu Frühpädagogik*. Berlin: Cornelsen.

Franke, M. (2007). *Didaktik der Geometrie in der Grundschule—Mathematik Primar- und Sekundarstufe* (2nd ed.). München: Spektrum Verlag.

Fuys, D., Geddes, D., & Tischler, R. (1988). The van Hiele model of thinking in Geometry among adolescents. *Journal for Research in Mathematics Education Education Monograph Series, 3*.

Gasteiger, H. (2010). *Elementare mathematische Bildung im Alltag der Kindertagesstätte: Grundlegung und Evaluation eines kompetenzorientierten Förderansatzes*. Münster, u.a.: Waxmann.

Ginsburg, H.P., & Opper, S. (1998). *Piagets Theorie der geistigen Entwicklung* (8th ed.). Stuttgart: Klett Cotta.

Gutiérrez, A., Jaime, A., & Fortuny, J.M. (1991). An alternative paradigm to evaluate the aquisition of the van Hiele levels. *Journal for Research in Mathematics Education, 22*(3), 237–251.

Hannibal, M. A. Z., & Clements, D. H. (2008). Young children's developing understanding of basic geometric shapes. *Teaching Children Mathematics, 5*(6), 353–357 (Focus issue: Geometry and geometric thinking (February 1999)).

Heiland, H. (1991). *Maria Montessori*. Reinbek: rororo Monographien.

Heiland, H. (1998). *Die Spielpädagogik Friedrich Fröbels*. Hildesheim: Olms.

Hoffmann, E. (ed.). (1982). *Friedrich Fröbel: Die Spielgaben*. Stuttgart: Klett.

Krajewski, K., Nieding, G., & Schneider, W. (2007). *Mengen, zählen, Zahlen. Handreichung zur Durchführung der Förderung*. Berlin: Cornelsen.

Laurendau, M., & Pinard, A. (1970). *The development of the concept of space in the child*. New York: International Universities Press.

Lehrer, R., Jenkins, M., & Osana, H. (1998). Longitudinal study of children's reasoning about space and geometry. In R. Lehrer & D. Chazan (Eds.). *Designing learning environments for developing understanding of geometry and space*. Mahwah: Lawrence Erlbaum Associates.

Lovell, K. (1959). A follow-up study of some aspects of the work of Piaget and Inhelder on the child's conception of space. *British Journal of Educational Psychology, 29*, 104–117.

Page, E. I. (1959). Haptic perception. A consideration of one of the Investigations of Piaget and Inhelder. *Educational Review, 11*, 115–124.

Piaget, J., & Inhelder, B. (1975). *Die Entwicklung des räumlichen Denkens beim Kinde*. Stuttgart: Ernst Klett.
Piaget, J., Inhelder, B., & Szeminska, A. (1975). *Die natürliche Geometrie des Kindes* (1st ed.). Stuttgart: Ernst Klett.
Preiß, G. (2006). *Guten morgen, liebe Zahlen. Eine Einführung in die "Entdeckungen im Zahlenland"*. Kirchzarten: Klein Druck.
Preiß, G. (2007). *Leitfaden Zahlenland 1. Verlaufspläne für die Lerneinheit 1 bis 10 der "Entdeckungen im Zahlenland"*. Kirchzarten: Klein Druck.
Presmeg, N. (2012). A dance of instruction with construction in mathematics education. http://cermat.org/poem2012/main/proseedings_files/Presmeg-POEM2012.pdf. Accessed 12 July 2012.
Puhani, P. A., & Weber, A. M. (2005). *Does the early bird catch the worm? Bericht Nr. 151*. Darmstadt: Arbeitspapiere für Volkswirtschaftslehre.
Razel, M., & Eylon, B.-S. (1991). Developing mathematics readiness in young children with the Agam Program. Paper presented at the meeting of the Fifteenth Conference of the International Group for the Psychology of Mathematics Education, Genova, Italy.
Rigall, A., & Sharpe, C., (2008). *The structure of primary education: England and other countries* (Primary Review Research Survey 9/1). Cambridge: University of Cambridge Faculty of Education.
Sarama, J., & Clements, D. H. (2009). *Early childhood mathematics education research. Learning trajectories for young children*. New York: Routledge.
Schäfer, G. E. (Ed.). (2010). *Frühkindliche Lernprozesse verstehen: ethnographische und phänomenologische Beiträge zur Bildungsforschung*. Weinheim: Juventa-Verlag.
Schäfer, G. E. (2011). *Bildungsprozesse im Kindesalter: Selbstbildung, Erfahrung und Lernen in der frühen Kindheit* (4th ed.). Weinheim: Juventa-Verlag.
Schneider, W. (2008). *Entwicklung von der Kindheit bis zum Erwachsenalter: Befunde der Münchner Längsschnittstudie LOGIK*. Weinheim: Beltz.
Steenberg, U. (2008). *Montessori—Pädagogik im Kindergarten*. Freiburg: Herder.
Szagun, G. (2008). *Sprachentwicklung beim Kind. Ein Lehrbuch* (2nd ed.). Weinheim: Beltz.
Tirosh, D., Tsamir, P., Tabach, M., Levenson, E., & Barkai, R. (2011). Geometrical knowledge and geometrical self-efficacy among abused and neglected kindergarten children. *sciEd: Scientific Journal for Science and Mathematics Educational Research, 2*(1), 23–36.
Van Hiele, P., & Van Hiele, D. (1986). *Structure and insight: A theory of mathematics education*. New York: Academic Press, Inc.
Vinner, S., & Heshkowitz, R. (1980). Concept images and common cognitive paths in the development of some simple geometric concepts. In R. Karplus (Ed.), Proceedings of the Fourth International Conference for the Psychology of Mathematics Education (pp. 177–184). Berkeley: Lawrence Hall of Science, University of California.

Chapter 12
Identifying quantities—Children's Constructions to Compose Collections from Parts or Decompose Collections into Parts

Christiane Benz

Introduction

Identifying quantities of collections is a well-accepted mathematical content in early childhood education. Many pre-school teachers think immediately of the process of counting every single item as a way to determine the quantity of the representation of the collection. Therefore, pre-school teachers think that one main part of their instructions in early childhood education should be to support children to develop counting competences (Benz 2010, 2012). The acquirement of counting principles (Gelman and Gallistel 1978) reveals both the aspect of instruction and the aspect of construction in early childhood mathematics. Learning the number words of the counting sequence is not possible without any instruction. However, without their own constructions, children cannot develop the different counting principles. Counting is an important competence, which can be seen as a milestone in the arithmetical learning process. However, counting is not the only way to determine quantities, as we can see below. There are different processes possible, which are based on children's constructions of perceiving or determining quantities. If we analyse the different processes, which can be used for identifying quantities of representations, it becomes clear that there are other valuable competences and constructions which should be in the focus too. In this chapter, children's constructions of different kind of processes in identifying quantities will be analysed. The insights in the children's construction shall provide a basis for instruction in terms of realizing and using learning opportunities and creating learning environments within mathematical early childhood education.

C. Benz (✉)
University of Education, Karlsruhe, Germany
e-mail: benz@ph-karlsruhe.de

Theoretical Background—Different Processes to Identify the Quantities of Collections

In order to describe different aspects and competences in identifying quantities of representations of concrete objects, here we will theoretically distinguish between two different steps (Benz 2011; Steffe and Cobb 1988):

- Step 1: The process of perception of the representation of the quantity.
- Step 2: The process of judgement or determination of the whole quantity of the collection.

The first step—the process of perception—will be discerned in three different kinds of perception and then the various processes of determination will be assigned. (see Table 12.1), First, the collection can be seen as a conglomerate of lots of separate single objects as one possibility of perception, the quantity can be seen also as a whole or as a composition of different parts. Then, there are different possibilities to determine the quantity: counting, knowing or calculating.

If the quantity is perceived as lots of different single items, the process of determination can be done through counting every single item. However, the collection can also be perceived as single items and simultaneously the quantity can be determined. Researchers speak about subitizing, spontaneous subitizing, perceptual subitizing or simultaneous recognizing. This means, "recognizing a number without consciously using other mental or mathematical processes and then naming it" (Clements and Sarama 2009, p. 44). Still, there are different theories about the mental processes which are behind the ability to subitize, but "regardless of the precise mental processes, subitizing appears to be phenomenologically distinct from counting and other means of quantification" (Clements and Sarama 2009, p. 44). For subitizing, the process of perception and determination seems to be one act. Even if research results vary regarding how many objects can be subitized at once, no one speaks about subitizing of a set of more than six objects (Clements and Sarama 2009). So, the process of subitizing is limited to a small number of objects. Some research suggests that sets with more than three objects will be decomposed and recomposed without the person being aware of the process (Clements and Sarama 2009, p. 45).

If the collection is perceived as a whole figure and the figure is recognized immediately because it is well known or memorized, like dice or finger patterns, some researchers speak also of subitizing. But it is not sure if the children are indeed aware of the quantity of the single items of this arrangement and if this representation is a composition of different parts (like 4 and 1). They could also just have learnt the "name" of the figure without being aware of the quantity (von Glasersfeld 1987, p. 261).

Next, to perceive the quantity as a whole entity, there is another way of perception of a quantity. A set of collections can be decomposed through structuring this collection and identifying different parts in this collection. The idea of structuring and decomposing a representation in different parts can lead to different ways to

12 Identifying quantities—Children's Constructions ...

Table 12.1 Different processes in identifying the quantity of a collection

Step 1: Process of perception	Step 2: Process of determination
Perception of the quantity as every single item	*Counting* every single object—counting all
	Knowing for sets with quantities up to 3–4 on the basis of subitizing (perceptual subitizing)
Perception of the quantity as a whole	*Knowing* because the figure or pattern of the representation is already known (e.g. dice patterns up to 6 or finger patterns) on the basis of subitizing (perceptual subitizing)
Perception of the quantity as a composition of different parts	*Counting* every single object
Identifying the parts	*Counting* on
Structuring the quantity in substructures or in different parts	*Calculating* the result
Parts can be perceived as single items	*Knowing* the result
Parts can be perceived as a whole	

determine the quantity of a collection. After identifying different substructures or parts, still every item can be counted. Another possibility is to perceive one or two parts of the substructures with subitizing and then counting every item or counting only the second part and starting with the quantity of the first part or knowing the result.

The mental act of decomposing a collection in its constituent parts can also be described as identifying, seeing, perceiving or creating a structure in the collection so that different parts or substructures can be identified. Sometimes, the arrangement of the objects or the spatial structure of the collection can lead to the grouping but still the identification of the structure is an individual constructive act (Söbbeke 2005). Structuring a quantity into different parts or substructures is seen as a powerful mathematical activity. In previous research and mathematical theories, different reasons for supporting the perception of structures and the ability of decomposing a collection into parts are evident and will be discussed in the next paragraph.

The Importance of Perception of Structures—Decomposing a Collection into Parts

In terms of a part–whole understanding, decomposing a quantity into parts or substructures is an important ability. Resnick (1983) points out that an interpretation of numbers in terms of part and whole relationships is very important. She mentions that a primitive form of part–whole reasoning occurs in early counting routines when children are able to maintain a partition on a collection of items: those items already counted and those items yet to be counted. She proposes that later on the basis of this basic part–whole schema, a quantitative part–whole schema will be established, which can be observed when dividing a collection into parts. Gaidoschik

(2010) and Young-Loveridge (2002) point out the connection between the structuring of a collection of items and the development of a quantitative part–whole understanding. The quantitative part–whole understanding is to be seen as one important component for building mental calculation strategies, another important step in school (Gaidoschik 2010; Gerster and Schulz 2004).

The competences in part–whole understanding and the competence of perception of structured quantities are—next to advanced counting competences—evaluated as predictors for arithmetical competences in year 2 (Dornheim 2008). The particular relevance of identifying structures in collections of quantities was also investigated by Mulligan et al. in the project Awareness of Mathematical Pattern and Structure (AMPS) (Mulligan et al. 2010). They were able to show that children who are low achievers in mathematics had problems perceiving structures in visual representations (Mulligan 2002). A general connection between awareness of structures and pattern and mathematical abilities is stated by Mulligan and Mitchelmore (2009, p. 35).

A link between spatial structuring abilities of children aged 4–6 years and developing number sense is suggested by van Nes (2009). She investigated spatial structuring ability in different tasks with 38 children aged 4–6 years and postulated four phases in spatial structuring ability. In these phases, she also focused on the ability to produce structures in unordered quantities with reference to determination of quantities. Lueken (2010) interviewed 74 first graders (aged 5 years 8 months to 7 years 2 months) at the beginning of school with a semi-structured interview about early structure sense. The interview contained tasks in visual, tactile and audio patterns and asked for explanations and reproduction of structured didactical material which is used in primary school like a ten-chain and the twenty-field. The results of Lueken's study showed that there is a correlation between early structure sense and mathematical competences, tested with the standardized OTZ test 3 months before the children entered school. She also showed that an early structure sense can be seen as a predictor for mathematical achievement at the end of year 2.

These theoretical and empirical studies show evidence for the relevance of identifying structures in representations and the connection with children's arithmetical development. Many researchers of these studies indicate that their research is done with a small group of children in special settings, thus the analyses are rather exploratory than confirmatory and offer only trends. They lead to further research questions

Research Questions

In most of the reported studies, the abilities to structure small quantities were tested mainly by reproducing structured representation or by determining their quantity when the representations were shown only for a short time to the children. This made it necessary to use subitizing for determining the quantity of parts or the whole. The memory can also play an additional role because the different parts must be memorized for determination.

Considering the difference between the processes of perception and determination of quantities (see Table 12.1), this study will be focused on the process of perception of quantities. Therefore, we will investigate children's constructions at the age of 4–6 years, if and how they perceive (de)composition or structures of quantities in representations as a help for determination. This leads to the following research questions:

1. *Do pre-school children perceive arranged structures in collections and can they use this perception to determine the quantity?*
2. *Do pre-school children use the idea of decomposing or structuring a collection into parts to create a representation of a collection so that they can easily see how many objects are there? What kind of structures do they use?*

Most of structured didactical material which is used later on in school for instruction is designed with structures of parts of 5 and 10 in order to enable children to (de)compose quantities easily for perception. This kind of structure is an important structure in terms of perception for numbers up to 100. Because perception of structures even in structured representations is an individual act, a third research question will be raised with reference to the idea on building further competences on informal strategies:

3. *What kind of structures do children use or perceive in a ten-frame to represent a collection so that it can be easily seen how many objects are presented?*

To answer children's constructions in perceiving and using structures, the following study was conducted.

Design

Although it was planned to interview only children at age 4–6, some younger children were asked to be interviewed as well, so they were included in the study. Altogether 189 children at the age of 3–6, all attending German kindergarten, were interviewed individually. In the interview, they had to solve different tasks. To answer the research questions above, the analyses of three tasks of the interview were selected.

To investigate the first research question—do children at the age of 3–6 perceive arranged structures in representations of quantities and can they use this perception to determine the quantity—a task of the study of Gasteiger (2010) was chosen. Here, the children were given cards with blue and red dots. The blue dots were structured (line above in Fig. 12.1) and the red dots were without structures (line at the bottom in Fig. 12.1).

Then, the children were asked to find a card with blue dots that corresponds to a card with red dots: *For every blue card there is a red card. Do you have an idea, which of these cards belong together?* This question does not address the perception of structures directly. With this question, it is investigated if children focus on

Fig. 12.1 Task "Grouped Quantities"

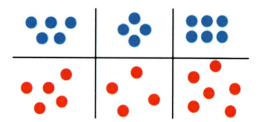

the aspect of quantity in general. The children had to identify the quantity so that they could reflect about the process of perception. If the children did focus on the aspect of quantity and tried to make pairs with the same quantity, they were asked: *On which cards could you identify easier how many dots there are?* Then, they were asked to explain their opinion. The children could take as much time as they needed.

With the second task, the children's ability to decompose a quantity into parts was investigated in a reversible way. Therefore, it was examined if children at the age of 3–6 already use the idea of decomposing or structuring a collection into parts to create a representation of a collection so that other people can easily see how many objects there are. It also was investigated what kind of structures the children used. First, the children were asked to create a collection with seven counters so that another person can easily see how many items there are. Then, they were asked why they think it can be easily seen how many counters are on the table.

The collections were categorized in different categories. If the children put the counters in a row so that no decomposition was clearly shown, then it was categorized as *not structured into parts,* also if they created a circle. If any decomposition into parts could be seen so that someone had the chance to determine the quantity without counting every single item, then it was categorized as *structured representation.*

In order to see what kind of structures young children see and use when they deal with structured material of formal school mathematics, the children were also asked to sort five eggs in an egg carton. In Germany, egg cartons usually contain six or ten eggs. We used a carton for ten eggs because it is equivalent to the didactical material of a ten-frame (Gerster and Schultz 2004). Here, the children are forced to use the structure of the ten-frame. Still, it was in our interest to investigate the children's constructions: how they "use" the structure to create quantities which can be seen easily, whether they can explain afterwards if and how they used the structure of the ten-frame for (de)composition. They were asked to put five eggs in a carton so that it can be easily seen and then to explain their representation. In the analysis, the structures are described. To categorize the explanations, it was investigated if and what kind of structure or (de)composition the children referred to.

The interviews were conducted in two parts to avoid too much strain on the children. The children could stop the interview at any time, thus not every task was solved by every child. All tasks were posed in the same order. The interviewers took care to ask the children also whether they could explain why they solved the task in the way they did. The solving process was videotaped and transcribed. Later on, a qualitative and quantitative analyses of the solutions and explanations were undertaken. The results of these analyses will be presented in the following section.

Results

Perception of Structures as a Help for Determination Quantities

As it can be seen in Fig. 12.2, 67% of the children made pairs with the same quantity correctly. Eleven percent of the children tried to make pairs with the same quantity but not every pair was correct. Nine percent of the children made pairs on the basis of other criteria (like "nice–not nice"). Thirteen percent of the children did not deal with the task; (e.g. they had no idea or said, "I cannot do that").

It can be stated that many children (78%) between the age of 3 and 6 see quantity as a criteria for correspondence and that they can make right correspondences in terms of same quantity.

Table 12.2 illustrates what it looks like if the children are divided into age groups.

With increasing age, the children perceive quantities rather as criteria for correspondence. Also, with increasing age the number of correct pairs of the same quantity rises.

If the children did focus on the aspect of quantity and tried to make pairs with the same quantity, they were asked: *On which cards could you identify easier how many dots there are?*

If we look only at the children who dealt with that task in terms of focusing on the same quantity, it can be stated that 75% of the children who focused on the same quantity responded that they could identify the quantity easier at the grouped representations. Sixteen percent of the children who focused on the same quantity preferred representations without arranged structures, and 9% of the children who focused on the same quantity did not see any difference.

Then, the children were asked to explain their decision:

Twenty-seven percent of the children who focused on the same quantity gave explanations, which did not refer to the arrangement or structure like *I can already paint dots*. Some of them made a connection to colours like *Blue is my favourite colour* or *I wear a blue T-shirt*.

Fifty-four percent of the children who focused on the same quantity did refer in their explanations to the structure in the representations. Different aspects of the arrangements are described:

- Structure in general
  The red cards are disordered
  The blue ones were easier painted
  The blue cards are more correct
- Dice pattern
  The 4 and the 6 look like a correct 4 and 6
- Describing the structure—Quantity of the parts
  (Card with four dots): *2 and 2*
  (Card with five dots): *If you look skewed, you can see 2 and 2 and then 1*

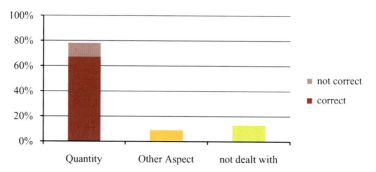

Fig. 12.2 Aspects of correspondence

Table 12.2 Aspects of correspondence—children at different age groups

Age of children (year; month)	N	Pairs of same quantity		Other correspondence	Not dealt with
		Correct	Not Correct		
3;6–3;11	8	3 (37.5%)	–	3 (37.5%)	2 (25%)
4;0–4;11	74	44 (60%)	10 (13%)	6 (8%)	14 (19%)
5;0–5;11	87	63 (72%)	10 (12%)	5 (6%)	9 (10%)
6;0–6;11	20	16 (80%)	1 (5%)	1 (5%)	2 (10%)

(Card with five dots): *Because on the bottom there are 3 and above there a 2*
(Card with six dots): *Here are 3 and here are 3 too*

The results show that pre-school children can already perceive structures in representations and they can use them to determine quantities. However, for interpreting these results in terms of ability to decompose a collection into parts through structuring, it must be considered that the cards with the four and the six dots are very similar to dice patterns. It cannot be stated clearly if they perceive these collections of quantities as a structured composition of different parts or as a whole figure which they recognize again as memorized pictures or figures (von Glasersfeld 1987). Thus, for the next task, the quantity of seven counters was chosen so that not only one dice pattern as a whole figure could be reproduced.

Structures Used to Create Representations

The children were asked to create a representation with seven counters so that they can easily see how many objects there are. All the counters had the same colour so that a composition only can be demonstrated through spatial structures. The children were not given seven counters; they first had to count seven counters out of a bowl with many counters (Table 12.3 and 12.4).

12 Identifying quantities—Children's Constructions ...

Table 12.3 Representations which can be seen easily

		Structured representation	Not structured into parts	Wrong quantity represented	Not dealt with
All children	189	108 (57%)	43 (23%)	22 (12%)	16 (8%)
Age of children (year; month)					
3;6–3;11	8	3 (37.5%)	4 (50%)	–	1 (12.5%)
4;0–4;11	74	34 (46%)	14 (19%)	14 (19%)	12 (16%)
5;0–5;11	87	56 (64%)	21 (24%)	7 (8%)	3 (4%)
6;0–6;11	20	15 (75%)	4 (20%)	1 (5%)	–

Table 12.4 Structures of five eggs in an egg carton

		Five in a row	●●● ●●	●●●● ●	Other structures	Wrong quantity	Not dealt with
All Children	189	77 (41%)	66 (35%)	12 (6%)	10 (5%)	8 (4%)	16 (9%)
Age							
3;6–3;11	8	1 (12.5%)	1 (12.5%)	–	–	–	6 (75%)
4;0–4;11	74	35 (47%)	24 (32%)	1 (1%)	2 (3%)	5 (7%)	7 (10%)
5;0–5;11	87	37 (43%)	33 (38%)	7 (8%)	4 (5%)	3 (3%)	3 (3%)
6;0–6;11	20	4 (15%)	8 (45%)	4 (20%)	4 (20%)	–	–

Here, the same tendency can be seen as with the first question. Many children, especially the 5- and 6-year-old children, already used a structure to create a representation which can easily be seen. They decomposed the collections in different parts.

Most children used a composition of the dice pattern of 6 and then placed one counter next to the dice pattern. Here, I do not distinguish the different possible orientations.

(Number of children who created this representation is in brackets)

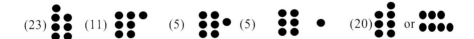

Most of the children (51) explained their (de)composing with explanations like *One more than six*. For the last representation in this line, the children gave different explanations because they used different structures. A total of 7 of the 20 children explained their representation as a composition of 6 and 1, and 13 children saw a substructure of 3 and 4.

The structure of 3 and 4 could be seen with other representations too, whereas the 3 and the 4 were represented differently. They sometimes used the dice pattern for 4 but no child used the dice pattern for 3:

Altogether 24 children used the composition of 3 and 4. The composition of dice patterns of 5 and 2 was created by 12 children. Other representations, which were used quite frequently, divided the dice pattern of 6 into rows and then one point was put between the rows:

Nine children placed the counters so that the digit was represented:

Here, the children did not use the idea of structuring a quantity but rather the idea of using digits to describe quantities which is an obvious solution for the task.

In this chapter, not all compositions are reported but only the most frequent compositions.

Summing up, it can be stated that children at pre-school age are able to decompose representations of quantities in different parts to facilitate for other people the perception of the quantity, whereupon in most of the structured representation, dice patterns were used in some way.

Different Perceptions of Structures in Structured Material

In order to see what kind of structures young children perceive and use when they have to deal with structured material with a structure of 2×5, the children were asked to sort five eggs in an egg carton which looks like a ten-frame. Thereafter, they were asked to explain why it can be seen easily. Through the structure of the ten-frame, they could not reproduce the dice pattern of 5 which some already know as a whole figure. So they were forced to find another way of representation.

Most children put the five eggs in one row; one third of the children put three eggs in one row and two eggs in the other row. These were the most frequent representations.

With increasing age, the use of this structure ●●● is more frequent and the representation with five eggs in a row decreases. How the children perceive their representation cannot be concluded from their representation because the perception of a structure and (de)composing the quantity into substructures and different parts individual constructive acts. The given structure of the ten-frame automatically produces a kind of structured representation. But if the children perceive the quantity as a conglomerate of single items, then as a whole figure or as (de)composition of different parts with a structure cannot be answered only through interpreting the created representation. Therefore, the interviewers asked the question *Why do you*

12 Identifying quantities—Children's Constructions ...   199

Table 12.5 Answers referring to structures or compositions

Answers referring to structures (Explanations in grey rows refer to a (de) composition)	Five eggs in row	●●● ●●	●●●● ●	Other structure
No explanation	$N=36$	$N=12$	$N=1$	$N=0$
Referring to no structure—Mention of counting every single egg	$N=28$	$N=4$	$N=1$	$N=0$
Referring to the row without reference to the ten-frame	$N=5$			
Structure of a ten-frame	$N=5$			
(De)composition in 2 and 3	$N=3$	$N=8$	$N=3$	$N=3$
(De)composition in 2, 2 and 1		$N=4$	$N=3$	$N=2$
(De)composition in 4 and 1 without explicit mention dice pattern		$N=6$	$N=4$	$N=3$
Dice pattern of 4		$N=13$		$N=1$
Dice pattern of 5		$N=12$		$N=1$
Dice pattern of 6		$N=7$		
	$N=77$	$N=66$	$N=12$	$N=10$

think, it can be easily seen, that there are five eggs? In order to get an indication of what kind of structures the children perceive in their representation.

As it can be seen in Table 12.5, most of the children using the representation of five eggs in a row did not refer to a composition of a quantity in different parts. Sixty-four children gave no explanation or gave an explanation which can be interpreted as a perception of the quantity as single eggs because they counted every single egg. But we cannot be sure if this really is the case. It is just an assumption. Only ten children referred to the structure as a row. Five of these children used the structure of the ten-frame in their explanation like *It is a carton for ten eggs and therefore five eggs are in a row* or *ten eggs are in the carton and five is the half.*

At this point, it must be stated that the structure of the ten-frame like it is often used in primary school, where the quantities are perceived as composition of two quantities of five items, is not used very much by children aged 3–6. Three children explained that they perceive a (de)composition of 2 and 3 in a row.

Fifty of the 66 children using the representation ●●●● / ● referred in their explanations to a structure. Only 16 gave no explanation or referred to counting every single object. Eight children perceived the two rows as a division into the parts in 2 and 3. The structure of the dice patterns of 4, 5 or 6 were mentioned in most of the explanations referring to a structure.

Children using the representation ●●● / ●● also referred proportionally quite frequently to a structure in their explanation.

Discussion

In the theoretical background, different processes in identifying quantities are discerned. In this chapter, we tried to investigate the process of perception, especially the perception of structures in order to identify different parts in a collection. It is not easy to gain insight into how children perceive a collection of objects—because there is no obvious action to observe. Therefore, we only can draw conclusions out of the explanations of the children or through careful interpretation of their way of determination or (re)producing representations, still having in mind that there is no one-to-one correspondence between perception and determination. In summary, it can be stated that half of all children of this study at the age of 3–6 already discern between structured and not structured representations and that they can use this perception to determine quantities. As already mentioned at the first task, not only the perception of structures but also the perception of quantities as a whole figure was investigated because the representation of the quantity 4 and 6 was similar to dice patterns which are mainly recognized first as whole figures (see Table 12.1). Some children already referred in their explanation to the quantity as a decomposition of parts even for the dice-like representation of 4 and 6. In the reversible task where children should create a representation of seven items, the children had to (de)compose the quantity because a dice pattern of the quantity of 7 does not exist. Here, the same tendency can be seen: More than half of the children already used a structured composition for their representation. With increasing age, the perception and the use of structure increased. Looking on the structures and decompositions which are used or explained by the children for the quantity of 7 the decomposition of the dice pattern of 6 was dominant. A possible interpretation for the preference of this use can be the fact that children used 6 as the number next to 7. Another possible interpretation can be that 6 is the largest quantity which can be represented with one dice pattern and the children used the largest possible quantity. Interestingly, the composition of 5 and 2 was used less frequently as the composition of 3 and 4. A possible explanation for the preference of the composition of 3 and 4 can be the proximity to 3 and 3. The (de)composition of 3 and 4 then can be seen as nearly dividing into halves or nearly doubling (Rottmann 2006). The structure of the finger-pattern with 5 and 2 was not transferred to create a structured representation with seven items. In this setting, it has now to be noticed that the quantity of 5 did not play a big role in children's ideas of (de)composition with round counters. Looking at the explanations of the children about the structures they used for the representation in the ten-frame, it can be stated that most of the children who used the structure of five items in a row in the structured ten-frame as a structure did not explain the representation of the quantity with reference to a structure or (de)composition. If they gave an explanation, then they referred to counting every single item. This can be interpreted in the way that they did not use a structure or (de)composition to perceive the quantity with different parts. Children who explained the quantity with (de)composition either used the two rows to structure the quantity in two parts or they referred to dice patterns. Most of the children did not perceive and use the structure of a ten-frame in the conventional way of perception which refers to decomposition of ten in two parts of 5 and refers to a row as a whole quantity of five items. The composition in parts of 5 and 10 is used in most didactical materials to represent numbers up to 100, so that conceptual subitizing is possible. If the children in this study used the row for the five eggs, then most of the children had to count. Only very few children could "use" the knowledge of the fact that there are parts in terms of rows which are representing five items in this ten-frame. This is not astonishing. It emphasizes the fact that children's perception of structures is an individual act. Also, it becomes clear that the decomposition and perception of quantities in parts of tens, fives and ones, which is used in didactical material, have to be learned.

Conclusion

What conclusions can be drawn on the basis of these results in terms of instruction or construction on the domain of identifying quantities?

In this study, children's own constructions of recognizing or perceiving collections of objects was investigated. It was carefully interpreted how the children probably could have perceived the representation. The bases for this interpretation are the children's created representations of quantities and their explanations of their way of determining the quantity of the representations. For the interpretation, we still had in mind that there is no one-to-one correspondence between perception and determination. The study reveals that many children could already perceive structures in representations. They could explain structures in quantities and they also could explain how they used the idea of (de)composing a representation of a quantity into different parts for determination. However, it must be noted that there are also children who do not obviously perceive or use structures. This shows, on the one hand, that it is possible for children at this age to construct knowledge in this domain. But it also shows, on the other hand, that many children need additional support. Therefore, it is a challenge for professionals to support children in the perception and usage of structures through questions and reflections about the perception of structures and through providing materials where children can perceive structures (like egg cartons).

The different possible interpretations why children did not use the idea to decompose quantities in a part with five items very much are already discussed above. A conclusion which can be drawn from this fact is that the idea of decomposing quantities in parts of tens, fives and ones is a content which perhaps has to be discussed because this idea is not concluded in children's own perceptions and constructions. Professionals must have in mind that many children have their own constructions regarding perceiving structures even in didactical material. Referring to this observation, children's own constructions have to be an important point of discussion for mathematical instruction not only in pre-school setting, but also in school settings when using didactical material with an arranged structure.

References

Benz, C. (2010). Kindergarten educators and math. In M. M. F. Pinto & T. F. Kawasaki (Eds.), *Proceedings of the 34th conference of the international group for the psychology of mathematics education* (Vol. 2, pp. 201–208). Belo Horizonte: PME.
Benz, C. (2011). Den Blick schärfen. In A. Peter-Koop & M. Lueken (Eds.), *Mathematischer Erstunterricht: Empirische Befunde und Konzepte für die Praxis* (pp. 7–21). Offenburg: Mildenberger.
Benz, C. (2012). Attitudes of kindergarten educators about math. *Journal für Mathematik-Didaktik. 33*(2), 203–232.
Clements, D., & Sarama, J. (2009). *Early childhood mathematics education research: Learning trajectories for young children* (Studies in mathematical thinking and learning) (1st ed.). New York: Routledge.
Dornheim, D. (2008). *Prädiktion von Rechenleistung und Rechenschwäche: Der Beitrag von Zahlen-Vorwissen und allgemein-kognitiven Fähigkeiten*. Berlin: Logos.
Gaidoschik, M. (2010). *Wie Kinder rechnen lernen—oder auch nicht: Eine empirische Studie zur Entwicklung von Rechenstrategien im ersten Schuljahr*. Frankfurt a. M.: Peter Lang.
Gasteiger, H. (2010). *Elementare mathematische Bildung im Alltag der Kindertagesstätte: Grundlegung und Evaluation eines kompetenzorientierten Förderansatzes*. Münster: Waxmann.
Gelman, R., & Gallistel, C. R. (1978). *The child's understanding of number*. Cambridge: Harvard University Press.
Gerster, H.-D., & Schultz, R. (2004). Schwierigkeiten beim Erwerb mathematischer Konzepte im Anfangsunterricht. Bericht zum Forschungsprojekt Rechenschwäche—Erkennen, Beheben, Vorbeugen. Pädagogische Hochschule, Freiburg. http://opus.bsz-bw.de/phfr/volltexte/2007/16/pdf/gerster.pdf
von Glasersfeld, E. (1987). *Wissen, Sprache und Wirklichkeit*. Braunschweig: Vieweg.
Lueken, M. (2010). The relationship between early structure sense and mathematical development in Primary School. In M. F. Pinto & T. F. Kawasaki (Eds.), *Proceedings of the 34th Conference of the international Group for Psychology of Mathematics Education* (pp. 241-248). Belo Horizonte, Brasil.
Mulligan, J. T. (2002). The role of structure in children's development of multiplicative reasoning. In B. Barton, K. C. Irwin, M. Pfannkuch, & M. Thomas (Eds.), *Mathematics education in the south pacific. Proceeding of the 25th Annual Conference of the Mathematics Education research Group of Australasia Inc.* (pp. 497–503). Auckland: MERGA.
Mulligan, J. T., Mitchelmore, M. C., English, L. D., & Robertson, G. (2010). Implementing a pattern and structure awareness program (PASMAP) in kindergarten. In L. Sparrow, B. Kissane, & C. Hurst (Eds.), *Shaping the future of mathematics education. Proceedings of the 33rd annual conference of the mathematics education research group of australasia* (pp. 797–804). Fremantle: MERGA.
Mulligan, J. T., & Mitchelmore, M. (2009). Awareness of pattern and structure in early mathematical development. *Mathematics Education Research Journal, 21*(2), 33–49.
van Nes, F. (2009). *Young children's spatial structuring ability and emerging number sense*. Utrecht: All Print.
Resnick, L. B. (1983). A development theory of number understanding. In H. P. Ginsburg (Ed.), *The development of mathematical thinking* (pp. 110–151). New York: Academic Press.
Rottmann, T. (2006). *Das kindliche Verständnis der Begriffe "die Hälfte" und "das Doppelte". Theoretische Grundlegung und empirische Untersuchung*. Hildesheim: Franzbecker.
Schipper, W. (2009). *Handbuch für den Mathematikunterricht an Grundschulen*. Braunschweig: Schroedel.
Söbbeke, E. (2005). *Zur visuellen Strukturierungsfähigkeit von Grundschulkindern: Epistemologische Grundlage und empirische Fallstudie zu kindlichen Strukturierungsprozessen mathematischer Anschauungsmittel*. Hildesheim: Franzbecker.

Steffe, L. P., & Cobb, P. (1988). *Construction of arithmetical meaning and strategies*. New York: Springer.

Young-Loveridge, J. (2002). Early childhood numeracy: Building an understanding of part-whole relationships. *Australian Journal of Early Childhood, 27*(4), 36–42.

Part IV
Tools and Interaction

Chapter 13
Children's Engagement with Mathematics in Kindergarten Mediated by the Use of Digital Tools

Per Sigurd Hundeland, Martin Carlsen, Ingvald Erfjord

Introduction

In the last few years, Norwegian authorities have emphasised the importance of implementing mathematics and the use of information and communication technology (ICT)in kindergarten (Ministry of Education and Research 2006a,b). The former document adopts a broad view upon ICT and includes in the notion, for instance, computers, digital cameras, and copy machines. Moreover, the document contains recommendations and ideas for how to implement ICT in kindergarten. The latter document introduces mathematics as a separate subject area in kindergarten. However, a combined emphasis on mathematics and use of ICT is not explicitly elaborated.

This study reports on our conducted research within a project called ICT Supported Learning of Mathematics in Kindergarten.[1] In our study, ICT means computers together with digital tools displayed by way of web-based applications. According to Sarama and Clements (2004), there is a need for research aiming at identifying the role of digital tools and their contributions with respect to mathematics learning. Our study aims at gaining insights from implementing and using digital tools as regards children's mathematical learning within the kindergarten setting. In general, our hypothesis is that kindergarten children's engagement with digital tools may support their learning of mathematics. More specifically, our tenet is that the studied children may encounter and experience mathematics concepts as regards comparison of weights through the use of a digital pair of scales in interaction and collaboration with a more capable adult. The literature has so far not offered this topic careful attention. In their meta-analysis, Plowman and Stephen (2003) argue that mathematics and the use of digital tools in preschool settings have not frequently been an object of study.

---

[1] This project was funded by the LA2020 programme at the University of Agder.

P. S. Hundeland (✉) · M. Carlsen · I. Erfjord
Department of Mathematical Sciences, University of Agder, Kristiansand, Norway
e-mail: Per.S.Hundeland@uia.no

Our study addresses the overall theme of this book in several ways. Mathematics education within the kindergarten context is in our perspective situated exactly within the poles of *instruction* on the one side and *construction* on the other side. With our theoretical position, we view mathematics education in kindergarten from an activity-oriented perspective (van Oers 2002). Kindergarten teachers aim at developing and orchestrating mathematical activities to create mathematical learning opportunities. In our view, the term instruction carries connotations in direction of teachers giving students orders to carry through. From our perspective, the kindergarten teachers' role takes the form of orchestration of mathematical learning opportunities for the children. The term construction is, to us, associated with a constructivist view upon learning. From our theoretical position, learning is seen as an ongoing process of appropriation (Moschkovich 2004; Rogoff 1990, 1995). By participating in learning activities, the children get opportunities to make the mathematical tools and actions their own. Children experience number, shape, and measuring, by making sense in what contexts they are used, by trying them out for various purposes in problem solving and communication (Säljö 2001; Wertsch 1998).

We believe the children in our study are involved in a learning process when engaging with the digital tools mediated by the interactive whiteboard (IWB). Hennessy (2011) explored interaction possibilities of the IWB used in teaching and she lists their affordances, among others, the direct manipulation of objects and multimodal nature of interaction. These affordances offer "strong support for cumulative, collaborative and recursive learning" (p. 483). However, we believe it is a challenge to explore to what extent the users of the IWB, in our case children aged 4–5 years, engage in the learning of *mathematics*, i.e. whether the children become participants in processes of appropriating mathematical concepts.

From these considerations, we have formulated the following research question for our study: In what ways did the use of a digital pair of scales in kindergarten give learning opportunities in mathematics as regards comparison of weights?

Learning as Appropriation

In our study, we adopt a sociocultural perspective on learning. We view learning as a situated and social process in which individuals, i.e. in our case kindergarten teachers and children, appropriate (mathematical) concepts, tools, and actions by collaboration and communication (Rogoff 1990; Wertsch 1998). Our reason for adopting this theoretical perspective is that a sociocultural stance offers a lens through which learning activities involving the use of digital tools may be analysed.

Appropriation as a sociocultural metaphor of learning is viewed as an individual process of 'taking something that belongs to others and making it one's own' (Wertsch 1998, p. 53). In order for this process to be nurtured, the individual has to participate in social interaction with others where communication and contributions regarding ideas and arguments are essential elements. Appropriation is describing the process through which individuals gain from participating in sociocultural activities (Rogoff 1995). To become a cultural knower, i.e. in our case to become a novice participant within mathematics, one has to: (1) involve oneself in a joint activity with others; (2) establish together with others shared foci of attention; (3) develop agreement with others regarding shared meanings for words and concepts, (4) reason with respect to the words and concepts used by others and transform these in future, purposeful actions; and (5) attend to the relationship between their individual sense of mathematical concepts and tools and the mathematical meanings of these (Moschkovich 2004; Rogoff 1990). Moreover, when a child encounters and makes initial contact with a new cultural tool, such as measuring and comparison of objects with different weights as is the case in our study, she/he is dependent on external support by more competent peers. As the child's experience increases and she/he comes farther in the process of appropriating the tool, the need for external support decreases.

However, the emergence of digital tools within educational practices, such as kindergartens and schools, transforms the way we learn and come to know new things (Säljö 2010). In a digital world, the interesting thing is our abilities to make productive and insightful use of digital tools in locally suitable ways. Learning in technological environments is a process of performative actions, which applies to children's engagement with digital tools in kindergarten. Learning is about mastering the tools and performing in appropriate ways when interacting with the ICT applications, or as Säljö (2010, p. 62) puts it: 'our mastery of such tools is a critical element of what we know'. These claims suggest that becoming familiar with digital tools at an early stage, in kindergarten, is important for the children in an educational perspective. In order to become a competent participant in an increasingly sophisticated and specialised society, the upcoming generation is in need of skills and competence regarding digital tools, their affordances, and constraints.

According to Plowman and Stephen (2003), the use of ICT in educational practices is a valuable supplement, or 'benign addition', to existing resources. Nevertheless, they claim, employing these tools does not transform kindergarten practice. Moreover, they assert that there is a scarcity regarding research on kindergartners' use of ICT tools. Other researchers, in reviewing studies on young children's learning with digital tools, have found that digital tools are effective in improving mathematical and problem-solving skills for children aged 3–6 (Lieberman et al. 2009). Clements and Sarama (2007) studied the effects of a preschool mathematics curriculum focused at creating technology-enhanced mathematics materials. They argue that early mathematical interventions contribute to children's developing mathematical knowing.

Sarama and Clements (2004) found that when children were engaging with computer software, opportunities for mathematics learning were provided. In using the digital tools, children's appropriation of mathematical concepts and skills was nurtured. The software helped the children to mathematise their everyday activities and supported the children in their participation in mathematical activities interacting with computers. The digital tools the children worked with supported them in representing mathematical ideas as well as modelled mathematical activity with objects, i.e. numbers and shapes, and mathematical actions such as counting, adding, and subtracting. Nevertheless, Sarama and Clements point to a critical issue concerning children's play and use of digital tools. In order for the children to make meaning of the digital tools, it is crucial the way they interpret and grasp the objects, actions, and screen design represented and offered through the software. Careful observations and conversations with the children are thus necessary in order to explore their meaning making.

The Mediating Role of Digital Tools

Within a sociocultural perspective, one tenet is the mediating role of cultural tools such as computer software and interactive boards (Säljö 2010; Vygotsky 1986). Children's interaction and collaborative participation is fundamentally dependent on the use of these tools. The ICT applications become digital tools by way of their mediating function. These tools mediate mathematical concepts and ideas. According to Leont'ev (1979, p. 56), "The tool mediates activity and thus connects humans not only with the world of objects but also with other people". The mediating role of digital tools is quite evident in that children interact with each other through communication and with the software by way of the dynamic mathematical objects incorporated in the software.

Plowman and Stephen (2003) argue that with accessible technologies with tangible interfaces, such as interactive boards, a distinction between playing with digital tools and embodied play in kindergarten may be neglected. In a kindergarten environment where these new technologies are available, the notion of children's play ought to be enlarged in order to encompass playing with digital tools as a mediated, physical, and embodied activity. The software applications are used as digital tools which children ought to mathematise in order to develop their mathematical thinking. The applications mediate reality in a particular way that the children need to make mathematical sense of. Displayed pair of scales, cars, trucks, buses, toy bears and dolls, footballs, and violins ought to be made sense of as objects that may be compared relative to their individual weights.

The children also have to consider various semiotic contexts in order to make sense of the ICT applications, the semiotic context of real toys and pair of scales as well as the semiotic context of the application. The children's sense making in the former context has to be mapped onto the semiotic context of the application, e.g. the weights of violins, teddy bears, dolls, cars, and trucks, their internal weight relationships and how the producers of the application have implemented various weights of these toys, not necessarily in the same manner as the children reason. Additionally, these issues have to be related to the pair of scales and its functionality as well as the boxes or areas (labelled heavy/light, heavier/lighter, and heaviest/lightest, respectively) in which the toys ought to be placed after the comparisons of toys' weights. From a sociocultural perspective, the reliance on symbolic tools such as interactive screens with manipulative objects exemplifies the crucial role that semiotic tools play in mediating a physical world with physical objects for the children (Säljö et al. 2009). Moreover, we will argue that the children are involved in inter-semiotic work, i.e. the coordination of iconic categories and mathematical ideas and operations.

Interacting with the Digital Tools Through the Zone of Proximal Development

Links between learning as appropriation and the mediating role of tools are, in a sociocultural perspective, found in the Vygotskian notion of the *zone of proximal development* (ZPD). In order for children to learn something, Vygotsky (1978) argues that interaction with more capable peers needs to take place within this zone. ZPD is the difference between what a child is able to do alone and without assistance and what she is able to do in collaboration with adults or more competent others. With this notion, Vygotsky addresses the potentiality in the child's appropriations and actions. This zone therefore could be seen as the adult's guiding of the child within a culture and the collective knowing of that culture (Säljö 2001). The notion of ZPD is useful when analysing children's interaction with digital tools and the collaboration with the kindergarten teacher(s) within that interaction, because this notion may be used to describe the communicative qualities of their interaction. In a social setting and collaboration with the adult, the children are exposed to reasoning and actions that they gradually appropriate by becoming able to make those arguments and carry out those actions themselves. According to Chaiklin (2003), it is the quality of the interaction that takes place within the ZPD among children and adults that makes the notion fruitful for analysing children's engagement with ICT tools. The interaction has to be ontogenetically adaptive in order to be purposeful, both with respect to the current situation of the child and with respect to future developments: an interactive creation of an intellectual space (Zack and Graves 2001). Sarama and Clements (2004) found that children of a particular age often seemed to be more competent than the software designers assumed them to be at that age. The age indicators associated with different programs do not meet the competences appropriated by children at that particular age in their ZPD (Vygotsky 1978).

Co-learning as a Methodological Approach

Our methodology in conducting this research is based on what Wagner (1997) calls a co-learning agreement among us as researchers and kindergarten teachers as practitioners. Researchers and kindergarten teachers collaborate in order to develop new forms of mathematical practice in kindergarten, a practice in which children interact with and use digital tools to appropriate mathematical concepts and actions. The reason for establishing a co-learning agreement is that, according to Wagner (1997, p. 16), within this agreement:

…researchers and practitioners are both participants in processes of education and systems of schooling. Both are engaged in action and reflection. By working together, each might learn something about the world of the other. Of equal importance, however, each may learn something more about his or her own world and its connections to institutions and schooling.

We argue that a co-learning agreement is useful when aiming at exploring the subtleties of the children's opportunities for appropriating mathematical concepts and actions by way of using the digital tools on the IWB. Working with digital tools on the IWB to stimulate learning of mathematics was a new experience for the children, kindergarten teachers, and researchers. Thus, a co-learning agreement was fruitful for common explorations of the new area of practice and research, in which both parties contributed with ideas and arguments.

More particularly, we used observations, video data of the sessions, field notes, and conversations with the kindergarten teachers as data collection methods to address our research question. In our opinion, these various methods complemented each other in our ongoing efforts to do an in-depth analysis of naturally occurring talk in interaction. The context of our project is collaboration with three kindergartens called Bee Pre-school centre, Swan Pre-school centre, and Frog Pre-school centre. We collaborated with two kindergarten teachers at each of these kindergartens.

In this chapter, we analyse data collected in an IWB session on Frog Pre-school centre planned and led by one of the researchers. The researchers had observed this group of children and their kindergarten teachers several times working with different digital tools on IWB ahead of this session.

Results

The digital tool used on the IWB was a Norwegian software package for mathematics, Multi 1b.[2] The software package Multi 1b is supposed to be appropriate for grade 1 students in Norway, which means an age of 6–7 years. At this age, many children are able to read in Norway. However, the children that engaged in the activity we observed were 4–5 years old. Thus, we did not expect any of the children to be able to read. Consequently, all the written instructions in the digital tool were explained by the adult who lead the session. In this chapter, we consider the work with the three afforded levels of difficulty 1, 2, and 3 in an application within the digital tool Multi 1b treating measuring, particularly measuring of weights.

In the following, we will present two transcribed excerpts from video data and our analyses of those in order to address aspects of our research question. The digital tool displayed a pair of scales and the users were supposed to use the scales to compare the weight of displayed toys. Three levels of activities are presented in the tool. In excerpt 1, we present children's work with level 1 where the tool asks the user to weigh two different, displayed toys and based on their weighing and

---

[2] http://web3.gyldendal.no/multi/1-4nettoppgaver/multi1b/kapittel7/oppgaveC/

reasoning drag the toys to two boxes labelled "HEAVIEST" and "LIGHTEST", respectively. At level 2, which was not engaged with in the session presented below, the users of the tool were supposed to use the pair of scales to compare the weight of one specific toy to four other toys. Each of these four toys was supposed to be dragged to either a box labelled "HEAVIER THAN" or LIGHTER THAN" the toy they compared with. At level 3, engaged with in excerpt 2, the mathematical challenges for the users of the tool are to relate the weights of three different, displayed toys with each other.

In the observed session, three children were placed close to the IWB. Immediately before this session, the children had engaged with a physical pair of scales and weighed various objects and compared their weights. In that session, the three children were made to experience, as regards the functionality of the pair of scales, that the pan with the heavier toy went downwards and the pan with the lighter toy went upwards. These children thus had some prior experience that they could relate to when exposed to the digital tool involving a pair of scales in a digital context. The adult started off the session by briefly demonstrating the functionality of the digital tool, pointed at the various elements of the screen and labelled them. Throughout the session, he read the written text presented within the application, called forward one child at a time to the touchable screen, and asked questions while the child interacted with the IWB. The session lasted for approximately 15 minutes before a new group of children accomplished the same activity. Both sessions followed the same pattern of interaction, addressing similar mathematical contents, and for convenience of the reader, we refer to only one of them in the two excerpts below.

Excerpt 1 Familiarisation with the Application and its Use on the IWB

In the following excerpt, four persons are interacting, one boy, Peter, two girls, Christina and Helen, and Ove (researcher).

1. Ove: Now we are supposed to be weighing with the help of the computer, and we are supposed to figure out which one of these two things is *lightest* and which is *heaviest*.
2. Christina: A ball
3. Ove: A ball and a doll. Here it says: Put the toys in the correct box (Ove points to the text at the top of the screen and reads). Here it says lightest and here it says heaviest. But this thing here, do you know what that is? (Points at the pair of scales)
4. Helen: The thing they are supposed to be laying at.
5. Ove: The thing they are supposed to be laying at. It is a pair of scales, it goes upwards and downwards as we put the toys into the pans. I will show you. Let's take the doll and drag it onto the left pan. Then it goes downwards. Let's then take the football and drag it onto the other, right, pan. What do you think will

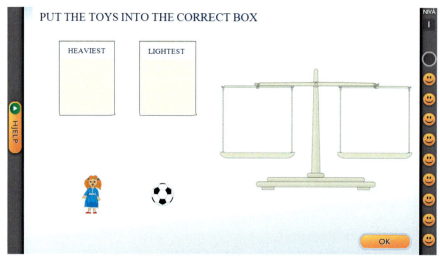

Fig. 13.1 The screen relative to excerpt 1 at level 1 in Multi 1b, measuring with scales (Translated by the authors). Source: http://web3.gyldendal.no/multi/1–4nettoppgaver/multi1b/kapittel7/oppgaveC/nivaa1

happen? (No response). It went just a little downwards. Which one of the two toys do you believe is the heaviest one?
6. Christina: The doll
7. Helen: The doll
8. Ove: The doll. Why do you mean that?
9. Helen: Because it went furthest down.
10. Ove: Yes, because it went furthest down.

This excerpt starts off by Ove demonstrating and explaining the functionality of level 1 in the application and the associated drag-and-drop affordance to use when interacting with the IWB. Ove emphasises the comparison words *lightest* and *heaviest* in relation to comparisons of the weights of toys (this is the reason why the comparison words are written in italics in the excerpt), in order to focus the children's attention to what the comparisons are about. At the screen (see Fig. 13.1), the following elements are displayed: A pair of scales to the right, two side-by-side boxes to the upper left corner labelled "HEAVIEST" and "LIGHTEST", respectively, in which the toys are supposed to be put after the weighing, and two toys—a football and a doll. Ove asks the three children's opinions regarding the displayed pair of scales. It seems as if Helen makes sense of it even though she has never tried the application out before. However, she had seen and engaged with a physical pair of scales some minutes ago. The visualisation of the pair of scales seems to communicate with her in such a way that she rationalises on its functionality. Ove is confirmative with respect to her reasoning and exemplifies the functionality of the pair of scales. Ove drags the two toys onto the two pans, first the doll onto the left pan and afterwards the football onto the right pan. Just before he drops the ball onto the pan,

Ove asks the children what they believe will happen. There is no recognisable response from the children to that question. But after having dropped it (there is only a small movement visible in the pair of scales when the football is placed onto the right pan), Ove asks a question addressing the conclusion that can be drawn from what they saw happen. Which one of the toys is heaviest? Both the girls conclude that it is the doll that is heaviest. Ove confirms their reasoning by repeating their answer, but continues by asking them to argue for their conclusion. Helen then utters her argument. We interpret this utterance to explicate the following conclusion: The doll is heaviest because the pan in which the doll is laying got further down than the pan with the ball. The pan with the doll is visually lower on the screen than the pan with the ball. In this situation with two different toys, a mathematical underlying element is the concept of pair of contrasts. One of the toys is lighter and the other one is therefore, logically, heavier.

From this excerpt, it seems as if the children have made sense of the application, both the functionality of the pair of scales and what they are supposed to do when interacting on the application through using the drag-and-drop affordance in the IWB. It seems as if the children quite spontaneously master the digital tool (Wertsch 1998). After a few repetitions of similar tasks at level 1, Ove decided that the children needed greater mathematical challenges. The children's engagement with the tasks at level 1 did not result in significant difficulties for them, and the tasks were solved with few actions on the IWB by the children. Thus, we find indications that the children were not met in their ZPD to any significant degree (Vygotsky 1978). This might be due to the children's recent experience with the physical pair of scales. The engagement with the digital tool at this level may thus be seen as an activity that repeats what the children experienced in the former session. The decision was then taken to continue with the application at the most difficult level, level 3, to enrich the intellectual space created in the interaction between the children and Ove (Zack and Graves 2001).

Excerpt 2 Engaging with the Application on the IWB

This excerpt sort of continues where the previous excerpt ended. The same four persons are interacting, but now with the application at level 3. At the screen (see Fig. 13.2), there are currently three boxes to the upper left corner, labelled from left to right "HEAVY", "HEAVIER", and "HEAVIEST".

Helen and Peter had already tried the application out in interaction and collaboration with Ove when Christine approached the IWB.

78. Ove: (Ove informs about the screen seen in Fig. 13.2, reads the text and indicates where the toys are supposed to be dropped according to their weights). Now it says that the heaviest object ought to be placed here (points at the box to the right). The object that is midmost ought to be placed there (points at the midmost box). And the object which is lightest (even though it says "heavy" on the box) ought to be placed here (points at the box to the left). Do you want to compare them?

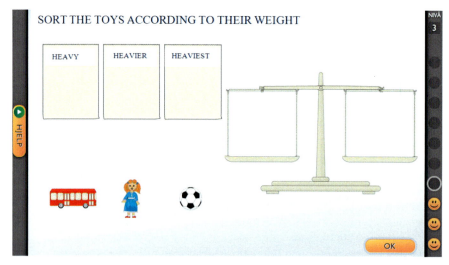

Fig. 13.2 The screen relative to excerpt 2, at level 3 in Multi 1b, measuring with scales (Translated by the authors) Source: http://web3.gyldendal.no/multi/1–4nettoppgaver/multi1b/kapittel7/oppgaveC/nivaa3

79. Christina: (She drags the doll to the left pan and the bus to the right pan)
80. Ove: Wow. Which one of those is the lightest one?
81. Christina: (She immediately points at the left pan, which is correct)
82. Ove: Yes, that's correct. It is the doll. But we still don't know what the relationship is between the ball (points at the ball) and the doll. Shall we weigh the ball and the doll?
83. Christina: (She removes the bus and replace it with the ball)
84. Ove: Which one of them is the lightest one?
85. Christina: (She immediately points at the ball, which is correct)
86. Ove: Yes, it's the ball. Then the ball has to go over here (points at the left box)

This excerpt is characterised by Christina's action-oriented approach to solve the measuring problem. She does not say anything, but she performs actions as responses to Ove's questions. We consider these non-verbal actions as ways through which Christina externalises her thinking. She communicates her reasoning by dragging and dropping the toys where they are supposed to, and she correctly answers two of the questions by a pointing gesture. In this dialogue, we also recognise that Ove holds back some of the apparent difficulties in the task. He deliberately uses the word "lightest" when Christina compares the weights of the ball and the doll, rather than asking for what toy to be heavier. Their attention is then focused at the pair of contrast 'heavy–light' or 'heaviest–lightest'. In this situation with three different toys, the children, in particular, Christina, but also Helen and Andreas who carefully watched the interaction among Christina and Ove, are exposed to the transitive ordering relation of quantities: If $a>b$ and $b>c$, then $a>c$. In this particular case, Christina concluded that the doll is lighter than the bus. In the second weighing, suggested by Ove, she compares the weight of the doll and the ball. She then found that the ball is the lighter of those two toys, i.e. ball<doll. Algebraically, if the bus is quantity a, the doll is quantity b, and the ball is quantity c, she did the following: In the first weighing she found that $a>b$. In the second weighing, she kept the lighter toy, b, and compared that toy with c. She concluded that $b>c$. If that had not been the case, that the second weighing led to the conclusion that $b<c$, then a third weighing would be necessary in order to decide the ordering of the quantities. Mathematically, the following conclusion about the transitivity might be drawn, that since $a>b$ and $b>c$, then $a>c$. That is, the ball (quantity c) is the lighter one and ought to be placed at the left box.

In this excerpt, we observe how the more capable peer and the child are collaborating in order to solve the problems. Christina is apparently in need of assistance in her problem solving, and Ove raises questions to explicitly involve Christina in their joint activity. The interaction takes place within the ZPD of Christine as her encounter with the pair of scales is guided by the more competent adult. Their shared focus of attention is the comparisons of the toys' weights to order them accordingly. Both, the ICT application and the goal-directed activity of weighing by way of a digital tool in this case were new to Christina and the other children. The ICT application mediated mathematical ideas with respect to the concept of measuring in a new way. Christina (and the other children) was confronted with measuring tasks in a digital setting. We therefore argue that the children, by being involved in this activity, have made initial contact with the implicit mathematical concepts such as pair of contrasts and the transitive ordering relation. Thus, opportunities are established from which Christina and the other children may start their individual process of appropriating the mathematics involved (Moschkovich 2004, Rogoff 1990).

Discussion

We set out in this study to come up with possible answers to the question: In what ways did the use of a digital pair of scales in kindergarten give learning opportunities in mathematics as regards comparison of weights? Through the two excerpts analysed in this study, we have seen how the children make meaning of the ICT applications, but also mathematical meaning. We argue that the children, through their utterances and actions, reveal that they make meaning of the digital tools offered and represented at the screen. It is decisive to oblige and surpass this critical issue, as argued by Sarama and Clements (2004), in order for the children to appropriate mathematical meaning mediated by the digital tools (Plowman and Steven 2003; Säljö 2010). The children seem to immediately interpret and grasp the meaning of the displayed pair of scales and its functionality. If the pan moves upwards, the toy in that pan is lighter than the toy in the pan that moves downwards at the screen. Particularly, the children investigate and experience the functionality of the pair of scales and how it mediates that various objects have different weights. The children are in need of support by the more capable adult in their testing of the material features of the digital tool(s). The balance between instruction and construction is delicate in this situation as the children's mathematical and digital background is limited. Instruction is thus needed in order for the children to make sense of the displayed digital tool. The delicate balance between giving a too limited versus a too extensive mathematical instruction must thus be considered by the adult. However, opportunities have to be established in which the children themselves may initially appropriate features of the tool, its functionality, and the mathematical concepts implicitly mediated by the tool.

When the children use these digital tools, opportunities are made in which they externalise their mathematical thinking. The children are offered possibilities to establish shared meanings for mathematical concepts due to the flexible displaying of these concepts by way of the computer. The digital tools also make powerful links between the per se abstract mathematical concepts and visual concretising by various representations. In using digital tools, these children may establish shared focus of attention as well due to their dynamic and multimodal nature. Interaction with digital tools may encourage the children to pose problems and conjecture regarding mathematical actions and objects. Due to the interaction with the digital tools and the more capable peer, the children become participants in an initial process of appropriating (Moschkovich 2004; Rogoff 1995) the mathematical tool of measuring, in particular comparison of weights, pair of contrasts, and the transitive ordering relation.

In this application, both at level 1 and level 3, mathematical problems with similar cognitive demands were engaged with repetitiously. At level 1, different toys appeared in each turn and the order of the labels heaviest and lightest on the screen changed (sometimes heaviest was written on the left-hand side and sometimes on the right-hand side). While engaging with the tasks at level 3, the labels of the boxes changed into light, lighter, and lightest (from left to right). Nevertheless, it seems as if the children do not have severe difficulties with that. From a mathematical point of view, the ordering of the toys relative to their weight is opposite of each other on these occasions. In the first situation, the heaviest toy ought to be placed to the left-hand box, but in the second situation the heaviest toy ought to be placed in the box to the right (in both situations the middle-sized toys ought to be placed in the box in the middle—whether the toys are characterised as lighter or heavier). These issues are deliberately hidden by Ove in the excerpts above, in order to competently guide and assist the children within their ZPD (Vygotsky 1978). The level of difficulty in the application is competently adapted to the children's level of competence. An intellectual space (Zack and Graves 2001) is thus interactively created in order for the children to competently participate with ideas, actions, and arguments.

However, from a mathematical point of view it is problematic that the web-based application introduces the words "heaviest" and "lightest" when the children are supposed to compare two objects regarding their weight. According to the meaning of the notion weight, the words "heavier" and "lighter" respectively should have been used and displayed within the application. The same mathematical problematic issue occurs when the children are supposed to compare the weight of three objects and these are pre-classified as "heavy", "heavier", and "heaviest".

A displayed object is in this context not "heavy" per se, but heavy with respect to an implicit comparison to a reference norm. These shortcomings of the digital tool, as well as the lack of comments by the adult in this respect, ought to be described as mathematically problematic. If we want children to develop proper conceptualisations of mathematical concepts and ideas as well as being able to use such notions properly and in accordance with the mathematical community, we argue that it is important to already in kindergarten introduce and use the mathematical correct words and notions both by adults and by way of software. Nevertheless, in the Norwegian language, as is the original language of both the application and the adult, it is usual when comparing two objects to denote the heavier one as the heaviest one and the lighter one as the lightest one (literal translations of the Norwegian words "tyngst"—"heaviest" and "lettest"—"lightest").

Additionally, these excerpts reveal that the children are challenged by the displayed toys, the correspondence of the toys with reality, and the weight of different toys in reality compared with what the application shows. Thus, the children are involved in inter-semiotic work (Säljö et al. 2009). The displayed buses and trucks, are they supposed to be interpreted as toy buses and toy trucks or real buses and trucks? What about the violin—is it supposed to display a real playable violin or some toy violin with a much smaller size? What images and thoughts are aroused among the children when displaying these objects? From the dialogues, we argue that the children, through inter-semiotic reasoning, are able to relate to the world of objects within the application and their representatives in the physical world, respectively. The digital displaying of the pair of scales and the objects by way of the computer constitute both affordances and constraints as regards the children's mathematics learning opportunities. Through inter-semiotic work, the children have to coordinate semiotic categories with the implicit mathematical concepts and ideas. The digital tool(s) as well as the more capable adult supported the children to some extent to mathematise their experience of measuring in this case (Samara and Clements 2004).

From the excerpts, we observe how Ove challenges the children mathematically through asking questions directly and indirectly linked to the mathematical issues implicitly imbedded in the applications. In competently assisting the children's engagement with the ICT applications, Ove nurtures possible links between the challenges and previous experience. Thus, Ove emphasises the mathematical potentials through which the children get opportunities to participate in processes of appropriating the imbedded mathematical tools. In terms of instruction, the adult in our study carries out his role through the orchestration of mathematical activities and thereby challenges the children within their ZPD. As regards the children's construction, we describe this process as an interactive, individual process of appropriating the offered mathematical tools and actions.

From our analyses of the children's interaction with the ICT applications, it is evident that in excerpt 1 there is a mismatch between the competencies of the children involved and assumed competence of children of that age by the software designers. This finding is in accordance with the result of Sarama and Clements (2004). It seems as if the children are able to master applications designed for children who are from 2 to 3 years older. An intellectual space (Zack and Graves 2001) where the children are appropriately challenged is established in excerpt 2. Kindergarten teachers therefore need to make an effort to choose software programs and applications that meet and challenge the children within their ZPD (Vygotsky 1978). It is needed in order for children to continue their individual process of appropriating the mathematical tools and actions incorporated in the digital tools.

References

Chaiklin, S. (2003). The zone of proximal development in Vygotsky's analysis of learning and instruction. In A. Kozulin, B. Gindis, & V. S. Ageyev (Eds.), *Vygotsky's educational theory in cultural context* (pp. 39–64). Cambridge: Cambridge University Press.

Clements, D., & Sarama, J. (2007). Effects of a preschool mathematics curriculum: Summative research on the Building Blocks project. *Journal for Research in Mathematics Education, 38*, 136–163. doi:10.2307/30034954.

Hennessy, S. (2011). The role of digital artefacts on the IWB in mediating dialogic teaching and learning. *Journal of Computer Assisted Learning, 27*, 463–489. doi:10.1111/j.1365-2729.2011.00416.x.

Leont'ev, A. N. (1979). The problem of activity in psychology. In J. V. Wertsch (Ed.), *The concept of activity in Soviet psychology* (pp. 37–71). Armonk, NY: M. E. Sharpe.

Lieberman, D. A., Bates, C. H., & So, J. (2009). Young children's learning with digital media. *Computers in the Schools, 26*, 271–283. doi:10.1080/07380560903360194.

Ministry of Education and Research (2006a). *Rammeplan for barnehagens innhold og oppgaver* [Framework plan for the content and tasks of kindergartens]. Oslo: Ministry of Education and Research.

Ministry of Education and Research (2006b). *Temahefte om "IKT i barnehagen"* [Thematic booklet on "ICT in the kindergarten"]. Oslo: Ministry of Education and Research.

Moschkovich, J. N. (2004). Appropriating mathematical practices: A case study of learning to use and explore functions through interaction with a tutor. *Educational Studies in Mathematics, 55*, 49–80.

Plowman, L., & Stephen, C. (2003). A 'benign addition'? Research on ICT and pre-school children. *Journal of Computer Assisted Learning, 19*, 149–164.

Rogoff, B. (1990). *Apprenticeship in thinking. Cognitive development in social context*. New York: Oxford University Press.

Rogoff, B. (1995). Observing sociocultural activity on three planes: Participator appropriation, guided participation, and apprenticeship. In J. V. Wertsch, P. del Río, & A. Alvarez (Eds.), *Sociocultural studies of mind* (pp. 139–164). Cambridge, MA: Cambridge University Press.

Säljö, R. (2001). *Læring i praksis. Et sosiokulturelt perspektiv* [Learning in practice. A sociocultural perspective]. Oslo: Cappelen Akademisk Forlag.

Säljö, R. (2010). Digital tools and challenges to institutional traditions of learning: Technologies, social memory and the performative nature of learning. *Journal of Computer Assisted Learning, 26*, 53–64. doi:10.1111/j.1365-2729.2009.00341.x.

Säljö, R., Riesbeck, E., & Wyndhamn, J. (2009). Learning to model: Coordinating natural language and mathematical operations when solving word problems. In L. Verschaffel, B. Greer, W. Van Dooren, & S. Mukhopadhyay (Eds.), *Words and worlds: Modelling verbal descriptions of situations* (pp. 177–193). Rotterdam: Sense Publishers.

Sarama, J., & Clements, D. H. (2004). Building blocks for early childhood mathematics. *Early Childhood Research Quarterly, 19*, 181–189.

van Oers, B. (2002). Teachers' epistemology and the monitoring of mathematical thinking in early years classrooms. *European Early Childhood Education Research Journal, 10*, 19–30.
Vygotsky, L. S. (1978). *Mind in society: The development of higher psychological processes.* Cambridge, MA: Harvard University Press.
Vygotsky, L. S. (1986). *Thought and language.* Cambridge, MA: The M. I. T. Press.
Wagner, J. (1997). The unavoidable intervention of educational research: A framework for reconsidering research-practitioner cooperation. *Educational Researcher, 26*, 13–22.
Wertsch, J. V. (1998). *Mind as action.* New York: Oxford University Press.
Zack, V., & Graves, B. (2001). Making mathematical meaning through dialogue: "Once you think of it, the z minus three seems pretty weird". *Educational Studies in Mathematics, 46*, 229–271.

Chapter 14
Mathematical Situations of Play and Exploration as an Empirical Research Instrument

Rose Vogel

Introduction

The long-term study early Steps in Mathematics Learning (erStMaL) is based at the Individual Development and Adaptive Education of Children at Risk (IDeA) Research Center in Frankfurt am Main[1]. In the context of erStMaL, children will be accompanied from the age of 4 years up to the age of about 9 years. Working out development lines of mathematical thinking stands at the centre of the study. The mathematical situations of play and exploration are designed as special empirical research instruments for the study erStMaL. They offer an action framework for children and the guiding adult which permits them to construct a situation context in the interaction in which processes of mathematical thinking can take place. The children cooperate in tandems or smaller groups (up to four children). Every half year with each child two situations of play and exploration are carried out in the described settings. The composition of the tandems and the groups remains constant during the complete investigation period. At the first data collection point, 144 children were involved in the study (see Acar Bayraktar et al. 2011).

Each situation of play and exploration focuses on one mathematical task or problem, which is presented in a playful or exploratory context according to the age of the children and represents the starting point of a common process of dispute. This format was chosen because the discussions themselves are distinguished by a relatively high degree of "close communication" (Koch and Österreicher 2007, p. 350;

---

[1] The IDeAResearch Center is funded through the "LOEWE" initiative of the federal state government of Hessen. LOEWE is a national initiative in the development of scientific and economic excellence. The cooperation partner in the IDeA Research Center is the German Institute for International Educational Research (DIPF), the Goethe University Frankfurt/Main and the Sigmund Freud Institute Frankfurt/Main. Further information can be found under www.idea-frankfurt.eu

R. Vogel (✉)
Goethe-Univesity Frankfurt a.M. and IDeA-Center Frankfurt a. M., Germany
e-mail: vogel@math.uni-frankfurt.de

Vogel and Huth 2009, pp. 38, 39). On the one hand, the increased intensity of communication can be used motivationally, and on the other for the discursive adaptation of the mathematical problem (see also Vogel and Huth 2010, pp. 184, 185).

Furthermore, the conception of the mathematical situations of play and exploration provides that the arrangement has its root in one of the following five mathematical domains: numbers and operations, geometry and spatial thinking, measurements, patterns and algebraic thinking or data and probability (including combinatorics). The mathematical domain is being expressed by a suitable selection of materials and arrangement of space and by the mathematical task. In addition, the guiding adult gives thriftily verbal and gestural impulses and encourages the participating children to engage in activities.

The tandem situations always take place in the same mathematical domain. The group situation is chosen from two further alternating mathematical domains. So every child is confronted with mathematical situations of play and exploration from three mathematical domains. The mathematical situations are further developed over time as described in the section.

Approaches and support for the development and conceptualization of the mathematical situations of play and exploration in the erStMaL long-term study come from a number of sources. These include the results of empirical studies (Clements and Sarama 2007; Sarama and Clements 2008; Schuler and Wittmann 2009), and practical information for work in day-care centres from operational books (e.g. Hoenisch and Niggemeyer 2007; Benz 2010). Additional publications include those in which concepts are described for the creation of a mathematical teaching and a learning environment (Hülswitt 2006; Wollring 2006), together with publications in the field of early education (Fthenakis et al. 2009; Korff 2008).[2]

The mathematical situations of play and exploration are carried out by specifically trained members of the project's staff and will be videotaped. The video material delivers the data material for the development of theories of mathematical thinking within the framework of mathematics education (Krummheuer 2011; Vogel and Huth 2010).

At first, the mathematical situations of play and exploration are introduced as an empirical research instrument in the context of a long-term study with two examples. The staged situations establish the starting point for children for the first encounter with the mathematical world. The mathematical world is caused situational and is characterized as the interplay between construction and instruction. With the detailed descriptions, the guiding adults gain confidence which open a scope of action for them. These two aspects are introduced in the following and illustrated by the empirical data material. This has arisen in the two exemplarily selected situations of play and exploration "animal polonaise" (data material from the data collection point T1) and "wooden sticks" (data material from the data collection point T3).

---

[2] This is only a selection of the literature that was evaluated in the preparation of the mathematical situations of play and exploration. The development of the mathematical situations is continued. In this context, there is also an ongoing process of feedback to the current discussion of mathematical education in child-care centres, and the transition to primary school.

At the data collection point T1, the observed children are approximately 4 years old; at the point T3, the children are approximately 5 years old.

Mathematical Situation of Play and Exploration in the Context of a Long-Term Study

The mathematical situations of play and exploration for the erStMaL long-term study will be developed further from data collection point to data collection point in the context of the mathematical domain. This continuing development will occur from various points of view. Therefore, the goal of development lines research involves a certain requirement for consistency and variation for investigation. In reality, this means that the situations of play and exploration must remain consistent within their mathematical frameworks, however, developing in the materials (artefacts) and arrangement of space and in the mathematical task. In this way, the developmental changes, such as the cognitive and communicative potential of the children, are taken into account. In addition, at each data collection point the children acquire progressive experiences in situations of play and exploration. These experiences can be included in the situation at the next data collection point. Therefore, appropriate continuing development must be designed specifically for each situation of play and exploration in consideration of its respective degree of freedom.

The continuing development of mathematical situations of play and exploration can add to the characteristic components of a situation of play and exploration described here: (1) of the mathematical task, (2) the materials (artefacts) and arrangement of space and (3) the stimuli set by the guiding adult during the performance of the situation.

The Mathematical Task Every mathematical situation of play and exploration shares a need of mathematical tasks that originates from the respectively selected mathematical domain. The mathematical task shows different degrees of freedom that will be strengthened by the degree of freedom of the material (artefacts) or rather the tools which are contemplated for the situations. This degree of freedom influences the scope of construction of the mathematical area of action for all actors (see sections Example 1: "Animal Polonaise" and Example 2: "Wooden Sticks" in this chapter). The advancement of the mathematical task can occur within the selected mathematical domain as variation of the task by the addition of more aspects.

The Materials (artefacts) and the Arrangement of Space The material (artefacts) and the arrangement of space are so selected that the processing of the mathematical task is initiated and supported. The chosen artefacts offer the children points of contact, since they usually originate from the world of the childlike play. So, for example, toys from plastic, which run on podiums (see section Example 1: "Animal Polonaise"), chipmunks made of plush, which want to distribute fairly nuts and cards with ladybugs, which can be sorted according different criteria, are selected. At the

Fig. 14.1 Animals and podium from the mathematical situation of play and exploration "animal polonaise"

same time, this material can be used to stimulate mathematical activities. Usually, the materials (artefacts) remain constant over several data collection points. Further developments of the materials for example consist of expanding from the plane to the space (see the situation "wooden sticks").

The Multimodal Stimuli The guiding adult, who accompanies the implementation of the mathematical situation of play and exploration, is urged to initiate the employment with the mathematical problem through open stimuli, but he/she should offer as little guidance as possible in order to provide the most potential freedom for the mathematical situations of play and exploration. This offers the children the possibility to choose a way of adapting the mathematical task which is suited to the situation. Thus, in the process, they can produce connections to other mathematical domains or to other worlds of ideas.

The components of the multi-modal stimuli must continue to be developed in a certain manner by the guiding adult. Thus, the initial stimuli remain in the repertoire of the guiding adult throughout and will be documented in the description of the situations for the subsequent data collection point. In addition, progressive stimuli will be supplemented from data collection point to data collection point. The guiding adult is confronted with the often-difficult task of making concrete decisions about which of the stimuli formulated in the pattern should be used, or rather be replaced by more appropriate, spontaneous stimuli.

Example 1: "Animal Polonaise"

The mathematical situation of play and exploration "animal polonaise" has to be assigned to the mathematical domain of combinatorics. On a podium, animals shall be brought in an order (see Fig. 14.1). At the first two data collection points, the mathematical task consists in finding all possible sequences that can be made using a given number of animals (at the first data collection point were used three animals, rather than four animals). In this situation, the level of mathematical freedom is rather small, since the task is defined clearly. The scopes are here rather in the processing of the mathematical task which can be solved using different combinatorial solution strategies. These, in turn, are linked to the available materials. The task will then be extended for the third data collection point by the requirement of documenting the sequences found with the help of cards, on which the animals are displayed. In doing so, the question as to how many such sequences there are can be approached systematically. Optimization of the solution strategies for finding all of the sequences can result through such documentation.

An extension at the fourth data collection point will then include limitations on the arrangement of the animals on the circus podium, such as always placing the elephant at the front. This will be introduced into the situations of play with the help of a dice as a random generator.

This example shows how that material and the arrangement of space will change in parallel with the extension of the mathematical task. Thus, the first data collection point begins with three animals, which increases to four, then the addition of animal cards for documenting the various sequences and the addition of a random generator in the form of a dice for creating conditions at the fourth data collection point.

The guiding adult has the task of introducing the mathematical task in this situation using the non-mathematical context of the circus as the framework for the activity. This should encourage the children to discover the potential sequences of animals on a circus podium as a form of exploration and symbolic play. In this situation, the guiding adult has the task of deciding at each data collection point and for each individual group of children the extent to which the circus context will be used and at which intensity. By adding the animal cards at the third data collection point, explanations will be required on the part of the guiding adult, who will create a connection between the plastic animals on the podium and the animal cards.

Example 2: "Wooden Sticks"

If one considers the "wooden sticks" situation as an additional example of a mathematical situation of play and exploration, then this mathematical task exhibits a greater degree of freedom. Patterns can be created, by arranging the coloured wooden sticks (see Fig. 14.2). Since the wooden sticks differ only in colour but not in shape, colour is an obvious criterion for the development of the patterns. Patterns can be created, by placing certain sequences of colours side by side (Hülswitt 2006). Another possibility would be to create geometric shapes from the wooden sticks that in turn serve as a unit of pattern development. The objectives of the play situations show that the mathematical task allows many possibilities that have increased even more scopes in connection with the materials.

Fig.14.2 Material from the mathematical situation of play and exploration "wooden sticks"

The mathematical task as soon as the material and the arrangement of space will remain consistent over multiple data collection points, since both the task and the materials contain a great degree of freedom for the solution. The materials will first be changed for the fourth data collection point by extending the creation of patterns in the space. Flat wooden sticks will no longer be used, but rather wooden sticks of a certain shape (rectangular prisms), in order to create spatial patterns.

Mathematical Situations of Play and Exploration—Area of Action between Construction and Instruction

Mathematical Area of Action

The central goal of the mathematical situations of play and exploration of erStMaL is to create an area of action that makes encountering mathematics as a culture possible. The perception of mathematics as an independent cultural orientation system is not new and has been handled in a special manner by ethno-mathematics (see Prediger 2001, p. 126). For learning mathematics, this means that points of access into this culture must be found with regard to the way of thinking, the values and the behaviour in this culture. Prediger (2001) introduced one such approach in her "Concept of Intercultural Learning".

> "Mathematics instruction should be used to teach students to know and to understand mathematics as an own culture. To do this, they should experience this culture and socialize as much as possible within it so that they can move safely within certain limited areas. The acquisition of implicit knowledge about the approaches, standards and values is also necessary." (Prediger 2001, p. 129; translated by R.V.)

Above all, intercultural overlap situations, in which the culture of mathematics meets other parts of cultural life, provide students with the ability "…to gather their own experiences in those overlap areas between mathematics and the world" (Prediger 2001, p. 130; translated by R.V).

The mathematical situations of play and exploration constitute such overlap areas between mathematics and the children's world of experience (see Prediger 2001). The mathematical discourse as a part of the situations of play and exploration should permit the children to participate in the mathematical concepts that are presented in a multi-modal manner by the guiding adult. Participation is used here in the sense that an area of learning will be created, where "knowledge learning" and "human being learning" and in the same way "acting learning" and "common life learning" can be connected (see Wulf and Zierfas 2007; translated by R.V.) and a narrative argumentation becomes possible (Krummheuer 2011; Tomasello 2008; Bruner 1986).

The experience world of the children is determined by the play. In the play, children discover the "physical world" (Samuelsson and Carlsson 2007, p. 33) as well as the world of the living together. In the free play, they test their own physical borders and the quality of objects. Role plays enable the actors to leave the pure object relation and to agree on a subject of the play; thereby, a common context as a reference point is possible (see Oerter 2011, p. 99). So the play can be described as a possibility to understand the world (see Samuelsson and Carlsson 2007, p. 31) and still the play remains free of purpose (see Oerter 2011, p. 5). These described aspects of the play are considered in the concept of the mathematical situations in the research study "erStMaL". They should create a space in contrast to learning situations, which makes free mathematical explorations possible.

Example—"Animal Polonaise"

The chosen scene in the transcript section (see Fig. 14.3) describes a situation in which the guiding adult introduces in the situation "animal polonaise". The animal figures should run above the podium, as well as they do in the circus. Besides, the fact that they run in different orders through the podium should be taken into account.

The situation ties up with the context circus. Here animals make tricks and run over podiums. With the plastic animals and the podium from cardboard the real circus becomes a situation of play in which the animals are controllable and these can be led in different orders about the podium. For the play situation, the podiums are so formed that the plastic animals can be put up only one after the other. In this manner, a mathematical interpretation is initiated for the purposes of a combinatorial situation "in order without repeating".

At the beginning of the example, the guiding adult puts three animals one after the other beside the podium. With this, a mathematical interpretation is given. The repeated walk one after another on the podium should support the children in finding other variations. The context enables the emergence of different variations, because the same animals can go several times differently about the podium. Thus, a real situation can be used in the play as a starting point for mathematical interpretations.

001			
002	>	B	*lift the tiger and put him down* and now in the circus
003			the animals want to make once a trick
004			on the podium\ *lift shortly the elephant and the monkey*
005			*(from left to right: elephant – monkey – tiger)*
006			*put them up again and push the podium more nearly to*
007			*the children* and namely they should run sometimes
008			in a row through it *put the animals in a*
009			*row next to the podium (from left to right):*
010			*(monkey – elephant – tiger)* and balancing about this
011	>	Kai	*looks on the carpet in the direction of the animal figures*
012	>	Ayse	*looks on the carpet in the direction of the animal figures*
013		B	*looks at Kai and Ayse* want you
014	<		help me sometimes/
015	<	Ayse	*looks at B*
016			y e s
017		B	na\ put this onto the podium that these can run about in **a**
018	>		row\

Fig.14.3 Transcript from the situation "animal polonaise" implemented with the children Kai und Ayse at the data collection point T1 (see Vogel and Huth 2010, S. 191 et seqq.). Explanation for understanding the transcript:/—lifting the voice,\—lower the voice, action are in italics and <—happened at the same time

Material and the Arrangement of Space

The activity-oriented approach described by van Oers (2004, pp. 316, 317) for early mathematical education, which touches on the cultural–historical approach for learning and development Vygotsky (1978), assumes that mathematical thinking is not limited by genetics. Mathematical thinking arises from the idea that "activities resulting from specific actions or situations" will be designated as "mathematical" by the adults (teachers or parents) (van Oers 2004, 317; translated by R.V.).

> "These activities, in turn, achieve a certain meaning in the understanding of the individual. The process of selection, designation and assessment of certain activities as 'mathematical' is in principle a socio-cultural process. [...] Consequently, mathematics is learned through social interaction and that in the context of meaningful activities." (van Oers 2004, p. 317) (translated by R.V.)

Meaning is not attributed to the materials themselves for the relevant activities in this theoretical context, but rather is given a meaningful value by the people participating in the situation (see also van Oers 2004, p. 321).

> "Learning processes are required to be able to use an aid properly. The behaviour of the students is supported by the aid in a manner specific to the culture in such a learning process, and simultaneously, the advantages that are connected with the culture structure of the aid become obvious." (van Oers 2004, p. 321; translated by R.V.)

Fig. 14.4 Stills from the situation "wooden sticks" at the data collection point T3 (two boys at the age of approximately 5 years are involved in the situation)

The materials and aids become a bridge between the strange culture (in this case, the culture of mathematics), in which experts (in this case the adult) demonstrate handling the material with reference to the task and deliver one interpretation with it. In this manner, the material has significance for the problems to be solved. Thereby, they create connecting factors for childlike thinking and the children's development and they introduce them to the thinking and activity processes of the relevant culture.

> "Higher mental functions exist for some time in a distributed or 'shared' form, when learners and their mentors use new cultural tools jointly in the context of solving some task." (Bodrova and Leong 2001, p. 9)

Through the interpretation of the guiding adult, the chosen materials and tools become artefacts of a culture of mathematics. They constitute connection points for the kindergarten children either to join the mathematical interpretations of the guiding adult or to make modified interpretations of the arrangement and to bring their own ideas as well as the storylines and rules of their child-like world into the situation (see also Vogel 2013).

Example—"Wooden Sticks"

The left picture (see Fig. 14.4) shows figures like houses and lanes, which the two boys have laid spontaneously with the wooden sticks at the beginning. The bicoloured pattern (see marking, red–yellow–red–yellow) is being laid by the guiding adult. This pattern shows the mathematical interpretation intending for the situation: the sticks are used for putting a tape ornaments. The figures of the children can be also interpreted mathematically. After statements of the children, they represent three-dimensional objects. In the mathematical interpretation, the boy could have laid down the front elevation of a building.

The children take up the impulse of the guiding adult and extend the pattern (see the right picture of Fig. 14.4). On inquiry, the children describe the lined up

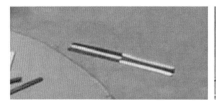 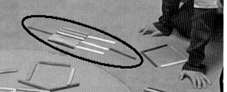

Fig. 14.5 Stills from the situation "wooden sticks" at the data collection point T3

sticks as people. Thereby, they tie in with a situation, e.g. a human queue in which people stand close to each other. With it, the children take up the mathematical interpretation at the action level and interpret them in their childlike world of experience.

The second pattern (see Fig. 14.5), which is pretended by the guiding adult, is taken up by one of the two boys in the manner that he lies down a structure which shows colour sample at one point (see the left picture of the Fig. 14.5). At the end of the laying sequence, the boy puts a square with the wooden sticks. The other boy has put another bicoloured pattern in the meantime. In this, the boy takes up a colour from the original pattern and chooses another colour as the second colour usage (yellow–lilac–yellow–lilac). While one boy at the action level is following up the pretended mathematical interpretation, the other boy also integrates elements from his world of experience at the action level. Thus, the resulted structure could be interpreted, e.g. as a rocket (see marking, Fig. 14.5).

Altogether, in the select sequences it becomes apparent that the children follow the mathematical interpretations of the guiding adult in their visible actions at time but absolutely also find their own mathematical interpretations. Thus, a boy of the tandem remains true to his original use of the wooden sticks as a representation of geometrical objects.

Mathematical Situations of Play and Exploration— Research Areas Between Instruction and Construction

The mathematical stagings shall be able to be repeated in the research context comparably several times. With it, the instructional view point gets more important if the mathematical situations of play and exploration are used as an empirical research instrument. For the implementation of this requirement of openness and standardization, a uniform structure for the description of the situations in the form of "didactic design pattern" (see Wippermann 2008) was chosen. This "design pattern" will be designated in the context of mathematical learning and thinking as "design patterns of mathematical situations" in the future. Alexander (1977) developed the theory of "Pattern Language". It was adapted for the area of teaching and learning and is used here especially to document and to relay expert knowledge about the

14 Mathematical Situations of Play and Exploration ...

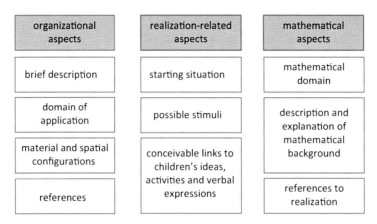

Fig. 14.6 Structure for the "design pattern of mathematical situations" in the erStMaL project

arrangement of teaching–learning environments (see Wippermann and Vogel 2004; Vogel and Wippermannn 2005).

In the erStMaL project, the mathematical situations of play and exploration will be described by the research team along a structure which has been specially developed.[3] The "design patterns of mathematical situations" are sub-divided into the following central groups of categories (see also Vogel 2013): (1) organizational aspects, (2) realization-related aspects and (3) mathematical aspects (see Fig. 14.6). The organizational aspects are important for the organization of the research. The realization-related aspects refer to the actual implementation of the play situations and the mathematical aspects support the guiding adult in their decision-making during the situation.

The individual descriptive categories are related to each other. Thus, a repertoire is described by possible stimuli in the realization-related categories. In the specific situation, selections can be made between them. Which of the possible stimuli for activities, gestures and spoken instructions in the "design patterns of mathematical situations" are appropriate must be decided for each situation and assumes a certain measure of mathematical knowledge in the respective mathematical domain and, furthermore, in the mathematical domains that might be used for creative solution of the task, as well as a good feeling for accompanying the mathematical learning process.

On the one hand, detailed instructions are given for the situation by the "design patterns of mathematical situations" and on the other the descriptions shall put the guiding adult in a position to react situatively and creatively to the mathematical constructions of the children.

---

[3] All the mathematical situations of play and exploration will be developed from the researcher group of the project erSTMaL

Conclusion

For the children, the mathematical situations of play and exploration are areas of common construction of the meaning, which receives a mathematical dimension by the instruction of the guiding adult. At the same time, these instructions are products of construction on the part of the guiding adult who interprets the descriptions of the situations in form of "design patterns of mathematical situations" in the context of the research process at different points. Such points are the preparations for the concrete data collection stage or several sequences in the implementation of the situations of play and exploration.

The exemplarily selected situations of play and exploration give an impression of this, like the children in the data collection stage meet the construction of mathematics which is determined by the material (artefacts), the mathematical task and the impulses by the guiding adult. The construction of mathematical spaces of exploration on the part of the guiding adult is initiated by instructions in the situation descriptions of the "design patterns of mathematical situations". The children themselves partially take up this mathematical interpretation or develop own interpretations.

Besides the use as an empirical research instrument, the mathematical situations of play and exploration are currently used in seminars of the primary teacher education in mathematics at the Goethe University, Frankfurt am Main. The work with the children is prepared in detail by the exact description of mathematical teaching and learning situations in the form of "design patterns of mathematical situations". For following analyses, the situations will be videotaped. In this way, the teacher students can observe and analyse the mathematical work of the children according to research-based learning. At the same time, they can experience what it means to accompany children in their mathematical learning.

Acknowledgements The preparation of this paper was funded by the federal state government of Hessen (LOEWE initiative).

References

Acar Bayraktar, E., Hümmer, A.-M., Huth, M., Münz, M. & Reimann, M. (2011). Forschungsmethodischer Rahmen der Projekte erStMaL und MaKreKi. In B. Brandt, R. Vogel, & G. Krummheuer (Eds.), *Die Projekte erStMaL und MakreKi. Mathematikdidaktische Forschung am „Center for Individual Development and Adaptive Education" (IDeA)* (pp. 11–24). Münster: Waxmann.

Alexander, C. (1977). *A pattern of language. Towns, buildings, construction.* New York: Oxford U.P.

Benz, C. (2010). *Minis entdecken Mathematik.* Braunschweig: Westermann.

Bodrova E. & Leong, D.J. (2001). Tools of the mind: A case study of implementing the Vygotskian approach in american early childhood and primary classrooms. Genf: International Bureau of Education. http://www.ibe.unesco.org/publications/innodata/inno07.pdf. Accessed 15 Mar 2011.

Bruner, J. (1986). *Actual minds, possible worlds*. Cambridge MA: Harvard University Press.
Clements, D. H., & Sarama, J. (2007). Early childhood mathematics learning. In F. K. Lester Jr. (Ed.), *Second handbook of research on mathematics teaching and learning* (pp. 461–555). Charlotte, NC: Information Age Publishing.
Fthenakis, W.E., Schmitt, A., Daut, M., Eitel, A., & Wendell, A. (2009). *Natur-Wissen schaffen*. Band 2: Frühe mathematische Bildung. Troisdorf: Bildungsverlag EINS.
Hoenisch, N., & Niggemeyer, E. (2007). *MATHE-KINGS. Junge Kinder fassen Mathematik an.* 2. vollst. überarbeitete Auflage. Weimar: verlag das netz.
Hülswitt, K. (2006). Mit Fantasie zur Mathematik—Freie Eigenproduktionen mit gleichem Material in großen Mengen. In M. Grüßing & A. Peter-Koop (Eds.), *Die Entwicklung mathematischen Denkens in Kindergarten und Grundschule: Beobachten—Fördern—Dokumentieren* (pp. 103–121). Offenburg: Mildenberger Verlag.
Koch, P. & Oesterreicher, W. (2007). Schriftlichkeit und kommunikative Distanz. *Zeitschrift für Germanistische Linguistik, 35*(3), 346–375.
Korff, N. (2008). *Entwicklung, Diagnose und Frühförderung mathematischer Kompetenzen im Elementar- und Primarbereich*. Reihe „Handreichungen zur Entwicklung der Mathematikdidaktik im Elementarbereich" (Hrsg. von D. Bönig). Bremen: Universität Bremen.
Krummheuer, G. (2011). Die empirisch begründete Herleitung des Begriffs der „Interaktionalen Nische mathematischer Denkentwicklung" (NMD). In B. Brandt, R. Vogel, & G. Krummheuer (Eds.), *Die Projekte erStMaL und MakreKi. Mathematikdidaktische Forschung am „Center for Individual Development and Adaptive Education" (IDeA)* (pp. 25–89). Münster: Waxmann.
Oerter, R. (2011). *Psychologie des Spiels. Ein handlungsorientierter Ansatz*. Weinheim: Beltz Taschenbuch.
Prediger, S. (2001). Mathematiklernen als interkulturelles Lernen—Entwurf für einen didaktischen Ansatz. *Journal für Mathematik-Didaktik, 22*(2), 123–144.
Samuelsson, P. I., & Carlsson, A. M. (2007). *Spielend lernen. Stärkung lernmethodischer Kompetenzen*. Troisdorf: Bildungsverlag EINS.
Sarama, J., & Clements, D. H. (2008). Mathematics in early childhood. In O. N. Saracho & B. Spodek (Eds.), *Contemporary perspectives in early childhood education* (pp. 67–94). Charlotte, NC: Information Age Publishing.
Schuler, St., & Wittmann, G. (2009). Forschung zur frühen mathematischen Bildung—Bestandsaufnahme und Konsequenzen. In M. Neubrand (Ed.), *Beiträge zum Mathematikunterricht 2009* (pp. 419–422). Münster: WTM-Verlag.
Tomasello, M. (2008). *Origins of human communication*. Cambridge MA: MIT Press.
van Oers, B. (2004). Mathematisches Denken bei Vorschulkindern. In W.E. Fthenakis & P. Oberhuemer (Eds.), *Frühpädagogik international. Bildungsqualität im Blickpunkt* (pp. 313–329). Wiesbaden: VS Verlag.
Vogel, R. (2013). Mathematical Situations of play and exploration. Educational Studies in Mathematics 84 (2), pp. 209-225. doi:10.1007/s10649-013-9504-4.
Vogel, R., & Huth, M. (2009). Können wir auch rot-rot-rot nehmen? Die Grundschulzeitschrift, 23 (222.223), 38–41.
Vogel, R., & Huth, M. (2010). "... und der Elefant in die Mitte"—Rekonstruktion mathematischer Konzepte von Kindern in Gesprächssituationen. In B. Brandt, M. Fetzer, M. Schütte (Eds.), *Auf den Spuren Interpretativer Unterrichtsforschung in der Mathematikdidaktik* (pp. 177–207). Münster: Waxmann.
Vogel, R., & Wippermann, S. (2005). Transferstrategien im Projekt VIB—Didaktische Design Patterns zur Dokumentation der Projektergebnisse. In Ch. Bescherer (Ed.), *Einfluss der neuen Medien auf die Fachdidaktiken* (pp. 39–60). Baltmannsweiler: Schneider Verlag.
Vygotsky, L. S. (1978). *Mind in society. The development of higher psychological processes*. Cambridge: Harvard University Press.
Wippermann, S. (2008). *Didaktische Design Patterns*. Saarbrücken: VDM.
Wippermann, S., & Vogel, R. (2004). Communicating didactic knowledge in university education—"Didactic Design Patterns" as Best Practices. In L. Cantoni & C. McLoughlin (Eds.),

Proceedings of World Conference on Educational Multimedia, Hypermedia and Telecommunications 2004 (pp. 3231–3234). Chesapeake, VA: AACE.

Wollring, B. (2006). Kindermuster und Pläne dazu—Lernumgebung zur frühen geometrischen Förderung. In M. Grüßing & A. Peter-Koop (Eds.), *Die Entwicklung mathematischen Denkens in Kindergarten und Grundschule: Beobachten—Fördern—Dokumentieren* (pp. 80–102). Offenburg: Mildenberger Verlag.

Wulf, Chr., & Zirfas, J. (2007). Ausblick: Lernkulturen im Umbruch. Zur Bedeutung von Ritualen und performativen Praktiken in Lernsituationen. In Ch. Wulf, B. Althans, G. Blaschke, N. Ferrin, M. Göhlich, B. Jörissen, R. Mattig, I. Nentwig-Gesemann, S. Schinkel, A. Tervooren, M. Wagner-Willi, & J. Zirfas (Eds.), *Lernkulturen im Umbruch. Rituelle Praktiken in Schule, Medien, Familie und Jugend* (pp. 323–328). Wiesbaden: VS Verlag.

Chapter 15
Number Concepts—Processes of Internalization and Externalization by the Use of Multi-Touch Technology

Silke Ladel and Ulrich Kortenkamp

Introduction

In Germany, the use of ICT in kindergarten (as well as in primary school) is still seen to be very controversial. There are various reasons for this, but a crucial point is that "traditional" technology (that is, computers and software) only offers indirect manipulation through the mouse, while it is generally preferred to offer manipulatives that children can hold, touch, feel, etc. With virtual manipulatives, children might not focus on the content but on the (artificial) way to interact with it. In the beginning, it is even a challenge for children if the mouse reaches the border of the table or mouse pad. The fine motor skills of the young children are not fully developed yet, for example, the hand–eye coordination still needs additional training. It is difficult for children to coordinate their eyes and what they see on the screen with their movements with the mouse. This problem is amplified by the fact that the scale of the distances moving the mouse does not correspond linearly to the distances on the screen.

Touch-sensitive interfaces enable children to work directly with virtual manipulatives, that is, interactive visual representations of dynamic objects that provide opportunities for constructing mathematical knowledge (Moyer et al. 2002). Touching and working with manipulatives meet the way young children learn. Children who cannot express knowledge in speech could express knowledge in gestures (Goldin-Meadow 2009). *"Interactive gestures allow users to interact naturally with digital objects, in a physical way, like we do with physical objects."* (Segal 2011, p. 7). Multi-touch technology gives children better control of their interaction. In a study with 128 children at the age of 6 and 7 years, Segal examined the variable direct-touch interaction vs. mouse interaction (Segal 2011). She concluded that children

---

S. Ladel (✉)
University of Saarland, Saarbrücken, Germany
e-mail: ladel@cermat.org

U. Kortenkamp
CERMAT, Martin-Luther-Universität Halle-Wittenberg, Halle, Germany
e-mail: kortenkamp@cermat.org

using direct-touch outperformed children using the mouse, in particular for strategy use in a counting and addition task. Segal reasons that the children using the touch interface had more time to concentrate on the task itself than to concentrate on the manipulation.

A further possible improvement in interface design can be multi-touch technology, as opposed to single-touch technology. Multi-touch means that the interface is able to detect and process the input of several touches at the same time, so it can be possible to handle a virtual manipulative with up to ten fingers, or more if several persons work with the same device. Single-touch, allowing for a single finger at a time, is still similar to a mouse movement, as it only removes the indirection. As it is not possible to use several fingers at once in single-touch environments, the single finger induces ordinal number concepts. As we will see below, representing a quantity by touching the screen with many fingers all at once can also support a cardinal concept of numbers.

Another reason for the controversial issue of ICT in kindergarten and primary school is that applications for early mathematics often do not match the consolidated research results of mathematics education and what we know about the development of mathematical knowledge. Segal (Segal 2011, p. 15) defines "Gestural Conceptual Mapping" as the *"mapping of gestures (actions) to mental operations and representations with the learned concept."* External representations must map to mental representations. In her research, Segal showed that children in the environment with direct-touch *and* gestural conceptual mapping delivered the best performance.

As an example for such a mapping, we refer to the "power of five" (Flexer 1986; Krauthausen 1995). Children are able to subitize small numbers of items. To conceive bigger numbers without the need to count, quantities should be structured, e.g., in blocks of five and x. Appropriate gestures must take that into account, for example, by grouping the tokens created by five touching fingers into blocks of five.

In our research, we consider multi-touch-technology, for example, multi-touch tables like Microsoft Surface, Evoluce One, or similar. It also applies to mobile devices, in particular the iPad or others based on the Android operating system. These affordable devices make the double-improvement (direct vs. indirect, multi-touch vs. single-touch) available in the classroom or kindergarten setting. Another requirement for sensible use of these devices is software that uses this technology based on educational research in mathematics. Starting from our initial hope that the way children use these devices can give us more information about the concepts of numbers they use, and maybe help them to fluently change between different concepts, we formulated three research questions:

- Can the usage data collected help reveal and distinguish the number concepts that children use?
- How must a multi-touch environment be designed to collect the appropriate data?
- Can we support the development of the part–whole number concept with such environments?

Didactical Background

Development of Number Concepts

The analysis of the object is a necessary requirement for understanding human activities. We focus on number concepts because this mathematical content is very important for further learning of mathematics. According to the ordinal concept, numbers describe positions in an ordered row (Fuson 1992; Dornheim 2008). Coming along with that is the knowledge of which number is the successor or predecessor and where a number is located on the number line. Objects can now be brought into a relative position to each other. This is very important for estimation as well. Children develop this concept about the age of 2–5 years. Parallel to this (ca. 3–6 years), children acquire also a cardinal concept of numbers. They understand that number words can be used not only to count but also to name a quantity. The last number counted corresponds to the cardinality of a set (Gelmann and Gallistel 1987). The part–whole concept of numbers is based on those developments. If a child already acquired a part–whole concept of numbers, then he/she knows that several parts are composed to a whole, e.g., the parts 3 and 5 are composed to the whole of 8. Especially the part–whole concept provides the basis for several fundamental mathematical principles like commutativity and associativity of addition, or the complementarity of addition and subtraction (Resnick et al. 1991, p. 32). The part–whole concept is also important to understand the decimal number system because this uses a decimal part–whole concept. It combines the part–whole concept with the decimal structure of our number system (Fig. 15.1) (Ladel and Kortenkamp 2011b; Ladel 2011).

Finger Symbol Sets

All three concepts can be externalized using fingers. Fingers are a very famous working material for young children and medium to represent quantities. There are numerous ways to do this (Brissiaud 1992; Ladel and Kortenkamp 2011a). According to the ordinal concept of numbers, the child may show his fingers *one by one*. Brissiaud called this *Counting-Word Tagging to Number*. Another way to represent quantities with fingers is to show them *all at once—Finger symbol sets*. This approach is according to the cardinal concept of numbers, if the child knows that all fingers belong to the quantity. If a child realizes that the seven fingers are shown with two hands, thus two parts, e.g., existing of five fingers and two fingers, and these two parts add up to the whole of seven, then he/she appropriated a part–whole concept. We also asked the children to produce tokens of an amount between 11 and 20. If they separate the quantity in tens and ones, it would be a grouping that tends to the decimal part–whole concept.

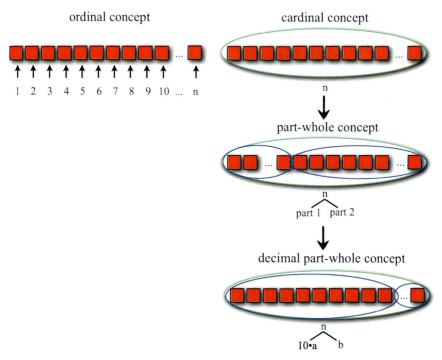

Fig. 15.1 Ordinal and cardinal number concept development

The starting point of our development of the multi-touch environment is to survey the way children work with their fingers. In a first step, we just observe and recognize the touches and the spatial and temporal distances caused by a child laying his/her fingers on the table surface. It is thus the externalization of the child's activated concept of numbers.

Theoretical Framework

> Studying the changes that learning environments undergo when technology-based artefacts are introduced means analyzing how activity changes as consequence of tools' introduction and how this change is meaningful for the students and the teachers.
> (Bottino and Chiappini 2008, p. 841)

Using a multi-touch table in kindergarten leads to a very complex environment. This calls for a theoretical framework that is able to capture this environment and gives more orientation. Within activity theory, we are able to identify relevant key issues. According to the "orchestration" approach, "learning is seen as the result of an active exploration and construction from the student, mediated by the tools made

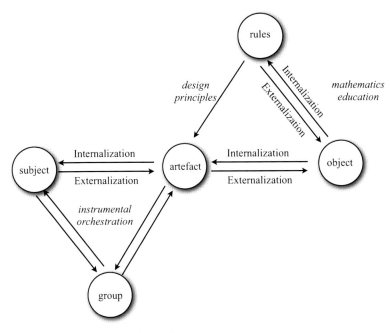

Fig. 15.2 Artifact-centric activity theory diagram

available in the activity and by the social interaction that develops within it" (Bottino and Chiappini 2001, p. 3).

For our experiments, we developed a first prototype environment where children can produce tokens on a multi-touch table.[1] In this section, we will give a short introduction to our theoretical framework, artifact-centric activity theory (ACAT) and point out the connection to the instruction and construction processes that we could observe in the experiments.

Artifact-Centric Activity Theory

An activity is a form of acting directed toward an object (Bottino and Chiappini 2008). In our experiments, the activity is to produce a given quantity of tokens, where the number is given either in verbal or nonverbal symbolic representation. The activity is carried out through an artifact, here a multi-touch table, and is orientated to an object, here the concept of a number. We are using a framework based on activity theory and activity systems (Engeström 1987) that considers the artifact as a central component in the activity, ACAT (Ladel and Kortenkamp 2013). We will give only a brief sketch of the framework here (Fig. 15.2).

---

[1] At http://cermat.org/acat/videos.html you can see children working with the environment.

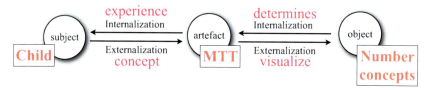

Fig. 15.3 The main axis of ACAT

Instead of measuring the outcome of the activity system—an educated student (Bellamy 1996)—we try to assess the processes that occur during the activity. ACAT gives us a framework to describe and analyze the interactions of children with the object mediated through the artifact.

ACAT enables us to consider the whole learning environment. The community (group), including the (nursery) teacher and the partner, influences the way children act (see the lower left triangle of Fig. 15.2). Especially the verbalization of the teacher may change the number concepts the children activate. The partner may impact the chosen number concepts as well. In the next section, we will exemplify how this impacts the design of the tasks we gave the children.

Construction

Within the activity, the number concepts are mediated through the artifact. Using the theoretical framework of ACAT, it is possible to point out the different processes of internalization and externalization that take place while learning with ICT and to focus on the mediating role of the artifact (Fig. 15.3).

The whole activity is based on interaction between subject and object. Here, we have to emphasize the two facets of an object. On the one hand, there is the object itself, which are number concepts, and this is independent of the subject, and, on the other hand, there is the psychological reflection, that is the concept[2] of the object that the subject has.

The child develops its number concept during the work with the artifact. It externalizes its *concepts* during the interaction with the virtual tokens, those form a tangible *visualization* that is *determined* by the object "itself." This gives the children a chance to *experience* the concepts necessary for their development.

This interaction axis captures also the congruence principle of Tversky et al. (Tversky and Bauer Morrison 2002, p. 3) that says that

> the structure and content of the external representation should correspond to the desired structure and content of the internal representation.

According to Segal (Segal 2011), this should yield a better construction of mental representations and operations of abstract concepts and thereby support performance.

---

[2] Do not confuse this with *number concept*.

Fig. 15.4 Rules

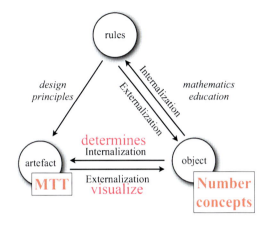

Instruction

As already stated in the introduction, it is mandatory to use mathematic-didactic-specific design for the multi-touch environment. ACAT helps us describe how these rules can be derived and analyze how they influence the activity.

The object is not only what the children should learn, but it also determines the way the multi-touch table software has to be programmed. Therefore, we have to follow certain rules, e.g., mathematic-didactical rules and multimedia design principles (Ladel 2009). The properties of the mathematical object, that is, number and its different concepts, and the way they are used in practice determine the design of the multi-touch interface and hence the external representation.

The design of our prototypical environments was following the theoretical considerations based on results from both mathematics education and general multimedia design principles. Within ACAT, the design of the artifact underlies certain rules, which are derived through mathematics education from the object of interest. The externalization and internalization, described in the previous section, are complemented by these design rules (Fig. 15.4).

Internalization occurs through the activity of the child also within a social community. That is why we have to consider, e.g., the nursery teacher and the team partner as well. The communication between two children in our environment is significant in the observation of the development of number concepts. We can observe if a child is able to solve a task with the help or in cooperation with another child or not. We refer to Vygotskys zone of proximal development (ZPD) that

> is the distance between the actual development level as determined by independent problem solving and the level of potential development as determined through problem solving under adult guidance or in collaboration with more capable peers.
> (Vygotsky 1978, p. 33)

The design and the social community aspects described above constitute the means of instruction. The construction process of the child can be shaped through this

Fig. 15.5 Tokens: The left tokens appear as one block; the tokens on the right seem to be separate

instruction. Part of it takes place in the design phase *before* the actual activity, the other part during the activity. So, instruction is based on the *rules* and the *group* in ACAT.

The Design of Multi-Touch Environments for Early Mathematics Learning

For first experiments, we used several variants of a prototype-learning environment. This was created not for actual teaching or learning, but just as a first step into understanding the interaction processes and the chances and pitfalls for learning in such environments. Basically, in all environments, pairs of children were asked to produce tokens using their fingers. A researcher posed the tasks and the experiments were recorded on video for later analysis. The video recordings are available on request from the authors.

In this section, we will describe some aspects of the design of these environments and some first findings that are based on the analysis of the videos. Without jumping to the conclusion already we note that the interaction is even more complex than we expected, which also proves the necessity of further detailed inspection of such interactions.

Design: Grouping of Tokens

A fundamental visualization question is the design and behavior of the virtual tokens on the table. According to the one-to-one principle (Gelmann and Gallistel 1987), we decided that each finger touch produces exactly one token.

While working with the multi-touch table, the children experience the structure of the external representation that offers the possibility to develop a meaningful mathematical discourse about the properties of the mathematical object (Chiappini and Bottino 1999). Therefore, the external representation (visualization of numbers) and the internal representation should be compatible (Segal 2011). In this way, it can support the development of the child's mental representation of the object. Our tokens have the shape of a square (and not of a circle) to make it possible to place one side of the square next to another one and make it possible to stick them together. Then, they can be recognized as one block (law of closeness) (Fig. 15.5).

15 Number Concepts—Processes of Internalization and Externalization ...

Fig. 15.6 A. tries to move the fourth token

Analysis: Influence of the Artifact

In the following example, we asked the children to put a certain number of tokens on the table. They can either produce tokens one by one using any finger or produce several tokens simultaneously using several fingers. We were hoping to deduce the number concepts used by the child through analyzing their actions.

Task: "Please put x tokens on the table."		
1	Interviewer	A., please put six tokens on the table
2	A.	*Ok. First the first finger*
		(A. uses the thumb to move one token on the table)
3		*then the second finger*
		(A. uses the index finger to move another token on the table)
4		*then the third finger*
		(A. uses the index finger again and moves another token on the table)
5		*ah*
		(she shakes her head and wants to take the token back with her middle finger, but the table does not react)
6		*I just take the forth*
		(A. takes her ring finger and wants to move one token on the table, but the token on the table does not move due to technical reasons, Fig. 15.6)
7		*then I just take this one*
		(A. uses the index finger to move a fourth token on the table.)
8		*and this one*
		(A. looks at her fingers and uses the index finger again to move one token on the table.)
9		*One, two, three, four, five. One more*
		(A. uses the index finger again to move the sixth token on the table)
10		*and six. One, two, three, four, five, six.*
		(Counting the tokens)

A. began by moving tokens one by one in the center of the table. However, she did not rely on counting "one, two, three," but she connected the tokens 1-to-1 to the fingers and used the ordinal numbers "the first, the second." This stands to reason that the ordinal concept of numbers dominates in this particular case, where the number word "one" corresponds to the first finger, "two" to the second finger, etc.

But in line 4, we see an adjustment event: A. made a mistake by using the 'wrong' finger. She used her index finger, which is "the second" for her, to produce "the third" token. She recognized her 'fault' and wanted to correct it by removing the token with her middle finger. A. externalized her concept of numbers via putting her fingers on the MTT and the MTT visualized the fingers through the tokens. At this stage, we do not know if A. really identifies only the sixth finger or the whole quantity with the number six. But then, the visualization through the MTT did not work well, which leads to the situation that A. had to change the concept she uses. She either knows or experienced that it does not matter with which finger the token is moved and accepted to let the third token remain on the table.

Next, she switched back to her ordinal concept and tried to move a token with her ring finger. At this point, there is a second adjustment event shown by the change of concept, this time caused by a technological fault of the MTT that caused A. to use her index finger again instead of her ring finger. When she wanted to place the fifth token, she first thought about which finger to take and then decided to use the index finger again, assumedly because her experience now tells her that the table reacts best with this finger and it is easier as well for the fine motor skills. Most importantly, she already learned that it does not matter if she uses the 'wrong' finger. The unresponsive table caused a transition of concept.

In the end, A. proved her work by counting all tokens on the table. She corresponded the sixth token with not only the number six but also the whole quantity of all tokens on the table. This means that she already connected the ordinal with the cardinal concept of numbers.

This example shows very well how the artifact can influence the way children work and also evoke changes of concepts (Fig. 15.1). If the MTT would have worked well and recognized A.'s fingers, there would never have been the need to change the concepts.[3] We could observe some children who paid attention to which finger they took to produce tokens, but then changed their concept and took any finger. The experience with the MTT led to the fact that the children were able to abstract and knew, that it does not matter, with which finger a token is produced.

Concerning the influence of the artifact and its design, we could observe problems that the young children did have producing tokens. In our first environment, the users produce tokens by touching the green border of the screen. Tokens that are moved into the center of the table will remain. If a finger is released while still on the green area, then the token will vanish again. We could observe that it was not easy for the children to move the fingers on the screen and therewith the to-

---

[3] We do not dare to claim that technology causes learning due to it insufficiencies, we just point out how complex the interactive process of working with an electronic learning environment can be, both in the intended and in the unintended way.

kens away from the body. The children could not see the tokens because they were covered by their hands (Dohrmann 2010). Also, the multi-touch technology had problems with the recognition of the fingers, because the young children touched the screen too weakly. Hence, the table did not visualize all the fingers as tokens. This led to the fact that children preferred using the one-by-one method (counting) instead of all-at-once and hence a simultaneous or rather quasi-simultaneous representation. So the experience the children made with the artifact changed their behavior in a way we did not intend. We had to change the design of the MTT environment for the second experiment: The children could now produce tokens in the middle of the table and if the tokens should remain, they had to be pulled to the border of the table. We could observe that this changed user interface encouraged more children to create several tokens at once.

Analysis: Influencing the Partner

It is not always possible for a child to adopt or use or transition to a new concept even if it is shown to the child by a teacher, a partner, or the artifact. In the following transcript, we can see how V. resists the different number concept of A. The researcher in this task explicitly asks for placing tokens all at once and not one by one.

Task: "Please put *x* tokens on the table *all at once*."		
1	Interviewer	*A., please put five tokens on the table, but this time all at once*
2	A.	(A. puts all five fingers of her right hand on the screen and moves the tokens on the table.)
3	Interviewer	*V., could you please put four tokens on the table, all at once?*
4	A.	*Like this.* (A. puts four fingers all at once on the table and lifts her hand again.)
5	V.	(V. uses her index finger and moves tokens one by one on the table.)
6	A.	*No, like this.* (A. shows V. four fingers all at once, Fig. 15.7)
7	V.	(V. looks at A.s fingers and continuous to move tokens one by one)

A. moved five tokens at the same time and V. watched her doing it. But as it was her turn, she did not do it the same way but moved them one by one, even when A. insisted that she should use four fingers and showed it to her again. V. could not change her concept but persisted moving one by one.

We must respect and observe whether a child is able to change his/her concept with help or not. In the example above, A. was able to use the cardinal concept and use several fingers at the same time on the screen. V. was not able to switch to this concept, even when A. showed her how to do it. *The new concept was not yet within the zone of proximal development of V.* In our setup, we are able to distinguish children that can reach certain concepts from those who are unable to do this yet even with the help of their peers.

Fig. 15.7 A. shows four fingers to V.

Analysis: Sharing Quantities

Regarding the task to produce a quantity of tokens "together," we could not only observe different kinds of agreements between the children, but also different ways to decompose:

1. **Halving:** The children decomposed into halves, e.g., "Six, that is twice three." This way to decompose is used for even numbers between 5 and 10. With quantities larger than 10, the kind of decomposition changed.
2. **Decimal part–whole concept:** Quantities higher than ten were decomposed into tens and ones, as the following transcript of P. shows.

Task: "Please put *x* tokens on the table *together*."		
1	Interviewer	*Can you put twelve tokens on the table, together?*
2	P.	*One, two, three, four, five, six, seven, eight, nine, ten.* (P. counts and tips his fingers.)
3		*Eleven, twelve.* (P. continues counting the fingers of his partner.)
4		*S. you have to put two.*
5	Interviewer	*So how do you decompose the twelve?*
6	P.	*I make ten, and S. makes two.*
7	Interviewer	*And can you also move 14 tokens on the table, together?*
8	P.	*One, two, three, four, five, six, seven, eight, nine, ten.* (P. counts and tips his fingers again.)
9		*I make ten, and S. makes four.*

P. did not know or maybe was not sure how many fingers he has on two hands and hence had to count them twice. The first time—representing 12—he just went on counting up to 12, but the second time—representing 14—he immediately knew that S. has to produce four tokens if he produces ten. He was then able to decompose 14 into ten and four (Fig. 15.8).

Fig. 15.8 P. working with the multi-touch table. He is using the decimal part–whole concept for sharing quantities with his partner

3. **'Power of five':** A third way of sharing a number we observed was the use of the 'power of five' (Krauthausen 1995).[4] The task was to put twelve tokens on the table together. Before moving the tokens on the table, E. said: "I make five and she makes five then and then I make two." E. did already have a sophisticated part–whole concept that she could use in the sense of addition. But she did not use the decimal part–whole concept and decomposed in ten and two but took the 'power of five' approach which corresponds to using one hand as bundling unit.

The Role of the Nursery Teacher

ACAT also enables us to clear up the role of the nursery teachers. In this theoretical framework, she has to supervise the work of the children, and to take care of aspects that cannot be handled by technology. For example, to analyze the processes we implemented automatic recording of the children's touch actions. We are thus able to analyze the externalization process of the students also using the collected data. The recorded data are demonstrated in Fig. 15.9, where you can see when and how long a finger touched the screen. On the left, the screen was touched with three fingers at the same time. On the right, we can see that five fingers touching one by one. This data and its visualization may help analyze the applied concepts a posteriori.

In our experiments, we could observe children changing their concepts when they were first representing numbers with their fingers and then representing the

---

[4] In German "Kraft der Fünf" is unambiguous, as Kraft does not mean power in the sense of the arithmetic operation, but only power in the sense of force.

Fig. 15.9 Log-data of finger touches. On the left, three fingers touched simultaneously; on the right, five fingers touched one after the other

same numbers with their fingers on the MTT: Some children first counted their fingers one by one and then put them all at once on the table. Other children did the opposite, showing fingers all at once when asked for a certain number, and working one by one on the MTT. Therefore, the actions done with the fingers *before* touching the screen cannot be recorded by the computer. The teacher has to observe these actions and these observations can be included in the analysis. From this, we deduce the need for a nursery teacher to work with the children and to observe them, as it is impossible to capture the full picture with technology alone. We have to be aware of the fact that the fingers are already a mediating artifact on their own. Using them creates a first externalization (Fig. 15.10).

Conclusions

Although our current multi-touch environments are not immediately usable for teaching, but only for our early experiments, they proved very useful for understanding the complex interaction that takes place. With regard to our first research question—*Can the usage data collected help reveal and distinguish the number concepts that children use?*—we saw that the data indeed give hints about the number concepts used directly on the table, but this is only a part of the number concept used by the child. Due to the fact that the fingers act as another mediating artifact, we cannot get computer data about the whole activity, but only about the direct interaction with the table. As our analysis shows, the children switch between different number concepts and the concepts used on the table are not necessarily the concepts they prefer to solve a task.

Nevertheless, it was very important to see how the design of the artifact (the table, not the fingers) can force children to switch between concepts. The failing

15 Number Concepts—Processes of Internalization and Externalization ...

Fig. 15.10 A child showing all fingers before switching back to the ordinal concept

finger recognition of the multi-touch table lead to children using any finger instead of a specific one (the first one, the second one, the third one), which is a favorable step in their development of abstraction. Changing the software enabled children to use the concept they prefer and to develop their understanding in their own pace. It is conceivable to use such a specific "failing" design to guide the construction process of the children, even if we cannot claim that this was the case in our experiments. This results in "more instruction" in the construction process.

The second research question—*How must a multi-touch environment be designed to collect the appropriate data?*—has to consider not only the artifact and its programming, but also the design of the learning situation as a whole. Teacher and group are indispensable components of the learning arrangement and thus must contribute to the data collection. The log data of the computer environment alone are not sufficient to capture the learning process of the children, as it only captures the interaction through *one* artifact, the multi-touch table. The whole mediation is usually done through a chain of artifacts. In our experiments, children used a certain number concept with their hands as a first artifact and then used a different number concept with their hands on the multi-touch table. A teacher can and should observe such transitions. In an experimental setup, it is necessary to complement the computer data with video recordings of the children's actions.

Finally, we are far away from answering the most important one of our questions—*Can we support the development of the part-whole number concept with such environments?* A very easy action like placing a certain number of tokens on a table is surprisingly complex to analyze, and there are many design decisions that have to be backed by media-pedagogic and (mathematics) didactic principles. Without knowing the proper design of such a simple action, it is impossible to create an environment that not only demonstrates but also changes the use of certain number concepts by children. Also, learning with the computer is not an asocial activity. Teachers and peer groups participate in that process and must be taken into account. We are convinced that the recent progress in technology, in particular the availability of multi-touch devices, can affect learning with the computer positively, as the computer steps back and integrates itself into a social context.

References

Bellamy, R. K. (1996). *Context and consciousness, chapter designing educational technology* (pp. 126–146). Cambridge: MIT Press.
Bottino, R. M., & Chiappini, G. (2001). Studying changes in learning environments brought about by ict-based systems. In H. Ruokamo, N. Ossi, P. Seppo, & H. Pentti (Eds.), *Intelligent computer and communications technology* (pp. 170–176). Tampere, Finland. PEG 2001 international conference.
Bottino, R. M., & Chiappini, G. (2008). *Handbook of international research in mathematics education, chapter using activity theory to study the relationship between technology and the learning environment in the arithmetic domain* (2nd ed., pp. 838–861). New York: Routledge.
Brissiaud, R. (1992). Pathways to number. Children's developing numerical abilities. chapter *A toll for number construction: Finger symbol sets* (pp. 41–65). Lawrence Erlbaum Associates.
Chiappini, G., & Bottino, R. M. (1999). Visualisation in teaching-learning mathematics: The role of the computer. In *Graphs and visualization education*. Coimbra, Portugal (pp. 147-152).
Dohrmann, C. (2010). *Über die didaktische Konzeption interaktiver Geometriesoftware angesichts substantieller Entwicklungen von Mensch-Maschine-Schnittstellen.* Diplomarbeit, Pädagogische Hochschule Schwäbisch Gmünd.
Dornheim, D. (2008). *Prädiktion von Rechenleistung und Rechenschwäche: Der Beitrag von Zahlen, Vorwissen und allgemein-kognitiven Fähigkeiten*. Berlin: Logos-Verlag.
Engeström, Y. (1987). *Learning by expanding: An activity-theoretical approach to developmental research*. Orienta-Konsultit.
Flexer, R. J. (1986). The power of five: The step before the power of ten. *Arithmetic Teacher, 2*, 5–9.
Fuson, K.C. (1992). Research on whole number, addition and subtraction. In D. A. Grouws (Ed.), Handbook of research on mathematics teaching and learning (pp. 243-275). New York: Macmillian
Gelmann, R., & Gallistel, C. R. (1987). *The child's understanding of number*. MA: Harvard University press.
Fuson, K.C. (1992). Research on whole number, addition and subtraction. In D. A. Grouws (Ed.), Handbook of research on mathematics teaching and learning (pp. 243-275). New York: Macmillian.
Goldin-Meadow, S. (2009). How gestures promotes learning throughout childhood. *Child Development Perspectives, 3*(2), 106–111.
Krauthausen, G. (1995). *Mit Kindern rechnen*. Arbeitskreis Grundschule – Der Grundschulverband – e. V. Frankfurt a. M.
Ladel, S. (2009). *Multiple externe Repräsentationen (MERs) und deren Verknüpfung durch Computereinsatz. Zur Bedeutung für das Mathematiklernen im Anfangsunterricht* (Vol. 48) of *Didaktik in Forschung und Praxis*. Hamburg: Verlag Dr. Kovacs.
Ladel, S. (2011). Multiplex-R: Zum Wechsel zwischen verschiedenen Darstellungsformen von Zahlen und Operationen bei 5- bis 8-jährigen Kindern. In R. Haug & L. Holzäpfel (Eds.), *Beiträge zum Mathematikunterricht* (pp. 527–530). Münster: WTM-Verlag.

Ladel, S., & Kortenkamp, U. (2011a). Finger-symbol-sets and multi-touch for a better understanding of numbers and operations. In M. Pytlak, T. Rowland, & E. Swoboda (Eds.), *Proceedings of the seventh Congress of the European Society for Research in Maths Education*. ERME, University of Rzeszów.

Ladel, S., & Kortenkamp, U. (2011b). Implementation of a multi-touch-environment supporting finger symbol sets. In M. Pytlak, T. Rowland, & E. Swoboda (Eds.), Proceedings of the seventh Congress of the European Society for Research in Maths Education, pp. 1792–1801. ERME, University of Rzeszów.

Ladel, S., & Kortenkamp, U. (2013). An activity-theoretic aproach to multi-touch tools in early maths learning. *The International Journal for Technology in Mathematics Education, 20*(1).

Moyer, P., Johnna, B., & Mark, S. (2002). What are virtual manipulatives? *Teaching Children Mathematics, 8*(6):372–377.

Resnick, L. B. et al. (1991). *Teaching advanced skills to at-risk students: Views from research and practice*, chapter Thinking in arithmetic class (pp. 27–53). San Francisco: Jossey-Bass.

Segal, A. (2011). *Do gestural interfaces promote thinking? Embodied interaction: Congruent gestures and direct touch promote performance in math*. PhD thesis, Columbia University.

Tversky, B., & Bauer Morrison, J. (2002). Animation: Can it facilitate? *International Journal of Human-Computer Studies, 57*, 247–262.

Vygotsky, L. S. (1978). *Mind in society: The development of higher psychological processes*, chapter Interaction between learning and development (pp. 79–91). Harvard University Press.

Part V
Intervention

Chapter 16
Intentional Teaching: Integrating the Processes of Instruction and Construction to Promote Quality Early Mathematics Education

Jie-Qi Chen and Jennifer McCray

Disputes about the roles of instruction and construction in teaching and learning processes have been ongoing for more than half a century (Ausubel 1964; Craig 1956; Kirschner et al. 2006; Kohlberg and Mayer 1972; Mayer 2004; Phillips 2000; & Richardson 2003). Although points of argument vary, there is a general consensus about the definition of these two processes. Instruction usually refers to classroom practices that are designed by the teacher to furnish knowledge through systematic methods and with specific goals. Teacher in this discussion means one who works with all aged learners from young children to adults in a collective educational setting, such as a daycare center, elementary school, or university. Construction, on the other hand, often describes a learning process in which children actively engage to build their own concepts and skills (Phillips 2000). Focusing primarily on teachers and their practices, instruction, while it has implications for learning, is essentially concerned with teaching. Attending to students and their sense making, construction, on the other hand, is a theory about learning.

Historically, instruction and construction were regarded as separate and competing processes with distinctive terms and practices associated with each. *Teacher initiated, goal oriented, explicit teaching*, and *established* are terms often associated with instruction, whereas *child initiated, interests oriented, incidental learning*, and *personal* are words typically used when describing construction (see Table 16.1). Nowadays, instruction and construction are rarely considered to be mutually exclusive processes in classroom practice. Rather, they are seen as complementing each other to strengthen teaching and learning for children's knowledge acquisition as well as their understanding (Richardson 2003; Sztajn et al. 2012).

Agreement in principle does not always lead to fully realized practice, however, and this is especially the case when subject matter enters into the equation. Instruction and construction do not occur in a vacuum; they are applied to content areas in the classroom context and must deal explicitly with content knowledge. What does it mean to integrate instruction and construction while dealing thoroughly and rigorously with a content area? To what extent does deep understanding of subject

---

J.-Q. Chen (✉) · J. McCray
Erikson Institute, 60654, Chicago, IL, USA
e-mail: jchen@erikson.edu

Table 16.1 Terms Associated with Instruction and Construction

Instruction	Construction
Teacher initiated	Child initiated
Teacher active	Child active
Teacher guided	Child directed
Teacher centered	Child centered
Explicit teaching	Incidental learning
Goal oriented	Interests oriented
Knowledge delivery	Knowledge construction
Common	Unique
Established	Personal

knowledge affect teachers' integration of instruction and construction? What kind of teacher professional development is needed to prepare teachers to teach specific subject matter in ways that combine the benefits of instruction and construction? To advance the field, discussion regarding instruction and construction needs to take these questions seriously. Further, to improve practice, the field needs mechanisms to help teachers integrate instruction and construction processes in their daily teaching practices.

Providing such mechanisms is particularly pressing in the field of early childhood education, as it has traditionally given relatively little attention to teachers' content knowledge (Bowman et al. 2001; Chen and McNamee 2006; McCray and Chen 2011). Instead, early childhood educators as a whole have long been focused on the processes of teaching, as opposed to the knowledge to be taught. This traditional early childhood approach was substantiated by a Position Statement by the National Association for the Education of Young Children in the United States (Bredekamp 1987). Calling it developmentally appropriate practice (DAP), the Position Statement supported a child-centered approach to teaching. While not tied to any specific curricula or content learning, it proposed a set of principles in alignment with constructivism. Specifically, it recommended that teaching be responsive to the needs and capabilities of individual children, emphasizing teacher observation and support over the instruction of skills. Though not without controversy, the influence of DAP on early childhood practice in the USA has been pervasive and far reaching (Bowman et al. 2001; Bredekamp and Copple 2009; Elkind 1987). Early childhood, then, is particularly "behind the curve" when it comes to a meaningful integration of instruction and attention to subject matter generally.

In this essay, we describe our effort to integrate instruction and construction in early childhood education through fostering intentional teaching around Big Ideas in early mathematics. We begin the chapter with a brief history of the debate about the roles of instruction and construction, highlighting the theoretical foundations for each argument. Situating issues in the historical context, we move the discussion to the current state of teaching in early mathematics, focusing on reasons why the debate tilts heavily in favor of construction and how that has affected early childhood classroom practice. Next, the chapter presents our argument for intentional teaching in early mathematics as a framework that effectively integrates instruction and construction in teaching and learning processes. We share evidence suggesting the effectiveness of this approach based on our work at the Early Math Collaborative at Erikson Institute in Chicago and conclude with a discussion of the renewed importance of articulating the relationship of instruction and construction in light of the accountability movement driving much of contemporary education.

A Brief History of the Instruction vs. Construction Debate

Two terms critical to understanding the idea of instruction are "teacher" and "acquisition" (Richardson 2003) as they emphasize the primary agent—teacher—in the process and the central action—acquiring knowledge—that students are meant to take. Two theories of learning—cultural transmission ideology and behaviorism—provide the conceptual framework for this sense of instruction. From the perspective of cultural transmission ideology, the primary task of education is "the transmission to the present generation bodies of information and rules of value collected in the past" (Kohlberg and Mayer 1972, p. 458). Knowledge and rules from the past may be rapidly changing or remain static; regardless, in instruction, education should focus primarily on the transmission of the culturally given. The teacher's job, then, is the direct instruction (DI) of such information and rules, whereas the student's primary responsibility is the acquisition of the given (Kohlberg and Mayer 1972).

Behaviorism supports the cultural transmission ideology by offering a psychological explanation of the learning process. Children learn through the imitation of adult behavior models, or through explicit instruction and reward or punishment. Of critical importance to this learning process is behavioral modification, which can be achieved most efficiently through classroom instruction designed by the teacher. In this framework, it is the teacher who supplies the model, sets the expectation, and presents the distilled knowledge and skills required to function successfully in society (Skinner 1974; Todd and Morris 1995). The child's role is to accept, or take in, this knowledge and skills.

A well-known example of teaching by explicit instruction is the Direct Instruction System for Teaching Arithmetic and Reading (DISTAR), developed by Siegfried Engelmann and Wesley Becker in the 1960s (Wesley et al. 1975). Today, DI has become a model for teaching. It emphasizes "well-developed and carefully planned lessons designed around small learning increments"; and it asks teachers to teach "clearly defined and prescribed teaching tasks" (National Institute for Direct Instruction 2012). DI is currently in use in thousands of schools across America and some of its components have been adapted by other popular intervention programs such as Success for All and the Knowledge is Power Program (Kirschner et al. 2006).

In contrast to instruction, the focus of construction is on "students" and their central activity in this context is "participation" (Richardson 2003). John Dewey (1963) and Jean Piaget (1952) are the primary architects of the philosophical and psychological foundations for this educational practice. Often referred to as a constructivist approach, this view holds that children are not passive receivers of knowledge. Rather, they actively construct knowledge through interaction with the environment, including both its physical and social dimensions (Piaget and Inhelder 1969). Knowledge is acquired, not by listening to others, but through individuals' active participation. Because knowledge construction is an idiosyncratic process, it involves a great deal of self-exploration and self-discovery. Accordingly, instruction that disregards children's prior experiences and their individual differences can have little effect on learning and development.

There are many constructivist approaches to teaching, including child-centered learning, discovery learning, problem-based learning, inquiry-based learning, and experiential learning, to name a few. All of these practices refer to an essentially equivalent pedagogical approach, namely, challenging students to solve "authentic" problems and acquire knowledge in information-rich settings (Kirschner et al. 2006). The emphasis in each of these practices is the self-directed activity of learners and the importance of the creation of personal meaning.

In the 1990s, a great deal of work on constructivism was done in different subject areas, including mathematics (e.g., Ball 1993; Cobb et al. 1991), reading and writing (e.g., Freedman 1994; Barr 2001), history (e.g., Wilson 2001; Wilson and Wineburg 1993), and science (e.g., Tobin 1993; White 2001). Many of these authors compare constructivism with the instruction transmission model, drawing attention to significant differences in the two pedagogical approaches. They highlight various distinctive features, including attention to individual differences, respect for students' background knowledge, provision of opportunities for students to challenge, change, or add to existing beliefs, achievement of understandings through engagement in tasks, and development of students' meta-awareness of their own learning process and understanding (Richardson 2013).

Moving into the new millennium, the discourse on instruction and construction made headway on two fronts. On one front, more and more scholars have come to realize that arguing over which of the two processes—instruction or construction—is more conducive to learning is counterproductive (Lampert 2001; Phillips 2000; Richardson 2003). Instead, the current zeitgeist presumes that students can learn and develop through constructive processes as well as teacher-directed instruction, and may learn best through a combination of these types of experiences. Teachers play a critical role in the constructive learning model, not only by providing information-rich environments and by serving as facilitators, but also by setting clear expectations, teaching specific skills, and helping to transform students' spontaneous concepts into more complex, analytical types of thought (Vygotsky 1978).

On a second front, the discussion has started to pay attention to how teachers' subject matter knowledge affects the way instruction and construction are integrated in practice. Many educators acknowledge that the single most important determinant of what children learn is what teachers know (Darling-Hammond and Bransford 2005). Recently, a body of literature has demonstrated the positive relationship between teachers' content knowledge and student outcomes in such areas as mathematics (e.g., Chen and McCray 2012; Hill et al. 2005) and language and literacy (e.g., Coburn et al. 2011; Taylor et al. 2011). Findings such as these have drawn the field's attention to the role of teachers' content knowledge in teaching. This has affected the discussion of the relationship between instruction and construction, which has become not only more focused on their effective integration but also more cognizant of how specific content might affect their implementation in teaching.

Instruction and Construction Practices in Early Mathematics Education

Because it is more congruent with DAP, the constructivist view has dominated the discussion of instruction versus construction in the field of early mathematics education (Clements et al. 2004; Copley 2010; Ginsburg et al. 2008). One of the most prominent and vocal scholars in this discourse is Constance Kamii, who bases much of her work on mathematics education on the writing of Jean Piaget. According to Kamii (2006), there are three kinds of knowledge: physical, social, and logical–mathematical. Physical knowledge is knowledge of objects in external reality, such as the color or weight of an apple, and it can be acquired empirically through observation and hands-on experience. Social knowledge, such as the alphabet and numerals, is created by convention among people. The child does not invent this kind of knowledge. She or he acquires it through instruction. Logical–mathematical knowledge, including number and arithmetic, is constructed by each child. For example, when presenting a child two counters, she or he can see the attributes of each counter, including things like color, size, or shape; these are present in the objects themselves. However, the child cannot see the "twoness" in the objects; the "twoness" results from the mental creation of a set—the set of two counters. In this way, numeracy requires a creative mental act beyond mere perception. While the child needs to have adults around to interact with to obtain conventional mathematics knowledge and skills, the ultimate source of mathematical understanding is the mental construction process within each individual (Kamii 2006).

Kamii's position is supported, explicitly or implicitly, by early childhood educators for at least three reasons. First, it resonates with the strong sentiment in the field that play and self-directed exploration are central in young children's learning. Early childhood educators as a group firmly believe that young children learn through play. In play, children develop a range of social and cognitive skills without risking failure (Bodrova 2008; Hanline et al. 2008; Miller and Allmon 2009). Play, by definition, is pleasurable, spontaneous, and child initiated. It is unlike instruction, which, for the most part, is planned and teacher initiated, with obligatory participation and no guarantee that it will be a pleasurable experience. Conceptually, play and construction are related but not identical. In early childhood practice, however, the two concepts are often seen as synonymous. To help children learn mathematics concepts and skills through play, for example, teachers provide mathematics-rich environments, including the provision of mathematics manipulatives in different learning centers. Though teachers observe children and encourage them to play with the materials, children's learning tends to be more incidental and less focused.

Another reason that early childhood teachers favor construction over instruction in mathematics teaching is related to preschool curriculum and teacher preparation. Until recently, most preschools and daycare centers—educational settings for 3–5-year-olds—in the USA did not use specific curricular texts for teaching. Instead, teachers created activities based on curriculum resource books and drew from their years of teaching experience. This means that to provide coherent mathematics instruction, teachers must have sufficient mathematical knowledge to design activities and plan their implementation. Unfortunately, mathematics as a topic is formidable and anxiety producing for many early childhood teachers. Unlike their peers at the elementary and high school levels, a majority of early childhood teachers have received little training in teaching mathematics, even those that have a bachelor's degree in early education (Copple 2004; Ginsburg et al. 2006). This general lack of preparation and knowledge in early mathematics causes many early childhood teachers to feel uncomfortable and inadequate when they are asked to instruct mathematics, particularly in group situations. They are more confident and comfortable when children take the initiative to learn mathematics through self-guided play situations.

A third reason that early childhood teachers favor construction in early mathematics teaching is their misunderstanding of what early mathematics is and what teaching early mathematics entails. In part due to inadequate preparation and knowledge, many early childhood teachers think of early mathematics as simple, consisting primarily of counting and simple arithmetic (Copley 2004). While opportunities for learning how to count are numerous throughout the day in the early childhood classroom, teaching such skills through specific instruction seems unnecessary to teachers. In addition, preschool teachers often think that the main focus of mathematical teaching should be children's memorization of number facts (Sarama and Dibiase 2004). In contrast to the larger mathematics education community that has moved toward "redefining mathematics as a dynamic discipline full of opportunity for inquiry and discovery" (Feiler 2004, p. 399), the early childhood community still views mathematics as static and rigid with little relevance or meaning in children's lives. This view of what mathematics is leads early childhood teachers to believe that it is developmentally inappropriate to instruct mathematics to preschoolers.

In 2000, when the National Council of Teachers of Mathematics (NCTM) first included standards for early education in its recommendations, it shocked the early childhood community that mathematics for young children involves more than counting and simple arithmetic. Reading through the content strands identified by NCTM, few early childhood teachers understand their relevance to young children, since terms such as "algebra," "data analysis," and "probability" sound foreign to them. Many early mathematics curricula have been developed to help teachers, but without sound knowledge of mathematics' content strands, early childhood teachers approaching mathematics from a child-guided constructivist perspective continue to do little to develop children's deep mathematical understanding. Teacher's inadequate preparation and their resistance to DI were the biggest challenges to effective early mathematics education a decade ago at the birth of the NCTM standards, and unfortunately, they remain the biggest challenges today.

Intentional Teaching: A Means to Integrate Instruction and Construction in Early Mathematics

To help early childhood teachers understand the content of early mathematics and how it develops in the thinking of young children, we launched the Early Math Collaborative in 2007. Designed primarily for preschool teachers who serve children aged from 3 to 5 years, the program supports teacher development in early mathematics by providing yearlong, bimonthly workshops and on-site coaching between workshops. During the coaching session, classroom video is used to engage the teacher in a reflective practice. Workshop instructors are Erikson faculty and coaches are experienced preschool teachers, who participate in content training alongside their teachers. The program promotes *intentional teaching* as a mechanism for integrating instruction and construction with a deep, connected understanding of early mathematics in classroom teaching.

Intentional teaching is a relatively new concept in the field of early education. It was developed to establish a middle ground in the long-standing debate that pits instruction against construction in discussions of what and how to teach children in early education. While stopping short of describing teaching as instruction, it makes clear that effective constructivist education relies on an active teacher who has goals for what children will learn and specific plans for how that might occur. In her 2007 book, Epstein describes the intentional teaching method as a blended approach that combines what she calls a child-guided and adult-guided learning experience (Epstein 2007). Intentional teaching, according to Epstein (2007), does not happen by chance. Rather, it is "planful, thoughtful, and purposeful," and that purpose is to achieve specific outcomes or goals for children's learning and development.

In our project, we have come to see that the biggest impediment to the intentional teaching of early mathematics is a lack of content knowledge on the part of most early childhood teachers. We believe teachers need information on what the mathematics content is, how it manifests in the thinking of children as they become familiar with it, and how they might best support its development in children's thinking. We operationalize this needed content knowledge as three integrated components: what to teach (content), whom to teach (learner's developing understanding of the content), and how to teach (strategies for supporting thinking about the content). We describe each component briefly below.

What to Teach What to teach focuses on the issue of content knowledge. Because early childhood teachers are traditionally trained as generalists, they are ill prepared in the area of mathematics knowledge. Confronted with the range of NCTM's content strands, they often feel anxious and incapable. Recognizing the challenge that early mathematics knowledge presents to teachers, our team developed a list of Big

Table 16.2 Sample big ideas by mathematics content strand

Content strand	Big idea text
Algebraic thinking	The same collection can be sorted in different ways
Number and operations	A collection can be made larger by adding items to it and smaller by taking items away from it
Measurement	Many different attributes can be measured, even when measuring a single object
Geometry	Two- and three-dimensional shapes can be used to represent and understand the world around us
Data analysis and probability	How data are gathered and organized depends upon the question that is addressed

For a complete list of Big Ideas, see *"Big Ideas of Early Mathematics: What Teachers of Young Children Need to Know"* by Erikson's Early Math Collaborative (2014), Upper Saddle River, NJ: Pearson

Ideas within each of the content strands identified by NCTM (2000). Our Big Ideas are key mathematical concepts with four distinctive characteristics: (1) they convey core mathematics ideas that serve as organizing structures for teaching and learning mathematics during the early childhood years; (2) they connect to each other in a coherent and systematic fashion; (3) they elaborate and solidify the mathematical experience and thinking of young children between the ages of 3 and 6 years; and (4) they provide foundations for further mathematics learning that facilitate long-term mathematical understanding.

Table 16.2 lists a sample Big Idea in each of the mathematical content strands identified by NCTM. To help teachers understand Big Ideas, we constructed adult learning tasks that engage teachers in exploring, analyzing, and applying the Big Ideas. For example, when studying geometry, teachers are asked to describe a shape without using its name, focusing their attention on noticing and naming shape attributes, such as number of sides and size of angles. Similarly, in the study of algebraic thinking, teachers challenged to name as many different sets of objects as they can find in the children's story "Goldilocks and the Three Bears." Teachers then analyze these sets to discover size and sequence patterns among them. We introduce these adult learning tasks to teachers during bimonthly workshops through hands-on experiences. In these workshops, teachers from different schools work together, participating in a community of learners focused on the understanding of Big Ideas.

In their joint statement on early mathematics, the National Association for the Education of Young Children (NAEYC) and NCTM (2002) pointed out that "Because curriculum depth and coherence are important, unplanned experiences with mathematics are clearly not enough. …Depth is best achieved when the program focuses on a number of key content areas rather than trying to cover every topic or skill with equal weight." Big Ideas help to ensure depth by providing teachers with a tool that focuses on foundational mathematics concepts. Equipped with such a tool, teachers can make the teaching and learning process more intentional. Teachers are more likely to specify and clarify their goals for teaching, distinguish the core from the trivial, engage in thoughtful curriculum analysis, and create meaningful

Table 16.3 Learning trajectory of pattern

Activity type	Child's behavior	Teacher's talk
Recognize	Detects regularity, applies the word "pattern" to simple repeating sequences	Do you see a pattern here? Do you notice anything that repeats?
Copy	Duplicates simple patterns alongside a model pattern	Can you copy this pattern? Does yours follow the same rule?
Complete	Fills in missing element of pattern	How can you fix this pattern? How do you know what's missing?
Extend	Continues a pattern	What comes next? How would this pattern keep going?
Describe	Identifies the rule of a pattern by naming the smallest unit that repeats	How could we name this pattern? What is its rule?
Translate	Uses new media to construct pattern with the same structure as model pattern	Can you make this pattern another way? How are they the same?

mathematics activities. Further, Big Ideas in mathematics help teachers articulate the underlying purpose of students' work and create multiple pathways for student understanding. Teachers become more flexible and responsive to children's mathematical thinking and behaviors.

Whom to Teach Focusing on whom to teach calls teachers' attention to understanding where children are in their thinking about mathematical concepts and their mastery of mathematical skills. The field of early childhood education has long taken pride in making child development knowledge the center of early education. This knowledge, for the most part, concerns the general developmental progressions in cognitive, language, social and emotional, and physical domains. Though fundamental in early education, such knowledge is too general to help teachers design classroom activities (Chen and McNamee 2006). Teachers need to supplement general knowledge of child development with an understanding of the learning trajectories in the development of children's mathematics thinking, integrating their analysis of children's behavior with the landmarks of conceptual understanding within content domains.

Learning trajectories refer to "paths by which learning might proceed" in a content area (Simon 1995). Learning trajectories are neither linear nor random. Developed through empirical research, they represent expected tendencies that describe probable steps children will follow as they develop their initial ideas into formal concepts within a content area such as mathematics (Maloney and Confrey 2010; Sztajn et al. 2012). Table 16.3 presents a learning trajectory that describes the growing understanding of pattern and regularity among 3–6-year-olds. It starts with recognizing patterns by detecting regularity and applying the word "pattern" to simple repeating sequences, then moves through copying, completing, extending, and describing, culminating in using new media to construct a new pattern that has the same structure as a model pattern. This learning trajectory, while recognizing that each child's path may be unique, describes a trend in how young children progress as they grasp the central mathematical concepts of pattern and regularity.

To help teachers integrate learning trajectories into their classroom practice, we developed a set of "research lessons." Designed for teachers to use in the classroom, each research lesson is a series of developmentally appropriate mathematics activities that share the following three features: (1) all activities correspond to the adult learning tasks by addressing similar Big Ideas in the same content strand; (2) they respect the learning trajectory of a particular content strand by building on children's existing knowledge and leading them to a more sophisticated understanding of the concept; and (3) they invite children to construct mathematical understanding by involving them in a challenging yet fun learning experience.

In the "Who is Napping" research lesson, for example, the Big Idea focus is that patterns are sequences (repeating or growing) governed by a rule, and identifying a pattern leads to predictability and allows one to make generalizations. *The Napping House* by Audrey Wood is a cumulative tale in which characters, such as a grandma, a boy, a cat, and a flea pile on a bed, one by one, to nap. The +1 growing pattern is easy for children to describe because the illustrations distinctly show the growing, linear sequence and foreshadow "what comes next." In the research lesson, children first review the book "*The Napping House*" that they read previously. They then represent the growing pattern using characters in the book on a piece of chart paper. They can also act out the story so that they are able to visualize change in the sequence. Aligning with the learning trajectory for pattern, teachers ask children to start the activity by identifying the pattern in the book. They can then copy, extend, and translate the pattern. Throughout the process, they are encouraged to talk about their experience (see Appendix for "*Who is Napping*" research lesson).

After learning the research lesson during the professional development workshops, the teacher implements them in the classroom. The coach observes, then reflects on the implementation process with the teacher using the videotape. The videotape helps to reveal clearly what children know and where they need further support. A teacher's reflection with the coach focuses on levels of progression in children's mathematics thinking and behavior. Engaging in reflective practice benefits teachers in a number of ways: It supports their growth in mathematical understanding as well as their intentional selection of instructional tasks, deeper interactions with children in the classroom, and more extensive use of children's responses to further learning (Sztajn et al. 2012).

How to Teach How to teach is about pedagogy best suited to key content. Responding to the developmental characteristics of young children, the teaching strategies early childhood teachers use routinely involve multisensory modes, hands-on learning, the use of manipulatives or props, and learning through play or games, to name a few. In most early childhood classrooms, these strategies are primary. They represent most of the intentional teaching that occurs. They are applied first, with teachers paying cursory attention to content and concepts, and adjusting complexity of challenge to meet children's understanding only as an afterthought and when time and attention allow. In these instances, what is being taught and who is learning it are both secondary considerations, taking a "backseat" to the means and modes of

WHO IS NAPPING?

Big Idea Focus: Patterns are sequences (repeating or growing) governed by a rule. Identifying a pattern brings predictability and allows one to make generalizations.

In this lesson, children:
- Create a visual representation of a growing pattern
- Discuss ideas about patterns

Materials
- o *The Napping House* by Audrey Wood
- o Character cards with felt, magnets, or tape on the back (see Blackline Masters, pp. 1—4)
- o Felt board, magnet board, or chart paper
- o Unifix cubes or inch cubes (optional)

1. **Review *The Napping House* and Introduce Activity**

   Remind children of *The Napping House* story. Ask children, *What happens at the napping house?* and *Who lives in the napping house?*

   Show children the character cards you have prepared and ask them to name each one. Tell children that you would like their help to figure out the pattern of the story.

2. **Represent the Growing Pattern**

   Turn to the page where the illustration shows the granny sleeping on the bed. Have a child display the granny character card on the board or chart paper to represent who is napping. For example, say:

   ➢ *Who is napping on this page?*
   ➢ *Let's show who is napping using a picture.*

   Continue to the next page with the granny and the child on the bed.

   ➢ *Who is napping now?*
   ➢ *Let's use two pictures now to show who is napping. Let's line them up.*

   Help children align the character cards so that a simple pictograph results. (All granny cards are lined up, all child cards are lined up, and so on.) Stop at the illustration with the flea; there are now six characters piled on the bed.

Planning Tips

Make sure that children are familiar with *The Napping House* prior to this lesson.

Introduce this activity to **small groups**. Once children are familiar with the materials, they can use them independently during center time to retell the story and represent the growing pattern.

Facilitation Tip

In order to focus on the math of the lesson, keep the book review brief. Do not re-read the book as you represent the growing pattern. Use the illustrations as a guide and have children tell who is napping on each page.

Math Note

Growing patterns change (increase or decrease) by a constant amount. The pattern of *The Napping House* is based on a constant change of plus one.

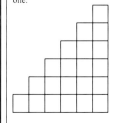

---

teaching. In our version of intentional teaching, decisions about how to teach are subordinated to what to teach and whom to teach. That is, the Big Ideas in a content strand and the learning trajectories that describe children's progression in understanding them drive the choice of materials, strategies, and grouping, not vice versa. Effective pedagogy is intentional pedagogy; it responds to the developmental needs of young children and facilitates the attainment of specific learning goals.

During workshops and coaching sessions, Erikson's instructors and coaches model a variety of teaching strategies appropriate for the Big Ideas and learning

3. **Discuss the Growing Pattern**

   Draw children's attention to the shape of the pictograph they have constructed. Ask questions to help them describe the growing pattern. For example:

   ➢ *What do you notice? How can you describe the pictograph we made?*

   ➢ *Why is this a pattern? Have you seen a pattern like this anywhere else?*

   ➢ *If this pattern continued, what would happen next?*

4. **Close the Lesson**

   Tell children that you appreciate their help in finding the pattern in the story. Remind them that finding patterns in stories helps them know what comes next. It helps them make predictions.

   Invite children to be on the lookout for other stories with a growing pattern. (See **Book Connections** for suggestions.)

Book Connections

> *I Went Walking* by Sue Williams
> *There Was an Old Lady Who Swallowed a Fly* by Simms Taback
> *This is the House that Jack Built* by Simms Taback
> *Bringing the Rain to Kapiti Plain* by Verna Aardema
> *Rooster's Off to See the World* by Eric Carle
> Other cumulative tales

Observation

Do children notice that the result looks like steps or a staircase?

Do any children use numbers to describe the pattern they see?

Can they explain what should come next in the pattern?

Math Note

It is important to identify what repeats in a pattern. In the case of a growing pattern, it's a quantitative change that repeats. This constant change brings predictability and allows one to make generalizations, just as with a repeating AB pattern.

Differentiation

Ask children to copy and extend the plus one growing pattern using unifix cubes or inch cubes.

For children who are ready, add numerals to label the pictograph or their cubes.

Teacher as Learner

The idea of growing patterns is new for many early childhood teachers.

Can you think of other examples of growing patterns?

---

trajectories. For example, Big Ideas are always introduced through activities with materials commonly found in preschool classrooms. Teachers learn different mathematics concepts not only by reading texts but also through acting out stories, working on number activities, comparing different attributes of everyday objects, and graphing classroom data for analysis. To enhance hands-on learning experiences, teachers engage in discussion and reflection about the Big Ideas embedded in the activity. They also consider how similar approaches to learning mathematics could be used when they work with children in other content areas.

The integration of children's books with mathematics education is one strategy that warrants special attention. Capitalizing on teachers' relative comfort with literacy activities, each of our workshops includes a featured children's book as a way to introduce mathematics Big Ideas. Books such as "*Goldilocks and the Three Bears*" and "*The Gingerbread Man*" offer high-quality illustrations and rich language. The stories also embrace a variety of mathematics concepts, such as sets, patterns, counting, and composing and decomposing numbers. At the end of each workshop, teachers receive a copy of the featured book and one or two other quality children's books emphasizing the same mathematics concepts. When teachers return to their classroom, they have materials to conduct an activity with children based on the mathematics concepts they explored during the workshop. Using children's books as an entry point to introduce mathematics concepts helps teachers see the connection between early mathematics education and the development of children's language and literacy skills. As well, it helps to ease teachers' anxiety toward early mathematics teaching, and increases their confidence in their ability to introduce diverse mathematics concepts and skills to young children.

Recent research has clearly demonstrated the positive relationship between the use of mathematics-related language by teachers and mathematical learning during the preschool years (Ehrlich 2007; Klibanoff et al. 2006; McCray 2008). Incorporating these findings, the workshops and coaching sessions emphasize both awareness and the use of mathematics-related verbalization. Teachers learn how to use mathematics language to describe children's daily activities during transition, snack, dramatic play, and outdoor time. Additional emphasis is placed on asking questions that invite children to describe their thinking using mathematical language.

Intentional pedagogy in early mathematics is not limited to mathematics lesson time or to activities in the mathematics learning center. Rather, it permeates all areas in the classroom throughout the day. The term "mathematizing" describes this approach. Mathematizing refers to the process of taking familiar situations or problems in daily life and framing them in mathematical terms (NRC 2009, p. 43). For example, the teacher might invite Jonah to compare the height of his tower with that of Tyrone's by describing the number and size of blocks each has used. To take another example, the teacher may ask children to help prepare for a snack by getting "as many napkins as there are children at your table," or children may be sent to wash hands through instructions such as "all children who are wearing red today may go line up now." Mathematizing involves children in the construction and re-construction processes of mathematical reasoning, problem solving, representation, connection, and communication (NRC 2009).

Impact of Intentional Teaching Rather than treating them as oppositional, intentional teaching embraces and integrates the processes of instruction and construction. In early childhood classrooms, "children need opportunities to initiate activities and follow their interests, but teachers are not passive during these child-initiated and child-directed activities. Similarly, children should be actively engaged and responsive during teacher-initiated and teacher-directed activities. Good teachers help support the child's learning in both types of activities" (Bowman et al. 2001, p. 8). Guided by the what, the whom, and the how of intentional teaching in early mathematics, early childhood teachers can set clearly defined mathematical goals for instruction while also attending to children's interests, listening to their ways of understanding, and helping them construct mathematical knowledge. Both children and their teachers play active roles in the learning process. When instruction and construction are integrated in the learning process, children experience greater gains in learning outcomes.

Our program evaluation, conducted during the 2008–2009 school year, found increased mathematics learning among children whose teachers participated in our yearlong professional development training designed to develop teachers' intentional teaching in early mathematics (Chen and McCray 2012; McCray and Chen 2011). A brief background about our intervention program in the context of the American educational system might be useful before we report the program evaluation results. In the USA as in many other countries around the world, there are a range of different early child care systems. In our early mathematics project, we worked with prekindergarten and kindergarten teachers who are part of the teacher workforce in the Chicago Public School system. That is, they are government employees and they are required to have a teaching certificate to work with children aged 3–8 years.

For our program evaluation, a total of 154 3–5-year-olds participated in the study. Of these children, 91 were randomly selected from 12 participating classrooms and served as the intervention group. An additional 63 children randomly selected from matched classrooms served as the comparison group. Children's mathematical abilities were measured using Subtest 10 of the Woodcock–Johnson III (WJ-III) Achievement Battery (Woodcock et al. 2001), a widely used, standardized, norm-referenced measure of mathematics ability. Two-level hierarchical linear modeling (HLM) was used to determine how much of the variance among changes in children's scores from fall to spring could be attributed to teacher participation in the intervention.

Results showed that participation in the intervention significantly predicted growth in WJ-III age estimate scores. Compared to children in comparison classrooms, children in intervention classrooms showed an average of 3 months additional growth in the WJ age estimate over the intervention year ($p<0.031$). The growth of children who began the school year behind national norms approached 5 additional months of learning. These results point to the positive impact of the intentional teaching professional development program in early mathematics on children's learning and its particularly significant effects on the children who are most in need of help.

Conclusion

The ongoing discussion of the relationship between instruction and construction reflects the paramount role of each in the process of teaching and learning. Due to concerted efforts to advance in the field of education, instruction and construction are seldom regarded as two separate entities; rather, they are often seen as two sides of the same coin. From years of research and field experience, we are clear that for certain kinds of knowledge and skills, such as creating, naming, and transforming shapes or counting or measuring to quantify differences, instruction with adult-initiated activities is more efficient and effective. On the other hand, child-initiated construction processes are more conducive to the acquisition of other kinds of knowledge and skills, including familiarity with two- and three-dimensional shapes and comparing or seriating without counting or measuring (Bowman et al. 2001; Epstein 2007). Regardless of whether children are engaged in instruction or construction experiences, teachers always play a vital role by creating supportive environments and purposefully challenging, scaffolding, and extending children's learning. Both instruction and construction are basic means in teaching and learning in early education. When they work in tandem, they both contribute to the attainment of meaningful learning goals (Richardson 2003).

Discourse on instruction and construction is not obsolete, however. In the "Race to the Top" initiative, the USA has once again entered into an accountability-driven school reform movement. What schools, teachers, and students are held accountable for, unfortunately, is measured largely in terms of standardized test scores. Standardized tests, by their nature, tend to focus on factual knowledge and discrete skills. Although the designers strive to give more attention to problem solving and in-depth understanding of content knowledge in the tests, limited time for test taking and a format for quick scoring make the task extremely difficult. Teaching to the test becomes inevitable for teachers when their performance evaluation and sometimes job security depend on their students' test scores. Teaching to the test is most prevalent in urban schools that serve minority and low-income students. In these schools, instruction involves more drill and practice, emphasizing what is on the test rather than inquiry and understanding. Knowledge construction through projects, experiments, and collaborative learning is largely ignored. As a result, while student test scores may increase in the short term, students' understanding and interest in learning suffer in the long run (Baker et al. 2010).

With education constrained by limited vision and "teaching to the test," there is a renewed significance for reflections on the meaning of instruction and construction. Good instruction always involves the students in a construction process. By the same token, construction can be effective only when instruction is carefully designed by teachers. While curriculum should not emerge solely from children's interests, the most meaningful and lasting learning occurs when children are engaged and invested in the topic of the study, regardless of the content areas. To ensure our children develop skills and the ability to thrive in the twenty-first century, we have no choice but integrate instruction and construction in the classroom teaching practice.

References

Ausubel, D. P. (1964). Some psychological and educational limitations of learning by discovery. *T00he Arithmetic Teacher, 11*, 290–302.
Baker, E., Barton, P. E. Darling-Hammond, L., Haertel, E., Ladd, H. F., Linn, R. L., Ravitch, D. Rothstein, R., Shavelson, R. J., & Shepard, L. A. (2010). *Problems with the use of student test*

scores to evaluate teachers (pp. 1–27). Washington, D.C. The Economic Policy Institute, http://epi.3cdn.net/724cd9a1eb91c40ff0_hwm6iij90.pdf.

Ball, D. L. (1993). With an eye on the mathematical horizon: Dilemmas of teaching elementary school mathematics. *Elementary School Journal, 93*(4), 373–397.

Barr, R. (2001). Research on the teaching of reading. In V. Richardson (Ed.), *Handbook of research on teaching* (4th ed., pp. 390–415). Washington, D.C., American Educational Research Association.

Bodrova, E. (2008). Make-believe play versus academic skills: A Vygotskian approach to today's dilemma of early childhood education. *European Early Childhood Education Research Journal, 16*(3), 357–369.

Bowman, B. T., Donovan, M. S., & Burns, M. S. (Eds.). (2001). *Eager to learn: Educating our preschoolers*. Washington, DC: National Academy Press.

Bredekamp, S. (Ed.). (1987). *Developmentally appropriate practice in early childhood programs serving children from birth through age 8* (Exp. ed.). Washington, DC: NAEYC.

Bredekamp, S., & Copple, C. (Eds.). (2009). *Developmentally appropriate practice in early childhood programs serving children from birth through age 8* (3rd ed.). Washington, DC: NAEYC.

Chen, J. Q., & McCray, J. (2012). A conceptual framework for teacher professional development: The whole teacher approach. *NHSA Dialog: A Research-to-Practice Journal for the Early Intervention Field, 15*(1), 8–23.

Chen, J. Q., & McNamee, G. (2006). Strengthening early childhood teacher preparation: Integrating assessment, curriculum development, and instructional practice in student teaching. *Journal of Early Childhood Teacher Education, 27*, 109–128.

Clements, D. H., Sarama, J., & DiBiase, A. M. (Eds.). (2004). *Engaging young children in mathematics: Standards for early mathematics education*. Mahwah: Lawrence Erlbaum Associates.

Cobb, P., Wood, T., Nicholls, J., Trigatti, B., & Periwitz, M. (1991). Assessment of a problem-centered second-grade mathematics project. *Journal for Research in Mathematics Education, 22*(1), 3–29.

Coburn, C. E., Pearson, C. P., & Woulfin, S. (2011). Reading policy in the era of accountability. In M. L. Kamil, P. D., Pearson, E. B., Moje, & P. P. Afflerbach (Eds.), *Handbook of reading research* (Vol. IV, pp. 561–593). New York: Routledge.

Copley, J. V. (2004). The early childhood collaborative: A professional development model to communicate and implement the standards. In D. H. Clements, J. Sarama, & A. M. DiBiase (Eds.), *Engaging young children in mathematics: Standards for early childhood mathematics education* (pp. 401–414). Mahwah: Lawrence Erlbaum Associates.

Copley, J. V. (2010). *The young child and mathematics* (2nd ed.). Washington, D.C.: NAEYC.

Copple, C. E. (2004). Mathematics curriculum in the early childhood context. In D. H. Clements, J. Sarama, & A. M. DiBiase (Eds.), *Engaging young children in mathematics: Standards for early childhood mathematics education*. Mahwah: Lawrence Erlbaum Associates, Inc (pp. 83-90).

Craig, R. (1956). Directed versus independent discovery of established relations. *Journal of Educational Psychology, 47*, 223–235.

Darling-Hammond, L., & Bransford, J. (Eds.). (2005). *Preparing teachers for a changing world: What teachers should learn and be able to do*. San Francisco: Jossey-Bass.

Dewey, J. (1963). *Experience and education*. New York: Collier

Ehrlich, S. B. (2007). *The preschool achievement gap: Are variations in teacher input associated with differences in number knowledge?* Unpublished doctoral dissertation, University of Chicago.

Elkind, D. (1987). *Miseducation*. New York: Alfred Knopf.

Epstein, A. S. (2007). *The intentional teacher: Choosing the best strategies for young children's learning*. Washington, DC: NAEYC.

Feiler, R. (2004). Early childhood mathematics instruction: Seeing the opportunities among the challenges. In D. Clements, J. Sarama, & A-M. DiBiase (Eds.), *Engaging young children in mathematics* (pp. 393–400). Mahwah: Erlbaum.

Freedman, S. W. (1994). *Exchanging writing, exchanging cultures*. Cambridge: Harvard University Press.

Ginsburg, H.P., Kaplan, R.G., Cannon, J., Cordero, M.I., Eisenband, J.G., Galanter, J., and Morgenlander, M. (2006). Helping early childhood educators to teach mathematics. In M. Zaslow and I. Martinez-Beck (Eds.), *Critical Issues in Early Childhood Professional Development* (pp.171 –202). Baltimore, MD: Paul H. Brookes.

Ginsburg, H. P., Lee, J. S., & Boyd, J. S. (2008). Mathematics education for young children: What it is and how to promote it. *Social Policy Report, 22*(1), 3–22.

Hanline, M. F., Milton, S., & Phelps, P. C. (2008). A longitudinal study exploring the relationship of representational levels of three aspects of preschool sociodramatic play and early academic skills. *Journal of Research in Childhood Education, 23*(1), 19–28.

Hill, H.C., Rowan, B., & Ball, D. (2005). Effects of teachers' mathematical knowledge for teaching on student achievement. *American Educational Research Journal, 42*(2), 371–406.

Kamii, C. (2006). Measurement of length: How can we teach it better? *Teaching Children Mathematics, 13*(3), 154–158.

Kamii, C., & Housman, L. (2000). *Young children reinvent arithmetic* (2nd ed.). New York: Teachers College Press.

Kirschner, P. A., Sweller, J., & Clark, R. (2006). Why minimal guidance during instructional does not.... *Educational Psychologist, 41*(2), 75–86.

Klibanoff, R., Levine, S. C., Huttenlocher, J., Vasilyeva, M., & Hedges, L. (2006). Preschool children's mathematical knowledge: The effect of teacher "math talk." *Developmental Psychology, 42*(1), 59–69.

Kohlberg, L., & Mayer, R. (1972). Development as the aim of education. *Harvard Educational Review, 42*(4), 449–496.

Lampert, M. (2001). *Teaching problems and problems of teaching*. New Haven: Yale University Press.

Maloney, A. P., & Confrey, J. (2010, June-July). *The construction, refinement, and early validation of the equipartitioning learning trajectory*. Paper presented at the 9th International Conference of the Learning Sciences, Chicago, IL.

Mayer, R. (2004). Should there be a three-strike rule against pure discovery learning? The case for guided methods of instruction. *American Psychologist, 59*, 14–19.

McCray, J. S. (2008). *Pedagogical content knowledge for preschool mathematics: Relationships between teaching practice and child outcomes*. Unpublished doctoral dissertation, Chicago: Erikson Institute/Loyola University Chicago.

McCray, J. S., & Chen, J. Q. (2011). Foundational mathematics: A neglected opportunity. In B. Atweh, M. Graven, W. Secada, & P. Valero (Eds.), *Mapping equity and quality in mathematics education* (pp. 253–268). New York: Springer.

Miller, E., & Allmon, J. (2009). *Crisis in the kindergarten*. Executive summary. Alliance for childhood e-report. http://www.allianceforchildhood.org/sites/allianceforchildhood.org/files/file/kindergarten_report.pdf.

National Association for the Education of Young Children/National Council of Teachers of Mathematics. (2002). *Early childhood mathematics: Promoting good beginnings*. http://www.naeyc.org/about/positions.asp.

National Institute for Direct Instruction. (2012). *About Direct Instruction*. http://www.nifdi.org.

National Research Council. (2009). *Mathematics learning in early childhood: Paths toward excellence and equity*. Washington: National Academy Press.

Phillips, D. (2000). *Constructivism in education*. Chicago: University of Chicago Press.

Piaget, J. (1952). *The origins of intelligence in children*. New York: International University Press.

Piaget, J., & Inhelder, B. (1969). *The psychology of the child*. New York: Basic.

Richardson, V. (2013). Constructivist pedagogy. *Teachers College Record, 105*(9), 1623–1640.

Sarama, J., & DiBiase, A.-M. (2004). The professional development challenge in preschool mathematics. In D. H. Clements, J. Sarama, & A.-M. DiBiase (Eds.), *Engaging young children in mathematics: Standards for early childhood education*. (pp 415-447) Mahwah: Lawrence Earlbaum.

Simon, M. A. (1995). Reconstructing mathematics pedagogy from a constructivist perspective. *Journal for Research in Mathematics Education, 26*, 114–145.

Skinner, B. F. (1974). *About behaviorism*. New York: Knopf.

Sztajn, P., Confrey, J., Wilson, P. H., & Edgington, C. (2012). Learning trajectory based instruction: Toward a theory of teaching. *Educational Research, 41*(5), 147–156.

Taylor, B. M., Raphael, T. E., & Au, K. H. (2011). Reading and school reform. In M. L. Kamil, P. D. Pearson, E. B., Moje, & P. P. Afflerbach (Eds.), *Handbook of reading research* (Vol. IV, pp. 594–628). New York: Routledge.

Tobin, K. (1993). *The practice of constructivism in science education.* Hillsdale: Lawrence Erlbaum.

Todd, J. T., & Morris. E. K. (1995). *Modern perspectives on B. F. Skinner and contemporary behaviorism.* Westport: Greenwood Press.

Vygotsky, L. (1978). *Mind in society.* Cambridge: Harvard University Press.

Wesley, C. B., Engelmann, S., & Thomas, D. R. (1975). *Teaching* (Vol. 1). Palo Alto: Science Research Associates.

White, R. (2001). The revolution in research on science teaching. In V. Richardson (Ed.), *Handbook of research on teaching* (4th ed., pp. 457–471). Washington, D.C.: American Educational Research Association.

Wilson, S. T. (2001). Research on history teaching. In V. Richardson (Ed.), *Handbook of research on teaching* (4th ed., pp. 527–544). Washington, D.C., American Educational Research Association.

Wilson, S. M., & Wineburg, S. S. (1993). Wrinkles in time and place: Using performance assessments to understand the knowledge of history teachers. *American Educational Research Journal, 30*, 729–769.

Woodcock, R. W., McGrew, K. S., & Mather, N. (2001). *Woodcock-Johnson III*. Rolling Meadows: Riverside Publishing.

Chapter 17
Professionalization of Early Childhood Educators with a Focus on Natural Learning Situations and Individual Development of Mathematical Competencies: Results from an Evaluation Study

Hedwig Gasteiger

Introduction

Nowadays, the importance to provide mostly all kindergarten children with basic mathematical competencies is recognized and early childhood mathematics education has been discussed in a broad way in the last years. This discussion was forced by several empirical studies which indicate that early numerical competencies are powerful predictors of later mathematical achievement (e.g., Dornheim 2008, Krajewski and Schneider 2009) and the fact that children bring heterogeneous prerequisites when they start school (Deutscher 2012) and even when they enter kindergarten (Anders et al. in press). While some children have rich experiences with mathematical learning in everyday life, others have almost none. Early childhood mathematics education has to compensate this lack of mathematical experiences (Stern 1998).

But what is the best way to organize early mathematics education, to ensure that mathematical learning is sustainable and provides children with basic mathematical competencies? Should early mathematics education follow a more instructive or a more constructive perspective on learning? Many ideas and programs for early mathematics education exist in Germany. They range from strong guided training programs with prescribed dialogues (e.g., Preiß 2007; Krajewski et al. 2007) to compilations of mathematical tasks which demand the responsibility of the educators to organize appropriate learning opportunities (e.g., Wittmann and Müller 2009). In this chapter, a way of early mathematics education is proposed which combines construction and instruction. It is founded on two basic ideas: on the one hand, using natural learning situations for early mathematics education (like play and everyday activities) which allows children to construct their mathematical knowledge, and on the other hand, being aware of individual competencies due to a purposeful observation which allows the educators to react instructively and to guarantee the support that children need for the best possible development of their mathematical competencies.

H. Gasteiger (✉)
Ludwig-Maximilians-University Munich, Munich, Germany
e-mail: hedwig.gasteiger@mathematik.uni-muenchen.de

This way of early mathematics education is difficult to realize for kindergarten educators. Empirical studies concerning teacher competencies (Ball et al. 2009; Shulman 1986) report that teaching requires a wide range of competencies. These competencies are bundled under the terms content knowledge, pedagogical content knowledge, and action-related competencies. There is every reason to believe that early childhood educators need similar competencies if learning is organized in the above-mentioned sense: They have to plan early mathematics education by using play and everyday situations, they have to detect mathematically relevant aspects in children's activities and conversations, and they have to be sensitive for important steps in the development of their children to be able to care for their further development. In Germany—in contrast to many other countries—mathematics education has not played an important role over time in preservice education of early childhood educators. Therefore, professional development programs are necessary to support them in their demanding tasks and to guarantee a substantial mathematics education for the young children. As a part of the academic support in a project aiming at improving the quality in kindergarten and in school (for further information: www.transkigs.de), a professional development program was designed and carried out. This program should help early childhood educators to implement early mathematics education based on a constructive understanding of learning and with instructive elements to foster children's development individually. It was evaluated through an empirical study and the results of the study will be reported in this chapter.

The foundation for the professional development program was the concept of learning mathematics in natural learning situations and the importance to assess children's individual stage of learning. Therefore, this concept and the conditions, which enable early childhood educators to support children in their individual learning processes, will be described below.

Theoretical Background

Early Mathematics Education in Natural Learning Situations

It is still unexplained which is the best way to guarantee sustainable mathematical learning in kindergarten, but there are several reasons to assume that early mathematics education in natural learning situations provides a solid base. Natural learning situations are distinct from learning situations as known in school context: In natural learning situations, the learner decides on his own what he would like to do; normally, he is highly motivated and reflects his own acting and learning (Schröder 2002, p. 18 f.). In contrast to this, learning in school context means to learn definitely more instructively: The teacher organizes learning processes, the content is given, and the learning goals are defined.

In early childhood education, learning mathematics in natural situations means to use learning opportunities in *everyday activities* and in *play situations* (Gasteiger 2010). Everyday activities with potential for mathematical learning are, for example, setting the table, comparing collected objects (amount, length, weight, colors,...), reflecting timetables for the day, and many else. As play is an appropriate way for preschool children to explore their environment (Fthenakis et al. 2009, p. 60) children also have many opportunities to develop mathematical competencies while playing (Seo and Ginsburg 2004; Siegler and Ramani 2008). This could be during free play while building blocks or playing shopkeeper and in directed play activities, for example, with board games.

But it is important to realize that natural learning situations are not only situations, which happen more or less by chance and learning in natural situations does not mean—in a misinterpretation of constructivism (Reusser 2006, p. 159)—to leave children alone. The crucial point is "the progressive development of what is already experienced into a fuller and richer and also more organized form, a form that gradually approximates that in which subject matter is presented to the skilled, mature person" (Dewey 1938, p. 48).

Therefore, the educators have to moderate and accompany the learning processes by explicitly *initiating* these learning situations (e.g., offering rhymes with numbers, describing ways, and measuring and comparing children's size) or by *using the potential* for mathematical learning that everyday activities offer (e.g., preparing food for the meal, free play, or playing board games). To judge the potential of natural learning situations, it could be very helpful for the educators to reflect these opportunities to learn based on the framework of the big or fundamental mathematical ideas like counting, pattern, shapes, or modeling (Clements and Sarama 2009; Wittmann and Müller 2009; Wittmann 2004).

There are some reasons, why natural learning situations can be seen as an adequate concept for early childhood mathematics: Children learn mathematics in meaningful contexts (everyday and play situations). If natural learning situations in early mathematics education are based on the big ideas of mathematics, then coherence and consistency in mathematical learning can be ensured (Clements 2004, p. 15) and children can enhance their conceptual and procedural knowledge in several mathematical content areas (Greenes 1999). Moreover, in natural learning situations children have the possibility to develop mathematical competencies in their daily life in dialogue with other children and adults. They can enhance important mathematical competencies like arguing or constituting in discussions with their peers (Steinweg 2008). Learning in this way corresponds to a constructivist perspective on learning (Reusser 2001), but nevertheless, appropriate instructional support can be very helpful or even indispensable. Especially if a child does not engage in activities with potential for mathematical learning, it is necessary to initiate adequate mathematical learning opportunities consciously. Findings on children's spontaneous tendency to focus on numerosity support this claim (Hannula et al. 2005).

Assessment of Children's Individual Stage of Learning

To recognize if a child needs individual support and in consequence to guarantee the best possible development of children's mathematical competencies, it is necessary to diagnose their individual stage of learning. Only then can the educators plan further steps and care for a suitable learning environment—including direct instructional advises appropriate to the child and the situation. This is necessary to ensure that natural learning situations can be used effectively and adequately to the individual processes of learning.

To gain a good overview of individual existing competencies, early childhood educators can use diagnostic tools like, e.g., OTZ (Osnabrücker Test zur Zahlbegriffsentwicklung, van Luit et al. 2001) or instruments, which allow a constant monitoring of children's performance like portfolios or "Lerndokumentation" (Steinweg 2006). The crucial point in this context is not to collect data to classify if a child's performance is in average or not, but to get enough information to foster further development. This form of diagnostic has a guiding effect (Wollring 2006) and it is called "pedagogical diagnostic" (Ingenkamp 1991, p. 760).

Requirements for Early Childhood Educators

To implement early mathematics education in natural learning situations and to ensure that children with different levels of knowledge and skills can profit, early childhood educators need wide-ranging knowledge and competencies.

First of all, they need content knowledge: They have to see the relations between mathematics in the early years and later on to guarantee coherent mathematical learning. Moreover, they have to judge if daily situations have the potential for further mathematical learning and they have to appraise if children's statements are mathematically correct (Ball et al. 2009): "Contrary to the views of many, young children's mathematical thinking is not limited to the concrete and the mechanical; it is often complex and abstract. Since this is the case, understanding the mathematics in children's thinking requires deep subject matter knowledge" (Ginsburg and Ertle 2008, p. 47).

Pedagogical content knowledge is necessary to identify individual learning difficulties, which in turn is an important precondition to foster children's mathematical development. A specific kind of pedagogical knowledge is "diagnostic knowledge" (Weinert et al. 1990, p. 172). It includes the knowledge of learning difficulties, misconceptions, and prerequisites and it helps to decide whether additional support is needed or not. Exactly this diagnostic knowledge is not really part of preservice education in Germany (Lorenz 2008, p. 29).

However, content and pedagogical content knowledge are not sufficient for successful action in concrete situations. To act adequately to the situation, to the individual person and to the subject, "action competence" (Weinert 2001, p. 51) is needed. This means to act, to a certain extent, spontaneously but appropriately. At first, action competence is needed to use the opportunities for mathematical learning in natural situations, because very often these situations only can be profitable for mathematical learning, if the educators ask relevant questions or encourage reflection (van Oers 2009; Baroody et al. 2006). Moreover, action competence is indispensable in case of individual learning difficulties: The educators have to identify adequate and necessary steps for further learning and react with inquiry, instructive help, or incitation by choosing an appropriate game or material (Lipowsky 2007, p. 30). Dewey describes successful teachers—and it could be assumed that the same could be said for educators—as "so full of the spirit of inquiry, so sensitive to every sign of its presence and absence, that no matter what they do, nor how they do it, they succeed in awakening and inspiring like alert and intense mental activity in those with whom they come in contact" (Dewey 1904, p. 23 f.).

Regarding the requirements educators should meet, it is clear that thinking of early mathematics education means not only to decide if a more constructive or a more instructive way would be better, it is not enough to design materials for early mathematics education, but it means especially to have in mind that professional development of educators is becoming more and more important.

Professional Development of Educators

While the importance of professional development programs in early childhood education is recognized, there is a research deficit concerning concepts and effectiveness of professional development of early childhood educators (Fröhlich-Gildhoff and Mischo 2011, p. 2). Mischo and Fröhlich-Gildhoff (2011, p. 10) identified the following demands for professional development in early childhood education: Development programs should satisfy educators' needs, they should be based on theoretical background, and they should include pedagogical content knowledge. Moreover, all efforts should be empirically evaluated with regard to the effectiveness.

Thinking about professional development programs for educators, it could be helpful to take into account the results of research on professional development of teachers. To change teachers' professional acting, it seems to be necessary to get input concerning content and assessment knowledge and to have many opportunities to learn something new. To try new materials, to train new patterns of activity, and to reflect on it are further aspects of effective professional development (Lipowsky 2012, p. 5 ff.). It is furthermore important to have the right framework conditions. Though it is not sufficient, it seems to be necessary that "learning opportunities for teachers" occur "over an extended period of time" and that teachers are involved "in a professional community of practice" (Hattie 2009, p. 120 f.; Garet et al. 2001). All in all, a constructive perspective on learning with instructive elements seems to be successful for educators as well as for children.

Professionalization of Early Childhood Educators as Part of the Project TransKiGs Berlin

If early mathematics education combines constructive and instructive elements (Presmeg 2014), while using natural learning situations and considering the individual stage of learning, it is indispensable to care for the professional development of educators (see Sect. "Requirements for Early Childhood Educators"). Therefore—as part of the academic support of the project TransKiGs in Berlin (www.transkigs.de)—a professional development program was worked out by the author, carried out and evaluated (see Sect. "Evaluation Study"). The foundation and the concept of this professional development program with all its accompanying measures will be described below.

First of all, the educators participating in the project TransKiGs were inquired to identify their needs (as demanded by Mischo and Fröhlich-Gildhoff 2011, p. 10). Based on this information, the professional development program was devised with four modules. The basis for this program was the above-mentioned concept for early childhood mathematics education: focusing on natural learning situations, encouraging mathematical learning essentially nonformal, and following primarily a constructive perspective on learning (see Sect. "Early Mathematics Education in Natural Learning Situations"). Another key aspect of the professional development program was to provide knowledge about the development of mathematical competencies in early childhood to enable the educators to focus on the mathematical learning process of each child and to care—in a more or less instructive way—for an appropriate support (see Sect. "Assessment of Children's Individual Stage of Learning").

In detail, the educators worked in three modules on content and pedagogical content knowledge in the domains 'number, counting, quantity', 'space and shape', and 'measurement and data'. The fourth module focused on observation, documentation, and possibilities of intervening if the observation shows special needs for some children. These four modules were devised considering that task orientation, opportunities to develop content, and pedagogical content knowledge, active learning, reflection, and discussion with other learners are fostering the impact and sustainability of professional development projects (Zehetmeier and Krainer 2011; Boston and Smith 2011, see above).

During the first year of the project TransKiGs, the educators could attend the modules 'number, counting, quantity', 'shape and space', and 'measurement and data'—the first one took a whole day, the others half a day (see Table 17.1). Because of employee turnover in the five participating day care centers, the modules were repeated after 1 year of work and supplemented by the module 'observation, documentation, intervention'. Interim, the educators had regular meetings with the teachers of their corresponding schools and with other participating educators—this was an essential element of the organizational structure of the project. So, participating persons had the possibility to reflect their own work and to share their experiences.

Table 17.1 Professional development program—an overview

	Module 1:number, counting, quantity	Module 2:space and shape	Module 3:measurement and data	Module 4:observation, documentation, intervention
Content	Counting Comparing Numbers Quantity and structures Pattern and change	Visual perception Spatial orientation Shape and space Symmetry	Measurement Length Weight Time Money Data and chance	Observation Diagnostic tools Documentation Encouragement Observation training (video-based)
1st year	6 h	3 h	3 h	–
2nd year	3 h	3 h	3 h	3 h

The three content-based modules (1–3) were structured as follows: The mathematical content was divided into smaller sections, e.g., for the domain 'number, counting, quantity' in counting sequence, counting process, comparing, quantification, and structures, pattern, and change. In each section, for enhancing their content and pedagogical content knowledge, the educators got information about associated mathematical competencies and their development from early childhood up to the first years of school. These information sections included thought experiments and self-reflection tasks like trying to count on, or calculating by, the letters of the alphabet. If possible, it was illustrated with short video sequences to reflect the development of children and to train observation. The theoretic input was enriched by everyday activities and play situations supposing to foster the mathematical learning in this special domain (e.g., counting children, steps, collected objects, pieces of fruit, …, or playing board games with a dice, card games to compare quantities, …). Many activities were carried out directly. So the educators had enough time to try them out for themselves and to analyze the demands and possibilities concerning the implementation of these activities in their daily work. Their experiences were reflected in a short discussion afterwards and supplemented by their own ideas. This approach was used to help the educators to improve their pedagogical and didactical action competence (see Sect. "Requirements for Early Childhood Educators"). At the end of each module, the educators were invited to contemplate the information and ideas they had gathered and to reflect in which situations in their everyday work they can observe mathematical development in the respective domain.

The fourth module aimed at a more conscious approach to mathematical competencies that children show. It provided information on observation and diagnostics in general—especially the reasons why this is indispensable in early mathematics education. Therefore, some diagnostic tools, like standardized tests, portfolios, or learning stories (Carr 2001), were presented and discussed in terms of early mathematics education. The main part of this module was a training to observe learning processes, to draw conclusions for further mathematical learning, and to reflect on which tasks or situations could help to foster it. For this training, video sequences were used. The participants were requested to describe the mathematical competencies they could recognize, to connect their observation with the content and pedagogical content knowledge in the content-domains, to judge whether it is necessary to react, and, if it is, to think about possibilities to intervene. Intervention in this regard means to think about natural learning situations serving as an enhancement adapted to the observed stage of learning. To support the educators in these challenging activities, the observation tool "Lerndokumentation" (Steinweg 2006) was offered to them. It is a chart, where many mathematical competencies are described as they can happen every day in early childhood education. The educators can use this tool to document their observations. In this module, discussion about the observed competencies and the possibilities to intervene, based on their content and pedagogical content knowledge, was seen as an important point to promote the pedagogical and didactical action competence of the early childhood educators.

The professional development program has to be seen embedded in a set of measures determined by the framework of the project. First of all, the project intended a network. All teachers and educators participating in the project cooperated in different kinds of meetings. Besides the professional development program, they had annual conferences, where they received expert input and had the possibility to exchange their experiences. Educators met furthermore regularly with teachers of the corresponding school to share information about their children and experiences in mathematics education. To support the educators in assessing children's individual stage of learning, they could use the observation tool "Lerndokumentation" (Steinweg 2006). It was offered to them almost at the beginning of the project with some information on how they can integrate it in their daily work. In addition, each participating kindergarten got three material packages (in annual intervals) with literature, materials, games, and picture books, helpful and suitable for mathematics education in natural learning situations (e.g., Wittmann and Müller 2009; Hoenisch and Niggemeyer 2004). These measures meet some of the requirements for effective professional development (see Sect. "Professional Development of Educators").

Evaluation Study

Research Question

The measures of professional development (see Sect. "Professionalization of Early Childhood Educators as Part of the Project TransKiGs Berlin") were evaluated. The aim of the professional development program with all supporting measures was to equip the early childhood educators with ideas for mathematical learning in play and everyday situations, to enable them to see important steps in their children's mathematical development, and to use this information for their further work. In consequence, it could be supposed that children enhance their mathematical competencies. So the main research question of the evaluation study was if the professional development program for educators—integrated in the framework of the project TransKiGs—has positive effects on the mathematical learning of children.

Sample and Methodology

A summative evaluation (Bortz and Döring 2006, p. 109) was used to evaluate the professional development program with reference to the research question. Therefore, a pre- and posttest design with treatment and control group was applied: Children's performance in a mathematics test was measured and compared with the performance of a control group. There were three points of measurement over a 3-year period in annual test intervals: a pretest (June/July 2006), a test during the intervention time (June/July 2007), and a posttest (June/July 2008).

As the evaluation took place in the field, only a quasi-experimental design was possible. All children in the 5-day care centers, participating in the project TransKiGs, defined the target population. A proportionally stratified sample (age, gender, migration-background; pretest: $N=21$, age 3–4 years; posttest: $N=19$, age 5–6 years) out of the target population formed the treatment group. The control group was stratified in the same way. For organizational reasons, the educators of children in this group had no possibility to participate in the project TransKiGs. The day care centers in both groups are located in comparable districts regarding some social data and the percentage of foreign nationals (Gasteiger 2010).

Three months after the pretest, the early childhood educators were introduced in the work with the observation tool "Lerndokumentation." The modules of professional development program as described above (intervention) were carried out by the author 8 months after the pretest and repeated after 1 year. As the evaluation took place under natural conditions, the posttest was carried out 4 months after the second intervention.

The educators had the choice to take part in the professional development program and there was a normal employee turnover during the 2 years of intervention. Most of the time, 17 educators took part in the project TransKiGs and 59–82% of these educators visited the different modules of the professional development program (first year: module 1: 71%, module 2/3: 76%; second year: module 1–3: 59%, module 4: 71%).

To measure the development of mathematical learning, a test instrument was designed (Gasteiger 2010) with items in the domains 'number and calculation' (19 items, Cronbach's $\alpha=0.89$, 0.86, 0.76), 'measurement' (5 items, $\alpha=0.55$, 0.40, 0.35), and 'shape and space' (6 items, $\alpha=0.62$, 0.55, 0.44)—30 items all in all ($\alpha=0.91$, 0.89, 0.78). The first part of the test was a guided interview, administered by the author and supported with some material, e.g., counting objects, number- and quantity-cards. Children were asked to count, to count objects, to quantify, and more. The second part was a paper–pencil test, where the children answered oral questions and they documented their answers by drawing or writing (for all test items see Gasteiger 2010, p. 270 ff.). For the data analysis, the whole test was videotaped. As same person interviewed all children, objectivity could be guaranteed. The reliabilities of the subscales 'measurement' and 'shape and space' are low. Therefore, for further data analysis, only the whole scale and the subscale 'number and calculation' will be used.

To assess whether changes in children's mathematical performance can be related to the intervention measures, questionnaires for the educators gave information, if the professional development program was seen as useful and if the educators use the observation tool "Lerndokumentation" in their daily work.

Results

The professional development program was positively evaluated. After finishing the professional development program, about 90% of the participating educators felt more competent to accompany children's mathematical learning, about 90% said their perspective on mathematical learning changed in a positive way, and 86–93% felt that they learned something for their daily work (Steinweg and Gasteiger 2007, 2008). The questionnaire concerning the use of "Lerndokumentation" showed that educators think more about mathematical activities in their daily work and improve in recognizing important steps in the mathematical development of their children (Gasteiger 2010, p. 194 ff.).

To analyze the findings of the summative evaluation study, the results of the mathematics test should be examined. Therefore, we used the data of the group of children who took part in the mathematics test three times ($N=19$ in treatment and in control group), with one exception: At the second point of measurement one child in the treatment group was not available for the test, but it took part at the pre- and posttest.

Pretest scores for treatment group ($M=28\%$, $SD=17\%$) and control group ($M=40\%$, $SD=22\%$) differ not significantly but considerably ($t(36)=1.89$, $p>0.05$), even though the samples were stratified in parallel ways. From the first to the second point of measurement, both groups' mathematical competencies are developing in parallel. At the third point of measurement, the results of both groups approximate to each other (treatment group: $M=80\%$, $SD=13\%$; control group: $M=84\%$, $SD=13\%$, $t(36)=.89$, $p>0.05$).

A two-factorial analysis of variance with repeated measures tends—if there are differences in the changing of mathematical development between the treatment, and the control group—to confirm or reject the hypothesis that children perform better in mathematics due to the professional development of their educators. The focus is on the interaction effect between group and point of measurement. Considering the whole scale of test items, the main effect of mathematical development over the period of 2 years is highly significant as expected ($p<0.001$). This is because children improve their mathematical competencies over time—independent from any intervention. The interaction effect is not significant ($F(1.730)=1.687$, $p=0.20$). For the whole scale of test items, that is to say the development of math-

Table 17.2 Analysis of variance, subscale 'number and calculation'

Factor	F	df	p
Time of measurement	210,595	2	0.000
Group*point of measurement (interaction effect)	4,468	1.924	0.016

Table 17.3 Comparison of means in the subscale 'number and counting'

M (SD)	Treatment group	Control group
1st point of measurement (pretest)	21 % (16 %) $t(36)=2.68, p<0.05, d=0.87$	39 % (23 %)
2nd point of measurement	55 % (22 %) $t(35)=2.29, p<0.05, d=0.75$	71 % (21 %)
3rd point of measurement (posttest)	83 % (14 %) $t(36)=0.46, p>0.05, d=0.15$	86 % (16 %)

ematical competencies over different content domains, the hypothesis must be rejected. If only the subscale 'number and calculation' is considered, in addition to the main effect of mathematical development in general, the interaction effect is significant as well (see Table 17.2).

Children in the treatment group differ significantly in their performance in the content domain 'number and calculation' from children in a control group (11 % explained variance in mathematical performance). The comparison of means shows that they can improve their mathematical competencies between the second and the third point of measurement (see Table 17.3).

Examining the subscales, it could be detected that the differences in the results of the two groups (whole scale) at the beginning of the evaluation study and also at the second point of measurement are caused by the differences in the subscale 'number and counting'. At the first and second points of measurements, the differences in this subscale are even significant (see Table 17.3), while the performances of treatment and control group in the two other subscales nearly do not differ (Gasteiger 2010).

Qualitative analysis of test results of low-achieving children shows that children in the treatment group can enhance their mathematical competencies more than children in the control group (Gasteiger 2010), p. 217 ff.). All children in the treatment group can count resultative and in a flexible way immediately before they enter school, while two children in the control group, for example, did not master the one-to-one principle in their counting processes.

Discussion

The question, whether measures of professional development for educators can have positive effects on the mathematical learning of children, is not easy to answer (s. Mischo and Fröhlich-Gildhoff 2011, p. 9). In this study, the intervention addressed the professional development of the *educators* but the mathematical competencies of *children* were the decisive factor to appraise whether the intervention was successful or not. This fact may explain why, from the first to the second point of measurement, both groups' mathematical competencies are developing almost in parallel (see Table 17.3). The professional development program aims to improve content knowledge, pedagogical content knowledge, and action competencies (Shulman 1986; Bass et al. 2009; Weinert et al. 1990). The educators considered this as successful (see Sect. "Evaluation Study"). So, it can be assumed that the educators taking part in the professional development program get ideas for implementing early mathematics education in natural learning situations, input about mathematical development in early childhood, and experiences in the observation of mathematical competencies (see Sect. "Theoretical Background"). The professional development program gave no explicit instruction how the educators should act when they are back at work. This decision was made consciously and based on the constructivist perspective of learning. But this means that changes in the daily work can only happen when the educators have in mind what they have learned about mathematical learning and development and, when they know how to act through their—hopefully—improved content and pedagogical content knowledge (see Sect. "Requirements for Early Childhood Educators"). There is a long way to children's improvement of mathematical competencies: The educators need to reflect on their daily work due to their new experiences, they need to try to realize early mathematics education in natural learning situations, to detect individual difficulties and competencies of the children, and to support their development. Not until then can the professional development have an effect on children's performance (s. Lipowsky 2012). So, it is remarkable that despite the long way, these effects on children's mathematical development can be detected.

Obviously, the effects of professional development on children's mathematical achievement do not emerge immediately (see Table 17.3), but there is reason to believe that this process has a sustainable impact on the daily work of the educators and may lead to an ongoing enhancement of children's mathematical development. If educators can see the impact of their efforts to improve their own acting, then it is extremely motivating and will reinforce their engagement in new teaching practices (Lipowsky 2012, p. 6 f.).

Another interesting point in this evaluation study is that the intervention only had effects in the domain 'number and calculation'. There are some ideas to explain this result. One reason may be that the test instrument was not balanced in the content domains. There were considerably more items in the domain 'number and calculation' than in the other two content domains and the subscales to 'shape and space' and to 'measurement' were not as reliable as the subscale 'number and calculation'. Maybe with a longer test instrument, effects could be detected in other content domains as well. It may also be assumed that early childhood educators rather think of numbers, counting, and calculating than of spatial thinking or measuring time when they engage with early mathematics education (Lee and Ginsburg 2007). Moreover, the domain 'number, counting, quantity' took more time in the professional development program than the other domains (see Sect. "Professionalization of Early

Childhood Educators as Part of the Project TransKiGs Berlin"). Possibly, it was or is easier for educators to think about natural learning situations in this domain than in the others. Discussions with educators during the professional development program confirmed this statement. They mentioned that they already had ideas about mathematical learning like counting all children in the morning or counting activities while setting the table, but that they learned in the professional development program that mathematics is everywhere and that many situations they know from their daily work, e.g., paper folding or building blocks, can be used for mathematical learning as well.

Conclusion

There are many ways to think about early mathematics education. Today, early childhood educators can use frameworks for an orientation, they have a choice between training programs which are generally highly instructive or several materials which support children in their constructive learning processes. Demanding that early childhood education should meet the requirements on sustainable learning and all activities in early mathematics should be based on individual prerequisites and the learning progress of children, it is indispensable to support the early childhood educators (Baroody 2004). They have to act competent—sometimes spontaneously—and to plan and initiate mathematical learning in a meaningful way, having in mind why some contents or skills are relevant for further mathematical learning, and others are not. Using materials, frameworks, and diagnostic tools without having in mind, which mathematical ideas are relevant for children and how they can learn them adequately and matched to their individual learning progress promises not to be successful (Siraj-Blatchford et al. 2002).

The results of the evaluation study show that professional development can have effects on children's mathematical learning though it is a long way from the development of educators' competencies to children's mathematical achievement and though it is highly demanding to realize early mathematics education between the poles of instruction and construction. The concepts of professionalization should reflect what is known about effectiveness of professional development programs and important framework conditions should be respected (Lipowsky 2012; Hattie 2009; Zehetmeier and Krainer 2011). Nevertheless, short-term effects could not be expected if early mathematics education is mainly guided by professionalization of educators, and not by strong-guided instructional advices. But there are good reasons to believe that in the long run, this approach can lead to a profound change in the thinking of early childhood educators and that they can successfully manage the integration of constructive and instructive perspectives on learning in their daily acting.

References

Anders, Y., Grosse, C., Roßbach, H.-G., Ebert, S., & Weinert, S. (in press). Preschool and primary school influences on the development of children's early numeracy skills between the ages of 3 and 7 years in Germany. *Special edition of school effectiveness und school improvement.*

Ball, D., Thames, M. H., Bass, H., Sleep, L., Lewis, J., & Phelps, G. (2009). A practice-based theory of mathematical knowledge for teaching. In M. Tzekaki, M. Kaldrimidou, & H. Sakonidis (Eds.), *Proc. 33th Conf. of the Int. Group for the Psychology of Mathematics Education* (Vol. 1, pp. 95–98). Thessaloniki: PME.

Baroody, A. J. (2004). The role of psychological research in the development of early childhood mathematics standards. In D. H. Clement & J. Samara (Eds.), *Engaging young children in mathematics. Standards for early childhood mathematics education* (pp. 149–172). Mahwah: Lawrence Erlbaum Associates.

Baroody, A. J., Lai, M.-L., & Mix, K. S. (2006). The development of young children's number and operation sense and its implications for early childhood education. In B. Spodek & O. Saracho (Eds.), *Handbook of research on the education of young children* (pp. 187–221). Mahwah: Lawrence Erlbaum Associates.

Bortz, J., & Döring, N. (2006). *Forschungsmethoden und Evaluation für Human- und Sozialwissenschaftler*. Heidelberg: Springer.

Boston, M. D., & Smith, M. S. (2011). A 'task-centric approach' to professional development: Enhancing and sustaining mathematical teachers' ability to implement cognitively challenging mathematical tasks. *ZDM Mathematics Education, 43*(6–7), 965–977.

Carr, M. (2001). *Assessment in early childhood settings. Learning stories*. London: Paul Chapman Publishing.

Clements, D. H. (2004). Major themes and recommendations. In D. H. Clements, & J. Sarama (Eds.), *Engaging young children in mathematics* (pp. 7–72). Mahwah: Lawrence Erlbaum Associates.

Clements, D. H., & Sarama, J. (2009). *Learning and teaching early math. The learning trajectories approach*. New York: Routledge.

Deutscher, Th. (2012). *Arithmetische und geometrische Fähigkeiten von Schulanfängern. Eine empirische Untersuchung unter besonderer Berücksichtigung des Bereichs Muster und Strukturen*. Wiesbaden: Vieweg & Teubner.

Dewey, J. (1904). The relation of theory to practice in the education of teachers. In *The third yearbook of the national society for the scientific study of education* (pp. 9–30). Chicago: University of Chicago Press.

Dewey, J. (1938). Experience and education. In J. A. Boydston (Ed.), *John Dewey. The later works, 1925–1953* (Vol. 13, 1938–1939, pp. 1–62). Southern Illinois University Press.

Dornheim, D. (2008). *Prädiktion von Rechenleistung und Rechenschwäche: Der Beitrag von Zahlen-Vorwissen und allgemein-kognitiven Fähigkeiten*. Berlin: Logos.

Fröhlich-Gildhoff, K., & Mischo, Ch. (2011). Schwerpunkt: Professionalisierung frühpädagogischen Personals. *Frühe Bildung, 0*(1), 2–3.

Fthenakis, W. E., Schmitt, A., Daut, E., Eitel, A., & Wendell, A. (2009). *Natur-Wissen schaffen. Band 2: Frühe mathematische Bildung*. Troisdorf: Bildungsverlag EINS.

Garet, M. S., Porter, A. C., Desimone, L. Birman, B. F., & Yoon, K. S. (2001). What makes professional development effective? Results from a national sample of teachers. *American Educational Research Journal, 38*(4), 915–945.

Gasteiger, H. (2010). *Elementare mathematische Bildung im Alltag der Kindertagesstätte. Grundlegung und Evaluation eines kompetenzorientierten Förderansatzes*. Münster: Waxmann.

Ginsburg, H. P., & Ertle, B. (2008). Knowing the mathematics in early childhood mathematics. In O. N. Saracho & B. Spodek (Eds.), *Contemporary perspectives on mathematics in early childhood education* (pp. 45–66). Charlotte.: Information Age Publishing.

Greenes, C. (1999). Ready to learn. Developing young children's mathematical powers. In J. V. Copley (Ed.), *Mathematics in the early years* (pp. 39–41). Reston: NCTM.

Hannula, M. M., Mattinen, A., & Lehtinen, E. (2005). Does social interaction influence 3-year-old children's tendency to focus on numerosity? A quasi-experimental study in day care. In L. Verschaffel, E. De Corte, G. Kanselaar, & M. Valcke (Eds.), *Powerful environments for promoting deep conceptual and strategic learning* (pp. 63–80). Leuven: Leuven University Press.

Hattie, J. (2009). *Visible learning. A synthesis of over 800 meta-analyses relating to achievement.* New Yourk: Routledge.

Hoenisch, N., & Niggemeyer, E. (2004). *Mathe-Kings. Junge Kinder fassen Mathematik an.* Weimar: verlag das netz.

Ingenkamp, K. (1991). Pädagogische Diagnostik. In L. Roth (Ed.), *Pädagogik. Handbuch für Studium und Praxis* (pp. 760–785). München: Ehrenwirth.

Krajewski, K., & Schneider, W. (2009). Early development of quantity to number-word linkage as a precursor of mathematical school achievement and mathematical difficulties: Findings from a four-year longitudinal study. *Learning and Instruction, 19*, 513–526.

Krajewski, K., Nieding, G., & Schneider, W. (2007). *Mengen, zählen, Zahlen. Die Welt der Mathematik verstehen. Förderkonzept.* Berlin: Cornelsen.

Lipowsky, F. (2007). Was wissen wir über guten Unterricht? In *Guter Unterricht. Maßstäbe und Merkmale—Wege und Werkzeuge, Friedrich Jahresheft, 25*, 26–30.

Lipowsky, F. (2012). Lehrerinnen und Lehrer als Lerner—Wann gelingt der Rollentausch? Merkmale und Wirkungen wirksamer Lehrerfortbildungen. *Schulpädagogik heute, 5*(3), 1–17.

Lee, J. S., & Ginsburg, H. P. (2007). What is appropriate mathematics education for four-year-olds? *Journal of Early Childhood Research, 5*(1), 2–31.

Lorenz, J. H. (2008). Diagnose und Förderung von Kindern in Mathematik—ein Überblick. In F. Hellmich & H. Köster (Eds.), *Vorschulische Bildungsprozesse in Mathematik und Naturwissenschaften* (pp. 29–44). Bad Heilbrunn: Klinkhardt.

Luit, J. E. H. van, Rijt, B. A. M. van de, & Hasemann, K. (2001). *Osnabrücker Test zur Zahlbegriffsentwicklung.* Göttingen: Hogrefe.

Mischo, Ch., & Fröhlich-Gildhoff, K. (2011). Professionalisierung und Professionsentwicklung im Bereich der frühen Bildung. *Frühe Bildung, 0*, 4–12.

Oers, B. van. (2009). Emergent mathematical thinking in the context of play. *Educational Studies in Mathematics, 74*(1), 23–37.

Preiß, G. (2007). *Leitfaden Zahlenland 1. Verlaufspläne für die Lerneinheiten 1 bis 10 der "Entdeckungen im Zahlenland".* Kirchzarten: Klein Druck.

Reusser, K. (2001). Co-constructivism in educational theory and practice. In N. J. Smelser, P. Baltes, & F. E. Weinert (Eds.), *International encyclopedia of the social and behavioral sciences* (pp. 2058–2062). Oxford: Pergamon/Elsevier Science.

Reusser, K. (2006). Konstruktivismus—vom epistemologischen Leitbegriff zur Erneuerung der didaktischen Kultur. In M. Baer, M. Fuchs, P. Füglister, K. Reusser, & H. Wyss (Eds.), *Didaktik auf psychologischer Grundlage. Von Hans Aeblis kognitionspsychologischer Didaktik zur modernen Lehr- und Lernforschung* (pp. 151–167). Bern: h.e.p. verlag.

Schröder, H. (2002). *Lernen—Lehren—Unterricht: lernpsychologische und didaktische Grundlagen.* München, Wien: Oldenbourg.

Seo, K.-H., & Ginsburg, H. P. (2004). What is developmentally appropriate in early childhood mathematics education? Lessons from new research. In D. H. Clements & J. Sarama (Eds.), *Engaging young children in mathematics. standards for early childhood mathematics education* (pp. 91–104). Mahwah: Lawrence Erlbaum Associates.

Shulman, L. S. (1986). Those who understand: knowledge growth in teaching. *Educational Researcher, 15*(2), 4–14.

Siegler, R. S., & Ramani, G. B. (2008). Playing linear numerical board games promotes low-income children's numerical development. *Developmental Science. Special Issue on Mathematical Cognition, 11*(5), 655–661.

Siraj-Blatchford, I., Sylva, K., Muttock, St., Gilden, R., & Bell, D. (2002). *Researching effective pedagogy in the early years.* London: Institute of Education/Department of Educational Studies.

Stern, E. (1998). Die Entwicklung schulbezogener Kompetenzen: Mathematik. In F. E. Weinert (Ed.), *Entwicklung im Kindesalter* (pp. 95–113). Weinheim: Beltz.

Steinweg, A. S. (2006). *Lerndokumentation Mathematik*. Berlin: Senatsverwaltung für Bildung, Wissenschaft und Forschung.

Steinweg, A. S. (2008). Zwischen Kindergarten und Schule—Mathematische Basiskompetenzen im Übergang. In F. Hellmich & H. Köster (Eds.), *Vorschulische Bildungsprozesse in Mathematik und Naturwissenschaften* (pp. 143–159). Bad Heilbrunn: Klinkhardt.

Steinweg, A. S., & Gasteiger, H. (2007). *2. Zwischenstandsbericht—Wissenschaftliche Begleitung der Implementierung der Lerndokumentation Mathematik im Rahmen des Projekts TransKiGs für das Land Berlin*. Senatsverwaltung für Bildung, Wissenschaft und Forschung. http://www.uni-bamberg.de/fileadmin/uni/fakultaeten/ppp_professuren/mathematik_informa-tik/Dateien/TransKiGS/Bericht_WissBegleitungTransKiGSBerlin_Dez07.pdf. Accessed 14 Nov 2012.

Steinweg, A. S., & Gasteiger, H. (2008). *3. Zwischenstandsbericht—Wissenschaftliche Begleitung der Implementierung der Lerndokumentation Mathematik im Rahmen des Projekts TransKiGs für das Land Berlin*. Senatsverwaltung für Bildung, Wissenschaft und Forschung. http://www.uni-bamberg.de/fileadmin/uni/fakultaeten/ppp_professuren/mathematik_informa-tik/Dateien/TransKiGS/Bericht_WissBegleitungTransKiGs_Berlin_Dez08.pdf. Accessed 14 Nov 2012.

Weinert, F. E. (2001). Concept of competence: A conceptual clarification. In D. S. Rychen & L. H. Salganik (Eds.), *Defining and selecting key competencies* (pp. 45–65). Seattle: Hogrefe & Huber Publishers.

Weinert, F. E., Schrader, F.-W., & Helmke, A. (1990). Educational expertise. Closing the gap between educational research and classroom practice. *School Psychology International, 11*(3), 163–180.

Wittmann, E. Ch. (2004). Design von Lernumgebungen zur mathematischen Frühförderung. In G. Faust, M. Götz, H. Hacker, & H.-G. Roßbach (Eds.), *Anschlussfähige Bildungsprozesse im Elementar- und Primarbereich* (pp. 49–63). Bad Heilbrunn: Klinkhardt.

Wittmann, E. Ch., & Müller, G. N. (2009). *Das Zahlenbuch. Handbuch zum Frühförderprogramm*. Stuttgart: Klett.

Wollring, B. (2006). Welche Zeit zeigt deine Uhr? Handlungsleitende Diagnostik für den Mathematikunterricht in der Grundschule. *Friedrich Jahresheft, 24*, 64–67.

Zehetmeier, St., & Krainer, K. (2011). Ways of promoting the sustainability of mathematics teachers' professional development. *ZDM Mathematics Education, 43*(6–7), 875–887.

Chapter 18
Employing the CAMTE Framework: Focusing on Preschool Teachers' Knowledge and Self-efficacy Related to Students' Conceptions

Pessia Tsamir, Dina Tirosh, Esther Levenson, Michal Tabach and Ruthi Barkai

Introduction

Concern for preschool mathematics education may be seen in the rise of national curricula in various countries which now make specific and sometimes mandatory recommendations for including mathematics as part of the preschool program. For example, in England, the non-statutory Practice Guidance for the Early Years Foundation Stage (2008) suggests ways of fostering children's mathematical knowledge from 0 to 5 years. In Israel, the National Mathematics Preschool Curriculum (INMPC 2008) is mandatory and contains specific guidelines and aims for children from 3 to 6 years. With new standards come new demands for teachers and the necessity for providing teachers with the tools to meet those demands.

In her plenary talk during the *mathematics education Perspective On Early Mathematics learning* (*POEM*) 2012 conference, Norma Presmeg discussed the "dance of instruction with construction in mathematics education" (Presmeg, personal communication). Continuing with the metaphor of dance, during the preschool years, there is ever the challenge of how the teacher can avoid 'stepping on the toes' of his or her young students. That is, can the teacher 'lead' the students without interfering too much and without crushing the children's independent thinking? Ginsburg et al. (2008) claimed that during the preschool years, children are interested in and develop mathematical ideas, often without adult assistance. Yet, while some of these ideas are in line with mathematical principles, others are not. They recommended that the preschool teacher create an environment whereby children can play with and construct mathematical ideas on their own but, in addition, teachers should take the time to "engage in deliberate and planned instruction" (Ginsburg et al. 2008, p. 8).

If we wish to guide young students in their mathematical discoveries, we need teachers who can lead this guidance. Yet, in Israel, as in many countries, attention to mathematics teacher education is mostly given at the elementary and secondary

P. Tsamir (✉) · D. Tirosh · E. Levenson · M. Tabach · R. Barkai
Tel Aviv University, Ramat Aviv, 6997801, Tel Aviv, Israel
e-mail: pessia@post.tau.ac.il

levels (Arcavi 2004; Kaiser 2002). All too often, preschool teachers receive little or no preparation for teaching mathematics to young children (Ginsburg et al. 2008). With this in mind, it is not surprising to find an increased call for strengthening the preparation of preschool teachers for teaching mathematics. The National Association for the Education of Young Children (NAEYC) and the National Council for Teachers of Mathematics (NCTM) recommend that "teachers of young children should learn the mathematics content that is directly relevant to their professional role" (NAEYC and NCTM 2002, p. 14). Similarly, the Australian Association of Mathematics Teachers (AAMT) and Early Childhood Australia (ECA) published a joint position paper recommending that early childhood staff be provided with "ongoing professional learning that develops their knowledge, skills and confidence in early childhood mathematics" (AAMT/ECA 2006, p. 3). Summarizing the above, some of the credentials necessary for teaching mathematics in preschool are knowing mathematics, knowing what mathematics young children are capable of learning, being skilled in planning an appropriate environment and activities, and having the confidence to engage students in mathematical activities. How can these requirements be framed, studied, and promoted?

This chapter describes a framework for professional development which takes into consideration the intertwining of instruction and construction that preschool teachers implement and facilitate in their classrooms. The chapter is divided into three sections. The first section introduces the *Cognitive Affective Mathematics Teacher Education (CAMTE)* framework, used in planning and implementing the program. Acknowledging that knowledge and beliefs are interrelated and that both affect teachers' proficiency (Pehkonen and Törner 1999; Schoenfeld 1992; Schoenfeld and Kilpatrick 2008; Törner 2002), the framework and program take into consideration teachers' knowledge as well as self-efficacy beliefs to teach mathematics in preschool.

The second part of this chapter demonstrates how the framework was used to study preschool teachers' knowledge and self-efficacy related to children's conceptions of counting and enumeration. The third part of this chapter discusses how results of investigating preschool teachers' knowledge and self-efficacy may be used in planning professional development and illustrates some of the ideas by presenting a case study of one preschool teacher who participated in our program.

The Cognitive Affective Mathematics Teacher Education (CAMTE) Framework

The framework used in our program takes into account both teachers' knowledge as well as their related self-efficacy beliefs. In this section, we present the theoretical framework which guides both our program as well as our investigation of teachers' knowledge and self-efficacy beliefs. The section begins with a brief discussion of teachers' knowledge for teaching mathematics and continues with a brief review of self-efficacy. We then present the model of the framework and how it relates to preschool teachers' knowledge for teaching mathematics.

Teachers' Knowledge for Teaching

In framing the mathematical knowledge preschool teachers need for teaching, we draw on Shulman (1986) who identified subject-matter knowledge (SMK) and pedagogical content knowledge (PCK) as two major components of teachers' knowledge necessary for teaching. In our previous work (Tabach et al. 2010), we found it useful to differentiate between two components of teachers' SMK: being able to produce solutions, strategies, and explanations and being able to evaluate given solutions, strategies, and explanations. Thus, our framework takes into consideration both of these aspects of SMK. Regarding PCK, we draw on the works of Ball and her colleagues (Ball et al. 2008) who refined Shulman's theory and differentiated between two aspects of PCK: knowledge of content and students (KCS) and knowledge of content and teaching (KCT). KCS is "knowledge that combines knowing about students and knowing about mathematics" whereas KCT "combines knowing about teaching and knowing about mathematics" (Ball et al. 2008, p. 401).

Within the domain of number, preschool teachers' SMK includes knowledge about counting, operations, and a variety of possible ways and methods of rationally examining and explaining found solutions. Teachers' KCS includes, for example, knowledge of young children's nonconservation of number (Piaget and Inhelder 1958). Within geometry, preschool teachers' SMK includes knowledge of defining geometrical concepts and identifying various examples and nonexamples of two- and three-dimensional figures (solids) as well as ways of justifying this identification. Teachers' KCS includes knowledge of which examples and nonexamples children intuitively recognize as such (Tsamir et al. 2008), as well as knowledge of children's commonly held concept images and concept definitions for geometrical figures (Tall and Vinner 1981). In both domains, KCT includes knowledge related to designing and assessing different tasks, providing students with multiple paths to understanding.

Self-efficacy

The framework used in our program also draws on Bandura's (1986) social cognitive theory, which takes into consideration the relationship between psychodynamic and behavioristic influences, as well as personal beliefs and self-perception, when explaining human behavior. Thus, besides investigating preschool teacher's knowledge, it is important to relate to their self-efficacy. Bandura defined self-efficacy as "people's judgments of their capabilities to organize and execute a course of action required to attain designated types of performances" (Bandura 1986, p. 391). Hackett and Betz (1989) defined mathematics self-efficacy as "a situational or problem-

Table 18.1 The cognitive affective mathematics teacher education framework

	Subject-matter		Pedagogical-content	
	Solving	Evaluating	Students	Tasks
Knowledge	Cell 1	Cell 2	Cell 3	Cell 4
Self-efficacy	Cell 5	Cell 6	Cell 7	Cell 8

specific assessment of an individual's confidence in her or his ability to successfully perform or accomplish a particular [mathematics] task or problem" (p. 262). The *CAMTE* framework takes into consideration teachers' mathematics self-efficacy as well as their pedagogical-mathematics self-efficacy, i.e., their self-efficacy related to the pedagogy of teaching mathematics. Teacher self-efficacy has been related to a variety of teacher classroom behaviors that affect their effort in teaching, and their persistence and resilience when facing difficulties with students (Ashton and Webb 1986). Studies report that teachers with a high sense of self-efficacy are more enthusiastic in teaching (Allinder 1994) and are more committed to teaching (Coladarci 1992).

Illustrating the CAMTE Framework Within the Domain of Number Concepts

The design of our program and the accompanying study was based on the framework presented in the following eight-cell knowledge and self-efficacy matrix (see Table 18.1). In Cells 1–4 and in Cells 5–8, we address teachers' knowledge and self-efficacy, respectively. In Table 18.1, we illustrate the different cells of the framework within the domain of number concepts, focusing on teachers' knowledge for teaching counting and enumeration.

Counting refers to saying the number words in the proper order and knowing the principles and patterns in the number system as coded in one's natural language (Baroody 1987). For the purpose of this chapter, we define "enumerating" as "counting objects for the purpose of saying how many." This is in line with the Hebrew terminology used in the Israel curriculum, which differentiates between counting (הריפס) and enumerating (הינמ). Gelman and Gallistel (1978) outlined five principles of counting, which in our terminology, we call enumerating. The three "how-to-count" principles include the one-to-one principle, the stable-order principle, and the cardinal principle. The two "what-to-count" principles include the abstraction principle and the order-irrelevance principle. For each cell, we offer specific examples.

Cell 1: producing solutions: compare the number of elements in two sets using a variety of strategies; count the following large collection of items using a variety of strategies.

Cell 2: evaluating solutions: evaluate the following strategies for comparing the number of elements in two sets; evaluate the following justifications for why one set has more elements than another set. (See Tirosh et al. (2011) for a review of possible strategies for comparing the number of elements in two sets and evaluations of those strategies.)

Cell 3: knowledge of students' conceptions: which number symbols are more difficult for children to learn; what are children's common mistakes related to the counting sequence.

Cell 4: designing and evaluating tasks: which tasks have the potential to foster children's acceptance of the one-to-one principle; which tasks will assess children's counting and enumeration skills.

Cell 5: mathematics self-efficacy related to producing solutions: teachers' beliefs regarding their ability to enumerate a large collection of items in multiple ways.

Cell 6: mathematics self-efficacy related to evaluating solutions: teachers' beliefs in their ability to evaluate various strategies for enumerating.

Cell 7: pedagogical-mathematics self-efficacy related to children's conceptions: teachers' beliefs in their ability to identify children's common mistakes related to counting.

Cell 8: pedagogical-mathematics self-efficacy related to designing and evaluating tasks: teachers' beliefs in their ability to design tasks that will promote children's correct and efficient enumeration strategies.

The above framework was used to plan and implement our professional development program as well as to investigate preschool teachers' knowledge and self-efficacy to teach mathematics in preschool. In the following section, we report on a study which focused on Cells 3 and 7 of the CAMTE framework (i.e., knowledge of students' conceptions and pedagogical-mathematics self-efficacy related to children's conceptions) with regard to the topics of counting and enumeration.

Studying Preschool Teachers' Knowledge and Self-efficacy Related to Students' Conceptions

At the heart of constructivist theories is that students build new knowledge upon existing knowledge (e.g., Simon and Schifter 1993; Von Glaserfeld 1991). When planning our professional development program, this central idea emerges twice. First, as we intend for teachers to plan activities for their young students based on their young students' existing knowledge, one of the objectives of our program is to increase teachers' knowledge of their students. However, before planning to increase teachers' knowledge of their students, we need to consider what the teachers already know about their students' conceptions. In general, in order for teacher educators to adequately plan a professional development program, it is essential to consider teachers' current knowledge. Therefore, we suggest that the CAMTE framework may be used to study preschool teachers' knowledge for teaching mathematics in conjunction with planning an appropriate program.

Table 18.2 Teachers' self-efficacy related to knowledge of students

Item	Question: I am capable of identifying…	Teachers $N=36$ M	SD
3	…which combinations of numbers that add up to 7 children find difficult to learn	2.4	0.03
5	…which numbers children find difficult to say the number which comes immediately beforehand	2.5	0.81
6	…counting skills that most children are competent performing (when considering counting up till 30)	2.6	0.93
2	…different arrangements of eight items which children find difficult to count	2.9	1.02
1	…which number symbols from 1 to 9 children find difficult to recognize	3.0	1.10
4	…which numbers children find difficult to say the number which immediately follows	3.2	0.73

Participants

Participants in this study were 36 practicing preschool teachers, who at the time of the study were all teaching 4–6-year-old children in municipal preschools. All had a Bachelor's degree in education. The study took place at the beginning of the year before they had attended any professional development courses which specifically addressed teaching mathematics in preschool.

Tools and Procedure

Based on the CAMTE framework, a two-part questionnaire was developed. The first part began with six self-efficacy questions related to participants' knowledge of children's conceptions of numbers (Cell 7 of the CAMTE framework). A four-point Likert scale was used to rate participants' beliefs in their ability to identify specific aspects of students' conceptions: 1—I do not believe at all in my ability; 2—I somewhat do not believe in my ability; 3—I believe somewhat in my ability; and 4—I completely believe in my ability. The actual questions are presented in Table 18.2. After participants completed this part of the questionnaire, they handed it in and received the second part of the questionnaire.

The second part of the questionnaire consisted of knowledge questions. These questions followed the self-efficacy questions in order to allow the participants to evaluate their self-efficacy before actually engaging in the task. Participants were asked to assess how many children at the end of kindergarten would be able to complete various number-related tasks (Cell 3 of the framework)—almost all children, many, about half, few, or almost none? Kindergarten is the last year of preschool. All questionnaires were completed in the presence of the researcher. The actual questions are presented in Table 18.3. Many of the items on the questionnaire were based on our previous work with young children. All items on the questionnaire

Table 18.3 Teachers' estimates of students' abilities to perform various tasks

Item	Question: How many students will be able to…	Teachers $N=36$ M	SD
6	say that changing the position of objects to be counted does not change the amount there are?	2.6	1.00
10	say how many apples to add to three apples in order to make seven apples?	2.8	1.03
8	say which number comes right before 6?	3.5	1.18
3	count from 6 to 15?	3.7	1.24
2	count backward from 7?	3.9	1.29
1	count from 1 to 30?	4.0	1.28
7	say which number comes right after 6?	4.0	1.07
9	identify the number symbol for 9?	4.0	1.15
5	say that it does not matter if you count objects from the left or from the right?	4.2	0.98
4	count eight bottle caps placed in a straight row?	4.4	1.02

were consistent with the requirements of the mandatory mathematics preschool curriculum.

Results

Pedagogical-Mathematics Self-efficacy Related to Children's Conceptions

As mentioned earlier, teachers were asked to assess on a scale of 1–4 (4 being the highest rating) their own ability to identify children's difficulties when performing various counting and enumerating skills. Teachers were told to take into consideration children at the end of their kindergarten year. Table 18.2 reports the means and standard deviations for each self-efficacy question related to this aspect of teachers' knowledge. Statements are arranged according to the level of self-efficacy reported by the practicing teachers, from low to high. Item numbers represent the order in which they were presented on the questionnaire.

Cronbach's alpha was used to measure internal consistency. A coefficient of $\alpha=0.743$ indicated that the items most likely formed a coherent group. We thus configured for each participant a mean self-efficacy score. The mean self-efficacy score for the group of teachers was 2.8 (SD=0.61) indicating that while teachers, for the most part, believed in their ability to identify aspects of students' conceptions, they were not absolutely sure of this ability.

Assessing Teachers' Knowledge of Students' Ability to Perform Number Tasks

Teachers were presented with various number tasks and asked to estimate on a scale from 1 to 5 how many students (1—almost none, 2—a few, 3—about half, 4—many,

Table 18.4 Comparing participants' estimates with children's performance

Item	Question: How many students will be able to…	Mean estimates translated to percents	Percent of children ($N=82$) who succeeded
6	say that changing the position of objects to be counted does not change the amount there are?	40	65
10	tell how many apples to add to three apples in order to make seven apples?	45	52.5
8	say which number comes right before 6?	62.5	59
3	count from 6 to 15?	67.5	68
2	count backward from 7?	72.5	60
1	count from 1 to 30?	75	49
7	say which number comes right after 6?	75	94
9	identify the number for symbol for 9?	75	88
5	say that it does not matter if you count objects from the left or from the right?	80	77
4	count eight bottle caps placed in a straight row?	85	93

and 5—almost all) would be able to complete the task correctly. The means of participants' estimations of students' abilities for each task and standard deviation are shown in Table 18.2. The table is arranged according to the teachers' estimation, from the tasks estimated to be most difficult to those estimated to be least difficult. The item number reflects the order of the questions in accordance to how they appeared on the questionnaire.

In general, teachers believed that for most tasks, more than half of kindergarten children at the end of their kindergarten year would be able to correctly solve the tasks. The exceptions were items 6 and 10. For those tasks, teachers believed that less than half of the children would be able to succeed.

In order to assess teachers' knowledge of kindergarten children's abilities to perform number tasks, we compared the participants' estimates with previous research we had conducted with kindergarten children (Tirosh and Tsamir 2008), which was much in line with studies by other researchers (e.g., Baroody and Wilkins 1999). (See Table 18.4.)

For example, in our previous research we asked children ($N=82$) to count from 1 to 30, to count backward from 7, and so on. In those studies, we configured the percentage of children who succeeded in the task. We then reconfigured the 1–5 scale the teachers used to reflect the results of the children's performance with the 0–100% scale. Reconfiguration was carried out in the following way. The lowest score on both scales was 1 and 0%, respectively, and the highest score was 5 and 100%, respectively. We transformed the 1–5 scale by using the linear equation: $y = 25(x-1)$ where x represents the scale used for teachers and y the scale used for children. We could then compare teachers' estimates of how many children would succeed at a task, with results of children's actual performances. This is presented in Table 18.4.

One-sample t tests were conducted in order to compare teachers' estimates with actual children's performance. Results, shown in Table 18.5, showed no significant

18 Employing the CAMTE Framework: Focusing …

Table 18.5 Comparing teachers' estimates with actual children performance

Item number	M	t value	Df	p value
6	40	−5.73	34	.000
10	45	−0.270	34	.788
8	62.5	0.851	35	.401
3	67.5	0.109	34	.914
2	72.5	2.102	34	.043
1	75	4.760	35	.000
7	75	−4.358	34	.000
9	75	−2.528	34	.016
5	80	0.751	33	.458
4	85	−2.114	35	.042

differences for items 3, 5, 8, and 10. In other words, for those items, teachers' estimations were in line with the actual amount of children that were able to perform those tasks at the end of kindergarten. For items 4, 6, 7, and 9, teachers significantly underestimated children's abilities. For items 1 and 2, teachers significantly overestimated children's ability.

The two items with the greatest difference between the teachers' estimation of children's knowledge and the children's actual performance were items 1 and 6. While teachers estimated that approximately three quarters of children would be able to recite the numbers from 1 to 30 (knowledge of counting) by the end of kindergarten, our investigation showed that only half were able to do so. Item 6 is related to knowledge of enumerating, specifically understanding the stable-order principle (Gelman and Gallistel 1978). Here, teachers believed that less than half of the children would have reached this understanding while in fact, more than half of the children exhibited knowledge of this principle.

Despite some of the specific differences between teachers' estimates of children's abilities and their actual abilities, it is important to note some general trends. First, with the exception of item one, counting from 1 to 30, teachers estimated that fewer children would be able to complete the tasks in items 6, 10, 8, 3, and 2 than would be able to complete the tasks in items 7, 9, 5, and 4. This general trend was in line with students' implementation of those tasks. That is, in a general sense, teachers correctly lined up the tasks in order of their difficulty. We also note that teachers knew that a greater number of children would be able to state which number comes after 6 than be able to state which number comes before 6. Our work with children demonstrated that, in general, children are more easily able to state which number comes after some other number than which number comes before that other number.

In addition to the questions described above, teachers were also asked to consider how much time they would dedicate to teaching number symbols and how much time they would dedicate to teaching which number comes before and after other given numbers. More specifically, regarding the teaching of number symbols, teachers were asked to consider the time period it would take to teach each number symbol and whether they would plan on spending an equal amount of time on each

Table 18.6 Time devoted to teaching number symbols

	Teachers (%) $N=36$
Would devote the same amount of time for teaching each number symbol	7(19)
Would spend more time teaching difficult-to-learn number symbols and less time on others	6(17)
Other	23(64)

Table 18.7 Time that would be devoted to teaching which number comes before and after a given number

	Teachers (%) $N=34$
Would devote the same amount of time for teaching both concepts	2(6)
Would spend more time teaching which number comes right <u>after</u> a given number	–
Would spend more time teaching which number comes right <u>before</u> a given number	12(35)
Other	20(59)

number symbol or perhaps they would plan to spend more time on symbols which are difficult to learn and less time on symbols which are easier to learn. Results are summarized in Table 18.6.

When it came to providing reasons for their decisions, a little over a third of the teachers (36%) answered this question based on pedagogical knowledge without taking into consideration the specific content. For example, T3 claimed, "[I would] first check what previous knowledge the group has and then I would choose my teaching strategy." T20 stated, "[I would teach] each child according to his pace." Approximately a third of the teachers considered the specific content; however, only 15% of the teachers specifically mentioned that they would spend more time on difficult-to-learn symbols such as 6 and 9.

Regarding time dedicated to teaching which number comes before and after a given number, participants were asked to consider if they would spend more time on teaching which number comes after a given number, more time on teaching which number comes before a given number, the same amount of time for both concepts, or something else. Results are summarized in Table 18.7. First, we note that none of the teachers wrote that they would dedicate more time to teaching which number comes right after a given number than which number comes right before a given number. This is in line with the relevant difficulties students find in completing each of the two tasks.

When considering their answers to this question, approximately 20% of the teachers exhibited general pedagogical knowledge but did not relate specifically to the content. For example, T15 stated that her teaching strategy and time considerations were "very dependent on the level of the children and their ability to learn." A third of the teachers took into consideration that it might take more time for children to be able to say which number comes before a given number than after a given number. For example, T31 claimed, "Because children can easily count (forward), it is easy for them to say the number which comes after [a given number] and more difficult for them to go backward and say the number which comes before."

Looking back at the results presented in both Tables 18.6 and 18.7, one notes that, in general, teachers did not choose any of the options shown to them. One possible reason for this occurrence could be that practicing teachers may draw on their experience, coming to different conclusions than those suggested on the questionnaire. In fact, as was noted above, many practicing teachers commendably mentioned that they would base the amount of time spent teaching different concepts on their students' abilities and background. In general, practicing teachers exhibited a flexible teaching plan based on the circumstances found in their class.

Using Results to Plan for Professional Development

Just as children bring their knowledge and experiences to the school classroom, teachers bring their knowledge and experiences to professional development courses. As mentioned above, none of the teachers had attended any professional development courses which specifically addressed teaching mathematics in preschool. In addition, given the fact that the mathematics preschool curriculum in Israel has only recently been authorized, few of the teachers had taken any mathematics education courses related to the curriculum when studying toward their teaching degree. And still, the teachers in this study displayed knowledge of their students' conceptions of number concepts. How can this be explained? We believe that teachers construct knowledge of their students by observing them doing mathematics, mathematics that arises spontaneously or is teacher directed. However, like children who construct their own knowledge, teachers' knowledge, in this case of their students, is not necessarily complete.

Considering Teachers' Knowledge

How could the results of the above study be used in planning professional development courses for those teachers? First, we might ask ourselves how those teachers came to be knowledgeable of certain aspects of students' number conceptions and not others. Perhaps, if we surmise that most of the teachers' knowledge came from their experiences while working with children, it might inform us of what types of number tasks teachers implement in their classes. For example, teachers correctly estimated how many children would be able to count backward from 7 but did not correctly estimate how many children would be able to count forward till 30. It could be that counting backward from 7 or from 10 is a more common task in kindergarten than counting forward all the way till 30. It could be that teachers are inclined to implement some tasks in a group setting and others individually. Group activities do not always give us accurate feedback of what each child is capable of doing on his or her own. Thus, we may plan during the professional development to discuss the difference between implementing activities in a group or with individuals.

In our program, we also discuss with teachers the difference between tasks which aim to teach or enhance students' knowledge as opposed to tasks which aim to assess students' knowledge. While the difference may be subtle, and perhaps any task could be viewed in both lights, we make this differentiation, and discuss this differentiation with teachers, in order to sharpen their knowledge of the different aspects of tasks that need to be considered before, during, and after implementing the task. We also review with the teachers the now mandatory curriculum, which includes many examples of tasks that can be carried out with children. This exposes teachers to additional ideas for mathematical activities that may be implemented in their classrooms. As can be seen, there is a relationship between Cells 3 and 4 of the CAMTE framework.

Another possible reason teachers' estimations did not always match students' implementations could be that teachers' mathematical knowledge is incomplete and therefore their assessment of children's abilities will be inaccurate. For example, teachers estimated that only 40% of children would know that changing the position of objects to be counted does not change the amount of objects. In Israel, because Hebrew is read from right to left and numbers are read from left to right, some teachers believe that children should be encouraged to count only from left to right in order to establish in them the directionality of reading numbers. Teachers may therefore believe that the positioning of objects is critical in counting. This example illustrates the relationship between Cells 1 and 3 of the CAMTE framework and emphasizes the need to investigate teachers' knowledge related to all cells.

Considering Teachers' Self-efficacy

Regarding self-efficacy, the teachers in our study felt reasonably able to identify aspects of children's number concepts but were not overly confident. For us, as teacher educators, this is a good starting point. We take this to mean that teachers believe in their abilities, an important characteristic for teachers to have. Yet, they also realize that continued learning on their part is necessary. Having teachers admit to a deficiency in their knowledge is not easy. One of the ways our program has dealt with this issue is by employing what we term the pair-dialog (P-D) approach to instruction, a specific form of team teaching in which two instructors teach cooperatively. In our interactions with teachers, we use a blend of pair performances (e.g., thought-provoking dialog episodes) and discussions that involve the teachers (segments of "inviting the audience," prospective and participating teachers, to express their views on different ideas that are presented and to "help us out" in resolving the dilemmas that we raise). (For examples of such dialogs, see Tsamir and Tirosh 2011.) A main gain of our approach is that the teachers are confronted, in a gentle and respectful manner, with their incorrect responses, and the P-D opening serves as a springboard for a thorough discussion of common errors.

An Illustrative Example: The Case of Maple

In order to enable teachers to construct knowledge of children's conceptions, as part of our program teachers are instructed to plan and record the implementation of a mathematical activity. Recordings are then shared and discussed collectively with the teachers and teacher educators.

To illustrate this final point, we present the case of Maple, a teacher with 7 years of experience and a Bachelor of Education (B.Ed.). For her final project, Maple chose to report on her assessment of a 4 1/2-year-old girl in her class. Her report included her prior assessment of that girl's counting and enumeration skills, "Gila can count till 10 without making mistakes. She also recognizes the number symbols up till 5." Maple then described seven different tasks which she chose to implement in order to assess different elements of her student's knowledge of enumeration. For each task, she wrote what specific element of enumeration skills she was assessing as well as what mistakes may possibly arise. For example, for her first task she planned to ask the child to count till 10 without placing any items before the child. She wrote, "The first task investigates consistent and acceptable counting...if the child cannot count, and the basis for enumeration is counting, then if the child cannot count as she should, she will not be able to enumerate." For the second task, she placed eight identical objects in a row and asked the child how many there were. She wrote, "The second task investigates the one-to-one correspondence principle and when I ask again how many there are, I am checking the principle of cardinality, that the child knows that the last number represents the total amount... [It could be that] a child will count the same object twice or, instead, skip an object." Maple also planned to assess the order-irrelevance principle by asking if the objects can be counted from right to left as well as from left to right and if the amount stays the same.

After writing up her analysis of the child's performance, she reflected on the process, noting not only the child's performance but also her own performance. For example, Maple is surprised at the strategy the child used when counting 20 bottle caps placed in a pile. The child first laid out all of the caps in a row and only then proceeded to count them. This was obviously a strategy Maple had not seen previously. She also remarked in her report that when talking to the child, she, the teacher, was not consistent in her terminology and sometimes mixed up the words for counting with enumerating. Maple also noted what she would change if she were to carry out the project again. She wrote, "I would emphasize the difference between counting and enumeration, before beginning to assess a child's knowledge. First I would strengthen my own knowledge and then the child's."

During the reflective interview at the end of the course, Maple was asked what she learned from the experience of videotaping her implementation of the assessment tasks and then watching the video. She noted, "It was interesting to watch myself. During class time I never see myself. It (the video) is a good tool. You can stop [the video-tape], think, watch it again, and then reflect. It really helped me to learn about myself and about the children." The interviewer also asked Maple, if she could point to some new insight that came about from her viewing the video. She answered, "First, about myself. As I conducted more assessment tasks, I saw that I was more confident in myself, more skillful with regard to conducting the assessment task. I see how I improved each time." At the end of the program, we see that Maple has begun to adopt a constructivist approach to instruction. As Cobb (1988) claimed, "the constructivist view of instruction implies that the teacher must be a reflective pedagogical problem solver who, in effect, conducts an informal research program" (p. 101).

Conclusion

The preschool teacher plays a major role in fostering children's mathematical abilities. "It is up to her to devote attention both to planned mathematical activities as well as mathematical activities which may spontaneously arise in the class and to pay attention to the mathematical development of the children" (INMPC 2008, p. 8). This is in line with Presmeg (2012) who claimed that "Effective instruction can facilitate students' making of constructions that lie within the canons of mathematically accepted knowledge, and yet there is room for creativity and enjoyment."

Being able to plan appropriate mathematical activities requires knowledge of mathematics as well as knowledge of students and tasks. However, it is one thing to implement a given curriculum with given activities and another to recognize opportunities for learning mathematics and make the most of these opportunities. If we want teachers to recognize such opportunities they need to be on the lookout for such opportunities. They need to be proactive. A high self-efficacy for teaching mathematics, based on actual experiences of solving mathematical problems and evaluating possible solutions, in turn based on effectively implementing planned tasks with children and seeing the results of their work with children, can help foster the positive drive we ask of our teachers. That is our aim as teacher educators—to promote a high self-efficacy for teaching mathematics in preschool which corresponds to a high level of knowledge for teaching mathematics in preschool.

Conflict of Interest This research was partially supported by The Israel Science Foundation (grant no. 654/10).

References

Allinder, R. M. (1994). The relationship between efficacy and the instructional practices of special education teachers and consultants. *Teacher Education and Special Education, 17*(2), 86–95.

Arcavi, A. (2004). Education of mathematics teachers. In R. Strässer, G. Brandell, B. Grevholm, & O. Helenius (Eds.), *Educating for the future. Proceedings of an international symposium on mathematics teacher education, The royal Swedish academy of sciences*, (pp. 227–238). Malmö, Sweden.

Ashton, P. T., & Webb, R. B. (1986). *Making a difference: Teachers' sense of efficacy and student achievement*. New York: Longman.

Australian Association of Mathematics Teachers and Early Childhood Australia (AAMT/ECA) (2006). *Position paper on early childhood mathematics*. http://www.aamt.edu.au/documentation/statements. Accessed 20 Jan 2009.

Ball, D., Thames, M., & Phelps, G. (2008). Content knowledge for teaching. *Journal of Teacher Education, 59*(5), 389–407.

Bandura, A. (1986). *Social foundations of thought and action: A social cognitive theory*. Englewood Cliffs: Prentice Hall.

Baroody, A. J. (1987). *Children's mathematical thinking: A developmental framework for preschool, primary, and special education teachers*. New York: Teacher's College Press.

Baroody, A. J., & Wilkins, J. L. M. (1999). The development of informal counting, number, and arithmetic skills and concepts. In J. V. Copley (Ed.), *Mathematics in the early years* (pp. 48–65). Reston: National Council of Teachers of Mathematics.

Cobb, P. (1988). The tension between theories of learning and instruction in mathematics education. *Educational Psychologist, 23*(2), 87–104.

Coladarci, T. (1992). Teachers' sense of efficacy and commitment to teaching. *Journal of Experimental Education, 60*, 323–337.

Gelman, R., & Gallistel, C. (1978). *The child's understanding of number*. Cambridge: Harvard University Press.

Ginsburg, H. P., Lee, J. S., & Boyd, J. S. (2008). Mathematics education for young children: What it is and how to promote it. *Social Policy Report, XXII*(I), 1–22.

Hackett, G., & Betz, N. (1989). An exploration of the mathematics self-efficacy/mathematics performance correspondence. *Journal for Research in Mathematics Education, 20*(3), 261–273.

Israel National Mathematics Preschool Curriculum (INMPC) (2008). http://meyda.education.gov.il/files/Tochniyot_Limudim/KdamYesodi/Math1.pdf. Accessed 7 Apr 2009.

Kaiser, G. (2002). Educational philosophies and their influence on mathematics education—An ethnographic study in English and German mathematics classrooms. *ZDM-Zentralblatt für Didaktik der Mathematik/International Reviews on Mathematical Education, 34*(6), 241–257.

National Association for the Education of Young Children and National Council of Teachers of Mathematics (NAEYC and NCTM) (2002). *Position statement. Early childhood mathematics: Promoting good beginnings*. www.naeyc.org/resources/position_statements/psmath.htm. Acceded 7 April 2009.

Pehkonen, E., & Törner, G. (1999). Teachers' professional development: What are the key change factors for mathematics teachers? *European Journal of Teacher Education, 22*(2–3), 259–275.

Piaget, J., & Inhelder, B. (1958). *The growth of logical thinking from childhood to adolescence*. New York: Basic Books.

Practice Guidance for the Early Years Foundation Stage (2008). www.standards.dfes.gov.uk/eyfs/resources/downloads/practice-guidance.pdf. Accessed 9 Apr 2009.

Presmeg, N. (2012). A dance of instruction with construction in mathematics education. Paper presented at *POEM 12 A Mathematics Education Perspective on early Mathematics Learning between the Poles of Instruction and Construction*. http://cermat.org/poem2012/main/proceedings.html. Accessed 24 June 2012.

Schoenfeld, A. H. (1992). Learning to think mathematically: Problem solving, metacognition, and sense-making in mathematics. In D. Grouws (Ed.), *Handbook of research on mathematics teaching and learning* (pp. 334–370). New York: Macmillan.

Schoenfeld, A. H., & Kilpatrick, J. (2008). Toward a theory of proficiency in teaching mathematics. In D. Tirosh & T. Wood (Eds.), *The international handbook of mathematics teacher education: Tools and processes in mathematics teacher education* (Vol. 2, pp. 321–354). Rotterdam: Sense Publishers.

Shulman, L. S. (1986). Those who understand: Knowledge growth in teaching. *Educational Researcher, 15*(2), 4–14.

Simon, M., & Schifter, D. (1993). Toward a constructivist perspective: The impact of a mathematics teacher inservice program on students. *Educational Studies in Mathematics*, 25(4), 331–340.

Tabach, M., Levenson, E., Barkai, R., Tirosh, D., Tsamir, P., & Dreyfus, T. (2010). Secondary school teachers' awareness of numerical examples as proof. *Research in Mathematics Education*, 12(2), 117–131.

Tall, D., & Vinner, S. (1981). Concept image and concept definition in mathematics, with special reference to limits and continuity. *Educational Studies in Mathematics*, 12(2), 151–169.

Tirosh, D., & Tsamir, P. (2008). *Starting right: Mathematics in preschool*. Unpublished research report. In Hebrew.

Tirosh, D., Tsamir, P., Levenson, E., & Tabach, M. (2011). From kindergarten teachers' professional development to children's knowledge: The case of equivalence. *Journal of Mathematics Teacher Education*, 14(2), 113–131.

Törner, G. (2002). Mathematical beliefs. In G. C. Leder, E. Pehkonen, & G. Törner (Eds.), *Beliefs: A hidden variable in mathematics education?* (pp. 73–94). Dordrecht:: Kluwer Academic.

Tsamir, P., & Tirosh, D. (2011). The pair-dialogue approach in mathematics teacher education. In P. Liljedahl, S. Oesterle, and D. Allen (Eds.), *Proceedings of the 2011 annual meeting of the Canadian mathematics education study group*. Burnaby: CMESG.

Tsamir, P., Tirosh, D., & Levenson, E. (2008). Intuitive nonexamples: The case of triangles. *Educational Studies in Mathematics*, 69(2), 81–95.

Von Glaserfeld, E. (1991). *Radical constructivism in mathematics education*. Dordrecth: Kluwer Academic.

Chapter 19
Early Enhancement of Kindergarten Children Potentially at Risk in Learning School Mathematics—Design and Findings of an Intervention Study

Andrea Peter-Koop and Meike Grüßing

Introduction

Children start developing mathematical knowledge and abilities a long time before they enter formal education (e.g. see Anderson et al. 2008; Ginsburg et al. 1999). In their play, their everyday life experiences at home and in childcare centres they develop a foundation of skills, concepts and understandings about numbers and mathematics (Baroody and Wilkins 1999). Anderson et al. (2008) reviewing international studies on preschool children's development and knowledge conclude that research

> (…) points to young children's strong capacity to deal with number knowledge prior to school, thus diminishing the value of the conventional practice that pre-number activities are more appropriate for this age group upon school entry. (p. 102)

However, the range of mathematical competencies children develop prior to school obviously varies quite substantially. While most preschoolers manage to develop a wide range of informal knowledge and skills in early numeracy, there are a small number of children who, for various reasons, struggle with the acquisition of number skills (e.g. see Clarke et al. 2008). Furthermore, clinical psychological studies suggest that children potentially at risk in learning mathematics can already be identified 1 year prior to school entry by assessing their number concept development (e.g. Krajewski 2005; Aunola et al. 2004). Findings from these studies also indicate that these children benefit from an early intervention prior to school helping them to develop a foundation of knowledge and skills for successful school-based mathematics learning. This seems to be of crucial importance as findings from the SCHOLASTIK project (Weinert and Helmke 1997) a longitudinal study on the development of primary school children suggest that students who are low achieving in mathematics at the beginning of primary school tend to stay in this position in

A. Peter-Koop (✉)
IDM, University of Bielefeld, Bielefeld, Germany
e-mail: andrea.peter-koop@un-bielefeld.de

M. Grüßing
Leibniz Institute for Science and Mathematics Education (IPN), Kiel, Germany

general. In most cases, a recovery does not occur. In addition, Stern (1997) emphasizes that with respect to success at school subject-specific knowledge prior to school is more important than general cognitive factors such as intelligence.

Theoretical Background: Number Concept Development

While pre-number activities based on Piaget's *logical foundations model* are frequently still current practice in first year school mathematics (Anderson et al. 2008), research findings as well as curriculum documents increasingly stress the importance of students' early engagement with sets, numbers and counting activities for their number concept development. Clements (1984) classified alternative models for number concept development that deliberately include early counting skills (Resnick 1983) as *skills integrations models*.

Piaget (1952) assumed that the development of number concept builds on logical operations based on pre-number activities such as classification, seriation and number conservation. He emphasized that the understanding of number is dependent on operational competencies. In his view, counting exercises do not have an operational value and hence no conducive effect on conceptual competence regarding number.

However, since the late 1970s this theory has been questioned due to research evidence suggesting that the development of number skills and concepts results from the integration of number skills, such as counting, subitizing and comparing. Studies by Fuson et al. (1983) and Sophian (1995), for example, demonstrate that children performing on conservation tasks who compare sets by counting or using a visual correspondence are highly successful. Clements (1984) investigated the effects of two training sequences on the development of logical operations and number. Two groups of 4-year-olds were trained for 8 weeks on either logical foundations focussing on classification and seriation or number skills based on counting. A third group with no training input served as a control group. Instruments measuring logical operations and number abilities were designed as pre- and post-test measures. It is not surprising that both experimental groups significantly outperformed the control group in both tests, however, the children that were trained on number skills significantly outperformed the logical foundations group on the number test while there were no significant differences between these two groups on the logical operations test. Clements' results comply with and extend previous research that had indicated that number skills, such as counting and subitizing, effect the development of number conservation (Fuson et al. 1983; Acredolo 1982). Hence, he concludes:

> (…) the counting act may provide the structure and/or representational tool with which to construct logical operations including classification and seriation, as well as number conservation. … Not only may explicit readiness training in logical operations be unnecessary, but well structured training in counting may facilitate the growth of these abilities as well as underlie the learning of other mature number concepts. (Clements 1984, p. 774–775)

An early training based on number abilities, like counting, comparing and subitizing, may be especially important for children who are likely to develop mathematical learning difficulties.

Krajewski (2008) provides a theoretical model that is based on the assumption that the linkage of imprecise nonverbal quantity concepts with the ability to count forms the foundation for understanding several major principles of the number system. The model depicts how early mathematical competencies are acquired via three developmental levels. In two longitudinal studies, Krajewski and Schneider (2009a, b) investigated the predictive validity of the quantity–number competencies of these developmental levels for mathematical school achievement. The results of the studies indicate that quantity–number competencies measured in kindergarten predict about 25 % of the variance in mathematical school achievement in grades 3 and 4. Moreover, a subgroup analysis indicated that low-performing fourth graders had already shown large deficits in their early quantity–number competencies (Krajewski and Schneider 2009b). It can be concluded that these early quantity–number competencies constitute an important prerequisite for the understanding of school mathematics. These results conform to different other longitudinal studies (e.g. Aunola et al. 2004)

Methodology

Based on relevant research findings reported in the previous section, the longitudinal study (2005–2008) that provided the background of this chapter aims at the following:

- To determine how 5-year-old kindergarten children potentially at risk in learning school mathematics can be identified one year prior to school enrolment.
- To implement an early intervention following two approaches—weekly one-on-one intervention by pre-service teachers versus (small) group intervention by the kindergarten teacher.
- To investigate possible effects of the intervention on children's number skills at the beginning of school, at the end of year 1 and year 2.

While key results with respect to the effects of the intervention on student achievement directly before as well as in the first two years of primary school have already been reported (Peter-Koop et al. 2008; Grüßing and Peter-Koop 2008), this chapter aims to explore how children potentially at risk learning school mathematics can be supported effectively in terms of their number concept development in early childhood education at kindergarten.

Hence, following a description of the concept and design of the intervention, results of the study with respect to three underlying research questions are addressed:

1. What are the effects of an 8-month intervention programme aimed at the development of number abilities for kindergarten children (5-year-olds) identified to be potentially at risk learning school mathematics upon school entry?

2. In how far has the early intervention a lasting effect with respect to their achievement in mathematics at the end of grade 1 and grade 2?
3. Do the two types of intervention—one-on-one support by a pre-service teacher versus small group intervention by the kindergarten teacher—lead to significant differences in mathematics achievement?

Overall, 947 5-year-old preschoolers from 35 kindergartens—17 in an urban and 18 in a rather rural setting—in the northwest of Germany took part in the first year of the study (September 2005–August 2006). With the permission of their parents, these children performed on three different tests/interviews conducted at three different days within a fortnight by pre-service primary mathematics teachers who had been especially trained for their participation in the study:

- The German version of the *Utrecht Early Numeracy Test* (OTZ; van Luit et al. 2001)—a standardized individual test aiming to measure children's number concept development that involves logical operations-based tasks as well as counting related items.
- The *Elementarmathematisches Basisinterview* for use in kindergarten (EMBI-KiGa) based on the *First Year at School Mathematics Interview* (FYSMI) [1] developed in the context of the Australian *Early Numeracy Research Project* (Clarke et al. 2006)—a task-based one-on-one interview aiming at 5-year-olds allowing children to articulate their developing mathematical understanding through the use of specific materials provided for each task, which in the meantime has been published by Peter-Koop and Grüßing (2011).
- The *Culture Fair Test* (CFT1)—an intelligence test for preschoolers to be conducted in groups between four and eight children (Cattell et al. 1997) in order to be able to control this variable with respect to the children identified as potentially at risk learning mathematics.

A total of 854 children performed on all three tests. Their data provided the basis of the quantitative analysis with the use of Statistical Package for the Social Sciences (SPSS). While the majority of the children interviewed demonstrated elaborate abilities and knowledge as described by Anderson et al. (2008), 73 children (about 8%) in the sample severely struggled with certain areas relevant to the development of number concept, such as seriation, part–part–whole relationships, ordering numbers and counting small collections. They were identified as 'children potentially at risk' with respect to their later school mathematics learning on the basis of their performance at the OTZ and the EMBI-KiGa. A total of 26 of these 73 children (35.6%) had a non-German speaking family background. However, only 13.6% of the children in the complete sample ($n=947$) had a migrant background. Hence, children from migrant families were over-represented in the group of children potentially at risk learning school mathematics.

Following an 8-month intervention (details regarding the intervention are outlined below), participants of the study were tested/interviewed again immediately before entering year 1. In order to monitor potential long-term effects, follow-up tests were conducted at the end of year 1 and year 2. Data on student achievement

Table 19.1 Measurement points, instruments and participants of the study

Measurement points	Instruments	Participants
September–November 2005 *T1*	CFT 1	Children participating in the study ($n=891$)
	OTZ	Children participating in the study ($n=947$)
	EMBI-KiGa	Children participating in the study ($n=854$)
January–June 2006	Intervention	($n=73$)
June/July 2006 *T2*	OTZ	Children potentially at risk ($n=60$)
	EMBI-Kiga	Children participating in the study ($n=715$)
June/July 2007 *T3*	DEMAT 1+	All year 1 classes with children participating in the study ($n=1916$)
		including the children participating in the study ($n=716$)
	EMBI	Children potentially at risk ($n=40$)
June/July 2008 *T4*	DEMAT 2+	All year 2 classes with children participating in the study ($n=1832$)
		including children participating in the study ($n=603$)
	EMBI	Children potentially at risk ($n=30$)

in mathematics after the first and second year of primary school were collected with the following instruments:

- *Deutsche Mathematiktests für 1. und 2. Klassen* (DEMAT 1+; Krajewski et al. 2002/DEMAT 2+; Krajewski et al. 2004)—German curriculum-based standardized paper and pencil tests to be conducted at the end of the school year with the whole class.
- *Elementarmathematisches Basisinterview Zahlen und Operationen* (EMBI; Peter-Koop et al. 2007)—a task- and material-based one-on-one interview assessing children's developing mathematical understanding in the four areas: counting, place value, addition/subtraction strategies and multiplication/division in grade 1 and 2 [2].

The data collection included four points of measurement (T1–T4). As it was to be expected that the number of children who took part in the first phase of the data collection would continually decrease over the following 3 years, a common experience with respect to longitudinal studies, an ample sample size taking into account this decline in numbers of participants was chosen at the start of the study (Table 19.1).

Paradigm and Content of the Intervention

The intervention for the 73 preschoolers identified to be potentially at risk learning school mathematics was conducted in two groups: Children in group 1 were visited weekly by a pre-service teacher who had been prepared for this intervention as part of a university methods course. The pre-service primary teachers were introduced to the children as 'number fairies' who wanted to show them games and activities that they could later share with their peers. This was done to ensure that the children did not feel any pressure and experience themselves as slow learners at a very early point in their education. The intervention for the group 2 children, in contrast, was conducted by the kindergarten teachers within their groups. While the intervention in group 1 was carried out one-on-one at a set time each week, the kindergarten teachers working with the children in group 2 primarily tried to use everyday-related mathematical situations, focussing on aspects, such as ordering, one-to-one correspondence or counting, as they arose in the children's play or everyday routine, in particular challenging the children identified to be at risk in these areas. The kindergarten teachers completed a diary in which they described these situations, noted how often they arose and what they did with the children in the whole group (or a small subgroup as in a game situation) and with the children at risk in particular. Like in group 1, the children of group 2 were not aware of the fact that they took part in an intervention. However, the parents of all children who took part in the intervention had been informed and had given their written permission. It is important to note that for ethical reasons it was not possible to establish a control group, i.e. children identified to be potentially at risk who did not receive special support in form of an intervention as parents would not have agreed for their children to be part of this group.

Before and during the intervention the pre-service as well as the kindergarten teachers were supported to the same degree by the researchers to ensure comparability of the two groups. While the pre-service teachers enrolled in a methods course on early mathematics learning, the kindergarten teachers took part in an in-service course dealing with the same content and covering a similar time, i.e. about 30 hours over 6 months. In both groups, the intervention was conducted over 6 months, involving about 45 min a week and based on individual *learning plans* developed by the pre-service and kindergarten teachers. These learning plans were based on the results of the assessment with EMBI-KiGa and OTZ and subject to gradual extension and adaptation. They usually provided the framework for 4–6 weeks and were extended or intensified based on the progress of the child. Figure 19.1 shows the first part of the individual learning plan for Marie (group 1) covering the first 4 weeks of the intervention by a pre-service teacher. The example of the learning plan (Fig. 19.1) also illustrates the activities chosen for the intervention which were based on number work and counting following the skills integration model described above. The intervention in both groups focussed on games and play-type activities (for some example, see Fig. 19.2) acknowledging that play is essential for children at this age (e.g. see Walsh et al. 2006) and therefore pedagogically appropriate for an intervention at kindergarten level while rather systematic-methodical approaches to learning as preferred at school [3] is regarded as not appropriate for kindergarten children, because it requires attitudes and makes demands that are not yet developed by preschoolers (Duncker 2010). Furthermore, research in the context of special education suggests that children with learning difficulties in mathematics benefit from games when learning to count (McConkey and McEvoy 1986).

19 Early Enhancement of Kindergarten Children Potentially ...

Content	Material/Games	Activities
Language of location (understanding of prepositions)	Teddy bear and a cardboard box and/or pictures of a teddy bear in different positions in a picture book	*Where is teddy?* The child has to use prepositions to locate where teddy is hiding (in, under, next to, above, behind)
Counting up to 10 One-to-one correspondence	Little plastic teddies from the EMBI, lego blocks, buttons etc.	Counting of various structured and unstructured quantities (teddies etc.)
Matching numerals and quantities	Memory (pairs consisting of a numeral and a set)	Matching numerals and quantities
	Domino (numerals on one side and dots on the other)	Matching numerals and quantities
	Dice	Identifying the dot patterns and naming the according numbers
Ordering	Tiles with numerals 1 – 10	Bringing the tiles in the right order, naming number before and number after a given number
Seriation	Pencils, candles, straws	Putting the objects in order from shortest to longest pointing out the smallest and the longest object
Ordinal numbers	String of coloured beads	Showing and naming different positions (first, third, fifth)
	Racing game with children from the group	Who comes first, second ...?

Fig. 19.1 Example of an individual learning plan

Fig. 19.2 Examples of games and play-type activities used in the intervention

Presentation and Discussion of Results

While it was to be expected that the performance of most children would increase from pre-test (T1) to post-test (T2) due to age-related advancement with respect to their cognitive abilities, the results of the study demonstrate that the total group of children identified to be at risk in learning mathematics showed the highest increase. Figure 19.3 shows the means of the pre- and post-tests conducted in September/October 2005 and June/July 2006 (i.e. the first two measuring points in kindergarten) comparing the complete sample with the children at risk. The analysis was based on the number of children that had completed the OTZ and EMBI-KiGa in

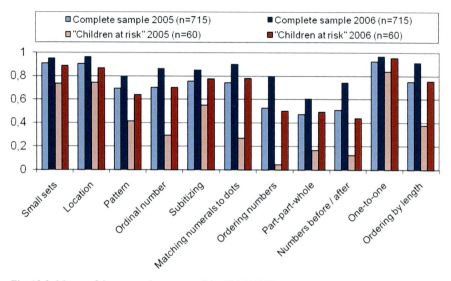

Fig. 19.3 Means of the pre- and post-test of the EMBI-KiGa

2005 as well as the EMBI-KiGa in 2006. Hence, the number in the complete sample decreased to $n=715$ with 60 children (8.4%) potentially at risk.

The data clearly show short-term effects of the intervention. The children potentially at risk have in particular increased their competencies in those areas that were addressed during the intervention, i.e. knowledge about numbers and sets as well as counting abilities, and performed significantly better in the post-test in tasks related to *ordinal numbers, matching numerals to dots, ordering numbers, numbers before/after* and *part–part–whole relationships* [4]. However, it is important to note that due to the fact that a control group was unavailable, a distinct effect of the intervention omitting other potential factors cannot be substantiated by this particular research design. Furthermore, ceiling effects hamper the comparison of the increase in mathematical competencies between the whole sample and the group of children identified to be potentially at risk in learning school mathematics. Despite this, the children potentially at risk undoubtedly demonstrated increased number knowledge and skills—domains which are seen as key predictors for later achievement in school mathematics (Krajewski 2005; Aunola et al. 2004).

Data from this study also suggest that children from non-German speaking background families show lower competencies in number concept development one year prior to school entry than their German peers. A comparison of the EMBI-KiGa pre-test data of the children with German as their first language and the children with a migration background based on a total of 854 children who completed the interview (see Fig. 19.4), shows a significant difference in achievement ($p<0.001$) in the areas *language of location, subitizing, matching numerals to dots, ordering numbers* and *numbers before and after*.

19 Early Enhancement of Kindergarten Children Potentially ...

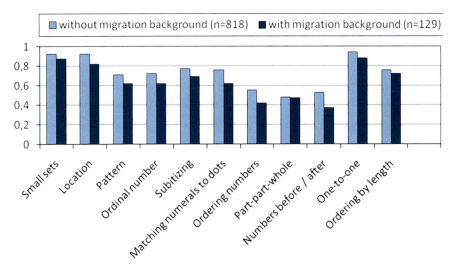

Fig. 19.4 Mean scores of children with a migration background and German speaking background children in the EMBI-KiGa pre-test

Complying with these results, children with a migrant background demonstrated significantly lower counting abilities with respect to the number-related items in the OTZ. A detailed investigation of these results indicates that language-related factors play an important role. In the subgroup of children from Turkish families [5] it was found that most of these children identified as potentially at risk in learning school mathematics, showed better performances in counting and number activities when they were encouraged to answer in Turkish (Schmidtman gen. Pothmann 2008). Thus, the intervention obviously proved beneficial with respect to their mathematical performance in the German language. The 23 children with a migrant background in the group of 60 children identified potentially at risk demonstrated a clear increase in achievement in the post-test (T2). While the achievement of both groups significantly increased ($p<0.001$) within the test interval, these children on average demonstrated an increase of 3.6 points between pre- and post-test compared to an increase of 2.9 points in the remaining group of the 37 children from German families. However, the difference in achievement between these two groups is not significant ($p=0.164$). In comparison, the growth in achievement in the group of children with a migrant background but without a potential risk factor in terms of their school mathematics learning is 1.3 points, while the mean score in this group of German children is 1.1 points. Again, the difference between those two groups ($p=0.629$) is not significant (Schmidtman gen. Pothmann 2008, p. 161). Immediately before school entry, the mathematical competencies of children with and without a migrant background obviously have converged—in some areas, i.e. *matching numerals to dots*, *ordering numb*ers and *part–part–whole*, they even show slightly (however, not significantly) better results (Schmidtman gen. Pothmann 2008, p. 121).

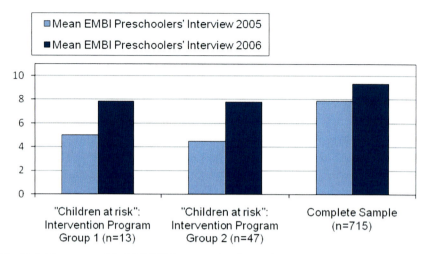

Fig. 19.5 Mean score of the EMBI-KiGa comparing the two intervention groups

And also another finding with respect to early intervention for preschoolers identified to be potentially at risk in learning school mathematics is encouraging. With respect to the substantial increase in achievement demonstrated by the 60 children with a risk factor in the EMBI-KiGa post-test (T2), no significant difference between the group of 13 children who worked once a week with pre-service teachers introduced as 'number fairies' (group 1) and the remaining 47 children who received remedial action within their groups by their kindergarten teachers (group 2) was found (Fig. 19.5).

This suggests that an intervention in the everyday practice by the kindergarten teacher who had received professional development in this area is as effective as a weekly one-on-one intervention by a visiting and hence more cost-intensive outside specialist. In addition, Fig. 19.5 shows a clear increase in achievement in both groups of an average 2.5 points in group 1 and even 3.2 points in group 2 which is clearly higher than the increase in the complete sample.

In addition to the short-term effect of the intervention, the study also aimed to investigate possible long-term effects at the end of grade 1 (T3) and grade 2 (T4). After the first and the second year in primary school as well, the group of children that had been identified as potentially at risk learning mathematics still shows lower achievements in the follow-up tests than the whole group of children participating in the study.

Taking a look at the different groups of children at the end of grade 1, there are only 20 children in the group of 40 children potentially at risk learning school mathematics beyond the weakest 25%. Another 19 children are now among the middle 50% and one child is among the top 25% in terms of their achievement in the DEMAT 1+. At the end of grade 2, 19 out of the still remaining 30 children potentially at risk belong to the group of the 25% of the weakest children, 6 of

Table 19.2 Results with respect to possible long-term effects at the end of years 1 and 2

	End of year 1 (max. 36)			End of year 2 (max. 36)		
	sample	M	SD	sample	M	SD
Overall	($n=1916$)	25.55	7.30	($n=1832$)	20.69	6.59
Children participating in the study	($n=716$)	26.08	7.09	($n=603$)	21.15	8.70
Peer groups in year 1/year 2	($n=1200$)	25.23	7.40	($n=1229$)	20.46	8.53
Children potentially at risk learning mathematics	($n=40$)	18.55	7.66	($n=30$)	11.65	9.12
Children potentially at risk with migration background	($n=15$)	18.93	7.99	($n=11$)	15.64	10.26
Children potentially at risk with German background	($n=25$)	18.32	7.62	($n=19$)	11.65	9.12

them with a non-German speaking background. Ten children—four of them with a migrant background—belong to the middle 50% and, like in grade 1, one child is still among the top 25%.

Implications

The findings of the study suggest that preschoolers who had been identified as potentially at risk in learning school mathematics one year prior to school entry could benefit significantly from an 8-month intervention programme based on the enhancement of number knowledge and counting abilities. Data from the pre- and post-tests clearly indicate increased knowledge, skills and understanding of numbers and sets, i.e. particularly those areas of number concept development regarded as predictors for later achievement in school mathematics (Krajewski 2005; Aunola et al. 2004). Further analyses suggest that for more than 50% of these children, this increase in their mathematical achievement prior to school entry proves to be of lasting effect at the end of grade 1 (Peter-Koop and Grüßing 2008). This percentage drops significantly after year 2 (see Table 19.2). One possible explanation for this finding relates to curriculum. In year 2 primary school mathematics in Germany, the focus shifts from number work to operations—an area that has not been trained in the intervention.

Furthermore, there were no significant differences in achievement found in the post-test between the groups of children who had experienced a one-on-one intervention by the pre-service mathematics teachers who had been particularly trained for this task and the children who had worked with their kindergarten teachers within their home groups. While clinical studies have already shown positive effects of early intervention (e.g. Krajewski 2005), this study suggests that there is not necessarily a need to bring external 'specialists' into kindergarten to work with individual children [6]. A comprehensive screening and respective enhancement of preschoolers potentially at risk by their kindergarten teachers is possible—given that the kindergarten teachers are prepared for this task during their initial and/or in-service training.

In addition, the findings show that children with a migrant background are not only over-represented in the group of preschoolers with a risk factor with respect to school mathematics, they also demonstrated the highest increase in mathematical achievement in the test interval. Hence, it appears to be important not only to focus on screenings that determine (German) language development prior to school as it is currently done in all German states, but also to investigate early mathematical abilities in order to identify children who need extra support in their number concept development. Since the Programme of International Student Assessment (PISA) study has emphasized that the group of migrant children is over-represented among the low-achieving students at the age of 15 (Deutsches PISA-Konsortium 2001) and findings from the SCHOLASTIK project (Weinert and Helmke 1997) indicate that low achievers in mathematics at the beginning of primary school in general stay in this position, this seems of crucial importance. While the German version of the *Utrecht Early Numeracy Test* (van Luit et al. 2001)—the OTZ—showed clear ceiling effects and also proved to be very difficult for non-German speaking background children due to its demands on German language comprehension, this study suggests that the EMBI-KiGa is a suitable instrument for the collection of information on preschoolers' number learning and the respective identification of children potentially at risk in learning school mathematics. This instrument allows children to articulate their developing mathematical understanding through the use of simple materials provided for each task in a short one-on-one interview that takes about 10–15 min for each child. Bruner (1969) has already highlighted the importance of material-based activities for young children who, for various reasons, cannot yet verbally articulate their developing and sometimes already yet quite elaborate (mathematical) understanding.

Furthermore, it can be stated that the design of the intervention which followed a play-oriented approach including traditional (mathematically slightly modified) games whenever suitable obviously had a positive effect on the children's number concept development. This is supported by findings of two studies in New Zealand that were designed to improve 5- and 7-year-old children's number knowledge through the use of mathematical games. It was found that games "appeared to be most effective as a way of enhancing children's learning when a sensitive adult was available to support and extend the children's learning as they played" (Peters 1998, p. 49). The conclusions of the study presented here with respect to the role of games and play-based activities are also supported by findings reported by a team of Swiss researchers who investigated the effects on learning outcome and motivation of two different approaches to fostering numeracy skills in kindergarten, comparing a training programme with a play-based approach. Their main results indicate that play-based fostering is as effective as a training programme in whole-group teaching in terms of learning outcomes in early numeracy (Rechensteiner et al. 2011). However, more detailed analyses are still needed to understand whether play-based early numeracy activities are of greater benefit for preschoolers potentially at risk learning school mathematics than a (whole-group based) training programme. Findings from the area of language education for preschoolers seem to suggest that whole-group training prior to school does not lead to compensational effects for slow learners (Röbe 1998).

Notes

1. The FYSMI is to be conducted in the first year of school, which in Australia is the preparatory grade preceding grade 1. This preparatory year is compulsory for all 5-year-old children. In Germany, in contrast, formal schooling starts with grade 1 when children are 6 years old. While a majority of German 5-year-olds attend kindergarten, this is not compulsory and involves fees to be paid by the parents.
2. This instrument is a German adaptation of the Australian *Early Years Interview* (Department of Education, Employment and Training, State of Victoria, 2001).
3. It is important to note that school-based approaches to mathematics teaching and learning in primary and junior secondary school also draw on games (e.g. Ainley 1990; Bragg 2006).
4. The analysis of the data from the standardised OTZ showed clear ceiling effects. Over 40 % of the children reached level A which supposedly represents the top 25 % of the children in this age group. However, in level E representing the bottom 10 % of the scale, the test differentiated sufficiently with respect to the sample.
5. The majority of the children with a migrant background in the sample were from Turkish parents, followed by families from Russia, Kazakhstan, Lebanon and Iraq.
6. However, it is acknowledged that there might be cases in which a specialist-based one-on-one training in addition to the help provided by the kindergarten teacher is expedient. In our study, we consider the pre-service teachers due to their extensive training in the area of children's number concept development and the high level of support and supervision that was provided before and during the intervention as specialists despite the fact that their teacher training had not been completed.

References

Acredolo, C. (1982). Conservation—nonconservation: Alternative explanations. In C. Brainerd (Ed.), *Children's logical and mathematical cognition: Progress in cognitive development* (pp. 1–31). New York: Springer.

Ainley, J. (1990). Playing games and learning mathematics. In L. Steffe & T. Wood (Eds), *Transforming children's mathematics education: International perspectives* (pp. 84–91). Hillsdale: Erlbaum.

Anderson, A., Anderson, J., & Thauberger, C. (2008). Mathematics learning and teaching in the early years. In O. N. Saracho & B. Spodek (Eds.), *Contemporary perspectives on mathematics in early childhood education* (pp. 95–132). Charlotte: Information Age Publishing.

Aunola, K., Leskinen, E., Lerkkanen, M.-K., & Nurmi, J.-E. (2004). Developmental dynamics of mathematical performance from preschool to grade 2. *Journal of Educational Psychology, 96*, 762–770.

Baroody, A. J., & Wilkins, J. (1999).The development of informal counting, number, and arithmetic skills and concepts. In J. Copley (Ed.), *Mathematics in the early years* (pp. 48–65). Reston: NCTM.

Bragg, L. (2006). Hey, I' learning this. *Australian Primary Mathematics Classroom, 11*(4), 4–7.

Bruner, J. (1969). *The process of education*. Cambridge: Harvard University Press.

Cattell, R. B., Weiß, R., & Osterland, J. (1997). *Grundintelligenztest Skala 1 (CFT 1)*. Göttingen: Hogrefe.

Clarke, B., Clarke, D., Grüßing, M., & Peter-Koop, A. (2008). Mathematische Kompetenzen von Vorschulkindern: Ergebnisse eines Ländervergleichs zwischen Australien und Deutschland. *Journal für Mathematik-Didaktik, 29*(3/4), 259–286.

Clarke, B., Clarke, D., & Cheeseman, J. (2006). The mathematical knowledge and understanding young children bring to school. *Mathematics Education Research Journal, 18*(1), 78–103.

Clements, D. (1984). Training effects on the development and generalization of Piagetian logical operations and knowledge of number. *Journal of Educational Psychology, 76*, 766–776.

DEET (2001). *Early Numeracy Interview Booklet*. Melbourne: Department of Education, Employment and Training.

Deutsches PISA-Konsortium (Ed.). (2001). *PISA 2000. Basiskompetenzen von Schülerinnen und Schülern im internationalen Vergleich*. Opladen: Leske + Budrich.

Duncker, L. (2010). Methodisch-systematisches Lernen im Kindergarten? Thesen zu einem schwierigen Balanceakt. In G. Schäfer, R. Staege, & K. Meiners (Eds.), *Kinderwelten—Bildungswelten. Unterwegs zur Frühpädagogik* (p. 26–37). Berlin: Cornelsen.

Fuson, K. C., Secada, W. G., & Hall, J. W. (1983). Matching, counting, and the conservation of number equivalence. *Child Development, 54*, 91–97.

Ginsburg, H., Inoue, N., & Seo, K. (1999). Young children doing mathematics: observations of everyday activities. In J. Copley (Ed.), *Mathematics in the early years* (pp. 88–99). Reston: NCTM.

Grüßing, M., & Peter-Koop, A. (2008). Effekte vorschulischer mathematischer Förderung am Ende des ersten Schuljahres: Erste Befunde einer Längsschnittstudie. *Zeitschrift für Grundschulforschung, 1*(1), 65–82.

Krajewski, K. (2005). Vorschulische Mengenbewusstheit von Zahlen und ihre Bedeutung für die Früherkennung von Rechenschwäche. In M. Hasselhorn, W. Schneider, & H. Marx (Eds.), *Diagnostik von Mathematikleistungen* (pp. 49–70). Göttingen: Hogrefe.

Krajewski, K. (2008). Vorschulische Förderung mathematischer Kompetenzen. In F. Petermann & W. Schneider (Eds.), *Enzyklopädie der Psychologie, Reihe Entwicklungspsychologie, Bd. Angewandte Entwicklungspsychologie* (p. 275–304). Göttingen: Hogrefe.

Krajewski, K., & Schneider, W. (2009a). Exploring the impact of phonological awareness, visual-spatial working memory, and preschool quantity-number competencies on mathematics achievement in elementary school: Findings from a 3-year longitudinal study. *Journal of Experimental Child Psychology, 103*(4), 516–531.

Krajewski, K., & Schneider, W. (2009b). Early development of quantity to number-word linkage as a precursor of mathematical school achievement and mathematical difficulties: Findings from a four-year longitudinal study. *Learning and Instruction, 19*(6), 513–526.

Krajewski, K., Küspert, P., & Schneider, W. (2002). *DEMAT 1 +. Deutscher Mathematiktest für erste Klassen*. Göttingen: Hogrefe.

Krajewski, K., Liehm, S., & Schneider, W. (2004). *DEMAT 2 +. Deutscher Mathematiktest für zweite Klassen*. Göttingen: Hogrefe.

McConkey, R., & McEvoy, J. (1986). Games for learning to count. *British Journal of Special Education, 13*(2), 59–62.

Piaget, J. (1952). *The child's conception of number*. London: Routledge.
Peter-Koop, A., Wollring, B., Spindeler, B., & Grüßing, M. (2007). *Elementarmathematisches Basisinterview (Zahlen und Operationen)*. Offenburg: Mildenberger.
Peter-Koop, A., Grüßing, M., & Schmitman gen. Pothmann, A (2008). Förderung mathematischer Vorläuferfähigkeiten: Befunde zur vorschulischen Identifizierung und Förderung von potenziellen Risikokindern in Bezug auf das schulische Mathematiklernen. *Empirische Pädagogik, 22*(2), 208–223.
Peter-Koop, A., & Grüßing, M. (2011). *Elementarmathematisches Basisinterview KiGa*. Offenburg: Mildenberger.
Peters, S. (1998). Playing games and learning mathematics: The results of two intervention studies. *International Journal of Early Years Education, 6*(1), 49–58.
Rechensteiner, K., Hauser, B., & Vogt. F. (2011). *Mathematics in kindergarten: Training or play?* Paper presented at Sig-5 Symposium "Maths in early childhood" at the EARLI Conference, Exeter, UK, 03 Sept 2011.
Resnick, L. B. (1983). A developmental theory of number understanding. In H. Ginsburg (Ed.), *The development of mathematical thinking* (pp. 109–151). New York: Academic Press.
Röbe, E. (1998). *Übergang von der Kita zur Grundschule: Eine vieldimensionale Entwicklungsaufgabe*. Impulsreferat auf der Tagung "Zwei Partner—eine Philosophie. Kita und Grundschule mit gemeinsamer Bildungsverantwortung", Staatskanzlei des Landes Brandenburg, 26 May 2008 (personal communication).
Schmidtman gen. Pothmann, A. (2008). *Mathematiklernen und Migrationshintergrund. Quantitative Analysen zu frühen mathematischen und (mehr-)sprachlichen Kompetenzen*. Doctoral thesis, University of Oldenburg, Faculty of Education.
Sophian, C. (1995). Representation and reasoning in early numerical development. *Child Development, 66*, 559–577.
Stern, E. (1997). Ergebnisse aus dem SCHOLASTIK-Projekt. In F. E. Weinert & A. Helmke (Eds.), *Entwicklung im Grundschulalter* (pp. 157–170). Weinheim: Beltz.
van Luit, J., van de Rijt, B., & Hasemann, K. (2001). *Osnabrücker Test zur Zahlbegriffsentwicklung (OTZ)*. Göttingen: Hogrefe.
Walsh, G., Sproule, L., McGuinness, C., Trew, K., Rafferty, H., & Sheehy, N. (2006). An appropriate curriculum for 4–5-year-old children in Northern Ireland: Comparing play-based and formal approaches. *Early Years—An International Journal of Research and Development, 26*(2), 201–221.
Weinert, F. E., & Helmke, A. (Eds.). (1997). *Entwicklung im Grundschulalter*. Weinheim: Beltz.

ERRATUM
Early Mathematics Learning

Ulrich Kortenkamp, Birgit Brandt, Christiane Benz, Gotz Krummheuer, Silke Ladel, Rose Vogel

Editors

U. Kortenkamp et al. (eds.) *Early Mathematics Learning*, DOI 10.1007/978-1-4614-4678-1© Springer Science+Business Media New York 2014

DOI 10.1007/978-1-4614-4678-1_20

The publisher regrets that in the Title page and the Copyright page of the print and online versions of this title, the names of the editors are listed incorrectly. Below is the correct order in which their names should appear.

Ulrich Kortenkamp, Christiane Benz, Birgit Brandt, Götz Krummheuer, Silke Ladel, Rose Vogel

The online version of the original book can be found at
http://dx.doi.org/10.1007/978-1-4614-4678-1

Index

A
Activity theory 115, 121, 240
Activity-oriented approach 230
Animal polonaise 226
Appropriation 10, 156, 208, 209
Arithmetic 111, 261, 262
Artefact-Centric Activity Theory (ACAT) 6, 241–243, 249
Artefacts 5, 25, 30, 225, 226, 231, 234, 241–243, 246, 247, 250, 251
Assembly-line instruction 41, 47–52
Assessment 51, 230, 278, 279, 294, 302, 303, 312
Attachment theory 126–129
Attachment–exploration behavior antagonism 130
Autodidactic processes 60

B
Big ideas 6, 15, 258, 264, 266–268, 277
Block building 102
Butterfly puzzle 66

C
CAMTE framework 294–296, 302
Canonical solution 80
Child development knowledge 265
Childlike world 232
Children 3–6, 23–29, 32, 33, 37–40, 43, 47–53, 55, 59, 60, 62, 63, 65–68, 71, 75, 76, 78, 82, 85, 89, 90, 93, 103–105, 111, 112, 114–119, 121, 125, 126, 130, 133, 134, 136, 137, 141–143, 154, 160, 161, 173, 175–180, 182–185, 189–194, 196, 198, 200, 201, 208–212, 214–220, 223–227, 229, 231, 232, 234, 237–252, 257–271, 275–287, 291–293, 295–304, 307–315, 317, 318

Classroom activities design 265
Cognitive construction 81
Cognitive development 89
Co-learning 211
Collaborative learning 271
Collection quantities 5
Collective educational setting 257
Communicative tools 111, 117
Component of content 80
Composition 93, 131, 190, 196, 198–201, 223
Construction 3–6, 10–15, 23, 32, 33, 56, 60, 65, 67, 116, 120, 143, 149, 154, 162, 169, 184, 189, 194, 201, 208, 218, 219, 224, 225, 234, 240–243, 251, 257–263, 269–271, 275, 287, 291, 292, 304
Construction knowledge 72
Construction plan 117
Constructivist approach 260
Constructivist learning model 260
Content knowledge 257, 260, 263, 271, 276, 278, 286
Content learning 258
Counting 6, 25, 48, 94, 119, 140, 155, 157, 174, 189–192, 194, 200, 209, 238, 246–248, 262, 269–271, 277, 280, 281, 283, 285–287, 292–295, 297, 299, 301–303, 308, 310–312, 314, 315, 317
Counting sequence 189
Counting skills 24
Counting-word tagging to number 239
Creative construction 121
Creativity 11, 113, 114, 125, 127, 133, 304
Cultural tools 231
Cultural-historical activity theory (CHAT) 5, 112, 113, 120

D
Dance metaphor 11
Decomposition 194, 200, 201

Design 3, 6, 79, 81, 86, 90, 126, 131, 133, 143, 193, 233, 234, 243, 244, 246, 247, 250, 251, 279, 294, 309, 314, 318
Development 6, 29, 34, 37, 73, 81, 91, 118, 120, 126, 318
Developmental education 112
Developmental niche 4, 58, 74, 75, 89, 100, 101, 104
Diagnostic knowledge 278
Diagnostic tools 278
Didactical design 102, 126, 131, 159
Digital tools 207, 209, 210
Documentation 6, 24, 29, 32, 227, 280
Dual inheritance 72

E
Early childhood development 127
Early childhood mathematics 189, 275, 277, 280, 292
Early learning 173
Early mathematics 112, 238, 258, 262–264, 269, 270, 276–281, 286, 287, 312
Early mathematics concepts 10
Early mathematics education 3, 5, 6, 24, 261, 275, 276
Early mathematics learning 3, 6, 10
Effective Practice of Pre-school Education (EPPE) project 22
Elementary education 173
Empirical research instrument 6, 223, 224, 232, 234
Enumeration 292, 294, 295, 303
Evaluation 130, 179, 270, 271, 282–287, 295
Everyday activities 209, 275, 277, 281
Exploratory data analysis (EDA) 12

F
Family 4, 27, 71, 79, 85, 86, 88, 89, 90, 133, 137, 139, 141, 310
Folk pedagogy 58, 59
Formal instruction 185
Functional mathematics 120

G
Geometrical knowledge 104
Geometry 61, 90, 102, 120, 131, 148, 154, 159, 160, 174, 224, 264, 293
German-Turkish family 94
Gestural conceptual mapping 238
Gesture 5, 29, 116, 148, 150–154, 156–158, 160–164, 167–170, 184, 216, 233, 237, 238
Goldin-Meadow's observation 154

H
Hierarchical Linear Modeling (HLM) 270
Horizontal mathematization 13

I
Idiosyncratic construction 15
Illuminative evaluation 9
Information and Communication Technology (ICT) 6, 207, 209–211, 217, 219, 237, 238, 242
Instruction 3–6, 11–15, 26, 32, 39, 51, 52, 58, 59, 61, 82, 111, 112, 118–120, 143, 154, 156, 169, 185, 189, 193, 201, 208, 212, 218, 219, 224, 234, 241, 243, 244, 257–263, 269–271, 275, 286, 287, 292, 302, 304
Instruction manuals 88
Instruction transmission model 260
Instruction–construction relationship 261
Intellectual autonomy 50
Intent participation 40–42, 47–51
Intentional teaching 258, 263, 266, 267, 269, 270
Interaction 3–6, 39, 40, 42, 48, 50–52, 56, 61, 63, 68, 72–75, 81, 91, 97, 102, 103, 105, 125, 131, 148–151, 153, 155–162, 164, 168–170, 207, 211–213, 216–219, 223, 237, 242, 244, 250, 251, 266, 284, 302
Interactional niche 56–58, 72, 82, 90–91
Interface design 238
Interlocutor design 160
Interpretation 61
Intervention 6, 39, 40, 178, 259, 270, 282–286, 307, 309–319

K
Kindergarten 6, 55, 59, 68, 71, 76, 81, 85, 86, 90, 133, 143, 177, 193, 207–210, 212, 217, 219, 238, 270, 275, 276, 282, 296–299, 301, 309, 312, 316–318
Kindergarten activities 55
Kindergarten children 85, 231, 275
Kindergarten education 173
Kindergarten educators 4, 57, 62–68, 185, 208, 211, 212, 220, 276, 319
Kindergarten teachers–children interactions 57
Kindergarten teachers–parents interactions 60
Knowledge 10, 13, 14, 21, 27, 33, 48, 51, 58, 60, 61, 63, 72, 112, 126, 133, 159, 179, 185, 201, 238, 239, 257–263, 266, 269–271, 275, 278–280, 291–296, 300–304,

307, 308, 310, 314, 317
Knowledge construction 271

L
Ladybug-situation 133, 134, 138
Language 4, 21, 25, 27, 29, 32–34, 39, 50, 116, 134, 153, 154, 219, 260, 265, 269, 294, 315, 318, 319
Language Acquisition Support System (LASS) 89
Language family members 88
Learning 5, 15, 22, 25, 26, 37–42, 49, 51–53, 56, 58–60, 68, 75, 81, 85, 90, 91, 117, 148, 150, 154, 173, 176, 184, 189, 208, 209, 212, 219, 224, 228–230, 232, 234, 240, 251, 252, 257, 259, 260, 263–271, 276–287, 292, 302, 304, 307–318
Learning centers 262
Learning environment 5, 157, 159, 189, 233, 240, 242
Learning methods 185
Learning opportunities 156, 262
Learning paradox 13
Learning styles 14
Learning tasks 264
Learning trajectories 265–267
Learning–appropriation links 211
Leeway of participation 73, 75, 91, 102
Level of involvement 113
Logical-mathematical knowledge 261
Longitudinal design 60, 81
Longitudinal study 85, 309
Long-term study 6, 223–225

M
Manchester Child Attachment Story Task (MCAST) 134
Manipulatives (resources) 4, 21, 24–27, 34, 237, 266
Math learning center 269
Mathematical activity 113
Mathematical argumentations 132, 149
Mathematical competencies 282
Mathematical creative ideas 5
Mathematical creativity 5, 76, 125, 127–131, 137, 142, 144
Mathematical culture 120
Mathematical development 90
Mathematical domain patterning 4
Mathematical instruction 5, 55, 68, 156, 228
Mathematical interactions 131, 148, 150, 155–158, 160, 165, 170
Mathematical knowledge 12, 81, 161, 233, 237

Mathematical language 156, 269
Mathematical learning 39, 40, 52, 57, 68, 71, 72, 89, 90, 275, 278–280
Mathematical learning environment 148
Mathematical problem solving 112
Mathematical reasoning 269
Mathematical situations 234
Mathematical stagings 232
Mathematical tasks 6, 125, 126, 128, 130, 133, 142, 143, 156, 225, 227, 275
Mathematical teaching 234
Mathematical teaching moments 40
Mathematical thinking 3, 4, 11, 21, 24, 26, 50, 56, 57, 60, 72, 73, 111, 113, 117, 120, 121, 144, 148, 210, 218, 223, 224, 230, 278
Mathematical tools 208, 209
Mathematics as play 120
Mathematics classroom 13, 27, 40, 111, 114–116, 119
Mathematics education 3–5, 9–13, 72, 75, 91, 111, 113, 127, 148–150, 153, 154, 156, 160, 208, 224, 238, 243, 261, 262, 268, 275, 276, 279, 281, 282, 287, 291, 301
Mathematics instruction 262
Mathematics knowledge 148
Mathematics learning 207, 208, 239
Mathematising 112–116, 118, 120, 269
Math-related language 269
Mediation 25, 251
Meta-environmental factors 125
Mother–daughter interactions 79
Multimedia design 243
Multimodality 148, 152, 158, 160, 167, 169, 208, 218, 226
Multi-Touch 6, 237, 238, 240, 241, 243, 244, 247, 250, 252

N
Natural Learning 142, 146 , 275–278, 280, 282, 286
Notion of language 73
Number concepts 238, 239, 242, 243, 250–252, 294, 301, 302, 308–310, 314, 317–319

O
Observation 6, 10, 12, 14, 27, 33, 58, 86, 121, 142, 201, 210, 212, 243, 250, 258, 261, 280–283, 286
Observation phase 85
Observation studies 118

P

Parental scaffolding 102
Parents construction 104
Parents–children interaction 91, 126
Partitioning 21, 24, 25, 28, 29, 30–33
Part-whole concept 239, 249
Part-whole-relationship 310
Pattern language theory 232
Pedagogical content knowledge (PCK) 4, 24, 25, 32, 276, 278–282, 286, 293
Pedagogical diagnostics 278
Pedagogical intervention 22
Pedagogical issues 4, 27
Pedagogical prescription 22
Physical knowledge 261
Picture–built objects relationships 101
Place value 4, 21, 24–26, 29, 30, 33, 34, 311
Place value cards 28, 29
Planning, national strategy model of 23
Play 37, 38, 114
Play-based curriculum mathematising 115
Playful activity 112, 114, 116, 118, 119, 121
Post-epistemological 10
Power of five 238, 249
Preschool interaction shows 52
Preschool teachers 6, 262, 263, 292, 293, 295, 296
Preschools 39, 51, 262, 296
Problem solving 67, 68, 111–114, 118, 217, 243, 269
Productive mathematising 5, 114
Professional Development 23, 258, 266, 270, 276, 279, 280, 282–287, 292, 295, 296, 301, 302, 316
Prototype learning 244
Prototypical environments 243

Q

Quantities 24, 117, 118, 189, 190, 192–196, 198, 200, 201, 216, 239
Quasi-experimental design 283

R

Research design 12, 130

S

Scaffolding 4, 40, 42, 43, 47, 49, 50, 52, 271
Screen design 210
Self-efficacy 6, 292–297, 302, 304
Semantic feature hypothesis 175
Semiotic process card 165
Semiotics 13
Sensitive instruction 121
Situational perspective 73
Social interaction 56, 241
Social-historical development 125
Socio-constructivist 72, 85, 89, 115
Sociocultural 208
Sociocultural activities 209
Sociocultural perspective 210, 211
Socio-cultural process 5, 230
Spatial development 104
Spatial orientation 93
Spatial thinking 4, 92, 93, 101, 104, 224, 286
Speech 5, 137, 142, 147, 148, 150–154, 156, 157, 160–164, 167–170
Speech knowledge 237
Spoken instruction 233
Subject knowledge 23, 33
Summative evaluation 283
Swedish preschools 4, 37, 38, 40, 52
Symbolic interactionism 73, 148
Symbolic tools 210

T

Tasks 39, 68, 75, 112, 114, 154, 175, 176, 178, 192–194, 215, 217, 218, 242, 244, 260, 266, 276, 281, 293, 295–299, 301–304, 308
Teacher–child interactions 22, 42
Teacher–pupil interactions 11
Teachers' content knowledge 258
Teachers' knowledge 23, 24, 292–295, 297, 298, 301, 302
Teachers' self-efficacy 302
Teachers–students interaction 40
Teaching moments 4, 40
Technology 5, 249, 250, 252
Theoretical edifices 10
Tools 5, 6, 25, 30, 32, 49, 113, 114, 207–212, 217–220, 231, 240, 281, 287, 291, 296
Traditional instruction 119
Traditional technology 237
Training programs 177, 275, 287
Transition 118, 154, 247, 251, 269
Triangulation 9

W

Wooden sticks situation 227

Y

Young learners 154

Z

Zone of proximal development (ZPD) 211, 217–220, 243, 247

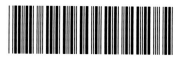